# Chepstow Castle

SU
COUNT

# Chepstow Castle
## Its History & Buildings

*Edited by*
Rick Turner & Andy Johnson

**Logaston Press**

LOGASTON PRESS
Little Logaston, Logaston,
Woonton, Almeley, Herefordshire HR3 6QH
logastonpress.co.uk

First published by Logaston Press 2006

ISBN
1 904396 52 6 (Paperback)


1 904396 53 4 (Hardback)

Set in Times by Logaston Press
and printed in Great Britain by
Biddles Ltd., King's Lynn

*Front cover illustration: Looking across the Main Gatehouse to the Middle Bailey
curtain wall and Great Tower beyond (© Skyscan)*

# Contents

# Preface and Acknowledgements

This book originated in a programme of research instigated by Cadw in 1998. It began in a rather unplanned way with Roland Harris, then of the Historic Building Research Unit, Reading University, undertaking the first measured survey of the Great Tower as part of a comparative study of early Norman keep towers. Dan Miles was commissioned to undertake a tree-ring analysis of the surviving doors. The results for the original Main Gatehouse doors caused great excitement as it led to a radical review of the development of the castle's defences and put Chepstow into the forefront of military design in the late 12th century.

Two things then stimulated a more concerted study of the castle. The first was two dayschools organised by Chepstow Museum and the Chepstow Society in 1999 and 2002. Here, those of us involved in individual strands of research, first presented our results to an enthusiastic audience. The second was the work needed to undertake a comprehensive revision to Cadw's guidebook to Chepstow Castle, published in 2002. Together these showed that it would be possible to undertake a comprehensive historical and architectural investigation of the whole of the castle and some of its appurtenances. This has not involved any large-scale archaeological excavations, but the great range of documentary resources and the extent of the standing fabric has enabled many new insights to be gained into one of Britain's best-preserved and most diverse castles.

The research programme has also stimulated and guided the conservation works at the castle. This has been particularly the case for the painted, plaster and carved decoration, which has been undertaken by Hirst Conservation and Nimbus Conservation. The consolidation of the masonry has been skillfully carried out by Cadwraeth Cymru, Cadw's direct labour force. Much remains to be done particularly on the south curtain wall and its towers to ensure future generations can review the results presented here.

Some of the results of this research have been published as papers in several academic journals. The authors would like to give particular thanks to the editors of the Society of Antiquaries of London (chapters III, IX, X and XVI), Colloque du Château Gaillard, (chapters V and VIII) and the Severn Estuary Levels Research Committee (chapter XII) for permission to adapt these papers for use in this book.

Much of the research reported here has been generously supported by Cadw, the historic environment division of the Welsh Assembly Government. They have also provided the majority of the illustrations, which are Crown Copyright without charge. The help provided by Cadw's photographic librarian, Chris Kenyon, and graphic designer, Ceri Staziker has been greatly appreciated.

Many others have provided help during the course of the work. The authors would like to thank the following: Jeremy Ashbee, Pascal Bidois, Kevin Blockley, Peter Brears, British Legion Chepstow, Richard Gable Forestry Commission, Jane Geddes, John Godbert, John Goodall, Ned Heywood, Peter Humphries, Alice Jarrett, John Kenyon, Maurice Llewelyn, Neil Ludlow, Tim Morgan, Nigel Nayling, David Park, Isobel Purcell, John Shipton, Mrs and Mrs G. Thomas, Cas Troggy Farm, Malcolm Thurlby, Kevin Trott, Helen Turner, James Turner, Keith Underwood, Diane Williams, Bill Zajac and the castle's custodial staff for their constant support and refreshment.

The majority of the original photography for this book was carried out by Ken Hoverd and Paul Highnam, the reconstruction drawings by Chris Jones-Jenkins and Terry Ball, and the final line drawings by Pete Lawrence.

The following have generously allowed for the reproduction of images in their collections: Amgueddfa Cymru - National Museum of Wales, Bayeux City Archive, British Library, Cardiff Central Library, Chepstow Museum, Corpus Christi College Cambridge, English Heritage, National Library of Wales, National Portrait Gallery, Royal Commission on the Ancient and Historic Monuments of Wales, and Mr J.K. Wingfield-Digby, Sherborne Castle, Dorset.

# Notes on Contributors

**Emeritus Professor J.R.L. Allen**, a geologist by training, is a Visiting Professor in the Department of Archaeology in the University of Reading. He has worked increasingly with archaeologists over the past 25 years, specialising in Holocene coastal stratigraphy and environments and the geological provenance and socio-economic implications of building materials from Roman times onward, especially in Wales and southern England.

**Richard Avent** has been Chief Inspector of Ancient Monuments and Historic Buildings at Cadw since 1984. He directed a major programme of archaeological excavations at Laugharne Castle in Carmarthenshire between 1976 and 1993 and has published on Marcher castles and the castles of the Welsh princes.

**David Bates** is Director of the Institute of Historical Research in the University of London, having previously taught in the universities of Cardiff and Glasgow. He is the author of numerous books and articles on Anglo-Norman history and is currently working on a biography of William the Conqueror for the Yale University Press English Monarchs series.

**Nicola Coldstream** is an architectural historian and Fellow of the Society of Antiquaries. Her books include *Masons and Sculptors* (1991), *The Decorated Style. Architecture and Ornament, 1240–1360* (1994) and *Medieval Architecture* (2002). She is currently President of the British Archaeological Association.

**David Crouch** is Professor of Medieval History at the University of Hull. He is a native of Cardiff and has published a number of articles on southern Welsh history as well as an edition of the acts of the bishops of Llandaff with the South Wales Record Society (1987). He publishes principally on the socio-political history of the 12th and 13th centuries. The second edition of his biography of William Marshal was published in 2002.

**George D. Geear**, after a career in education and the military, now lectures, writes and works as a consultant in the field of ordnance, arms and explosives. He lives in a Victorian Coast Artillery Fort in Pembrokeshire which he is planning to open as a museum of military technology and as a memorial to the men who served and trained there.

**Andy Johnson** is the proprietor of Logaston Press and has co-authored and edited numerous books on the history of the Welsh Marches.

**Chris Jones-Jenkins** studied at the Welsh School of Architecture but decided not to go into practice. He learned the art of cutaway drawings whilst working on the reconstructed buildings at the Museum of Welsh Life, St.Fagans, and since 1984, he has used these techniques as a part-time freelance illustrator, mostly for Cadw, for whom he has worked on over 40 monuments, many of them with Rick Turner.

**Jeremy Knight** is a former Inspector of Ancient Monuments for Cadw, author of official guides to various castles, including Chepstow, and of books on late antiquity and Roman France. In 2002 he was presented with a Festschrift *The Medieval Castle in Ireland and Wales*. His book *Civil War and Restoration in Monmouthshire* was published by Logaston Press in 2005.

**Dr Daniel Miles** leads the Oxford Dendrochronology Laboratory and has analysed historic woodwork for over 20 years. Projects have included in-depth studies of the Tower of London, Westminster Abbey, Windsor Castle, and Salisbury Cathedral. The Laboratory has also undertaken extensive dendrochronological surveys in Wales as well as Shropshire, Hampshire, Somerset, and most recently New England.

**Marc Morris** presented the Channel 4 series *Castle* and wrote the accompanying book. He is also the author of *The Bigod Earls of Norfolk in the Thirteenth Century* (Boydell, 2005).

**Dr Richard K. Morris** is an Associate Fellow of Warwick University and a specialist in studying the building fabric of medieval architecture. He is the founder of the Warwick Mouldings Archive, a research collection of profile drawings from medieval and early Renaissance buildings and excavations.

**Stephen Priestley** MA studied history at Cambridge. He has worked as a research assistant at the Tower of London, for English Heritage and for Cadw where he investigated the history of various Welsh castles including Chepstow. He has also undertaken a research project for British Waterways on the history of Pontcysyllte Aqueduct. Since 2003 he has been working as research manager for Border Archaeology, an archaeological contractor based in Leominster, Herefordshire.

**Anne Rainsbury** BA AMA is Curator of Chepstow Museum and producer of many events at Chepstow Castle. Her interests cover all aspects of Chepstow and area's rich history, and she is committed to keeping its history 'alive' and relevant at the heart of the community, both inside and outside the museum, through a range of events, activities and projects.

**Bevis Sale** is an archaeologist, artist, and teacher. Since the 1960s he has been involved in archaeology in Britain and abroad, mostly on a freelance basis, and has specialised in fieldwork and illustration.

**Ron Shoesmith** worked as a freelance archaeologist for the then Department of the Environment in the early 1970s and directed excavations on the Chepstow Priory site for two years. He was Director of Excavations for the City of Hereford Archaeology Committee from 1974 to 1996. Since then he has worked as a private consultant and is Archaeological Consultant to the Dean and Chapter of Hereford Cathedral. He is a Fellow of the Society of Antiquaries of London.

**Rick Turner** is an inspector of ancient monuments for Cadw. He studied archaeology at Cambridge University and worked previously for Lancaster University, British Gas and Cheshire County Council. Famous for his discovery of Lindow Man, his research interests now centre on the study of medieval and later buildings in Wales.

# List of Figures and Plates

**Chapter I  Introduction**
1.  Map of the area around Chepstow showing Iron Age hillforts, postulated Roman roads, the surviving parts of Offa's Dyke and early medieval sites mention in the text. (P. Lawrence, Cadw)
2.  Map of Chepstow showing the position of Roman find spots, the castle, priory, early town and Port Wall.
3.  Millerd's plan of Chepstow, 1686.
4.  A geological map of the Chepstow area showing the sources of the building stone. (P. Lawrence after J.R.L. Allen)
5.  The forum-basilica at Caerwent. (P. Highnam, Cadw)

**Chapter II  William the Conqueror, William fitz Osbern and Chepstow Castle**
6.  Family tree of William fitz Osbern and William the Conqueror.
7.  Map of England, Wales and Normandy showing the places associated with fitz Osbern mentioned in the text. (P. Lawrence, Cadw)
8.  A feast of William the Conqueror's chief supporters as depicted in the Bayeux Tapestry. (Bayeux City Archives)
9.  Plan showing the location of fitz Osbern's castles in the Marches. (P. Lawrence, Cadw)
10. The west front of Chepstow Priory. (M. Thurlby)
11. Aerial photograph of King Harold's hunting lodge at Portskewett. (Crown copyright RCAHMW)
12. A reconstruction of the Norman castle. (C. Jones-Jenkins, Cadw)
13. The motte and later shell keep at Cardiff Castle. (Cadw)

**Chapter III  The Norman Great Tower**
14. The west external elevation. (P. Lawrence, Cadw)
15. The south external elevation. (P. Lawrence, Cadw)
16. The east external elevation. (P. Lawrence, Cadw)
17. The east doorway of the Great Tower. (Cadw)
18. The north external elevation. (P. Lawrence, Cadw)
19. The west internal elevation and a reconstruction of its Norman appearance. (P. Lawrence, Cadw)
20. The south internal elevation. (P. Lawrence, Cadw)
21. The Romano-British figures in the south wall of the Great Tower. (Cadw)
22. The east internal elevation. (P. Lawrence, Cadw)
23. The north internal elevation. (P. Lawrence, Cadw)
24. A reconstruction of the ground- and first-floor plans of the Norman Great Tower. (P. Lawrence, Cadw)
25. A reconstruction of the exterior of the Norman Great Tower. (C. Jones-Jenkins, Cadw)
26. An extract from Frame and Ellis' plan of the castle in 1865 showing the 'Keep'.
27. Chip carving on the west doorway of the Round Chapel at Ludlow Castle. (R. Turner)
28. The Norman doorway at St Leonard's Church, Hatfield, Herefordshire. (K. Hoverd, Cadw)
29. The hall of the Great Tower at Rouen with Duke William receiving Duke Harold Godwinson. (Bayeux City Archives)
30. Scolland's Hall, Richmond Castle, Yorkshire. (English Heritage)

**Chapter IV  Chepstow under the Marshals**
31. Plan of the medieval lordships of Gwent. ( P. Lawrence, Cadw)
32. Manuscript illustration of a tourney. (BL Add. 12228 ff.150v-151)
33. The Round Tower at Pembroke Castle. (R. Turner)
34. Plan of Caerleon Castle. (P. Lawrence, Cadw)
35. Tomb effigy of William Marshal I, Temple Church, London. (Cadw)
36. Tomb effigy of William Marshal II, Temple Church, London. (Cadw)
37. Gilbert Marshal's death from Matthew Paris' Chronicle. (Corpus Christi College, Cambridge, MS 16 f.148)

**Chapter V  The Main Gatehouse**
38. The doors to the Main Gatehouse: the outside photographed *c.*1958 when under repair at Caernarfon. (K. Hoverd, Cadw)
39. The doors to the Main Gatehouse: the internal view as now on display on the first floor of the Bigod apartments. (K. Hoverd, Cadw)
40. A detail of the hasp on the northern leaf of the doors. (K. Hoverd, Cadw)
41. A detail of the iron roves on the rear of the doors. (K. Hoverd, Cadw)
42. The exterior of the Main Gatehouse. (K. Hoverd, Cadw)
43. The ground- and first-floor plans of the Main Gatehouse. (P. Lawrence, Cadw)
44. The second-floor and parapet level plans of the Main Gatehouse. (P. Lawrence, Cadw)
45. The rear of the Main Gatehouse. (K. Hoverd, Cadw)

# Time Line

| NATIONAL EVENTS | | LOCAL EVENTS | | LORDS OF CHEPSTOW | |
|---|---|---|---|---|---|
| 1066 | Coronation of William I | 1067-71 | Work begins on castle Founding of Priory | 1067-72 | William fitz Osbern |
| | | 1071 | Death of William fitz Osbern | 1072-74 | Roger de Breteuil |
| | | 1074 | Roger, son of William fitz Osbern, deprived of his estates | 1074-1115 | In Royal hands |
| 1086 | Domesday Survey | 1081-93 | Building of Great Tower by William I | | |
| 1087 | Accession of William II | | | | |
| 1100 | Accession of Henry I | 1115 | Castle handed to the de Clare family | 1115-48 | Gilbert de Clare |
| 1135 | Accession of Stephen | | | | |
| 1139-41 | Civil war between Stephen and Matilda | | | 1148-76 | Richard de Clare (Strongbow) |
| 1154 | Accession of Henry II | | | 1176-89 | Richard's children wards of Henry II |
| 1189 | Accession of Richard I | 1189-1219 | Lower, Middle and Upper Baileys' gates, towers and curtain walls built by William Marshal | 1189-1219 | William Marshal, hereditary marshal of England and Earl of Pembroke |
| 1199 | Accession of John | | | | |
| 1216 | Accession of Henry III | | | | |
| | | 1228-c.1238 | Remodelling of the Great Tower by William II and Gilbert Marshal | 1220-48 | William Marshal II followed by his brothers, Richard, Gilbert, Walter and Anselm, then by Maud, wife of Hugh Bigod, 3rd Earl of Norfolk |
| | | | | 1248-69 | Roger Bigod |
| 1272 | Accession of Edward I | 1271 | Wentwood survey | 1270-1306 | Roger Bigod III, 5th Earl of Norfolk |
| | | 1274-78 | Probable building of Port Wall | | |
| | | 1278-85 | Lower bailey, domestic buildings and Gloriette on north side built | | |
| | | 1284 | Visit of Edward I | | |
| | | 1287-93 | Marten's Tower built | | |
| 1290 | Jews expelled from England | 1292-1300 | Upper part of great tower completed | 1306-12 | In Royal hands |
| 1307 | Accession of Edward II | | | 1312-38 | Thomas de Brotherton, Earl of Norfolk |
| 1327 | Accession of Edward III | 1326 | Visit of Edward II and Hugh Despenser fleeing his queen and Roger Mortimer | 1338-99 | Mary de Brotherton and her daughter, Margaret |
| 1348 | Black Death | | | | |
| 1377 | Accession of Richard II | | | | |
| 1399 | Accession of Henry IV | | | 1399-1400 | Thomas Mowbray, Duke of Norfolk |
| | | 1403 | Castle garrisoned against Owain Glyndwr | 1400-32 | John Mowbray, Duke of Norfolk |
| 1413 | Accession of Henry V | | | | |

| | | | | | |
|---|---|---|---|---|---|
| 1422 | Accession of Henry VI | | | | |
| 1455 | Beginning of Wars of Roses | | | | |
| 1461 | Accession of Edward IV | | | 1468 | Castle exchanged by Earls of Norfolk with lands held by Earls of Pembroke |
| 1483 | Accession of Edward V | | | 1469-91 | William Herbert I and II, Earls of Pembroke |
| 1483 | Accession of Richard III | | | | |
| 1485 | Accession of Henry VII | | | 1491-1507 | Walter Herbert |
| 1509 | Accession of Henry VIII | 1508-20 | Castle accommodation remodelled | 1508 | Passes to Charles Somerset by inheritance, then as Earls of Worcester and Dukes of Beaufort until 1914 |
| 1539 | Dissolution of major monasteries | | | | |
| 1547 | Accession of Edward VI | | | | |
| 1553 | Accession of Mary | | | | |
| 1558 | Accession of Elizabeth I | | | | |
| 1603 | Accession of James I | | | | |
| 1625 | Accession of Charles I | 1643-44 | Castle in front line of Civil War | | |
| | | 1645 & 48 | Castle besieged and captured | | |
| 1649 | Execution of Charles I | 1650-80 | Used as political prison | 1649-60 | Castle in the hands of Cromwell family |
| 1658 | Death of Oliver Cromwell | | | | |
| 1660 | Accession of Charles II | 1660s | Developed as an artillery fort | | |
| | | 1690 | Castle partly dismantled and abandoned as a ruin | | |
| | | 1770s | Castle cleared of industrial buildings and opened to visitors | | |
| | | 1899 | Castle put up for auction by Duke of Beaufort | | |
| | | | | 1914 | Acquired by the Lysaght family |
| | | | | 1953 | Castle placed in care of the state |

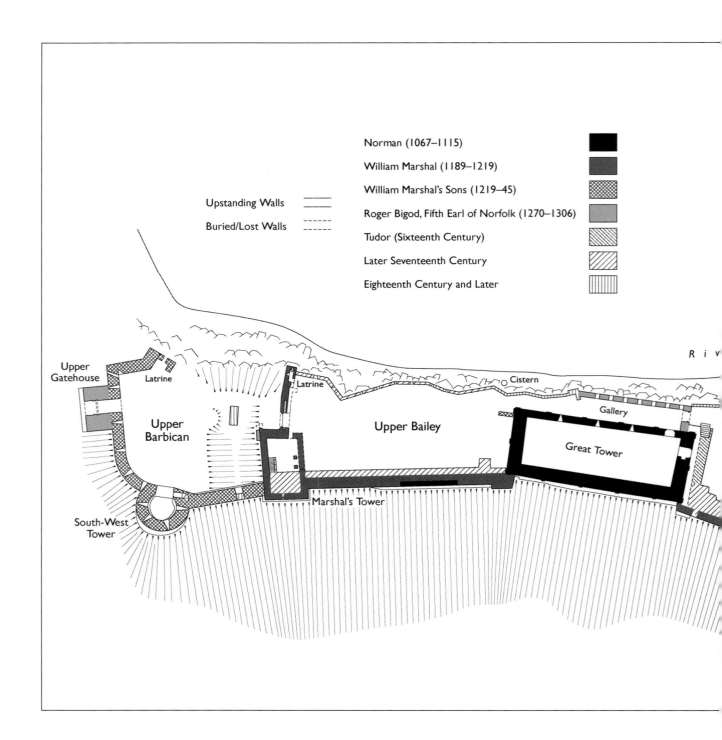

Norman (1067–1115)

William Marshal (1189–1219)

William Marshal's Sons (1219–45)

Roger Bigod, Fifth Earl of Norfolk (1270–1306)

Tudor (Sixteenth Century)

Later Seventeenth Century

Eighteenth Century and Later

Upstanding Walls

Buried/Lost Walls

Upper Gatehouse

Latrine

Upper Barbican

Latrine

Upper Bailey

Cistern

River

Gallery

Great Tower

South-West Tower

Marshal's Tower

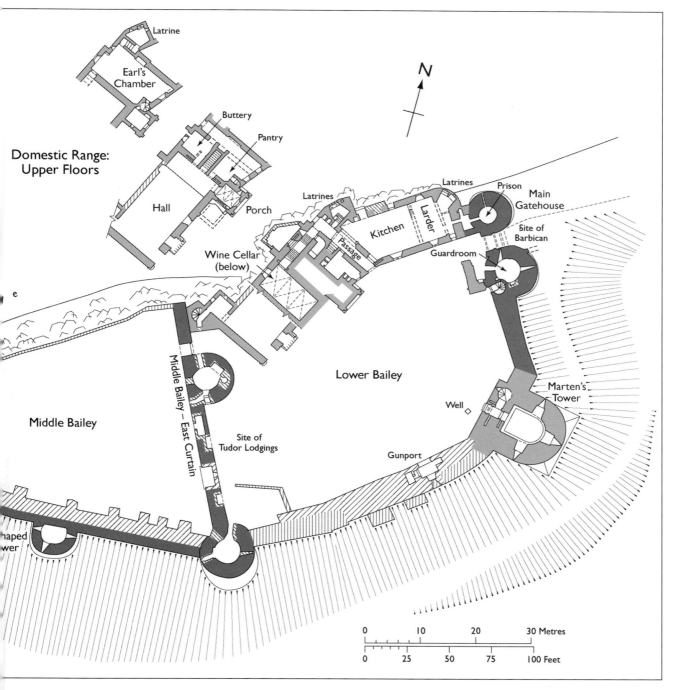

*Ground-floor plan of Chepstow Castle (with the upper floors of the domestic range)*

# CHAPTER I

# Introduction

*by* Ron Shoesmith *and* John R.L. Allen

The aim of this introductory chapter is to set the scene for the main part of this book which describes the various periods of occupation of the castle, the buildings and the people who lived and worked in them.

A short note on the physical background and topography of the Chepstow area is followed by a summary of the development of the area and town from its beginnings to the Norman Conquest. The local geology is discussed with reference to the stones used mainly in the construction of the Great Tower and completes the chapter.

The development of the town and its trading position on the Severn Estuary, its early buildings and its defensive Port Wall are described in chapter XVIII.

## Physical background

The most important geological event which has affected the lower Wye Valley area was caused by the uplifting of the landscape across which the River Wye meandered on its flood plain. The subsequent rejuvenation of the river and the new drainage pattern resulted in deeply-entrenched meanders which have had a great influence on communication, settlement and industry in the area.

The immediate Chepstow area had previously suffered from earth movements that produced faulting and folding which left various rock types exposed within a small radius of the town. These are described in more detail later in this chapter.

The geology of Chepstow's hinterland, especially the Forest of Dean, with its iron and coal fields and vast reserves of timber, has had a great influence on the development of the town and port.

The River Wye, stretching up to Hereford and central Wales has also been of continuing importance. Chepstow has acted as a port for onward transmission of wood and agricultural produce coming down the river, and as a base for the transmission of manufactured goods and such diverse items as wine to the landlocked and more remote regions upstream.[1]

## Topography

Chepstow stands on a peninsula which shelves down to the west bank of the River Wye near its confluence with the Severn. The river flows in a semi-circle around the town with the castle standing on the edge of a cliff overlooking the river. The town thus occupies a strategic position between England and Wales at the lowest bridge crossing of the Wye. The road which crosses the bridge and passes through the town was for many years a section of the main road from Gloucester into South Wales.

## Pre-Roman background

Chepstow is some 4km from the actual mouth of the Wye and it is to the south, on the west bank adjoining the final bend of the river, that signs of prehistoric occupation have been found. One Palaeolithic flint has been found within the

Chepstow area, whilst St. Peter's Cave, on the southern outskirts of Chepstow gives an indication of the pattern of hunter-gatherer activity better known from the King Arthur and Merlin Caves further north over the border in Herefordshire.[2] Activity continued in the same area in the Neolithic period, evidenced by a long barrow at Thornwell Farm, almost under the shadow of the Severn Bridge and only 2.5km south of the centre of Chepstow. Now incongruously next to a housing estate, this burial mound was only discovered in 1990. Similar mounds containing chambered tombs have been found at Heston Brake, a little further south near Portskewett.[3] It would seem that the area had a particular significance for a considerable time, for also at Thornwell Farm two cist burials and a round barrow of Early Bronze Age date have been found.[4] The Bronze Age is quite well represented in the area with several round barrows, standing stones and a stone circle recorded near Caerwent and round barrows near Tintern.[5]

Although there is no evidence for the use of the strategic promontory site at Chepstow during the Iron Age, the area around the town seems to have continued to be well used and well-populated. There are two substantial Iron Age camps at Piercefield—at Caer Hill and Porthcasseg—another called Bishop Barnet's Camp at St. Arvan's and the well-known one at The Bulwarks, all on the western banks of the Wye. There is also a promontory fort slightly further north in a strong position at Llancaut on the eastern bank. All are within some 3km of the centre of Chepstow (Fig. 1).

**The Roman period**
The area around Chepstow was generally well populated during the Roman period. It goes without saying that most of Monmouthshire must have been dominated by the large Roman town at Caerwent, the 'market town of the Silures', some 8km. to the south-west of Chepstow, but there are other sites even closer. On the Wyndcliff, to the north of Chepstow, there is a possible temple site, whilst on Portskewett Hill, some 6km south-west of the town 'walls and painted plaster in association with Roman coins and pottery' have been found.[6] Although Wales was essentially a military region throughout the Roman period, the countryside around Caerwent, the only Roman town in Wales, was subject to civil rule and the whole area must have benefited from this policy.

However, the extent of the Roman occupation in the immediate vicinity of Chepstow has been uncertain for many years. Leland, writing in the 16th century, found no evidence for a Roman origin at Chepstow, considering it more likely that

> when Cairguent (*Venta Silurum*) began to decay then began Chepstow to florisch. For yt stondeth far better as apon Wy there ebbyng and flowyng by the rage cummyng owt of Severn. So that to Chepstow may cum greate shyppes.[7]

Coxe, writing in 1801,[8] and Bradney, writing in the early 20th century,[9] both agreed with Leland.

However, sporadic Roman finds from within Chepstow help to paint a different picture. The finds include the well-known use of orange-red Roman tiles as a string course in the Great Tower (p.10) and the possible Romano-British carved stone on the south interior wall (Fig. 21); other masonry in the castle may also have a Roman origin (p.10-12). Close to the bridge, at 27 and 28 Bridge Street, Roman coins have been found.[10] On the edge of the castle ditch a late 3rd-century coin was found,[11] whilst a little further to the south, under the floor of 9 Bank Street two early 4th-century coins were unearthed. Other coins have been found to the west of the town,[12] inside a 'subterranean passage' underneath the George Hotel adjoining the Town Gate (the 'passage' is assumed to be a stone-built drain of uncertain date)[13] and, to the south of the town at 53 Green Street coins and pottery were found in a pit underneath the Port Wall.[14] A little more exotic was a harness mount, found when excavating foundations for a house somewhere in Chepstow in 1930.[15]

But the main evidence comes from the 1973–4 excavations just to the south of the priory church.[16] Here, underneath the remains of the monastic barn, were found three late 1st-century cremation burials associated with Roman pottery and a mid-1st-century coin.

These were not random or hurried burials, as one of them had been surrounded by a timber shrine. Roman tile and pottery were also found nearer the church.[17]

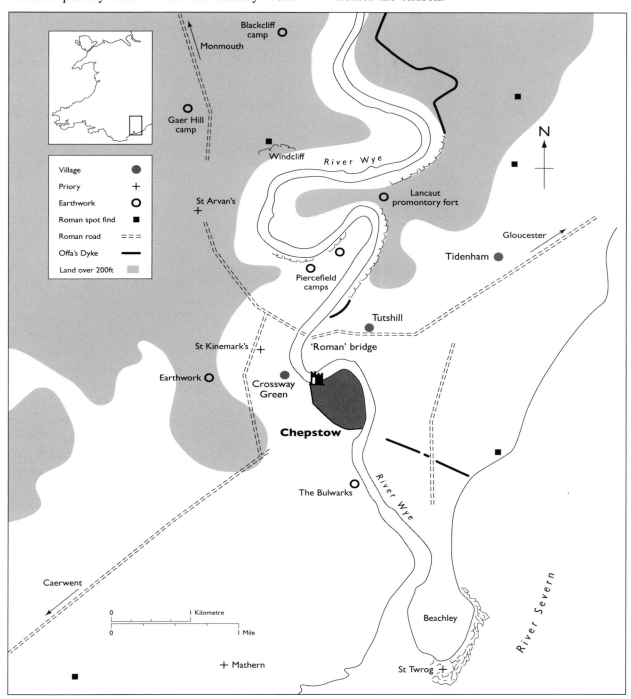

*Fig. 1 The area around Chepstow showing Iron Age hillforts, postulated Roman roads, the surviving part of Offa's Dyke and early medieval sites mentioned in the text*

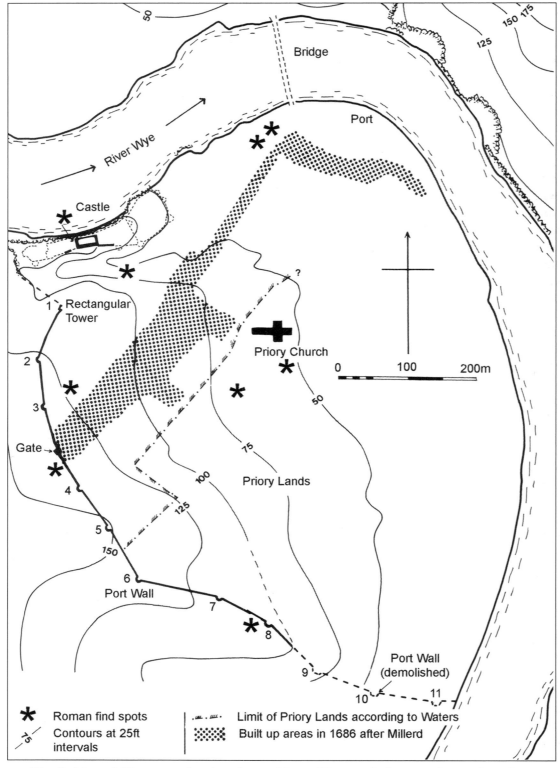

*Fig. 2  Map of Chepstow showing the position of Roman find spots, the castle, priory, early town and Port Wall*

4

The various finds seem to fall into two main periods. The earliest is during, or more probably just after, the final defeat of the Silures by the Romans in AD 78. This period includes the cremation burials in what was apparently a small cemetery, perhaps indicating the presence of a temporary fort in the immediate vicinity. The second set of finds, of late 3rd to early 4th century in date, may well relate to an expansion of the civilian area based on Caerwent and could suggest the possibility of a Roman villa in the immediate area. Robbing such a site for tile and stone for the castle in the late 11th century would have been much less laborious than bringing the material overland all the way from Caerwent.

Roman burials are often found alongside a road on the outskirts of a settlement or fort[18] and this raises the question of the course of the main Roman road leading from Gloucester to Caerwent and its crossing of the Wye. The general course of the road, indicated by straight alignments to the north-east and south-west of Chepstow, is readily apparent and has been described in some detail (Fig. 1).[19] On both sides of the Wye the road points almost directly to the old bridge crossing at Chepstow, but with no hard evidence for the last 1km of the route that would take them direct to the river. It has been proposed by several writers that the reason is that the bridge crossing was about 1.5km upstream of the present bridge. Here, at Castleford, traces of bridge timbers have been seen from time to time.[20] Although no dating evidence for this bridge is available, Fox suggests that the bridge, or a ford, may still have been in use in the 8th century when Offa's Dyke was constructed,[21] but it is considered unlikely that it was still in use when Chepstow Castle was built.

This does not preclude a crossing of the Wye at Chepstow at some time during the 350 years or so of Roman rule. Although the Wye is deep (and the tide exceptionally strong), the Romans were quite capable of building a timber bridge in such a position. Indeed Coxe, describing the Gloucestershire half of the bridge about 1800, noted that 'the carpentry of the piers ... is extremely ingenious and was probably formed on the Roman model'.[22] It may well be that the Roman road alignments did indeed lead to a ford (or even a bridge) at Chepstow, the road following the line of Nelson Street and Church Road within the town (Fig. 159) and thus directly past the subsequent Roman cemetery on its way down to the river. It may have been much later that the crossing of the Wye was moved upstream.

The evidence, although still sketchy, can be used to postulate a Roman basis for Chepstow, if only a small, 1st-century fort and river crossing followed by more settled occupation in the late 3rd and early 4th centuries.

**The Saxon period**

Although Leland thought Chepstow may have replaced Caerwent as the main town for the area after the end of the Roman occupation,[23] there is no evidence to substantiate a post-Roman, pre-Conquest, date for the town. However, the whole area, and especially the crossing of the Wye, must have been of considerable significance throughout the Saxon period. Fox suggests the Castleford crossing was still in use in the 8th century and cites as evidence that Offa's Dyke 'leaves the high ground ... and makes for the river just above the Roman road crossing', while on the west 'parish boundaries follow [the course of the Roman road] ... up the steep slope and for a considerable distance beyond'. The alignment of the Dyke is such that here, and here only in this southern sector, the Mercians carried their frontier down to the river bank.[24] Fox considered that the 'tree-clad limestone cliff opposite Chepstow ... undoubtedly represents throughout its length, the Mercian frontier'.[25] As the cliff declines, the Dyke recommences and cuts across the Beachley Promontory to the cliffs above the River Severn.

Several churches close to Chepstow have their origin in the late Saxon period including St. Arvan's, some 3km north-west[26] and St. Kinemark's, only 1km north-west of the town centre.[27] At Mathern, 4km south of Chepstow, the Bishop of Llandaff had a palace reputedly built on a site previously used by the early Christian kings of Gwent. On the opposite side of the river to Chepstow is the royal manor of Tidenham, given to the monks of Bath Abbey by King Edwy in AD 956. Shortly before the Conquest, the whole area around Chepstow belonged to Harold Godwinson, who had a hunting lodge at Portskewett some 7km south-west of Chepstow (Fig. 11).

**The Foundation of the Town**

Very shortly after the Norman Conquest, William fitz Osbern was created Earl of Hereford and Lord of Striguil. (Both castle and town, and apparently the area around, were originally called *Striguil*, the latter name apparently being a corruption of the Welsh 'ystraigyl' meaning simply 'the bend').[28]

There are no indications that there was any settlement on the Chepstow peninsula before the Conquest, so it is essential to view the location as one which was carefully chosen as the site of a castle to protect the southern end of fitz Osbern's palatinate and the crossing of the Wye rather than that for a town. The choice of the narrow site for the castle, with cliffs plunging precipitously for almost 100m to the river on the north and a parallel ravine on the south, must have been of prime importance. It will be shown (chapters II and III) that work on the castle must have started almost immediately after the Conquest, and certainly before 1070, when fitz Osbern returned to the continent and his eventual death.

However, fitz Osbern presumably had greater ideas for his new acquisition, for within that short space of time he also founded a priory at Chepstow—a dependent cell of his abbey at Cormeilles. Again, the choice of site was of

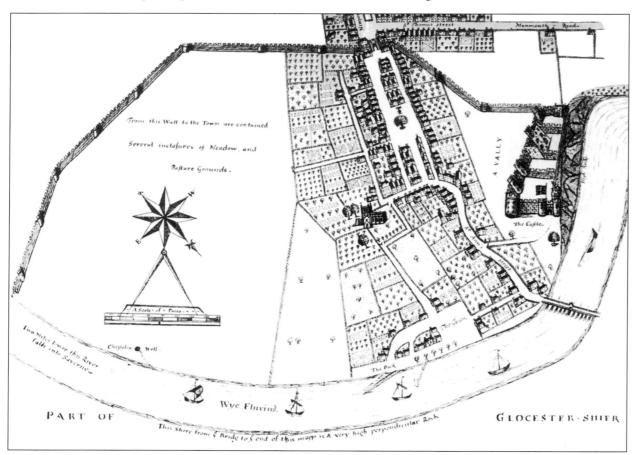

*Fig. 3  Millerd's plan of Chepstow in 1686*

6

importance. It would have to have been sufficiently far away from the castle so as not to affect the defensive potential of the site, but sufficiently close to come under the mantle of protection which the castle offered. The site chosen, almost central on the spine of the peninsula, and some 250m from the castle, fulfilled both these criteria and allowed the priory grounds to stretch away from the castle over the eastern part of the peninsula and down towards the river. It can even be suggested that the site was chosen to have its precinct boundary formed by the eastern edge of the line of the putative Roman road (the line of the present Nelson Street and Church Road) — an alignment that would have been well visible at that time. Indeed, the earliest buildings on the priory site, to the south of the church, were aligned with Nelson Street rather than with the church.[29]

The whole site, with its magnificent castle and church, must have been a magnet for settlers, and the town grew at a much greater rate than other border settlements such as Wigmore, Clifford and Ewyas Harold in the northern, more unsettled parts of fitz Osbern's estate.[30] The town is included in the Gloucestershire section of the Domesday survey, the only place west of the Wye to be so treated. The main entry reads:

> Earl William made the castle of Estrighoiel and it paid in his time only for vessels going to the forest. But in the time of Earl Roger, his son, this town paid sixteen pounds, and Ralph de Lumesi had half of it. The king has now twelve pounds from thence.[31]

From this it is evident that, within a few years of the Conquest, a small borough had grown, or been planted between the castle and the priory. An indication of the plan of this borough can be obtained by an examination of the plans of Millerd (Fig. 3) and Coxe, together with a consideration of the then existing buildings and the general topography. Accepting that the Great Tower of the castle and the priory church were the earliest and most important buildings in Chepstow, then the most logical situation for a

road would have been from the western doorway of the church (or an adjoining gatehouse) to the main gateway leading into the castle. It is suggested that the eastern part of this road still survives as Upper Church Street, which runs across the spine of the peninsula. This short street has all the appearance of an early road, for all the streets running down the hill suffer a break in alignment as they arrive at this street, as though they had to fit in around existing properties. There may well have been other roads leading to the castle from the west and from a river crossing. There is no record of the original construction of a bridge at Chepstow, the earliest dated reference being in 1234 when the bridge was repaired.

The development of the town from its Norman origins to the Civil War is covered in chapter XVIII.

**The Building Stone** *by* John R.L. Allen
A geological analysis of the building stones provides important insights into Norman and later medieval procurement and building practices and the changing circumstances under which the castle was created. Such an analysis involves five necessary steps, which may be taken at different levels of detail as circumstances dictate:

1. identification of lithology,
2. attribution of the lithology to a geological formation,
3. attribution of the lithology and formation to the geographical location of an exposure, quarry or mine, with its implications for possible routes and means of transport to the building site,
4. the relative abundance of the lithology in the building,
5. evidence for re-use.

The Great Tower at Chepstow was built directly after the Norman Conquest and seems to have remained largely unaltered for about 150 years. The Marshal family were responsible for heightening the Tower and putting in an extra floor in the early 13th century (chapter IX). The final phase of work was under Roger Bigod at the end of the 13th century, around the time that the domestic buildings were erected in the Lower Bailey (chapter XVI).

Within the Great Tower lithologies were identified by visual and hand-lens inspection of stone *in situ*, by the hand-lens inspection of small samples removed from blocks, and by the microscopic examination of thin-sections. Building stone has been re-used in all periods, either by importation from an older to a new building site, or by exploiting stone at the same site when either rebuilding or major repair works took place. Few of the many criteria advanced for re-use are conclusive (see below).

### The Lithologies and their Provenance in the Great Tower

Only sedimentary rocks were used in the Norman Great Tower, dividing almost exclusively between carbonate rocks (limestones and dolomites) and sandstones. They are discussed below in order of decreasing geological age. Colour is an important rock property and is given in the endnotes in terms of the colour names and codes of the widely used Munsell system.

The oldest formation represented in the first phase of the Great Tower is the Brownstones (upper Lower Old Red Sandstone, Siluro-Devonian).[32] The roughly-dressed blocks are of dull reddish-brown,[33] fine to medium grained, occasionally pebbly, laminated to structureless, lithic sandstone, frequently with a calcareous cement.[34] The nearest outcrop of the Brownstones yielding similar rocks is in the Tidenham-Woolaston area north-north-east of Chepstow. (Fig. 4).

The Upper Old Red Sandstone (Devonian) is formed of the Quartz Conglomerate overlain by the Tintern Sandstone Group.[35] The former is represented by roughly dressed blocks of a tough, off-white to light-grey[36] rock in which variable amounts of well-rounded, vein-quartz pebbles are set in coarse to very coarse grained quartz sand cemented with secondary quartz. The Quartz Conglomerate has an extensive but invariably narrow outcrop at a distance of not less than several kilometres to the west and north of Chepstow, and especially along the Wye valley upstream from Tintern. The Tintern Sandstone Group is represented by blocks of dark, reddish-brown,[37] medium to coarse-grained, occasionally pebbly, siliceous sandstones.[38] The outcrop of the Tintern Sandstone Group adjoins that of the Quartz Conglomerate (Fig. 4).

A number of stones belonging to the Carboniferous Limestone series[39] are represented. Roughly dressed blocks assigned to the Lower Dolomite range from massive, light brownish-grey,[40] dolomitic mudstones to pale yellow,[41] fine to medium-grained, slightly vuggy dolomites (i.e. having cavities lined by crystals). This formation outcrops close to Chepstow to the north-north-west, south and west (Fig. 4). The Whitehead Limestone (possibly with the oolitic Crease Limestone) is represented by structureless to striped or delicately laminated, reddish-grey,[42] greyish-red[43] or dark reddish-brown[44] calcite mudstones (some porcellanous), interbanded mudstones and oolites, oolites, quartzose mudstones and quartzose oolitic mudstones. The formation has a small outcrop at Chepstow, and others to the north and south. Interbedded among these carbonate facies is the Lower Drybrook Sandstone. Blocks from this formation in the earliest phase are massive to faintly-laminated, greyish-yellow,[45] greyish-yellow-brown[46] or dull yellow-orange[47], fine to coarse-grained quartz sandstones.[48] The Lower Drybrook Sandstone has scattered outcrops to the north, north-north-east and west of Chepstow Castle.

The Trias appears in the fabric as well-dressed blocks of a distinctive sandstone, mapped on the coast of the Severn Estuary from Portskewett to Llanfihangel Rogiet.[49] It is especially conspicuous in the plinth and in and around the decorated doorway on the exterior of the eastern wall. These Sudbrook beds were not formally named by the Geological Survey, but are now referred to as the Sudbrook Sandstone, after the quarried exposures on the coast (Fig. 4).[50] The rocks are soft, massive, dull to bright yellow-orange,[51]

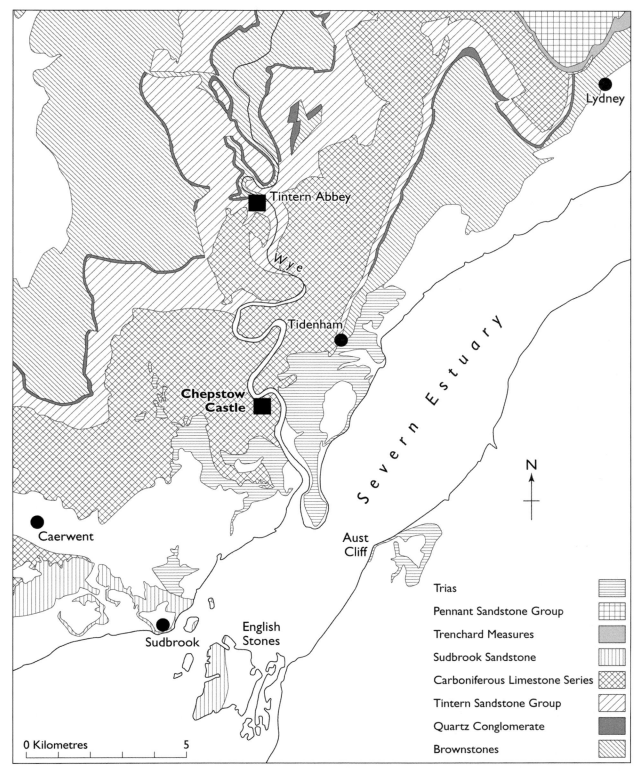

*Fig 4 A geological map of the Chepstow area showing the sources of the building stone used in Chepstow Castle*

medium to very coarse-grained, occasionally pebbly, quartz sandstones.[52] The Sudbrook Sandstone outcrops well to the south-west of Chepstow, but is readily accessible by water.

The youngest of the sediments are post-glacial tufas or travertines,[53] a range of calcareous deposits formed by the degassing of calcium bicarbonate-rich waters, commonly in the presence of algae and mosses. Tufa occurs in the Norman Great Tower as irregular to dressed blocks of off-white, cindery-textured limestone with occasional moulds recognizably of leaves and twigs. The source is unknown. Welch and Trotter[54] record only one occurrence of tufa in the area, from near Lydney,[55] but small deposits are common along streams and valleys that drain the Lower Old Red Sandstone, with its calcareous palaeosols, and the Carboniferous Limestone series.

One lithology from this phase that has not been satisfactorily provenanced is a hard, compact, chiefly medium- to coarse-grained, non-micaceous, lithic sandstone of variable colour, ranging from dull yellowish-brown[56] to greyish-brown[57] or greyish-yellow.[58] Feldspars are rare but rock fragments are abundant (25-35%), consisting of a variable mixture of mainly acidic lavas and tuffs with phyllites, schists and mudrocks. Some samples carry a little secondary quartz cement. Clearly different from the other sandstones present, the character and high proportion of lithic grains in the rock suggests an affinity with some Upper Carboniferous sandstones as described from the South Wales Coalfield.[59] The sandstones are unlike the micaceous rocks of the predominant Pennant Group, however, but a possible source is the underlying Trenchard Group,[60] outcropping along the rim of the Forest of Dean Coalfield to the north of Chepstow (Fig. 4).

In describing patterns of relative abundance, a sharp distinction can be made between the walls of the tower, and its partly battered plinth. It can confidently be stated that the massive plinth is composed almost exclusively of Sudbrook Sandstone, a presence recognised by North,[61]

with rare snecks of other stones inserted between some blocks. These coursed, monumental blocks reach up to $c$.1m in length and typically are 0.25-0.30m thick.

Substantially smaller, coursed blocks make up the walls above. Judgements about them are more subjective, as they display considerable local variation in composition on both the inner and outer faces of the building. Overall, however, the dominant rock-types in the early constructional phase are the carbonates of the Carboniferous Limestone series, excepting the dolomitic mudstones and dolomites, which are very rare. Quartz Conglomerate and tufa are also very rare and the Brownstones are uncommon. Blocks of the Tintern Sandstone Group, Lower Drybrook Sandstone, Sudbrook Sandstone and possibly the Trenchard Group seem no more than uncommon to common, although exhibiting local concentrations. The Sudbrook Sandstone is especially conspicuous on the east-exterior wall, whereas this role is played by the Tintern Sandstone Group on the interior of the west wall and by the possible Trenchard Group on the outside.

In addition to the long-established case of the orange-red Roman tiles, which form a conspicuous string course in the Great Tower, other claims have been made for the re-use of materials from Roman sources.[62] Putting aside inscribed or sculptured stonework, such as the possibly Romano-British figure group on the south-interior wall (Fig. 21),[63] the objective criteria for re-use are varied, subtle, best applied collectively, and generally suggestive rather than conclusive. Up to nine lines of evidence can be pursued, including comparative petrology/mineralogy, the presence of characteristic mechanical features on blocks, and the metrical properties of blocks.[64]

Eaton[65] thought that both the monumental and smaller blocks of Sudbrook Sandstone had been robbed from Roman sources, citing as evidence the (unquantified) scale of the blocks and the presence of mechanical features. The present survey confirmed the Lewis/clamp and dowel holes in the western plinth, although his figured dowel hole has since lost its mortar plug. In the south plinth the survey yielded two more Lewis holes and a possible dowel hole. Eaton's report of similar mechanical features on small blocks in the west and south interior walls was confirmed, including a block with 'faint traces of a feathered relief'.[66] It is questionable, however, whether the cable-decorated capital in one of the blind arches of the west-interior wall indicates re-use.[67]

A metrical analysis of the monumental blocks forming the plinth tends to support the idea of re-use.[68] Although Eaton[69] seems finally to reject the possibility that the blocks were robbed from Roman Caerwent (*Venta Silurum*),[70] it is worth examining comparative data from this site, where huge slabs of Sudbrook Sandstone survive as paving in the forum-basilica.[71] Allowing for the fact that one sample comes from walls, and the other from paving, two conclusions seem inescapable. First, the blocks in the Norman Great Tower, large as well as small, can all be accommodated within the dimensions of the slabs at Caerwent. Second, and perhaps most telling, the blocks at the two sites are indistinguishable in terms of thickness. The outstanding issue is perhaps the extent to which blocks of Sudbrook Sandstone from Caerwent may have been reshaped at Chepstow.

Other lithologies contributing to the fabric seem also to have been re-used, but not as proposed by Eaton,[72] who states that the 11th-century walls 'are for the most part faced in small, roughly-squared blocks of Old Red Sandstone'. On the basis of this claim he erects an elaborate model for the procurement of stone from the Roman religious complex at Lydney[73] to the north-east of Chepstow. These contentions are without evidence. First, the two lithologies attributed to the Old Red Sandstone in the earliest phase at Chepstow—the Brownstones and Tintern Sandstone Group—are markedly subordinate to

*Fig. 5 The forum-basilica at Caerwent which may have provided some of the building stone for Chepstow Castle*

carbonate lithologies and not more abundant overall, merely common. Second, the local Drybrook Sandstone[74] is seen to predominate in the fabric of the Lydney buildings.[75] A very little Quartz Conglomerate and Carboniferous Limestone are the only other rock-types present. Although the blocks used at Lydney are broadly similar metrically to the smaller blocks at Chepstow (see below), they are not represented petrographically there, either in the Old Red Sandstone lithologies, or in the Lower Drybrook Sandstone, in shades of yellow-orange.

Many if not most of the blocks of carbonate rock at Chepstow could have come from Caerwent. First, on the basis chiefly of the surviving facing of the Roman town's wall, the mix of lithologies at Caerwent, including a little Quartz Conglomerate and Lower Drybrook Sandstone, is closely similar in both range and relative abundance to that in the Great Tower. Second, as random samples of 50 blocks from each of Caerwent and Chepstow demonstrate, there are metrical similarities between the two sites.[76] The blocks at Caerwent are slightly the larger—smaller ones were used for buildings within the town and the blocks in the wall itself show signs of grading—but their form-ratio is the same as in the Great Tower.

What is most striking about the fabric of the Norman Great Tower is its great lithological diversity. Whether or not the materials represent Norman quarrying or the re-use to some degree of Roman stone, the builders appear to have been operating in an environment in which, although there was plenty of rock, there was no recognizable tradition of winning building stone from tried and tested sources. Alternatively, or indeed as well, the diversity can be seen as indicative of haste; the Norman Great Tower was to be completed speedily, so any stone of an acceptable quality was procured from wherever it could be quickly found.

The re-use of Roman building stone cannot be conclusively demonstrated. Several lines of evidence suggest the Sudbrook Sandstone was robbed from Caerwent, but there is less support in the case of other rock-types. If re-use is rejected altogether, it follows that all of the stone could have been procured from outcrops no more than 10–15km from the castle (Fig. 4). There was certainly no attempt to re-use Roman building stone from Lydney.

### The Marshals' Great Tower

Although above the Norman work there is an obvious change in the character of the dressing and laying of the stone, the relative inaccessibility of the higher walls inevitably means that less can be said geologically about the fabric of this phase. Reliance has been placed largely on indirect, binocular inspection with direct examination restricted to small areas around the central, internal archways on the northern and southern interior, where scaffolding was temporarily erected.

Inside, as well as outside, the predominant building materials in this phase are calcite mudstones and oolitic limestones comparable with formations of the Carboniferous Limestone Series of the Chepstow area (Fig. 4).[77] Scattered among these limestones are very occasional dressed blocks of the Tintern Sandstone Group (Upper Old Red Sandstone) and the Sudbrook Sandstone.[78]

As exemplified by the north-interior elevation, the relieving arches of the windows include two kinds of flaggy sandstone. One is a calcareous, fine to medium-grained, flaggy sandstone present to a very small extent in the Norman fabric. The other, used for window seats, appears in the Great Tower for the first time. It is closest to the Upper Carboniferous Pennant Sandstone Group,[79] best known from the South Wales Coalfield to the west.[80] The central arch and the dressings of the windows in the interior elevations, and many of the quoins of the exterior, are of a distinctive muddy limestone. Although the formation had been worked out by the end of the medieval period, the rock is identical to documented examples of the Dundry Freestone, of the Upper Inferior Oolite (Middle Jurassic) to the south of Bristol.[81] The Dundry

Freestone is accompanied in the blind archway against the west-interior elevation by white-pink alabaster, which forms the lowermost blocks.

Another limestone of the Upper Inferior Oolite appears to have been used for the exquisitely carved pieces which contribute to the springing of the two central arches of the interior of this phase, as seen on the north and south walls. Its combination of features suggests the rock is the Doulting Stone, a much-worked limestone outcropping near Shepton Mallet in the southern Mendips.[82] Also contributing to the springing are short shafts of typical Purbeck Marble. The formation, which yields the marble, is part of the Upper Jurassic outcrop of east Dorset.[83] The abacus of the northern corbel is made of Blue Lias Limestone and the southern corbel of a fine-grained, Upper Carboniferous Sandstone. Blue Lias was also used in William Marshal's buildings in the Upper Bailey, where it forms a window seat in Marshal's Tower and lintels to the latrine within the curtain wall.

The narrower range of building materials encountered in the Marshal phase of the Great Tower suggests two important changes in the approach to procurement by Marshal's sons as compared to the Norman builders. More time and greater wealth seem to have been available to these new builders.

First, the overwhelming dominance in the general fabric of stone from the local Carboniferous Limestone Series points to a simpler, more focused approach to the acquisition of building material for ordinary purposes. Quarries long-established in the local outcrops were probably being exploited, although some of the larger and better dressed limestone blocks resemble in size and proportion those in the Norman phase, and may represent re-use from that period of build.

Second, types of stone partly foreign to the Chepstow area were sought for specific and especially decorative purposes, in the latter case at what was with little doubt considerable expense. The flaggy Brownstones used in the relieving arches is probably local, but the platy sandstone from the Pennant Sandstone Group, employed also for window seating, outcrops no closer than 10km away from Chepstow. The occasional blocks of Triassic alabaster could have come from the cliffs either at Aust,[84] or from much more distant Penarth,[85] where there have been commercial workings in modern times. This material may have been imported primarily for the purpose of making plaster suitable for fireplaces and chimneys; an early 14th-century document records the use at Usk Castle of plaster of Paris made from 'sparstone' shipped from Aust Cliff.[86] A sample of plaster from one of the new window reveals proved to be made with plaster of Paris. The costliest and most remotely sourced materials are undoubtedly the Dundry Freestone, the Doulting Stone and the Purbeck Marble. After a short overland journey northward from the quarries, the Dundry Freestone was probably shipped to Chepstow from the banks of the Avon. The Doulting Stone pieces, perhaps already roughly carved at the quarry site, may have reached Chepstow by one of three possible routes. The most direct involved a lengthy overland journey northward across the Mendips, and thence by sea from the banks of the Avon. A second is by boat across the Somerset Levels down either the Axe or Brue to a port on the inner Bristol Channel. The third possibility is the old Roman route overland along the Polden Ridge to a haven on the Parrett.[87] The Purbeck Marble shafts, unless they were also shaped at and supplied from Doulting, could have been brought by sea to Chepstow from Wareham or Swanage on the Isle of Purbeck.

### Roger Bigod's Building Work

References in the building accounts for the period 1282–4 provide invaluable insights into the provenance and means of transport of Roger Bigod's material for his work in the kitchen range in the Lower Bailey. A similar procurement strategy for Marten's Tower and the Great Tower seems likely. Stone was quarried at Tintern (Tintern Sandstone Group) and Tidenham (presumably the Carboniferous Limestone

Series) and thence shipped to the castle.[88] Aust Cliff supplied sparstone directly by boat,[89] perhaps for the making of special plaster, as found in one of the window reveals of the Marshals' building phase. Lime was made with the aid of imported coal,[90] some of which came down the Severn from Lydney.[91] Sand was shipped from a number of places, including St. Arvan's on the Wye and Tidenham and Lydney on the Severn.[92] Lead, bought at Gloucester and Bristol, was shipped to the castle[93] and melted and cast there using some of the imported sand.[94]

Throughout the buildings of the Lower Bailey, the rubble stone is very largely Carboniferous Limestone. Much of it is pinkish in colour, porcellanous and brittle. Some Sudbrook Sandstone has been used in rough slabs, particularly in forming the vault below the cellar and in the relieving arches above the cellar doorway and window. The majority of the dressed stone is from the Tintern Sandstone Group, almost certainly from the Barbadoes Wood quarry 1½km north of the abbey where stone was being produced contemporaneously for the new church.[95] However, Jurassic oolite was used particularly in Marten's Tower for some of the finer openings and carvings such as the doorway from the courtyard, the chapel windows and the carved statues on the parapets. Some Old Red Sandstone is used in the dressed arches within the vault below the cellar.

Of Roger Bigod's building work at the Great Tower, only the Gallery is directly accessible. An examination of the remaining fabric has been limited to the use of binoculars. Generally speaking, the walls are composed of neatly coursed, regular blocks of what appear to be grey-weathering limestones from the local Carboniferous Limestones Series (Fig. 4).[96] Blocks of a similar size are grouped together into courses or sets of courses. Various lithologies occur in the quoins and dressings of windows and openings, but chief among these are dark reddish-brown sandstones from the Tintern Sandstone Group (Upper Old Red Sandstone) with a variety of other local sandstones.[97] By Roger Bigod's time building stone was being procured from an even narrower range of sources—all arguably well-established—than is evident in the early years of the 13th century.

# CHAPTER II

# William the Conqueror, William fitz Osbern and Chepstow Castle *by* David Bates

It is beyond doubt that William fitz Osbern built a castle at Chepstow and therefore that some kind of fortified structure existed there before his death at the Battle of Cassel in north-eastern France in February 1071. It is, however, now clear that his role at Chepstow can no longer be seen in straightforward terms as the builder of the Great Tower which still exists and that it must, among other things, take account of his wide range of commitments in England and France after 1066.[1] Not only is he unanimously portrayed in early sources as the closest of all the Conqueror's associates in Normandy and in England from the mid-1040s until 1071, he was also a key figure in the Norman Conquest of England, where charter evidence and Domesday Book show just how active he was between 1066 and 1071.[2] For his reputation it is worth citing the two great early 12th-century historians, William of Malmesbury and Orderic Vitalis. For the former, 'he might well be compared with the best of princes' and for the latter, he was 'the bravest of the Normans, renowned for his generosity, ready wit and outstanding integrity'.[3]

William fitz Osbern's birth-date was probably slightly later than William the Conqueror's; the early 1030s is a reasonable estimate.[4] He was a member of the uppermost ranks of the Norman aristocracy. His father was Osbern the steward, nephew of the future Conqueror's great-grandfather Count Richard I's long-lived second wife Gunnor, who had lived until c.1030 (Fig. 6). His mother was Emma, daughter of Rodulf—usually known as Count of Ivry, and the half-brother and closest associate of Richard I. Osbern was prominent at the ducal court from the later years of the reign of Duke William's grandfather Duke Richard II (996–1026), and perished dramatically by violence in the young William's palace in c.1041. Although such a murder in the ruler's presence was a spectacular invasion of princely space, its long-term political consequences appear to have been minimal. The perpetrators were members of the family of Roger II de Montgomery, the future earl of Shrewsbury, and a man whose collaboration with the Conqueror comes close to being as legendary as fitz Osbern's.[5]

The statement by William the Conqueror's contemporary biographer, William of Poitiers, that the close relationship between the two Williams went back to their respective boyhoods is likely to be correct.[6] Although charter evidence indicates that the young William fitz Osbern's formal protectors were his own family, he begins to appear in ducal charters in the mid-1040s, at the time that the young Duke William was asserting his personal rule.[7] He married Adeliza, daughter of Roger I de Tosny, at a date which may well have been in the mid-1040s; this union could not have taken place without the sanction of the ducal court.[8] In c.1046 he founded a

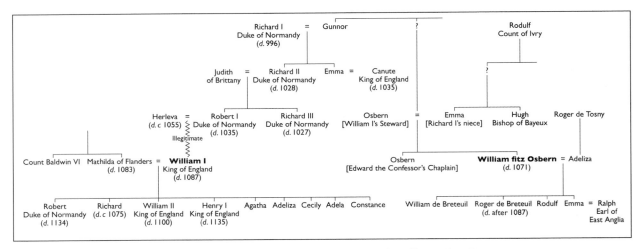

Fig. 6 Family tree of William fitz Osbern and William the Conqueror

monastery at Lyre in central Normandy; followed in c.1060 by the establishment of a second abbey at Cormeilles (Fig. 7).[9] All this suggests that cooperation and friendship between the two Williams pre-dated by several years William of Poitiers' reference to William and Roger de Montgomery as the two nobles despatched to negotiate with Count Geoffrey Martel of Anjou, as his army advanced northwards to seek to relieve Duke William's siege of the castle of Domfront in either 1049 or 1051–2.[10]

Fitz Osbern's subsequent rise in the 1050s was spectacular. His vast, inherited lands stretched throughout the whole of Normandy; the process of their transmission to him via his father, Osbern, and his uncle, Bishop Hugh of Bayeux (long debated) has now been convincingly determined by Pierre Bauduin.[11] He also inherited his father's title of *dapifer* (steward), and with

Fig. 7 Map of England, Wales and Normandy showing the places associated with fitz Osbern mentioned in the text

16

it his central role at the ducal court. Ducal intervention to exclude from the family inheritance William fitz Osbern's brother Osbern, who left Normandy for England in 1050 to become a chaplain of King Edward the Confessor, is likely.[12] Then, in or shortly after 1054, Duke William entrusted William fitz Osbern with the frontier castle of Breteuil, which guarded one of the most accessible entry routes into southern Normandy.[13] There has not been a modern study of this castle, which consists of two huge ringworks (140m x 120m and 70m x 50m), protected by a large earthwork to the north and two artificial lakes to the south and west.[14] While not in any way a precursor of Chepstow, it is notable as being a structure on a vast scale.

William of Malmesbury singled out fitz Osbern as the most forceful advocate of the invasion of England in 1066. He provided sixty ships for the invasion fleet (Fig. 8).[15] Soon after the Conqueror's coronation on 25 December 1066, he was made an earl, entrusted with Winchester and the Isle of Wight, and endowed with lands across most of the south of England; in all likelihood his power in considerable measure replicated that of the former King Harold as earl of Wessex.[16] These years after 1066 were beyond doubt the apogee of fitz Osbern's career. With the king's half-brother, Bishop Odo of Bayeux, whose base was at Dover, he was left in charge in England when the Conqueror returned to Normandy from February until December 1067. The Anglo-Saxon Chronicle comments on their oppressive behaviour and castle-building, activities which were surely to be expected in a kingdom much of which remained either hostile or untouched by the new regime's direct rule.[17] A charter dating from 1069 describes him as 'count of the palace' (*comes palatii*). This use of a Carolingian title signifying pre-eminence among the aristocracy at court must indicate that fitz Osbern was in effect the Conqueror's chosen deputy during the extraordinarily demanding times which followed the victory at Hastings.[18] An early 12th-century source, with seemingly special access to the traditions of William fitz Osbern's family, says that he had rule over

Normandy and England under the king.[19] And another early 12th-century source says that it was specifically on William's advice that the king had all the monasteries of England plundered in 1070 to remove the treasures which the defeated English had placed in them for safe keeping.[20]

William fitz Osbern's attestation of all the English royal diplomas which have survived from the period between 1066 and 1070, shows him to have been regularly in the king's company on great occasions. Not all of the diplomas can be dated, but on the basis of those which can, it is certain that he was present at Westminster at Whitsun in 1068 when William the Conqueror's wife Mathilda was crowned queen of the English and at the royal court at Winchester at Easter 1069.[21] It is also known that he took part in the military expedition to relieve York in the winter and early spring of 1069, since Orderic tells us that he was left behind as castellan at York after

*Fig. 8 A feast of William the Conqueror's chief supporters as depicted in the Bayeux Tapestry— one of which would be fitz Osbern*

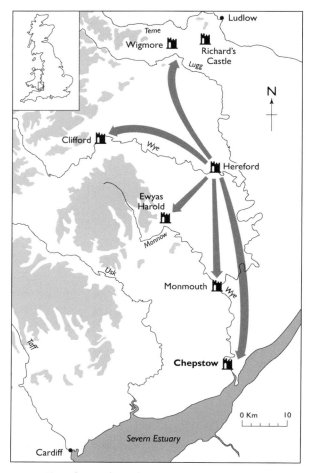

*Fig. 9 A plan showing the location of fitz Osbern's castles in the Marches, spreading out from the base of his earldom at Hereford*

*Fig. 10 The west front of Chepstow Priory, still retaining its Norman doorway and west windows*

the king departed for the south of England; his stay there was, however, a short one since, like the king, he was back at Winchester by 13 April.[22] He was active throughout this period in many counties of southern England, confirming property transactions, which included a grant to the abbey of Bath, of which record survives in a unique writ in which his name is paired with the king's.[23] His absence from any surviving charter written and confirmed in Normandy dateable to between 1066 and the end of 1070 suggests that he remained in England throughout the four years after the Battle of Hastings.[24] The one transaction involving property in France in which it is known that he was involved—his restoration to the abbey of Saint-Denis of the customs of the estate

of Berneval-le-Grand near Dieppe—almost certainly took place in England.[25] This vast range of responsibilities and activities is essential in the context of any estimate of his role at Chepstow.

Although directly involved on the Welsh border only for a short time, William fitz Osbern had a powerful impact there; William of Malmesbury, for example, noted that the laws he instituted were still in force in the 1120s.[26] From Domesday Book we learn that he built or re-fortified castles at Wigmore, Clifford and Ewyas Harold as well as Chepstow. *Liber Llandavensis* adds Monmouth to the list (Fig. 9). References to renders and settlement at both Chepstow and Monmouth indicate that what was involved was more than a simple fortification.[27] There are references in Domesday to his involvement in redistributing lands, usually to the main Norman settlers in the region.[28] A particular area of interest for him seems to have been the north bank of the Severn estuary where exchanges and reorganisation of lands at Lydney and Tidenham, taken alongside his known activities at Berkeley, suggest a policy of developing a sustained presence on both sides of the river.[29] His extensive grants to his two Norman monastic foundations of Lyre and Cormeilles are indicative of remarkable patronage at a notably early date after the Conquest.[30] The overall picture from evidence of this kind is of a far-reaching, co-ordinated effort to organise and dominate the society of the southern marches. Chepstow seems to have been especially important to him since it is reasonable to think that he founded a priory subject to Almenèches there as well as the castle and a small urban settlement (Fig. 10).[31]

Earl William inherited the results of Earl/King Harold's recent aggressive advances into Gwent. These included at least the coastal belt between the Wye and the Usk where Harold had built a hunting lodge at Portskewett (Fig. 11), and most probably other acquisitions elsewhere. The location of the castles of Chepstow and Monmouth on the west bank of the Wye shows his intention to hold at least what he already had. Orderic tells us that he invaded Wales, launching a campaign against the people of Brycheiniog and three kings, Rhys ab Owain ab Edwin, Cadwgan ap Meurig and Maredudd ap Gruffudd ap Llywelyn.[32] The territories controlled by these kings, which comprised parts of southern Powys, Morgannwg and parts of mid-Wales, indicate that this was a serious war against a substantial coalition of Welsh rulers. Careful attention to detailed evidence has shown further gains, which may well have amounted to most of Lower Gwent as

*Fig. 11  Aerial photograph of the earthworks of King Harold's 'hunting lodge' at Portskewett which would have had direct access to the Severn Estuary in the 11th century*

far west as the Usk.[33] These victories were accompanied by settlements with Welsh rulers. Caradog ap Gruffudd, king in Upper Gwent, who later appears as an ally of William's son Roger, may well have been among these. Another alliance is indicated by Domesday Book's record of three grants to King Maredudd ap Gruffudd ap Llywelyn, which were still in force in 1086 in the time of Maredudd's son Gruffudd.[34] The precise date of these many activities is unknown, but fitz Osbern's wider responsibilities in Wessex in 1067 and his itinerary thereafter suggest that he is most likely to have been closely involved on the Welsh March in the second half of 1068. The fact that the warfare in Herefordshire in late 1067 and early 1068 instigated by the man known as Eadric the Wild involved only conflict with local castellans supports this proposed chronology.[35] Indeed these troubles may well have led to a decision by the two Williams that more direct involvement by a heavyweight political figure was needed. Also,

the Conqueror is known to have hunted in the Forest of Dean in the late summer of 1069 and, although there is no direct evidence of William fitz Osbern's presence then, it is quite likely that the king's visit was connected with his consolidation of the region.[36]

William fitz Osbern crossed to Normandy, at a date likely to have been towards the end of 1070, to support Queen Mathilda as her husband's regent in the duchy.[37] His despatch to Normandy after his long sojourn in England suggests that serious matters were afoot. The king had joined them by the end of the year; there is every likelihood that the three of them spent Christmas at Rouen.[38] Top of the agenda must have been the conflicts which had erupted within the Flemish comital family in which the widow and children of Mathilda's recently deceased brother, Count Baldwin VI, were struggling against another brother, Robert the Frisian. The accounts differ in detail, but the essence is that fitz Osbern was sent

Fig. 12 A reconstruction of the Norman castle showing the Great Tower and surrounding structures as first built. Although there is no evidence for the timber stockade, it is a likely adjunct to the initial defences

with a small force to join the king of France, Philip I, and others in support of Baldwin VI's widow and children, with marriage to the widow for the widowed William fitz Osbern as a central element in the package.[39] Although Malmesbury treats the marriage project as a sign of excessive ambition on fitz Osbern's part, the whole business made excellent political sense given the strength of the connections between the Anglo-Norman realm, Flanders and Picardy.[40] William fitz Osbern's participation was simply one more reflection of how important he was to William the Conqueror.

Fitz Osbern's death at the Battle of Cassel on 20 or 21 February 1071, as several writers recognised, removed a man who had been of the utmost importance to the Norman Conquest of England.[41] His huge cross-Channel estates were divided among his two sons, with the elder, William de Breteuil, receiving the Norman lands and the younger, Roger, the English ones (Figs. 6 and 7).[42] A daughter, Emma, was married in 1075 to Ralph, Earl of East Anglia, and at the wedding-feast he and Roger hatched a plot against the king which led ultimately to defeat and forfeiture. The English lands once held by William fitz Osbern passed to the king and his descendants ceased to play any role in the affairs of the southern marches. In spite of Roger's fall, however, there is enough evidence to show that he had consolidated further and in all likelihood extended his father's achievements on the Welsh border.[43]

As far as the great tower of Chepstow Castle is concerned, it is hard to believe that William fitz Osbern could have presided over the erection of so elaborate a building with so much to occupy him elsewhere. It looks like the product of a time when the Norman take-over of England was more secure and when decisions had been made about the likely limits of military expansion into Wales in this sector. Everything therefore points to the later years of the Conqueror's reign for the main phase of construction. The king's one known visit to Wales, his combined military campaign and pilgrimage to St. David's in 1081, may well have expanded Norman territorial control further into Morgannwg and led to the construction of a castle at Cardiff (Fig. 13). However, it was essentially an exercise in the type of symbolic display and political consolidation which characterised almost every aspect of his rule in the last decade of his life. After 1072 he spent relatively little time in England,[44] attracted for a time in the 1070s by prospects of European adventures. In the event, from the last years of the decade he was tied down by the consequences of his quarrel with his eldest son and the dispute with his brother, Bishop Odo. He was also threatened by invasions of England from Denmark and of Normandy from France, and concentrated on holding what he had. In this context the Great Tower at Chepstow makes sense as a symbolic marker of the limits of conquest, and perhaps, as a commemoration of the achievements of the

*Fig. 13 The motte and later shell keep at Cardiff Castle. Construction possibly began with William the Conqueror's combined military campaign and pilgrimage to St. David's in 1081*

man to whom William the Conqueror owed a great deal and who he held in greater affection than any other man. In the end, however much stylistic and structural analyses show that William fitz Osbern is unlikely to have been directly responsible for the building and design of the Great Tower of Chepstow Castle, there can be no question that it was he who was responsible for developing Chepstow as the site where such a structure could be built and for creating the general conditions which made it possible. The association of castle, priory and borough, securely dateable to his time, makes it certain that he had singled out Chepstow for special treatment. It is pure speculation to suggest it, but it is quite possible that the Great Tower of Chepstow Castle fulfilled an ambition already formulated by William fitz Osbern.

# CHAPTER III

# The Norman Great Tower

*by* Rick Turner, Chris Jones-Jenkins *and* Stephen Priestley

The only direct documentary reference to the Norman castle at Chepstow comes from the Domesday Book and dates from 1086. Within the county of Gloucestershire are some entries covering territories in the lordship of Chepstow including the following:

> *Castellum de Estrighoiel fecit Willelmus comes et eius tempore reddebat xl. solidatas tantum de navibus in silvam euntibus. Tempore Comitis Rogerii filii eius reddidit ipsa villa xvi. libratas et medietatem habedat Rad(ulphus) de Limesi. Modo habet rex inde xii. libratas[1]*

This can be translated as:

> Earl William built the castle of Striguil and in his time paid only 40s from the ships going into the woodland. In the time of his son Earl Roger, this town paid £16 and Ralph de Limesy had half. Now the king has £12 from it.

Whilst this reference credits Earl William with building the castle, it does not say that he built the Great Tower. William fitz Osbern was one of the closest friends and confidantes of William the Conqueror, who granted him the Saxon earldom of Hereford. This had been founded by the Danes and then developed by the Saxon kings of England as a buffer against the Welsh. Other entries in Domesday show that he built or re-fortified four castles in Herefordshire: Richard's Castle, Wigmore, Clifford, and Ewyas Harold, and probably that at Monmouth (Fig. 9).[2] With Chepstow, these formed a formidable frontier on the southern March, complemented by the castles built by Roger de Montgomery, earl of Shrewsbury and later by Hugh d'Avranches, earl of Chester, in the central and northern March. The earldom of Hereford already had its own *caput* or castle-palace at Hereford, taken from the Godwinson family.[3] In addition to his earldom, William I granted fitz Osbern lands in Oxfordshire, Dorset, Berkshire, Somerset and Hampshire, including the Isle of Wight, where he built Carisbrooke Castle. At none of these other castles is there any evidence for stone buildings or defences to match those surviving at Chepstow. However, he had already developed a substantial castle, perhaps centred on a donjon, at Breteuil in Normandy in the 1050s[4] and would have been very familiar with the great towers of the region.[5]

Earl William fitz Osbern died in Flanders in 1071 after four years of campaigning, consolidating William the Conqueror's new kingdom in England and guarding the dukedom of Normandy. He was succeeded as lord of Chepstow by his son Roger de Breteuil, a much lesser and weaker man. Roger was involved in a conspiracy with Ralph, Earl of Norfolk and Suffolk and Waltheof of Northumbria, to overthrow King William. He was captured and imprisoned by the king and his estates were forfeited to the Crown. Chepstow was to remain in royal hands until about 1115, when Henry I granted the lordship to Walter fitz Richard de Clare (d.1138), whose family held the castle for most of the 12th century.[6] Throughout the period of the Crown's ownership, there are no direct references to Chepstow Castle.[7]

Except for the Great Tower, there is little to show the extent and character of the Norman castle. Along the base of the south curtain wall of the Upper Bailey, there is a low plinth with a convex profile, standing three or four courses high. It is similar but less massive than that below the adjacent Great Tower. Above the plinth is an irregular panel of coursed blocks of a wide variety of stone types, overlain by the Carboniferous Limestone rubble of William Marshal's later curtain wall. This suggests that the Upper Bailey, at least, had a stone curtain wall

contemporary with the Great Tower. It probably extended up to and returned by the present Upper Bailey ditch.

The imposing entrance on the east face of the Great Tower would imply that this was the direction of approach. It is hard to imagine that it was not defended by an outer ward in some way. Yet there is no clear evidence for such a ward in the Norman castle, except for a change of slope in the Middle Bailey (see chapter VI). The other problem resulting from siting the Great Tower on top of a porous limestone cliff was how to obtain water. This may have been solved by the remarkable cistern on the bank of the river immediately below the tower (see chapter XII).

**Description of the surviving fabric**
This section describes the surviving fabric identified as belonging to the Norman period, beginning with the exterior of the building starting with the west elevation and progressing anti-clockwise. The interior is considered in the same way.

*West external elevation* (Fig. 14)
This is the simplest and plainest of the external elevations, yet it sets the pattern that all the others follow but elaborate upon. Just above ground level the top of a plain plinth is visible, made of Sudbrook Sandstone. The same stone is used to form plain angle buttresses and a central plain pilaster, which divides the elevation into two equal bays, 5.5m wide. Both buttresses and pilaster have a simple chamfered base rising from the offset of the plinth. The stone was neatly dressed into square blocks and laid in courses consistently 300mm high. Sometimes pieces of Roman tile and snecks of Carboniferous Limestone are used to fill wide joints. The Norman wall top is marked by a V-shaped band, which steps around the buttresses and the pilaster, and two courses of squared blocks, forming a low parapet. Directly above this ashlar detailing sit two small circular lights, the one nearer the centre of the elevation retaining the two plain Sudbook Sandstone blocks through which the window was cut.[8]

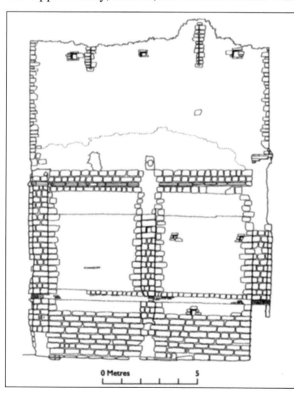

*Fig. 14  The Great Tower:*
*west external elevation*

Almost exactly one-third of the way up the bays of the Norman phase within this elevation is a band of four courses of re-used Roman tile. This band steps out to respect the buttresses and pilaster. Where the tiles are missing it can be seen that the band is only one tile in depth and does not pass into the core of the building. This implies that it was a decorative rather than a structural feature. There is a single course of squared Sudbrook Sandstone blocks above the band of Roman tiles. Within the bays the lowest courses are made of dressed blocks of Sudbrook Sandstone with lime-stone-snecked joints. However, from just below the Roman tile band the character of the facing stone changes dramatically with much smaller stones being used laid in rough courses.

*South external elevation* (Fig. 15)
This elevation formed part of the landward-facing defences of the castle. Though it stands upon the top of one side of a natural valley, the Dell, this part of the castle is overlooked from the slightly higher ground on the opposite side some 60m away.

The plinth is made of massive blocks of Sudbrook Sandstone laid in regular courses 300mm high. It has a convex profile so that at its base it stands 0.4m forward of the main wall face. The natural rock on which it stands slopes down-hill, so that only four courses of the plinth are present at the western end, rising to twelve courses at the eastern end. The top of the plinth runs at an angle of about 3° below the horizontal across the elevation.

This elevation has angle buttresses and is divided into five bays by plain pilasters. The three central bays are all 6.2m wide, but the end bay to the west is 5.8m wide and that to the east only 4m wide. The V-shaped horizontal band at the wall top of the Norman phase, with its two courses of sandstone blocks above and one below, partly survives above the two western bays, and the band projects a short distance beyond the second pilaster. This detail was removed when the wall top and pilasters were raised over the other bays in the Marshal phase.

There is a band of four courses of Roman tile one-third of the way up the Norman bays running parallel with the top of the plinth. There is a wide variety of building stones used with a lower proportion of Brownstones than represented on the west elevation.

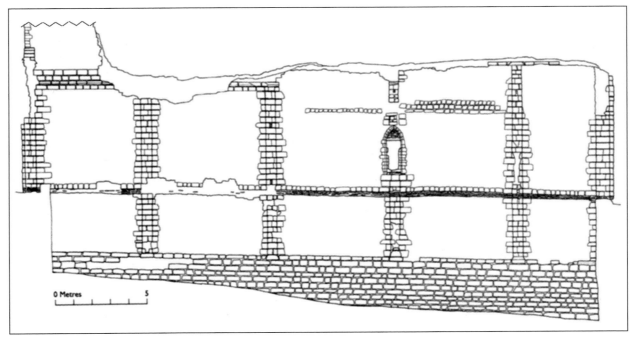

*Fig. 15 The Great Tower: south external elevation*

*East external elevation* (Fig. 16)

This is the most familiar and commonly illustrated elevation of the Great Tower. However, it is far more altered than either the west or the south elevations and the original fabric needs to be carefully unravelled.

The plinth of this elevation rose from the top of a terraced slope created in front of the Great Tower, giving an imposing appearance for anyone approaching by land or river. It rose perhaps twelve or more courses to form a convex profile, now hidden by the later walkway.

The elevation was framed by angle buttresses and divided into two equal bays by a plain pilaster. Their tops were truncated during the later Marshal phase of building work. The southern bay is divided by a band of four courses of Roman tile at one third of its height and contains one original opening, a slit window with a rounded head, which lights the head of the intra-mural staircase rising to the first-floor.

The northern bay is dominated by the massive Sudbrook Sandstone doorcase (Fig. 17). The head has a joggled lintel with a broad central key block. The lintel is decorated with two bands of chip carving in a saltire pattern. Above this lintel is a recessed, semi-circular tympanum made of lozenge-shaped blocks set into a distinctive pink mortar whose aggregate is made of crushed Roman tile. The saltire pattern is carved on these blocks at 45° to the lintel. The tympanum is framed by two semi-circular arches, with the inner being slightly recessed from the wall face. The individual blocks are carved with radiating bands of saltire decoration whose dimensions vary, implying that they were carved on the blocks before erection. The main doorway opens into an intra-mural anteroom with a staircase on the left leading up to the first floor and a similar door directly ahead, which gave access to the undercroft.

The three courses of Roman tile frame the outer arch of the doorcase. The remainder of the bay is faced with regular courses of large Sudbrook Sandstone blocks. These courses are

*Fig. 16 The Great Tower:*
*east external elevation*

*Fig. 17 The Great Tower:*
*the east doorway*

26

disrupted above the doorcase by a rectangular panel of rubble Carboniferous Limestone, characteristic of the Marshal phase of work. This implies the removal and blocking of a Norman window of the form to be found on the north elevation.

*North external elevation* (Fig. 18)

This is the most complex and revealing elevation of the Great Tower. Its unravelling has provided the key to reconstructing the exterior of the three phases of buildings that are represented in its ruinous state—the original Norman work, that of the Marshals and finally Roger Bigod's addition.

The plinth, like that on the west elevation, has a vertical not a convex face. The rock face runs downhill from west to east and the plinth accommodates this slope by both angling and stepping downhill. Below the second bay the foundation levels are exposed, showing that the rock surface was cut into broad steps before becoming eroded.

In the first bay the plinth forms a vertical edge and then a step to accommodate a rectangular doorcase with plain Sudbrook Sandstone jambs and what was probably a flat joggled lintel where the oak beams are now. This was the original ground-floor entrance into the Great Tower. Just visible behind the return of the Gallery wall is another vertical edge of Sudbrook Sandstone blocks, implying that the plinth stepped back up to a level consistent with that surviving on the east elevation.

The elevation is divided into five bays. The first four bays are similar, averaging 5.7m in width, whilst the fifth bay is smaller at 4.9m in width. The Norman wall top detail survives on the north-west buttress and the lower, single course runs partly across the fifth bay. The band of four courses of tile also runs across the fifth bay to a similar point as the stone-course above, where it ends with a series of stepped sandstone blocks. It only reappears again in the north-east

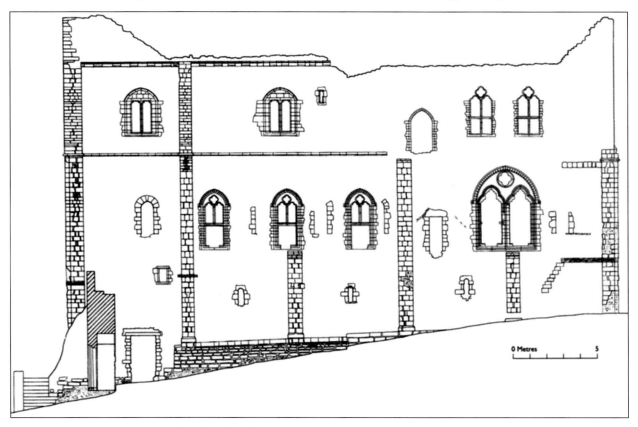

*Fig. 18 The Great Tower: north external elevation*

27

buttress, though a short band of three courses of tile runs across the first pilaster at a slightly higher level.

Each of the three central bays has a small, semi-circular headed window lighting the ground floor with metal bars but no glazing. The pattern of the openings at first floor can also be reconstructed with some confidence. A complete window survives unblocked in the first bay. It is 0.75m wide and 1.6m high to the springing point of a semi-circular arched head. The opening is framed by dressed Sudbrook Sandstone and occasional limestone tufa blocks. Parts of the dressed stonework of four other windows of identical form can be traced on this elevation. In the fourth bay is a rectangular doorcase, 0.75m wide and 2.05m high, with a monolithic lintel. To either side of the lintel are the remains of mortar fillets, which indicate the position and direction of the original staircase up to the porch of this doorway.

*West internal elevation* (Fig. 19)
The room is 8.9m wide and the large blocks of the plinth are just visible, built off the limestone bedrock. In the lower part of this elevation there is a large, centrally-placed socket, 0.5m square and 0.4m deep. This was to receive the end of the bridging beam which ran in sections along the length of the building, and which must have been supported at intervals on massive wooden posts. The sockets for smaller but still massive joists run down the long walls at a height showing the joints rested on top of the bridging beam. It is presumed that the Norman first-floor level was at the base of the piers of the niches. If so, this implies a floor thickness of 0.75m.[9]

The first floor is dominated by an arcade of four semi-circular headed niches made of plain sandstone. These are carried on plain piers with similar chamfered bases to the pilasters on the exterior. The capitals have a V-shaped profile, like the external eaves band, except for the

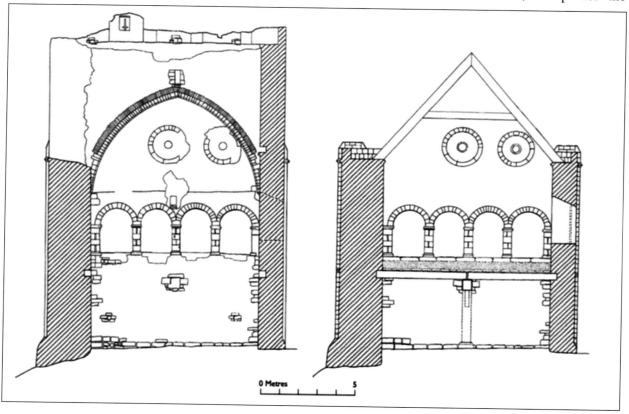

*Fig. 19 The Great Tower: west internal elevation*
*with a reconstruction of its Norman appearance (right)*

28

second pier, which has a cable moulding. The niches are 1.7m wide, 1.7m to the springing point, 2.5m high to the head of the arch, and 0.9m deep. They contain fragments of their original plaster decoration, which is described in more detail below (p.35; Plate 3).

About 1m above the head of these niches there is a marked change in build, with coursed brown-stone blocks below and irregular soft-edged blocks of rubble limestone above. This limestone contrasts with the smaller, more angular rubble limestone of the Marshal phase. Within this lime-stone are the remains of the two rear arches of the circular lights. These seem to be made of blocks of Sudbrook Sandstone and the inner faces are dressed to respect the reveals, which are made of long, pitched slabs of limestone. The left-hand window is just left of centre, and both windows do not relate to the pattern of the niches beneath. Nevertheless the form of these windows can be found in other Norman buildings[10] and the stone used in the dressings only occurs in the first phase of the Great Tower. The later blind arch hides the form of the gable end, and so some uncertainty about the reconstruction of this elevation remains (Fig. 6).

*South internal elevation* (Fig. 20)
This elevation is 27m long; the rear of the massive blocks of the plinth are visible in the eastern half and all the fabric up to the line of the sockets for the floor joists is Norman. The joists were on average 0.3m high, 0.4m wide and 0.4m deep and are at 1.8m centres except at the eastern end where the widths increase to up to 2.2m.[11]

The pattern of niches continues around from the west elevation, with four more open niches surviving at the western end and a blocked fifth niche lying behind the ruins of the magnificent double arch which spans the Great Tower in the Marshal phase. One more niche survives towards the eastern end of the elevation and the survival of the springing stones implies that there was a similar niche to either side. The central part of the first floor is complicated and multi-period, but it provides crucial evidence for the understanding of the disposition and possible function of the Norman Great Tower.

At the level of the capitals of the arcade of niches are two lengths of projecting band, which are chamfered on the lower side. The one to the left measures 1.5m long and the one to the right 1.1m long. The one to the left is long enough to

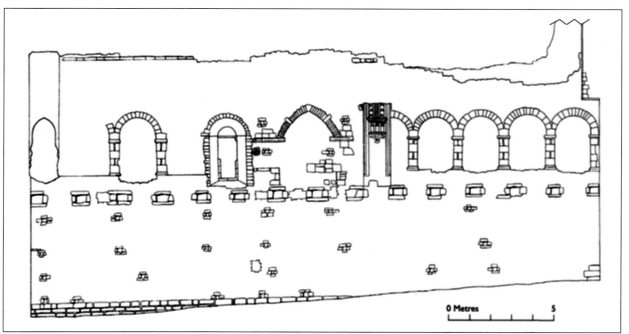

*Fig. 20 The Great Tower: south internal elevation*

receive the end of the arch of a fourth niche. If the one to the right was extended to be 1.5m long it would be short of receiving the arch of the fifth niche from the right. There are Sudbrook Sandstone blocks associated with these two lengths of projecting band. Joining the two lengths of projecting band and spanning a gap 2.1m wide is a pointed relieving arch with irregular and narrowed voussoirs. This archway respects two vertical joints, which pass below the level of the Norman floor. It is argued below that these belong to a fireplace created as part of the Marshal phase. The masonry within the area between the projecting band and the top of the vertical joints is jumbled and must reflect later blocking of the features. There are two putlog holes within this masonry and two higher up which may help confirm that this area was remodelled. Nearby is a piece of Romano-British sculpture identified by some as being Mithraic[12] but following a recent examination by Martin Henig,[13] thought to represent Venus and her nymphs (Fig. 21).

The pattern of the arcade of niches seems to require a wider niche or another feature in this area. The projecting bands and their associated blocks of Sudbrook Sandstone seem to be Norman fabric and the carving would fit with the

evidence for other re-used Roman materials in the Norman Great Tower. Together these features give emphasis to this part of the original building.

Entrance into the first floor from the intra-mural staircase within the east wall of the tower was through a doorcase—whose semi-circular relieving arch remains—in the south-east corner of the room. There is no doubt that the fabric of the straight flight of this staircase and the associated slit window on the east elevation (Fig. 18) is Norman. However, as the staircase turns towards the doorway, and certainly as it rises to form a spiral staircase to the wall walk, the fabric belongs to the later Marshal phase.

*East internal elevation* (Fig. 22)
Four courses of large Sudbrook Sandstone blocks at the base of this elevation represent the rear of the massive plinth. As at least twelve courses exist on the exterior it appears that the natural

*Fig. 21 The Romano-British figures in the south wall of the Great Tower*

*Fig. 22 The Great Tower: east internal elevation*

bedrock was cut away to create deep notches on the south and east sides into which the plinth courses were laid. The ground floor is again dominated by the elevated doorcase. It is identical in form and dimensions to that on the external elevation except that it is undecorated and the tympanum is formed by horizontally rather than diagonally laid courses. One voussoir in the outer arch has chip-carved decoration, but this must have been a spare block as it would have been obscured by the joists and floor of the undercroft. The socket for the end of the bridging beam replicates that in the west elevation. Given that the threshold of this doorcase is 2.3m above the bedrock floor, there must have been a wooden staircase down from this entrance.

The level of the first floor is marked by the base of a course of Sudbrook Sandstone blocks with a chamfered top. From this chamfered top spring what must be the jambs of another niche in the southern part of the elevation, measuring 1.7m wide. This must have been shallower than the remainder, so as not to have broken into the intra-mural stairway. On the north side is a similar but wider gap (2.2m) in the Sudbrook Sandstone. Whilst this may have been another niche, it was perhaps more likely to have been a window. The top part of the elevation has been comprehensively re-modelled in the Marshal programme of work.

*North internal elevation* (Fig. 23)
This part of the building is as complex and revealing as the equivalent external elevation. The ground floor remains almost unaltered from the Norman period. The rear of the plinth shows as a single course at the western end and six courses at the eastern end. Here it contains the rear of the doorway into the gallery. The reveal has a drawbar socket. The three windows are

*Fig. 23 The Great Tower: north internal elevation*

31

nearly symmetrically dispersed within the elevation. Each has a semi-circular headed plain rear arch and a stepped sill. A course of Roman tile gives emphasis to the sill level.

The line of joist sockets remains intact except where a rectangular was light inserted in the late 13th century. The spacing is consistently at 2m centres except at the eastern end when it becomes a little eccentric with one gap as large as 2.7m.

At the first floor, the fenestration can be partly reconstructed. The rear arch of a blocked window is partly obscured by the springing of a later arch in the north-west corner. It measures 1m wide, 2.2m to the springing point and 2.6m to the apex. The large double window of the Marshal's programme of work has removed any evidence for a window in this location, but the Norman doorcase remains intact. This too has a semi-circular headed rear arch measuring only 0.8m wide. Inside the doorway there is a shallow socket to receive a wooden bolt behind the door, not a full drawbar hole. Traces of three more rear arches are apparent to the right of the crossing arch and a complete window survives in the end bay. There is no evidence for glazing in these windows and the hangings for the shutters have eroded away. A building break exists between the distinctive coursed, squared, and mixed Norman building stone and the angular Carboniferous Limestone of the Marshal phase. This line runs 1.2–1.3m below the stringcourse. No evidence for the form or location of the roof trusses survives on this elevation.

## A Reconstruction of the Norman Great Tower

*Plan form* (Fig. 24)

The ground-floor, and to a lesser extent the first-floor, plan of the Norman Great Tower can be reconstructed with confidence. The tower is an irregular quadrilateral in plan measuring about 32m on both long sides externally, with the west end measuring 12.6m and the east end, 13.5m wide. Internally these measurements are c.27m long and between 8.8m and 9.3m in width. The walls are of different thicknesses varying between 1.2m for that on the north and 2.4m for

that on the south. These variations are accounted for by the increased defensive capabilities that the Great Tower required on its more vulnerable landward-facing southern side, and allowed for the intra-mural staircase and niches to be incorporated into the thickness of the walls.

The ground floor was entered from the line of the present Gallery on the north side, through the doorway in the north-east corner. This has a drawbar socket so that it could be barred from the inside. The sloping limestone bedrock always seems to have formed the floor of the undercroft with the height of the ceiling reducing from 6m at the east end to 4.2m at the west end (Fig. 19). An alternative entrance into the undercroft would have been through the elevated doorway in the east elevation and then out through the equivalent doorway on the inner face of the wall. The threshold of this doorway is over 2m above the floor and would have required a flight of wooden stairs down into the undercroft. The doorway through the north wall would have allowed for the easier access of heavy goods and materials. The undercroft was lit by three single round-headed lights in the north wall, which retain evidence for bars but no glazing and have stepped reveals. Within the undercroft there was a massive wooden substructure supporting the floor above. This consisted of a line of stout posts running down the centre of the room supporting a bridging beam, made of a number of large timbers, scarfed together and fitting into the sockets in the end walls. Halved across this beam would have been fifteen pairs of massive joists fitting into the sockets running along the long walls, which would have carried ceiling planks, layers of bedding sand, and probably a flagged floor above.

The first floor had two points of access. The most obvious was through the highly ornamental doorway in the east elevation and up the intra-mural staircase in the east wall to the rather modest doorway in the south-eastern corner of the first-floor room. The main door has a drawbar socket and there is another socket on the intra-mural stairway, indicating a lost door, providing a second barrier, so this route could be defended

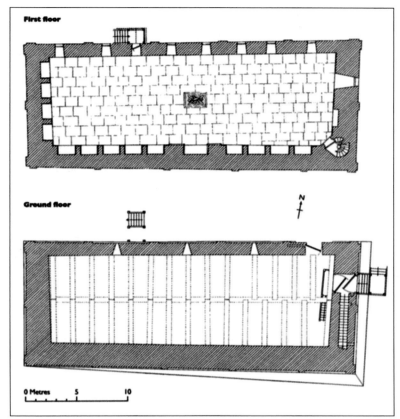

*Fig. 24 A reconstruction of the ground- and first-floor plans of the Norman Great Tower*

than elsewhere (Fig. 20). The east wall could have had a pair of niches, more widely spaced than in the west and south walls, or a niche and a window. In total this provides for fourteen or fifteen standard niches and one wider example. This vast and apparently undivided room would have opened up into the gabled roof. The two plain circular lights in the west end seem to have belonged to the original build and may have been matched by similar windows in the now missing east gable.

*The exterior*

The Great Tower was designed to be approached from the east. The east elevation stands on its plinth, at least twelve courses high, standing above a scarped bank. It would have looked very massive and imposing with its main entrance raised above the ground to about one third of the full height of the elevation (Fig. 24). This doorway with its highly decorated, chip-carved tympanum framed by the band of Roman tiles is the most ornate feature of the Great Tower. However reconstructing a stepped access up to it presents problems and all the alternatives that have been tried diminish the architectural massing of the building (see Fig. 25 and Plate 2 for alternatives). There must have been a causeway alongside the northeast corner. The simplest form of entrance was to have had a set of massive open timber steps leading from the causeway up alongside the plinth to the doorway. It is possible that these steps were only a temporary feature that could be dismantled and erected as need demanded. It must be expected that the lord of Chepstow would have used this entrance and that it had ceremonial as well as defensive significance.

The rest of the east elevation can be reconstructed from the surviving evidence and by transferring the form of the wall top from the west elevation. There was plenty of width for a

against attack. The second doorway is in the fourth bay of the north elevation. It must have been reached by a covered wooden staircase, standing in what is now the Gallery. This had a thin wooden door and no deep drawbar socket, making it apparently vulnerable to being stormed. The internal floor could have been flagged and so carried one or more open hearths. The room was lit by six, round-headed windows, regularly disposed in the relatively thin north wall. The west, south and part of the east wall were lined with round-headed niches (Figs. 19 and 20). They are on average 1.6m wide, 1m deep and rising up to 2.4m high from the flagged floor level. They have plain ashlar surrounds, with chamfered bases and springers, and some retain traces of their original plaster decoration. In the south wall there was an apparently wider niche (2m) at the centre, with longer chamfered springer blocks

*Fig. 25 A reconstruction of the exterior of the Norman Great Tower showing one possible form of entrance, with a probable causeway along the northern side*

wall-walk so the staircase must have risen to form a vice, and the gable end stood on the inner wall face. Nowhere on the Great Tower is there evidence for crenellations in this phase.

The plinth along the north elevation rises vertically and was stepped to create a space for the doorway into the undercroft. Whilst the break in the Roman tile band argues for a pentice, any roofed building would have reduced the light through the three small undercroft windows, and would have had to respect the stairs up to the doorway at first-floor level. There is no evidence for a roof crease or supports. On balance it seems more likely that there was no building against this side of the Great Tower until Roger Bigod's time.

Sufficient survives of all the windows to reconstruct their form and disposition. The bases of the pilasters are at different heights but the chamfered band at the wall top ran level with two courses of ashlar sandstone on top and one below. The rubble walls would seem to demand being rendered, but the existing render with its black gritty aggregate must belong to the Marshal phase of work as it covers the blocking of some of the Norman openings. To gain access to the first-floor doorway, a dogleg wooden staircase can be constructed within the fourth bay without compromising the fenestration. Traces of mortar fillets above the doorway show that the stairs were roofed and give the angle of the stairway. The north wall is half the thickness of the other walls at 1.2m as opposed to 2.4m, making any wall-walk much narrower. The long gabled roof would have required at least one louvre to vent any open hearths, with, perhaps, other ornamentation being restricted to any decorated ridge tiles.

*The interior*

There is no other room surviving in Britain, or even perhaps in northern France, which compares with the first floor of the Norman Great Tower. It has many quirks including its eccentric plan, the entrance in a corner, another through an understated doorway in the north wall, and no obvious orientation down the long axis. There is no evidence for any division, or any logical place to put one, so a single great room has to be imagined (Plate 2).

The room was lined with niches, with their thresholds at floor level so they could have accommodated either standing or seated figures. The postulated larger niche was nearly central to the south wall. This helps make sense of the two circular windows in the west gable, which would have been visible from this position. Those occupying the niches in the south wall could also look through the line of windows facing north. These were unglazed, so the room must have been dark (even in the middle of the day because of the use of shutters), cold, draughty and partly smoke-filled when any open hearth was lit.

Superficially, the interior was very sparsely decorated. The rear arches of the windows and door are plain. The arcade bases, piers and capitals of the niches are simply chamfered, except for the re-used, cable-decorated block in the west wall. The only decorative carving is the Romano-British panel alongside the central niche. However, the survival of primary plaster decoration in the four niches in the west wall gives some idea of what has been lost. This decoration is made up of two types of plaster. The first is white with a fine aggregate, whilst the second uses crushed Roman tile as the filler giving a pinky/orange colour and a coarser feel to the surface.[14]

It is in bay 2 of this arcade that this plaster Plate 3). The rear face of this niche up to the base of the capital mouldings, and the soffits of the jambs and the arch were covered with the white plaster. The tympanum of the niche was plastered with the crushed Roman tile plaster. This was then overlain in the upper third of the tympanum by a lunette of the white plaster so creating a band of the Roman tile plaster, which was then overlain by strips of white plaster to form a rather crude saltire pattern.[15]

The survival of this decoration is very remarkable. It is the oldest domestic internal decoration within a standing building in Britain and suggests that the interior of this first-floor room would have been plastered throughout. The band of Roman tile plaster passing across the tympanum of the niches, set within the white plaster, replicates the effect created on the exterior by the band of Roman tiles. The saltire pattern in bay 2 also echoes the saltire patterns of chip carving above the main east door, though it is much more crudely executed than on the stonework. Did this scheme provide for a new imperial building to impress those who knew the ruins of the great Roman buildings at Caerwent and Caerleon? Or was the decoration elaborated on the plain wall surfaces, to give a more sumptuous appearance to the interior, in contrast to the stark grandeur of the exterior (Plate 2)?

## The date, patron and function of the Norman Great Tower

Before considering the date of the building, and so the name of the patron and therefore the possible functions of the Great Tower in the Norman period, it is worth reviewing the ideas of antiquarians and architectural historians in the past. Both Leland and Aubrey considered the tower was the work of the Romans.[16] Camden described Chepstow as having 'a varie spatious castle situate over the river' but assumed that the Domesday Book entry referred to Cas Troggy or Striguil Castle which lies some 10km west of Chepstow.[17] Wyndham gave the fullest description of the early tourists to the site:

Chepstow Castle occupied several acres, and its ruins are still very considerable. The chief gateway has a venerable aspect, and the most antient part of the whole structure and of Norman origin, is nearly perfect. Several Roman bricks are intermixed with other materials; and particularly in the outward wall of the north west angle of the chapel, five or six courses of them appear between the facings of the stone; these were probably brought from Caerwent.

Within the chaple are twelve large niches with semicircular arches over them, formed in the walls. These seats were chair high above the floor of the room; the use of them is not very apparent, unless we might be permitted to imagine, that they were intended for the twelve Norman adventurers, who might probably do their *first* services in this castle, for the lands which they had newly conquered in Glamorganshire.[18]

In the early 19th century William Coxe dismissed the Roman theory.[19]

Some fanciful antiquaries have attributed the construction of the castle to Julius Caesar, without considering that he was never in these parts …

Coxe followed Wyndham in saying that the Great Tower was called the Chapel and 'the

whole building appears to consist of heterogeneous materials, collected from the remains of dilapidated structures'.[20] However, he countered Wyndham's suggestion that the niches were for the twelve knights of Glamorgan by identifying that there were fifteen niches in total. He concluded that the original character was Saxon or Norman.

Parker concentrated on the early English work in what he called a hall and did not credit anything to the Normans.[21] The south Wales castle expert, G.T. Clark, had a comprehensive plan of the castle drawn by A.S. Ellis and W. Frame in 1865 in which the Great Tower is called the Keep (Fig. 26). His papers in the National Library of Wales contain manuscript descriptions and sketches of the castle dated 1875,[22] but it was not until 1881 that he published an article on Chepstow. This gives a long and detailed description[23] before reaching his conclusions. Firstly, he thought that:

The large sandstone blocks, like the bricks, were probably brought from some Roman work.

And:

The basement of the keep has the appearance of early work, owing, probably to the employment of Roman material; but it seems more probable

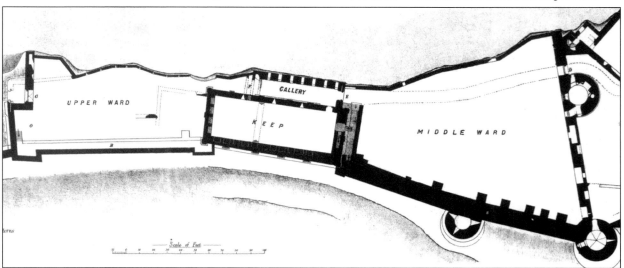

*Fig. 26 Part of Frame and Ellis' plan of 1865 showing the Great Tower, here labelled 'Keep'*

that the actual date is half a century or so after the Conquest, and that the original building included the walls, as they now stand up to the summit, contained a basement for stores, and a large hall above, probably with a high, but flat ceiling.[24]

Further on he considered the patron in more detail.

The oldest part of the Castle, and, indeed, the only part having distinct Norman features, is the keep, generally attributed to Earl William Fitz Osbern. More probably, however, judging from internal evidence, its builder was Gilbert de Clare, a nephew of the founder of Tintern Abbey, who died 1149.[25]

Sixty years passed before anyone attempted a comprehensive description and analysis of Chepstow Castle. This was undertaken by Clifford Perks.[26] When beginning his consideration of the architectural history of the castle, he concluded that the lower part of the Great Tower was undoubtedly the earliest.

In trying to date this work two main possibilities have to be considered; either it is the original castle of William Fitz Osbern that is mentioned in Domesday, or else it was built to replace that castle by the Clares early in the 12th century.[27]

He then listed the eminent scholars who had preferred one of the two options and concluded that the weight of authority was seen to be slightly in favour of the earlier date. Perks recognised the tower had no affinities with any other building in the British Isles and so was part of the great variability in castle design before the accession of Henry I. Having balanced the evidence again, he concluded:

… it is possible to say with confidence that we have here the original castle of William Fitz Osbern, which allowing for the possibility of its being incomplete at his death, may be dated 1067–1074.[28]

Perks went on to write the first Ministry of Works guide to Chepstow Castle,[29] in which he was more definite in attributing the Great Tower to fitz Osbern.

Much of Fitz Osbern's castle still survives. On the narrowest part of the ridge he built a large oblong tower of two storeys, the upper of which was his hall.[30]

From this date later authors came to accept this identification without question. It led to claims that the Great Tower is the oldest standing secular building in Britain.[31] Fernie[32] gave further support to this idea:

The great tower had no existence independent of the castle, whereas the hall was the central building in a dwelling of any pretensions. The earliest examples, Scolland's Hall in Richmond Castle and the hall at Chepstow, probably of the 1070s, are large and splendid two-storey buildings with a plain ground floor and a more sumptuous first floor for entertaining, with the entrance at one end and the high table or dais at the other, marked by an architectural feature such as blind arcading or a special window.

Given the extensive new study of the architectural evidence for the Norman phase of the Great Tower, it is time to review the case for Earl William fitz Osbern as the builder, and consider an alternative, that the tower was built during the Crown's ownership of Chepstow in the period 1075–1115.

The life of fitz Osbern and his close relationship with William the Conqueror has been described in chapter II. In the recent past undue emphasis has been given to the Domesday entry, and the assumption that the tower formed part of Earl William's new castle. How accurately can the Great Tower at Chepstow Castle be dated? The architectural and decorative evidence needs to be given much greater weight in this discussion. The most obvious decorative detail is the chip-carved saltire pattern in the tympanum over the main entrance (Fig. 17). Its first securely-dated use is at the church of La Trinité in Caen,

*Fig. 27 Chip carving on the west doorway of the round chapel at Ludlow Castle*

*Fig. 28 The Norman doorway at St. Leonard's Church, Hatfield, Herefordshire which parallels the east door at Chepstow*

Normandy in 1060,[33] whilst the earliest datable example in England occurs in St John's Chapel, Tower of London, in the late 1070s.[34] The motif then occurs quite widely and can be seen for example in one of the outer orders of the west door of Chepstow Priory. The furthest end of the date range for this detail may come from the round chapel at Ludlow Castle, where an almost identical pattern to Chepstow is visible on the soffit of the outer order of the west door (Fig. 27) and the chancel arch.[35] Coppack believes that, given the plan form of this distinctive chapel, it could not pre-date the 1120s or 1130s. This short review shows that the main decorative motif could have been used at any time within a sixty-year period, covering the various patrons previously suggested for the Great Tower.

The form if not the decoration of the east doorway of the Great Tower is exactly paralleled in a simpler way at St Leonards Church, Hatfield, Herefordshire.[36] This doorway is reset in the north nave wall (Fig. 15). It stands only 1.6m high and 0.95m wide and is made of dressed limestone tufa blocks. The lintel is formed by a T-shaped joggle rather than a wedge-shaped joggle as at Chepstow, but the blocks within the tympanum are arranged in diamond shapes at both sites. The manor of Hatfield was held by Hugh l'Asne in 1086. He was a member of fitz Osbern's household, and was made one of the tenants-in-chief in Herefordshire by the earl, as well as being an existing tenant on the earl's estate in Normandy.[37] There was therefore a personal rather than just a tenurial connection between the two sites, with the possibility that the St Leonard's doorcase was built in homage to that at Chepstow Castle.

Parallels for the form and plan of the Great Tower are very hard to find. Its construction, of a great mixture of stones and tiles at least some of which are re-used, has suggested to Allen (see chapter I) and others that the work was carried out hastily, and where there was no tradition of stone quarrying and masonry. However the deliberate selection of Roman building materials may also have been symbolic. The ruins of Caerwent were probably quite well preserved in the 11th century.[38] By producing a massive tower, articulated with plain ashlar buttresses, framing white-rendered walls with a bold band of Roman tile and a massive Romanesque entrance, the Great Tower was perhaps a statement of a new imperial presence at the gateway into south Wales. The great keep at Colchester Castle was built over and partly incorporates the vaults of the Roman imperial temple dedicated to Claudius. It also replaced a late Saxon *villa regalis*, and was partly built of Roman materials incorporating bands of Roman tiles.[39]

Chepstow's Great Tower is a massive building with very thick walls and could not have been constructed in a short period. By comparing the size of the tower with other contemporary works such as the White Tower, Harris has estimated that the Norman phase took perhaps four to five years to build, whilst Dixon estimated eight years.[40] Even if William fitz Osbern were to have made a prompt start in 1067, these estimates suggest that he could not have completed the tower, and this must have been left to one of his successors.

The plan of the first floor of the Great Tower is not a great hall in any traditional sense.[41] It is a single, very large room lined with niches rising from floor level on its west, south and perhaps east wall, and probably focussed on the larger, near central niche in the south wall (Fig. 23). Access from the main doorway in the east wall involved climbing an external flight of open, wooden stairs, passing through a barred doorway

into a porch, and up a narrow intra-mural stairs to emerge in the south-east corner, out of sight of anyone occupying the central niche. The other access was simpler, and involved climbing a covered wooden dogleg staircase to a rather small and plain doorway but emerging opposite but a little to one side of the central niche. The room must have been quite dark and cold. Equivalent great towers in Normandy, such as Langeais and Ivry-la-Bataille (the home of William fitz Osbern's mother), do contain a vast cellar and a hall, but also have a separate chamber, latrine, often a chapel and access to a kitchen and other service rooms.[42] None of these rooms is present at Chepstow.

An intriguing possibility, which might help explain the peculiarities of the plan of the first floor, is that the main doorway in the east elevation was not a permanent or even an entrance at all. If general access to the first floor was via the door in the north wall, then perhaps only the lord of Chepstow was allowed to use the decorated doorway and temporary steps were erected and dismantled for his needs. Alternatively, perhaps the intra-mural staircase led down to a porch and the door would be opened to frame the lord to the masses gathered on the ground below. Such elevated doorways, with no clear means of access are known in Saxon and other Norman buildings. The evidence for these doorways was gathered together by Renn[43] as a class of buildings for which he requisitioned the term *burhgeats*. These included a mixture of towers belonging to Saxon and Norman churches, and Norman keeps, gatehouses and town gates. The consensus view is that the Saxon term means an 'entrance to a protected enclosure', and 'its purpose might be either secular or religious or a joint corporate venture with compatible objectives. An open gallery or a large upper doorway can only have been for display (of people or relics) and not for defence, particularly if the openings go down to the floor level'.[44] The tradition continued at the royal keep of Norwich Castle where an elevated doorway at first-floor level overlooks the market place. Dixon and Marshall have argued that this doorway was intended as a balcony for Henry I to show off his Norfolk born queen, Alice, to the people below.[45] An arrangement of this form would have also increased the security of the undercroft at Chepstow as anyone entering or leaving the cellar when the north door was barred would have to have passed along the intra-mural staircase and through the first-floor room. So the form of the building suggests solely a ceremonial function rather than a domestic one. It could have been more comfortably built within the royal ownership of the lordship rather than the four brief and war-filled years of William's earldom. A case can now be made for William the Conqueror being the patron of the Great Tower.

Recent years have seen extensive research into the great buildings of William I and his two sons, and have led to a re-evaluation of their date and function. The Domesday Book only provides incidental evidence on the castles built or inherited by William I and never provides a description of the structures that they may have contained.[46] The greatest effort has centred on the White Tower in the Tower of London,[47] where work is now thought to have commenced in the late 1070s. There is evidence for a building break part way up the second floor of the tower, and documentary evidence suggests that it was not completed until William II's reign, perhaps as late as 1100. It may thus never have been used by William I as a residence. Its massive presence within the south-east corner of the Roman walls of London—with their bands of Roman tiles—must have made it a very imposing sight for anyone arriving in the city by sea.[48] The Great Tower at Chepstow occupies a similar position just above the port of Chepstow and dominating the access up the River Wye into the heart of the earldom of Hereford.

The White Tower is much larger than the Great Tower at Chepstow. It was three storeys high and double-pile in plan. Built over a secure and massive undercroft it contains parallel suites of rooms at first- and second-floor level, the latter incorporating the chapel of St John. Where there are similarities between the two buildings is in the presence of a massive plinth, the external walls being divided by pilasters and the relatively plain detailing to the ashlar work. The main doorway is at first-floor level and would have been reached by an open, and probably wooden, flight of steps, later superseded by a forebuilding.

Ashbee argues that the large room on the west side of each floor of the White Tower acted as a hall and general assembly area, with the king's chamber in the smaller room to the east. The first-floor chamber has a broad and tall recess in its south wall, a feature repeated in the west end of the chapel. These have been identified as possible

*Fig. 31 The hall of the Great Tower at Rouen with Duke William receiving Duke Harold Godwinson, from the Bayeaux Tapestry*

throne niches. In both chambers, the spine wall contains plain semi-circular niches rising from the floor level, though these are much larger than at Chepstow. With the exception of the chapel, none of the internal ashlar is carved or moulded. No trace of plaster has survived the later uses of the tower, but the survival of soot stains on the rubble stone which revealed the position of the original roof, may indicate that it was never fully decorated.[49] Unlike Chepstow, the White Tower is well provided with garderobes and has fireplaces in the main rooms. The main axes of these rooms were longitudinal, and processional routes can be reconstructed.

The motif which dominates the interior of the Great Tower is the line of niches. An arcade of this type is illustrated on the Bayeux Tapestry, within the hall where Duke William received Harold and his knights before the conquest.[50] This is taken to be a depiction of the hall within the now-lost Great Tower at Rouen, but the details are strikingly similar to what survives at Chepstow (Fig. 29). A more complex arcade incorporating windows has been reconstructed for the internal long walls of William II's enormous Westminster Hall, built in the 1090s,[51] but these features were well above floor level.

The only non-royal hall from Norman England, which can usefully be compared to Chepstow, is Scolland's Hall at Richmond Castle in Yorkshire. This first-floor hall (which is slightly smaller than Chepstow) was built by Alan of Brittany, earl of Richmond, probably sometime between 1071 and 1086, and incorporated into the defensive curtain wall. The undercroft contained a massive timber ceiling of the same form as Chepstow but the entrance into the first floor was via an external staircase through a large ornamented doorway opening directly into the hall (Fig. 30). Visitors on entry looked down the length of the hall to the lord's table with the windows built into the long walls. A doorway leads off from alongside the lord's table into a private chamber beyond, serviced by garderobes in a tower.[52] This arrangement of entrance, hall and chamber was to become the standard plan of lordly residences in medieval England and is in stark contrast to the first-floor plan reconstructed at Chepstow.

A final balancing of all this evidence is needed to try to identify who was the patron of the Norman Great Tower. The case for Earl William fitz Osbern rests heavily on the reference in Domesday. Domesday also records that Earl William erected two other castles in his earldom, at Clifford and Wigmore in Herefordshire,[53] but neither of these castles were to include any buildings on the scale of the Great Tower. The same is

*Fig. 30 Scolland's Hall, Richmond Castle*

41

also true at Carisbrooke Castle on the Isle of Wight, which was the centre of his second largest estate in England. One clue in support of the earl is the survival of the doorcase at St Leonard's Church, Hatfield, presumably erected at the expense of Hugh l'Asne, one of the earl's leading supporters. The date range for surviving parallels for the chip carving of this doorcase begins before Earl William's erection of Chepstow Castle, and the very varied sources for the building stone implies that the Great Tower was constructed at a time when no established supply of building stone was available.

The evidence against Earl William being the patron is extensive. He was only Earl of Hereford for four years (1067–1071), during which he was leading the suppression of rebellions across England and spent periods of time in Normandy. The border with Wales was a frontier, which needed to be defended with castles but did not lend itself to the erection of massive domestic or ceremonial buildings. Earl William would have taken over the site of the Saxon castle and palace in Hereford and there seems little need nor the time to build an alternative in the south-west corner of this earldom at Chepstow. The first-floor room did not provide a great hall, which can be compared to those known from a generation earlier in Normandy[54] or the only equivalent hall built for a Norman earl in England, at Richmond Castle. The absence of any secondary chamber, garderobe, chapel or obvious access to a kitchen seems to suggest that this room fulfilled only ceremonial rather than domestic functions.

Earl William's son, Roger de Breteuil also only held the earldom for four years and the arguments against him are the same as those against his father. Following Roger's arrest for treason in 1075, the earldom of Hereford was surrendered to the crown where it was to remain until 1115. This gives a forty-year period in which King William I, or his two sons, could have built the Great Tower. William I took over the Saxon royal palaces of Winchester, Westminster and Gloucester and was well-known for holding crown-wearing feasts in their great halls at Easter, Whitsuntide and Christmas, at which he entertained in state all the great men of England.[55] He was to rebuild the royal hall at Winchester in the 1070s and later start work on the great palace keeps at the Tower of London and Colchester. His son, William II, was to outdo his father with the greatest royal hall of all, at Westminster.

So the Norman kings built large ceremonial buildings with unusual plans in England from the 1070s onwards. Why should such a building be needed at Chepstow, right at the edge of the kingdom and not on an earlier royal site? The most likely historical context for the commissioning of this building would seem to be the expedition that William I made with a substantial entourage and army through south Wales in 1081. Ostensibly a pilgrimage to the shrine at St Davids, the visit was probably just as much a show of strength and an opportunity to exact tribute from the new prince of south Wales, Rhys ap Tewdwr (d.1093). They did indeed reach an agreement which helped bring relative peace over south Wales.[56] It is now generally accepted that William established the castle of Cardiff within the walls of the Roman fort from that date.[57] Was the decision to construct the Great Tower likely to have resulted from this expedition? Was it intended to represent the presence of the king at the entrance to south Wales? Is its unusual plan at first floor, solely for ceremonial purposes, where the king could have sat with his Norman lords and receive homage and tribute from the Welsh prince and his entourage? If so then its purpose may have been short-lived, for William died in 1087, and Rhys ap Tewdwr in 1093. After this, Wales fell into chaos, which provided an excuse for William II and his Marcher lords to break the treaty and expand their estates westwards.[58] Perhaps these events made the Great Tower at Chepstow redundant, and fix its construction and potential royal use to the period 1081–93. As with the White Tower, its building and appearance may have been far more important than its use.

# CHAPTER IV

# Chepstow under the Marshals

*by* David Crouch

William Marshal came into the possession of the castle of Chepstow and the lordship of Netherwent on his marriage to Isabel, the daughter of Earl Richard fitz Gilbert of Striguil late in the summer of 1189. After 40 years in royal hands, Henry I had granted the Marcher lordship of Striguil to Walter fitz Richard of the great family of Clare. Walter's most significant act was the foundation of Tintern Abbey in 1131. The lordship passed to his nephew Gilbert and in 1148 to Gilbert's son, Earl Richard fitz Gilbert de Clare, nicknamed 'Strongbow' and conqueror of Leinster, the south-eastern province of Ireland, in 1170–71. Richard had also taken the castle and lordship of Usk from Iorwerth, lord of Caerleon, consolidating the land holding between the rivers Usk and Severn in the lordship of Netherwent. When Richard died in 1176, his estates passed first to his son, Gilbert (died 1185), and then Isabel.[1] Both were wards of Henry II. No significant works may have been undertaken at Chepstow during this period beyond repairs to the tower and castle to the value of £10 13s. in 1185.[2]

The Marshal, as William Marshal was called, was in his mid-forties when he married Isabel. He already had behind him a long career as a courtier and soldier. Most remarkably, his life story can be followed in a biographical poem *L'Histoire de Guillaume le Maréchal*, written soon after his death by a man called John who had known the Marshal in his prime. This is an astonishing survival, being the first medieval biography of a layman who was not a king.[3] In the last years of Henry II's reign, the king had evidently decided that the Marshal was to be rewarded for his service by a profitable marriage. The first opportunity he had been given was the wardship of Heloise of Lancaster, heiress of the northern honor of Kendal in 1185 or 1186. Marshal seems to have thought carefully about it, but decided he could do better than this. A recently-discovered letter from Henry II to William Marshal has revealed that in the summer of 1188 he was in negotiation with the old king for the hand of Dionisia, heiress of the great French castle of Châteauroux, the dominant fortress of the region of Berry.[4] However, the Marshal's biography tells us that the king raised the stakes further in the days before he died by offering Marshal the marriage of Isabel of Striguil. It was this marriage which the new king, Richard the Lionheart, confirmed to the Marshal in the days immediately after Henry II's death on 6 July 1189, and which he accomplished in London perhaps early in August.[5]

**The Marshals in Gwent**

William Marshal acquired Netherwent at a difficult time for the Marcher lords in south Wales, and Gwent in particular (Fig. 31). The entire period of the Marshal tenure of the lordships of Netherwent and Usk was affected by rivalry with the Welsh dynasty of Caerleon. This difficulty

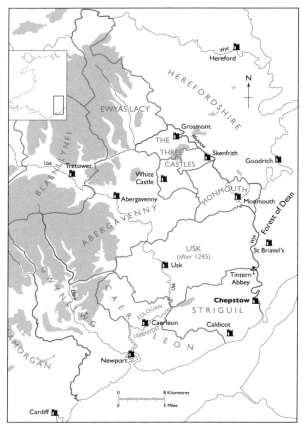

*Fig. 31 Plan of the medieval lordships of Gwent*

had begun to emerge on 25 July 1175, when Rhys ap Gruffudd of Deheubarth met King Henry II at Gloucester with the lesser princes of south Wales in an attempt to build a new peace in the southern March. With him he brought Iorwerth ab Owain, the dominant Welsh magnate of Gwent and long-time rival of Earl Richard fitz Gilbert. As a result of the meeting Iorwerth recovered his ancestral lordship of Caerleon after three years deprivation of it by the king. The new order was clearly not to everyone's liking. William de Briouze (or Braose), lord of Abergavenny and Brecon, demonstrated his annoyance by ruthlessly seizing and killing Iorwerth's brother-in-law, Seisyll ap Dyfnwal, at Abergavenny, sacking his house and killing two of his sons and many of his followers.[6] Although this massacre soured Anglo-Welsh relations for long after, Iorwerth ab Owain recovered his lands in Edlogan (which lay in the river valley between Caerleon and Usk) and

Lebenydd (south-east of Caerleon around modern Christchurch),[7] and, with the death of Earl Richard in 1176, a long period of stability and Welsh predominance began in Gwent.

When William Marshal established himself in Gwent, his principal political rival was therefore the new lord of Caerleon, Hywel ab Iorwerth, who had become a prominent loyalist to the Angevin regime in Wales. Loyalism was to be the leading policy of the house of Caerleon from the 1180s onwards, bolstered perhaps by the family connection between Hywel and the Angevin kings through Morgan, his nephew, son of Henry II and Nest ferch Iorwerth ab Owain. Hywel's local power and prestige in Gwent remained unchallenged until his death, which can be established from exchequer memoranda as occurring during the warfare between the barons loyal to King John and those promoting the claims of Louis of France. This war followed the sealing of Magna Carta in 1215 and continued after King John's death in 1216. William Marshal became regent and protector of the young King Henry III and led campaigns on land and at sea forcing Prince Louis and his men to withdraw. Most likely it was around this time in 1217 that Caerleon Castle was seized by the Marshal.[8]

Marshal promoted Chepstow as the principal focus of his power in the southern March and Severn valley. As it is now known, following the recent archaeological investigations of the castle, the Marshal invested heavily in expensive building works there in the early 1190s. In part this would have been to assert his lordship over a new honor and impress his neighbours. It was also a proclamation of his wealth. The source of the large amounts of cash he must have paid out on the building works at Chepstow would seem likely to have been the massive wealth he had accumulated on the tourneying circuit in north-eastern France in the 1170s and early 1180s (Fig. 32). This included a huge annual money fee he had acquired from Count Philip of Flanders in the city of St-Omer when he left the Norman tourneying team and joined the Flemings in 1182. He would have been able to add to this the rewards for being a successful royal servant between 1185

*Fig. 32 Manuscript illustration of c.1352 of a tournament scene—more akin to a melée—of the type in which William Marshal excelled*

and 1189. The Marshal was undoubtedly a very wealthy man already in 1189, even before he married Isabel. This fortune would also have been the source of his ability to buy the shrievalty of Gloucester early in 1190, when he had already appointed his household knight, Nicholas Avenel, as castellan of Gloucester.[9]

Through his marriage he gained a share of the Giffard honors in England and France which was his wife's inheritance. In 1199 he was made earl of Pembroke at King John's coronation, the lands and title which had been confiscated from Earl Richard fitz Gilbert by Henry II in 1153. Finally, in 1200, he set out on a journey to regain possession of his lands in both Pembroke and Leinster (Fig. 33). With the possession of the shrievalty of Gloucester and the keeping of the forest of Dean he had become by 1204 the most powerful

*Fig. 33 Pembroke Castle, the centre of Marshal's Pembrokeshire estates, with the prominent round tower for which he was responsible*

magnate in the March. Fortunately for the Welsh of Gwent, Marshal was principally a courtier and his appearances in Wales were infrequent. Further good fortune for the Welsh was the fall from royal favour in 1207-8 not just of Marshal, but also William de Briouze, lord of Abergavenny and Brecon. Both men retreated to Ireland, and the Marshal in the end was exiled there till the outbreak of the Barons' Wars in 1214.[10]

It was those same Barons' Wars which ultimately ended the long period of Welsh resurgence and dominance in Gwent. William Marshal no doubt resented the Welsh lordship over Edlogan and Lebenydd, but there was little he could do about it when John was king. Nest Bloet, sister of Hywel of Caerleon, was a particular favourite of the king and she and her children received numerous royal favours. The death of John and the appointment of Earl William Marshal as protector of the boy-king, Henry III, changed the situation radically in Gwent. During the civil wars of 1216–17 the Welsh of Deheubarth and Gwynedd allied with the invading French and the rebel barons. It seems that Hywel of Caerleon was unable to stay neutral when Rhys Ieuanc ap Gruffudd had the run of Glamorgan and Llywelyn ab Iorwerth had seized Brycheiniog, and so he joined the coalition. However, when the rebellion collapsed and the invading French were defeated in the summer of 1217, Hywel ab Iorwerth was left exposed. During the truce between himself and Louis (28

August–12 September) William Marshal raised a force from the knights of Gwent and sent it against Hywel. According to the *Histoire de Guillaume le Maréchal* there was fighting in which a number of English knights, including Hywel's nephew Sir Roland Bloet, were killed. Following this there was a siege of Caerleon conducted by the bailiff of Netherwent and the castle was stormed early in October 1217 (Fig. 34). Hywel died either in battle or in the siege of Caerleon and Morgan, his son and heir, was driven back on his castle of Machen.[11]

At the Treaty of Worcester in March 1218 a new political order was constructed, which would define the March for most of the 13th century. The power of the principality of Gwynedd over the Welsh was recognised, and its dominance over the English Marcher lords was tacitly accepted. But Gwent was to be an exception. Here, despite the intercession of Llywelyn and the earl of Chester, William Marshal refused to give up Caerleon to Morgan ap Hywel, citing Morgan's breaking of the truce with Louis's party the previous year.[12] Unlike the rest of Wales, English dominance was asserted and maintained in Gwent, where the Briouze family was re-established at Abergavenny, and the Marshal family became dominant along the middle and lower Usk valley.

So in 1218 Gwent came to be dominated by four powerful English magnates: Earl William Marshal was the greatest of them with castles at Usk, Caerleon and Chepstow; Hubert de Burgh was established in the Three Castles (White, Skenfrith and Grosmont), and Reginald de Briouze was at Abergavenny. The fourth magnate was a newcomer, Earl Gilbert de Clare of Hertford who in 1218 received the earldom of Gloucester by right of his mother Amice, daughter of Earl William of Gloucester. With Gloucester he received the lordships of Glamorgan and Newport.[13] Besides these great men, there were the lords of the lesser honors: John son of Gilbert son of Baderon was lord of Monmouth; Caldicot and Caerwent were under the rule of Henry de Bohun, created earl of Hereford in 1200. By 1218, the geography of

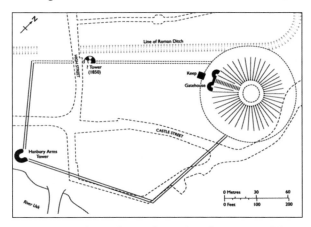

*Fig. 34  Plan of Caerleon Castle, stormed by Marshal's forces in October 1217*

lordship as it was to be for the rest of the Middle Ages was therefore established in Gwent, and remained the same up to the Act of Union.

The position of the Welsh dynasty of Caerleon in the new order was anomalous, and Morgan ap Hywel had to fight a long but ultimately successful legal struggle against the Marshals to repossess Caerleon. The settlement of 1218 had not deprived Morgan of all his lands in lowland Gwent. Although he had lost Caerleon, he would seem to have maintained his claim to a territorial overlordship in Lebenydd and Edlogan, and his castle at Machen remained in his hands. His opportunity to move against the Marshals soon came when the great Earl William died on 14 May 1219 (Fig. 35), and the lordship of Striguil and Netherwent came into the hands of his widow, Countess Isabel at the direction of the papal legate, Guala Bicchieri.[14] The countess enjoyed her free widowhood for less than a year, and died on 11 March 1220 after some weeks' illness. Morgan wasted no time and was challenging the new Earl William Marshal's right to Caerleon in the *curia regis*, early in May 1220, when he appointed attorneys to represent him.[15]

But with the new earl's marriage in 1224 to the king's sister, Eleanor, any chance of an early legal victory by the Welsh over the Marshals evaporated. It is to this time that the surrender by Morgan to the new earl of his rights to the castle of Caerleon can be dated, for revenues in Caerleon were part of the Marshal-Plantagenet marriage settlement.[16] The second Earl William Marshal was a figure of great power within England, Ireland and the March, but he died in 1231 without children (Fig. 36). His successor was his brother, Richard, lord of Longueville in Normandy and Long Crendon in England. Earl Richard rapidly fell foul of King Henry III and a war erupted between him and the king at the end of July 1233, when the earl attempted to muster an army at Wycombe to defy Henry. The failure of the muster confined the rebellion to the March and the South West, where Earl Richard was initially very much on the defensive, losing Usk to a royal army in September.[17] But in October the war entered a new phase. Chepstow was the

*Fig. 36 Effigy of William Marshal I*

*Fig. 36 Effigy of William Marshal II*

hold knight, which liberated Hubert de Burgh from his siege in Devizes church. Siward was picked up from Aust on his return to the coast by a fleet of galleys and other ships out of Chepstow, which drove off royalist vessels from Bristol.[18] Usk was recaptured and with the aid of Llywelyn of Gwynedd the war was taken into England in 1234. It was on a mission to secure the Marshal position in Ireland that Richard died in April 1234 after a battle with royalists near Dublin. In May 1234, Earl Richard's brother and heir, Gilbert Marshal, began negotiations that led to peace and royal acceptance of his succession to the earldom.

Morgan ap Hywel, naturally, was retained in the royal household for the campaign, and did great damage to the Marshal lands in Gwent. In August 1233 he had been prompt to pledge his loyalty to Henry III and had received assurances that the king would not make peace with the Marshals without including him. Early in September 1233 Morgan's suit against the Marshals for possession of Caerleon had once again come to the *curia regis* and his plea was heard at Worcester on 19 September. Earl Richard failed to appear, and Caerleon was ordered to be

earl's base for his forays into Glamorgan and England, and also the base for the spectacular raid in 1233 by Richard Siward, a Marshal house-

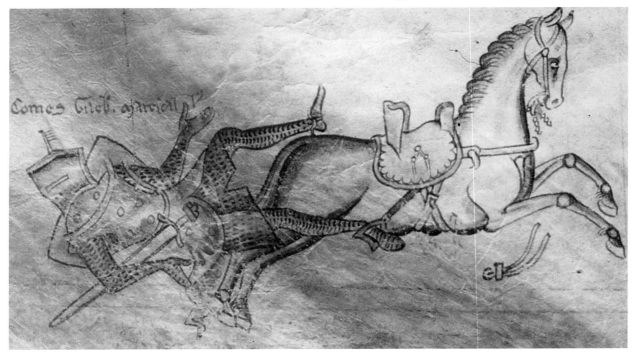

*Fig. 37 Gilbert Marshal's death at a tournament as illustrated in Matthew Paris' Chronicle*

seized, Morgan having a grant of an English manor of the Marshals until he could repossess it.[19] Yet it was not till after the conclusion of the Marshal war and the death of Earl Richard that Morgan was able to reoccupy the castle of Caerleon and lordships of Edlogan and Lebenydd. The new Marshal earl, Gilbert, the third son of the elder William Marshal, lost the castle of Caerleon to Morgan before September 1234 as a consequence of the peace. This is apparent from an action taken against the earl by his sister-in-law, Countess Eleanor, who had been deprived of her dower assignment on Caerleon, which had been agreed on her marriage in 1224.[20]

It was not long before Morgan and the new earl were at war, and in 1236 Morgan had to suffer the seizure of his Glamorgan castle of Machen by Earl Gilbert. Spurred on by Prince Llywelyn ab Iorwerth of Gwynedd, now Morgan's ally, the royal government began to move against the Marshals early in 1236 (the *Brut* noting that it was 'for fear of the Lord Llywelyn'). Morgan had damages assessed against Earl Gilbert over his seizure of Machen, which the earl paid (reluctantly) in September of the same year.[21] It seems that Earl Gilbert took the reverse badly, as seen in 1236, from a remarkable indenture between him and a local knight, Sir William de St Maur, by which Sir William undertook to support, by any legal means possible, the earl's attempts to oust Morgan from the manor of Undy, in Netherwent.[22]

Earl Gilbert died at a tournament near Ware in June 1241, the victim of his ambition to seem as great a knight as his father (Fig. 37). He was thrown and dragged by a horse that was beyond his skill to manage, and his ill-disciplined military household had scattered too far across the field to assist him. He was buried at the Temple Church in London with his father and eldest brother[23] His successor was the fourth Marshal brother, Walter, who King Henry III made some efforts to deprive of his full inheritance. Although the king delivered Walter's lands, late in 1241, still in 1245 royal castellans were in control of the Marshal castles in Gwent, including Caerleon (which the settlement of 1234 had apparently

allotted to Morgan as a subtenancy of the Marshals).[24] As a result of this continued dispute Walter Marshal seems to have resided in Herefordshire, where he held Goodrich by inheritance from his father's testament of 1219, not as heir of his brother, and so could not be denied it. Earl Walter's tenure of the earldom was relatively brief. He died in November 1245 at Goodrich and was buried at Tintern Abbey. He was followed to the grave within a month by the last surviving Marshal brother, Anselm, also laid at Tintern.[25] This ended the direct line of the Marshal family, and its great lands were partitioned between several female heirs, with Chepstow and Netherwent being allotted to the elder Marshal's grandson, Roger Bigod, earl of Norfolk.

## The Lordship of Netherwent under the Marshals

The investment by Earl William Marshal in building works at Chepstow is clear evidence that the first Marshal earl had singled it out to be his principal seat. But there are further indications that Chepstow was intended to be the centre of Marshal power. The *Histoire de Guillaume le Maréchal* recounts that it was at Chepstow that he had deposited his treasure, and there is some convincing evidence from the biography itself that in the 1220s the Marshal documentary archive was either held in the castle or in a nearby monastery. It was at Chepstow in the 1230s that the Marshal galleys which dominated the Bristol Channel were based, and it was at Chepstow that Earl Richard declared a grand tournament under his patronage in 1234, a tournament which was forbidden by the king's writ, but held nonetheless.[26]

It is not possible to gauge the frequency of the Marshal earls' stays at Chepstow. They lived an itinerant life, and they also visited their houses and castles at Hamstead Marshall in Berkshire, Caversham in Oxfordshire and Charing, near London. But when they were absent from Chepstow their seneschal or bailiff was present, and the identifiable seneschals of Netherwent were all powerful, trusted and high-ranking officials. In 1219, the seneschal was Sir John (III) of

Earley, son of John (II), the Marshal's friend and executor. In 1223, after 1234, and perhaps till as late as 1243 the seneschal was Master William of Christchurch, a noble cleric of Netherwent and Herefordshire, and in 1230 also a royal official in Brycheiniog and Buellt. His local importance is indicated by his election as bishop of Llandaff in 1243, although he did not secure royal assent.[27] In September 1244, the last Marshal seneschal of Netherwent was noted as Sir William of Wilton, who was still in office in the last days of Earl Walter in 1245. He was a particular intimate of Earl Walter, being named as one of the executors of his testament in 1245.[28]

There are a few references to the administration of the honor of Netherwent during the Marshal years. Perhaps the most illuminating is a list of exemptions granted by the younger Earl William Marshal in 1223, which projects a hierarchy of courts and officers at work. There are references to shire and hundred courts held by the earl, as well as the manorial courts of halimote and forest courts called *wodespeches*. There are also references to the earl's foresters, bailiffs and sergeants and their authority within Netherwent. A writ of Earl Gilbert Marshal is likewise addressed to his seneschal and all his bailiffs of Netherwent (*inferioris Went*).[29] A charter of Earl Walter of 1245 refers to the power of the seneschal of *Strugull* to distrain the bailiffs under his jurisdiction for any default of justice.[30] The reference to 'shire' and 'hundred' courts is anomalous in that Earl William did not control any shire in England at the time, although he did have a shire court in Pembrokeshire; however, Tintern had no lands there.[31] The 'shire' reference may in fact be to the honor court of Striguil, although it is hard to account for the idea that there might be subordinate hundred courts, unless they refer to subsidiary honorial courts at Usk, Caerleon and Trellech. A reference to the earl's judgement in the *comitatus* of Netherwent in a charter of Earl Gilbert (1234–1241) tends to support that suggestion.[32] In 1234 there is a mention of the 'laws and customs of Netherwent' which were administered at Magor from the court of the earl. At this time, the honor was being described as that of Netherwent and Tidenham, the manor on the Gloucestershire side of the mouth of the Wye.[33] A cirograph generated by the 'court of the lord earl at *Strigull*' survives from the time of Earl Walter, where on 28 September 1244 a settlement or concord was drawn up between Tintern Abbey and William of Durnford the younger concerning woodland near St Pierre.[34] A verdict in that court is mentioned in 1245 when the 'knights and free tenants of Netherwent' delivered an inquest on the extent of the lands of Tintern Abbey at Merthyr Gerain, near St Brides Netherwent.[35]

CHAPTER V

# The Main Gatehouse

*by* Richard Avent *and* Dan Miles

It is an encouraging reflection on the continuing development of castle research, particularly through the application of new technology, that even those castles considered to have well-established building chronologies still have the potential to provide further surprises. Nowhere has this been better demonstrated in Wales than here at Chepstow where important new discoveries have come to light, leading to a re-interpretation of major aspects of the castle's development. One of these, resulting from dendrochronological dating of its original doors, has been a re-assessment of the dating and function of the Main Gatehouse at the easternmost end of the castle.

## Main Gatehouse Doors

The starting point for this study of the Main Gatehouse was the constructional analysis and dendrochronological dating undertaken by Dan Miles of the Oxford Dendrochronology Laboratory on the pair of oak doors which, until they were replaced by replicas in March 1964, secured the main entrance to the castle.[1]

These are now on display in the earl's chamber on the first floor of the Bigod apartments (Figs. 38 and 39). Together they measure 2.75m across and 3.63m at their highest point and they fitted comfortably into the door rebates in the main gatehouse entrance passage. Each leaf is composed of a 'L'-shaped, substantial, hanging style with a rebate cut out of the back to leave an overlapping section on the front to run flush with the outer vertical boarding. This boarding varies between 15cm and 30cm in width and was originally covered with wrought iron sheets overlaid with horizontal iron straps (Fig. 38). On the rear of the doors, the hanging styles can be seen continuing around the top of the circular head of each leaf.

Each door is divided by two mid-rails separated by a 15cm gap within which the timber bar for securing the doors would have been locked in place by a hasp and padlock (Fig. 40). The original hasp may well be that still fixed to the rear of the northern door. Originally, the doors probably had a bottom rail which has subsequently been lost, perhaps when the wicket gate was inserted into the north door, with the addition of substantial timbers along the bottom of the front of both doors. The mid-rails divided the rear of the doors horizontally. The diagonal timbers of the lattice bracing in the upper sections runs equally at about 50° above the horizontal while the bracing in the lower section is not as consistent.

All the main structural elements of the doors, the iron straps, wrought iron sheathing, vertical boards and diagonal ledges were secured together with 1.5cm square nails with 2.5cm round dome-heads which were cold-riveted over roves (lozenge-shaped 'washers') on the inside (Fig. 41). Most of the roves were aligned horizontally, although some have loosened and slipped over the years. With all this iron, almost certainly locally derived, what must have been extremely heavy doors were hung on three pairs of pintles secured into the masonry just behind the stone jambs in the gatehouse passage.[2]

Elements in the design of these doors are consistent with the few other surviving examples of this period, all in ecclesiastical contexts. This is one of the earliest uses of lattice bracing and can be compared with the west doors at Peterborough Cathedral.[3] Aspects of the carpentry are also very advanced. The mortice and tenon joints securing the horizontal mid-rails into the hanging stiles and the use of a saw to prepare the timbers are the earliest provenanced examples of the use of these carpentry techniques identified anywhere in Britain or northern France.

The doors were constructed from two different types of oak trees. The outer planking, hanging stiles, and some of the diagonal ledges came from one or two large fast-grown trees, while the majority of the lattice bracing, the horizontal mid-rails and the arched heads were derived from several straight slow-grown trees.

There is no evidence to suggest that the doors had been made from re-used timber. The shrinkage visible in the timbers after the doors had been constructed is consistent with the use of green or unseasoned oak within a year or two of the trees being felled. It seems probable that they would have been hung in the entrance passage as soon as construction of the gatehouse had reached first-floor level.

The doors have been dated using dendrochronology. Fourteen timbers from the rear of the doors were selected for sampling using micro-boring—a method which involves removing a core with a diameter of only 5 millimetres compared with the usual 16 millimetre core. Twelve diagonal timbers, six from each door and the two mid-rails were sampled. Seven of the timbers had sufficient rings to combine to produce a site master of 107 rings giving an estimated felling date range of 1159–1189.[4]

*The doors to the Main Gatehouse:*
*Fig. 38 The outside photographed c.1958 when under repair at Caernarfon*
*Fig. 39 The internal view as now on display on the first floor of the Bigod apartments*

On the basis of its overall design, the construction of the main gatehouse at Chepstow has previously been dated to sometime between 1219 and 1245, when the castle was held by the sons of William Marshal. The dendrochronological dating now suggests that we should be

*Fig. 40 A detail of the hasp on the northern leaf of the doors*

*Fig. 41 A detail of the iron roves on the rear of the doors*

looking to a date for its construction either between 1159 and 1189 or very shortly after 1189.

There is a further piece of archaeological evidence, which has a bearing on this date. In 1991 Kevin Booth carried out an excavation in the southern guardroom and rear porter's lodge of the main gatehouse in advance of the creation of new facilities for the castle's custodians.[5] In a layer associated with its construction Booth found a silver Short Cross penny of King Henry II which was minted in the mid-1180s. Although it is not possible to determine when this coin was lost, it provides a *terminus post quem* for the construction of the gatehouse in the latest few years of the dendrochronological date range.

**The builder of the Main Gatehouse**
No comparisons can be found in Britain, Ireland or on the Continent for a gatehouse with this degree of sophistication as early as the third quarter of the 12th century. The lordship of Striguil, as Chepstow was then known, was held by Earl Richard de Clare, nicknamed 'Strongbow', until his death in 1176. His heirs were too young to inherit and his estates were taken into the custody of the king. Richard's son, Gilbert, died in 1185 leaving Gilbert's sister, Isabel, as a very rich heiress and a ward of the king. It is highly unlikely that any money would have been spent on a major programme of building works at Chepstow Castle during this period. The only recorded expenditure is in the Pipe Roll of 1185 when £10 13s. was spent on the repair of the Great Tower and some houses within the castle.[6]

However, in 1189, in accord with his father's wishes King Richard I granted Isabel in marriage to William Marshal. Marshal was a truly remarkable man. Born in about 1147 as a younger son of a fairly modest family, he had to build his career, most of the time in France, through his skills as a soldier, particularly on the tournament field, and through his unswerving loyalty to whichever English king was on the throne. His marriage to Isabel brought Marshal further wealth and major landholdings, most particularly the lordship of Striguil in the south-east corner of Wales.[7]

In 1189 Marshal found himself in possession of an old, outmoded castle which appears to have undergone very little development during the 12th century. With newly acquired wealth, a leading position in the governance of the English kingdom, and a very considerable knowledge of the most advanced military techniques gained during his years in France and the Holy Land, Marshal was ideally placed to modernise the castle. It is reasonable to assume that the first stage in that process involved construction during the 1190s of new outer defences, including a major gatehouse, to provide a much larger enclosed area for the additional buildings required by a magnate of Marshal's importance. This would have been followed by a strengthening of the Middle Bailey defences with round towers which, even if constructed some ten years later than has previously been thought, still represented an early use of the rounded mural tower in Britain and northern France. By the time of his death in 1219, Marshal may have also rebuilt the Upper Bailey defences adding his commodious south-west tower.

**Later Alterations**
It is clear that the rear of the gatehouse was completely rebuilt when Roger Bigod, fifth earl

*Fig. 42 The exterior of the main gatehouse*

of Norfolk, extensively remodelled the lower bailey in the late 13th century.[8] This involved the construction of an impressive range of apartments along its northern side, which connected to the rear of the gatehouse and, with the construction of Marten's Tower, probably replacing an earlier tower on the same site (chapters XIV and XV).[9] Booth's excavations clearly demonstrated that the foundations to the rear of the southern tower of the gatehouse were of later date and, apart from thickening the earlier wall to the north of the entrance passage, all the area behind the north tower was also rebuilt at this time.

The most obvious late 13th-century alterations to the gate towers are to the wall heads where the battlements were largely rebuilt with the inclusion of either a fixed or temporary hourd. The curtain wall to the south of the gatehouse, which must have originally extended to whatever preceded Marten's Tower, was also heightened to its present form. The Tudor remodelling of the gatehouse accommodation was part of an extensive campaign of work by Charles Somerset, earl of Worcester and is described in more detail below.[10] Finally the wall-walk level and the parapet walls were remodelled to create gunports and musketloops in the later 17th century.[11]

**Description**
The following description attempts to strip away the evidence of later modification to arrive at as accurate picture as possible of the original gatehouse arrangements.

*Exterior*
The Main Gatehouse, guarding the main entrance to the castle, stands at the eastern and lowermost end of a narrow spur with a vertical cliff to the north and the Dell, separating the castle from the town, to the south. It consisted of two round towers, the northern smaller in diameter than the southern, and an extended passage with rear chambers to either side (Fig. 42). There is no surviving evidence for an external ditch at this end of the castle and today's gentle grass slopes give a false impression of vulnerability. In the medieval period this area to the east of the castle

was almost certainly waterlogged for much of the year and one has to imagine an approach to the gatehouse along a raised causeway, probably close to the cliff edge. The first obstacle would have been a barbican, the only surviving evidence of which consists of toothing for a one metre wide wall in the face of the south gatehouse tower. Recent excavations have traced the foundations of this wall extending 2.6m forward of the face of that gate tower although it probably extended further. No comparable toothing can be found in the face of the northern tower and neither could wall foundations be located archaeologically, suggesting that the barbican wall probably stretched across the face of the north tower to the cliff edge. It is possible that the barbican gate at the end of the causeway was off-centre to the main gatehouse passage (Plate 4). This would have been a useful additional defensive feature, particularly given that the ground-floor room in the northern gate tower functioned as a prison and lacked the arrowloops of its southern counterpart. The first floor of this tower is set at a slightly higher level than that of the south tower and this may have had the incidental advantage of providing sufficient height for its arrowloops to have a field of fire over the barbican wall.

Both gatehouse towers have an external basal splay and are sited on ground which, although built up over time, still slopes down from west to east, most steeply from the base of the curtain wall on the south side of the south tower. Although later fireplaces and windows were inserted into both towers, it is still possible to reconstruct the original arrangements. The two ground-floor arrowloops in the south tower, one facing out to the field and the other immediately in front of the outer portcullis slot, consist of a plain, narrow slit with a rounded basal oillet. The only other slit in the gatehouse adopting this form is that at first-floor level on the cliff face of the north tower. All the other surviving first- and second-floor arrowloops are of the cross-slit with basal oillet form.

A row of square holes beneath the battlements of both gatehouse towers and two larger holes

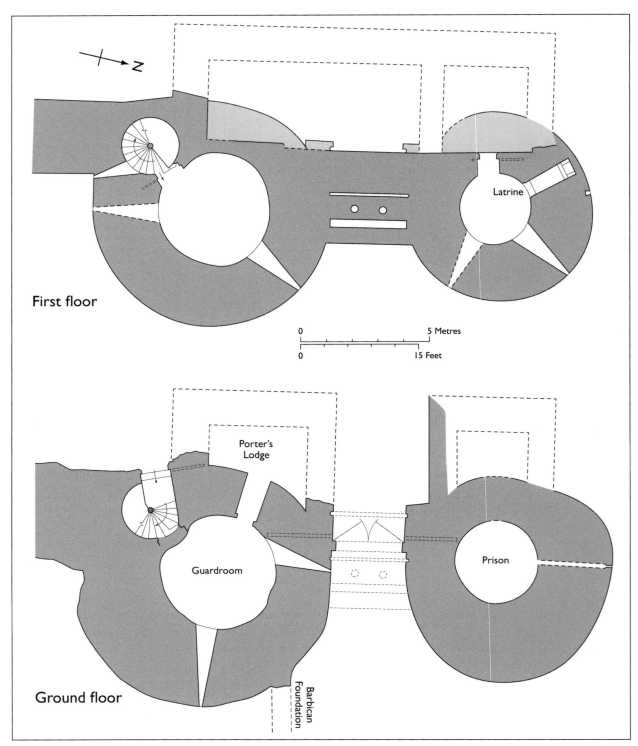

First floor

Latrine

0 ——— 5 Metres

0 ——— 15 Feet

Porter's
Lodge

Guardroom

Prison

Ground floor

Barbican
Foundation

*Fig. 43 The ground- and first-floor plans of the Main Gatehouse
showing the original pair of round towers and defended gate passageway,
with Bigod's rectangular range added to the rear*

56

above the entrance passage probably housed the timber beams of a late 13th-century hourd extending above the entrance as a pentice or projecting wooden turret.

*Gate passage*

Once through the barbican, an attacker would have faced an impressive set of defences (Fig. 43). First, at a high level behind a corbelled-out, chamfered segmental arch with bull-nose stops at the springing of its inner face, a narrow 'murder' slot extended up through the masonry of the front of the gatehouse to just behind the parapet. Next came the segmental outer arch of the passageway. This, too, was chamfered on both faces with bull-nose stops at the springing of its inner face. On the underside of the arch two perfectly symmetrical round holes extend right up through the masonry of the gatehouse to wall-walk level. These have previously been interpreted as murder holes but, given that this function could have been much more adequately performed by the murder slot, another alternative is proposed. This is that they may have housed counterweights for the outer portcullis immediately to the rear. At this point the passage was also defended from the southern gatehouse tower by an arrowloop. The pointed arch behind the portcullis is very similar to that of the gateway through the east curtain of the middle bailey. Beyond the portcullis the great oak doors hung within the inner square rebate of the main round-headed archway with its quarter-round outer profile. Once closed, the doors were secured by two drawbars located above one another. The upper was drawn back into the south tower and the lower into its northern counterpart. The passage was then extended a further metre inwards beneath its rubble soffit to its segmental rear arch and inner portcullis which was raised at first-floor level. The doors could not be fully opened unless the portcullis was raised. The grooves for both portcullises, cut into dressed masonry blocks, are of the same dimensions and profile and are clearly contemporary.

Beyond the inner portcullis the entrance passage widened out and extended for a distance

of 4.37m to the back of the gatehouse, with the last 1.32m on the north side containing the remains of the springing for the rear archway. The southern wall of the rear entrance passage has disappeared although its line can be traced in the toothing on the rear, west, wall of the southern gate tower. No evidence survives for doors at the back of the passageway and, given the width of the opening, these probably never existed. The rear passage must have had a wooden ceiling at first-floor level. Boards in that part not housing the winding mechanism for the rear portcullis could have been removed to drop missiles from above, in the event of an attack.

*Rear chambers and ground floor*
*of gatehouse towers*

The two rear chambers are small and cramped providing only very limited accommodation. In plan, they have the appearance of being later additions to the two curving rear walls of the gate towers (Fig. 43). However, although they have undergone extensive alteration, it is clear from the surviving wall junctions that chambers at ground level with suites of accommodation at first and second-floor levels were always part of the original design.

Booth's excavations to the rear of the southern gatehouse tower showed that the foundations of this room, probably the porter's lodge, were secondary and this alteration is probably part of Roger Bigod's late 13th-century rebuilding.

No evidence survives to indicate the position of the external doorway into the porter's lodge but this must have been from the entrance passage through the missing north wall. The doorway from this room into the south tower has an arch, which does not sit comfortably on the jambs to either side. By contrast, the doorway at the other end of this entrance passage is much lower and has a pointed head. The door opened outwards and was secured by a drawbar from the outside. It is possible that the stonework of neither doorway is original. However, the way the stone of the soffit of the passageway is carefully set on edge to carry the weight of the masonry above suggests that this was the original entrance to the tower and is not a later insertion.

As originally designed, the ground floor of the south tower functioned as a guardroom with one arrowloop covering the entrance passage and another facing due east out to the field. The present position of the inner door drawbar may point to a later use of the guardroom as a second prison. This room is now occupied by a free-standing unit providing facilities for the castle's custodians.

An examination at first-floor level of the nature of the masonry of the northern rear gate-house chamber and its relationship to the gate-

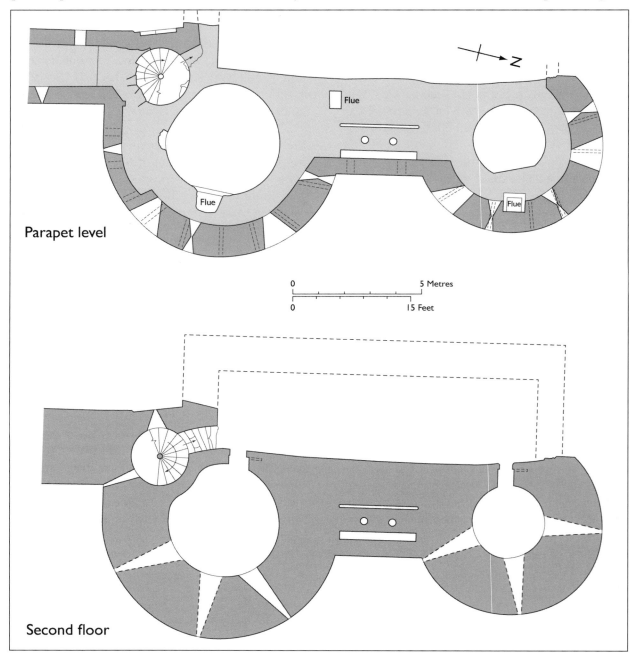

*Fig. 44 The second-floor and parapet level plans of the Main Gatehouse*

house tower reveals that only the wall along the entrance passage, with its arch springing at the inner end, is original and even this has a secondary internal thickening. The rear and northern walls were completely re-built, almost certainly when Roger Bigod incorporated the gatehouse into the adjoining kitchen and chamber block in the late 13th century. At the same time a ground-floor entrance to the prison was inserted replacing the original access by trap-door from the floor above. The only lighting in the prison came through a narrow shaft sloping down from outside in the thickness of the north wall. This shaft terminates in a fake arrowloop at first-floor level in the north wall (Fig. 43).

*Upper floors of gatehouse towers*
A ground-floor doorway in the inner face of the curtain wall just south of the gatehouse leads to a newel stair rising in a clockwise direction to the gatehouse's two upper floors and the battlements where it terminated in a small turret (Figs. 43 and 45). The remains of the original curtain wall are evident for a short distance to the right and above this doorway. The doorway is wider than the other late 12th-century doorways in the gatehouse, and its northern jamb has been set back slightly into the exterior face of the south wall of the porter's lodge. The door was secured by a drawbar, the slot of which is visible in the broken end of the remains of the south wall of the porter's lodge. The stairway is lit at three points.

The upper rooms in both gatehouse towers have been extensively altered with the insertion of later windows at both levels and fireplaces on the second floor. Despite these alterations, it is still possible to trace the original arrangements, particularly in areas where the later plaster is now missing. All were equipped with similar narrow embrasures for their arrowloops. The doors in the four original surviving doorways opened into the rooms and were secured from the inside with drawbars. The first-floor room in the northern tower has a garderobe built within the thickness of the wall and venting out over the river. The reveal is rebated for a thin wooden door. None of the rooms appear to have had fireplaces origi-

nally, and must have provided somewhat austere accommodation.

Access to the first-floor room in the south tower was from the newel staircase (Fig. 43). Two arrowloops are apparent at this level although both are now blocked. All but the upper part of the embrasure survives for the slit overlooking the entrance, but only fragments for the slit facing out along the line of the south curtain survived the insertion of a flue for the ground-floor fireplace. Based on the arrangements in the north tower, one would have expected another, east-facing, embrasure to have existed between these two where there is now a later, two-light window, but no trace survives on either the inner or exterior walls. The original floor of this room was 1.75m lower than that of the main first-floor chamber across the back of the gatehouse.

Entry to the upper room in this tower was via a doorway through its west wall from the gatehouse's rear chamber. The outer jambs of the doorway were chamfered with traces of much-eroded stops, probably of domed form. Two arrowslits are visible quite close together on the exterior of the tower at this level. That facing north-east is the best preserved embrasure and slit in the gatehouse. Traces of the arch for the embrasure of the blocked east-facing slit are apparent at the back of a later Tudor fireplace. The basal oillet of a third, south-east facing, slit survives on the exterior face of the tower just beneath the later window.

The northern gatehouse tower is smaller than its southern partner. In this case, there always appears to have been direct access to the tower from the rear chamber at first-floor level with the door being secured from inside by a drawbar. There were originally two embrasures for arrowloops at this level.[12] On the interior, the evidence for these has been destroyed by the insertion of a three-light window, leaving only traces of the left side of the rear arch of the north-east facing embrasure. However, the cross slit with its basal oillet can clearly be seen on the exterior of the tower; this is in contrast to the other, south-east-facing slit, where only the basal oillet survives below and to the left of the inserted window.

Access to the upper room in this tower, like that in the tower to the south, was from the main rear chamber, again with the door secured from inside by a drawbar. The insertion of two windows and a fireplace has destroyed all evidence on the interior walls of the original embrasures. However, an eastward-facing cross slit with basal oillet, blocked by the later fireplace, is apparent on the exterior of the tower. Basal oillets beneath both Tudor windows, one facing north over the cliff and the other overlooking the entrance passageway, are all that survive of the other two arrowslits at this level.

*Rear Accommodation Block*
Although the rear walls of the gatehouse have been destroyed at first- and second-floor levels, it is still possible to reconstruct part of the original arrangements from what survives. The eastern wall, of the rear accommodation block was built over the rounded backs of the towers below to create, with the now-missing long west, and short north and south walls, a rectangular space, which was approximately 3.5m wide.

There is no evidence in the surviving fabric of the gatehouse for the original means of access from the ground to the first floor of the rear accommodation block. There was no doorway off the newel staircase or between the rear room and the slightly lower first-floor room in the southern gatehouse tower. The first floor was divided into two rooms by an upward extension of the northern wall of the entrance passage. The larger room extended over the entrance passage, the porter's lodge and the rear of the south tower. The inner portcullis would have been raised against the eastern wall of its northern end. The smaller room was immediately above the later jailer's room. The upper floor, with its slightly bowed east wall, appears to have been undivided although timber partitions could have existed. Reveals for window openings are visible at both floor levels in the remains of the south wall and may have been matched in the missing west wall. At first-floor level the reveal is of similar proportions to those for the arrowloops in the gatehouse

towers and the stair lights, suggesting narrow openings. The taller, second-floor reveal points to a larger window.

The flue of the first-floor fireplace is visible at wall-walk level, but the blocked fireplace at second-floor level is very different in character. Only a monolithic lintel and the right jamb, with the possible stub of a lampholder survive. This cannot be accurately dated, but the substantial technical difficulties involved in inserting a lintel of this size at a later date may point to this fireplace being an original feature.[13] The pitched roof extended across the back of the gatehouse on a north-south alignment.

**Function**
At ground-floor level the gatehouse performed an essentially military function with control of the gateway being concentrated within the larger southern tower and associated porter's lodge. As a result of the later reconstruction of the rear of the structure, it is no longer possible to determine the nature of the original arrangements in the area behind the northern tower. What is clear is that it did not perform its later function as a jailer's room as access to the prison would have originally been from the floor above. The most likely scenario is that this is the location of the missing, presumably circular, newel stair to the first floor of the gatehouse. This may have extended up to the second floor although this was also accessible from the newel stair at the other end of the gatehouse. There are two possible alternatives, neither of which seem very likely. An external wooden or stone stair could have been constructed against the outer face of the west wall of the gatehouse, along the lines of that seen at Harlech Castle in the late 13th century.[14] This would be a very vulnerable feature in the event of the gate passage being stormed by attackers and the defenders having to resort to the gatehouse as a final stronghold. In the second alternative, access could have been, as it was in the late 13th century onwards, from buildings constructed against the north-western end of the gatehouse. This, too, is unlikely as, again for defensive

*Fig. 45  The rear of the Main Gatehouse*

reasons, earlier gatehouses tend to be free-standing, apart from where linked to adjoining stretches of curtain wall.

The main first-floor chamber served both a residential and a military function. Militarily, the portcullis would have been raised from within the northern half of the room over the entrance passage and alongside the fireplace. By comparison with the surviving mechanism in the Byward Tower at the Tower of London,[15] the winding gear may have occupied an area only about one metre wide behind the portcullis slot. The portcullis would have been kept in the raised position throughout the day, in order to allow the gatekeeper to open the castle doors. It is not unusual for a portcullis to be raised into a room of good quality, sometimes even including chapels over an east-facing gate. However, based on the evidence of the only surviving window reveal in the south wall, the only natural light entering this room would have been through this and similar narrow lights in the west and north-facing walls. This would be consistent with what is found at other castles where defence at this lower level was a paramount consideration at this early period. Only on the uppermost floors were any concessions made to greater light and comfort. All of this suggests that this room, in which the fireplace may or may not be an original feature, along with the first-floor room in the north tower, would have provided reasonable accommodation, but would not have been seen as one of the principal apartments within the building.

The first doorway off the newel stair led into the south tower, first-floor room. Set at a lower level than the accommodation block behind, there appears never to have been any intention to link the two. With an arrowloop set at a low level just above the entrance passage, this room would have supplemented that below it, in controlling the immediate approach to the castle gate. An arrowslit on the opposite side of the tower provided enfilading fire along the lower face of the curtain wall. The absence of any sign of an east-facing arrowloop is puzzling, particularly given that traces, however slight, survive of all the other slits in the gatehouse towers. The position of the embrasures in the floor above, cutting across the line of any potential flue, rule out the possibility of a fireplace and it has to be assumed that all trace of an original slit was destroyed when the Tudor window was inserted.

The newel stair continues directly up to the wall-head with a separate short stair leading into the second-floor, rear chamber. Immediately to the right another door provides access to the upper room in the south tower. The bases of the chamfered jambs of this doorway were decorated with stops. The rear chamber extends across the full width of the gatehouse, although there may have been a timber partition, extending up to the roof truss above, creating a separate north room on the same line as the stone partition on the floor below. The taller window opening in the south wall may have been reflected in the now missing west and north walls, with openings of the same general external dimensions as those surviving in Marshal's Tower in the Upper Bailey. This was clearly the principal apartment of the Main Gatehouse, possibly with a private chamber at its northern end, which could have contained a garderobe discharging over the cliff. Both tower rooms provided additional accommodation at this level.[16] The second-floor suite may well have been occupied by the constable of the castle.

One interesting aspect of all the original doorways leading into the tower rooms at both upper levels, and that at ground-floor level to the newel staircase, is that they were secured from inside by drawbars. No distinction seems to have been made between the doorways in the more private areas of the building and those in general use by the soldiery, such as that to the first floor in the south tower. These measures were probably designed to secure different parts of the building in the event of an attack.

# CHAPTER VI

# The Middle Bailey

*by* Richard Avent *and* Rick Turner

The Middle Bailey is triangular in shape, flaring out from the east front of the Great Tower (Fig. 46). It measures *c*.50m east-west and is 42m wide against its east curtain wall and is contained by impressive walls and towers on its eastern and southern sides, and a low modern wall along the cliff edge. The bailey does not contain any build-

ings today and this may have been the case during most of its history. However it does provide a natural gathering point below the east doorway of the Great Tower.

The grass-covered interior of the bailey is terraced (Fig. 47). The Great Tower stands on a raised platform of limestone bedrock, which was

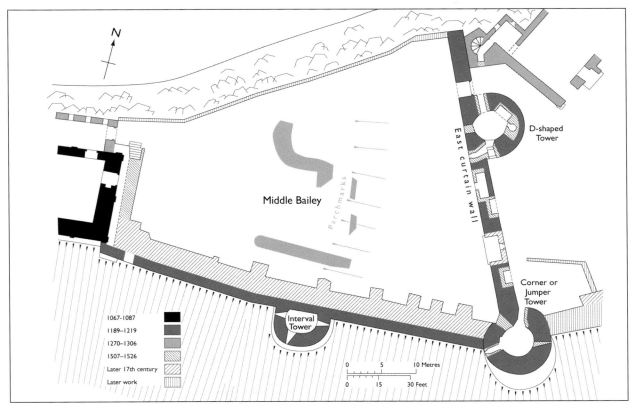

*Fig. 46 Plan of Middle Bailey showing parchmarks and names of towers*

*Fig. 47 The exterior of the Middle Bailey gateway framing the Great Tower*

Despite the extensive documentation now assembled for Chepstow Castle, there is no reference to the Middle Bailey until the late 17th century (see p.236). So for the medieval period, the discussion has to be limited to the standing fabric and the results of a small excavation in the north-east corner of the bailey.

**East Curtain Wall and Towers**

The Middle Bailey gateway lies on the line of the axis running through the Main Gatehouse. However, it is much plainer in form, consisting of a sharply-pointed, two-centred arch, 2m wide and 3.6m high at its apex. The jambs have two chamfered orders ending in pyramidal stops and contain a mixture of Dundry Limestone and Old Red Sandstone. The springer of the inner order is shouldered and the outer order has a pendant stop. The two orders of the arch are in plain ashlar limestone (Fig. 47). The rear of the gateway is rebated. The present doors are Tudor though their pintles and hinges may be original,[1] but the medieval doors were thinner—no deeper than 70mm—to respect the neatly-masoned, drawbar sockets (Fig. 48). These are 140mm square and the one to the north is 0.43m deep and to the south over 2.5m deep. The rear arch is plain and segmental, matching those in the Main Gatehouse and the Upper Bailey gateway.

The curtain wall ran north to the cliff edge where it was terminated with neat limestone quoins. It was lower that it appears today, following the Tudor remodelling which has removed any crenellated parapet and buried the wall-walk. There is a rectangular hole and shaft in the end of the curtain wall, which suggests there was a latrine at the end of the wall walk. Two chamfered limestone doorjambs are built into the rear of this length of curtain wall indicating there was a contemporary building at this point. A small-scale excavation was undertaken in 2003 in the corner of the curtain wall and behind the modern cliff edge wall.[2] The area of excavation was 2m wide against the curtain wall face and ran uphill for 6m (Fig. 49). The limestone bedrock was revealed within half the trench, but at its eastern end it had been levelled

cut into a notch to house the tall plinth on its eastern side (see pp.30–31). The land must have fallen away below the plinth, where the Tudor steps and terrace run across the face of the building, to a level perhaps 1m lower than today, to give access to the sallyport still visible on the outside of the south curtain wall. There is another significant break in slope about two-thirds of the way across the bailey which stands about 1.2m high. In dry weather, parchmarks appear on the upper terrace (see Fig. 46). These may represent the buried foundations of an earlier phase of defences of the Middle Bailey. If so they are the only evidence of a castle ward, east of the Great Tower before the late 12th century. Whether this was Norman and contemporary with the Great Tower or was added during the Clare family's ownership of the castle is a matter for speculation.

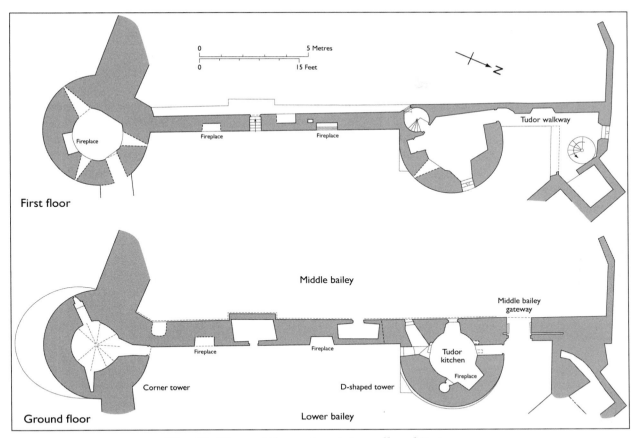

*Fig. 48 Plans of the east curtain wall and its towers*

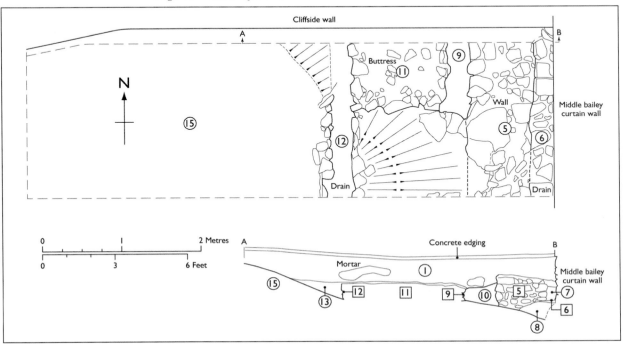

*Fig. 49 Plan of the excavation carried out in the north-east corner of the Middle Bailey in 2003*

up with a hard mortar layer on which the Middle Bailey curtain wall was constructed. Against the curtain wall was a narrow stone-capped drain (6 on Fig. 49), 0.3m wide with a low wall footing on its western side (5 on Fig. 49). Further to the west was a shallow gully (9 on Fig. 49). What was interpreted as a square buttress (11 on Fig. 49), and another drain (12 on Fig. 49). Only the last drain fell towards the cliff. These structures were contemporary with a layer of loam rich in smithing iron slag and part of a hearth cake. None of these structures could be related to the door jamb in the curtain wall, yet they contained sealed potsherds of late 12th- and 13th-century dates. This area was levelled with a late medieval demolition deposit. The function of this complex of structures is not clear, though an iron forge must have been close by.

The gateway was protected by a large, D-shaped tower projecting forward from the curtain wall. There was no ditch in front of this tower or the rest of the east curtain wall (Fig. 50). The tower has a plinth with a chamfered Dundry Limestone capping. It stands three storeys high with a chamfered band between the ground and first floor. Each storey retains a number of arrowloops—all with Dundry Limestone dressings—but others have been lost to Tudor alterations. At ground-floor level the loops are tall with a basal oillet. One survives intact (Fig. 51.1), and fragmentary reveals of others show that one will have covered the gateway and one viewed along the length of the remainder of the curtain wall. At first-floor level, there are two complete arrowloops with no oillets and parts of a third viewing along the curtain wall, later used as a jamb of a Tudor doorway (Fig. 51.3). The same plain slots are used on the second floor where two complete examples remain and one was lost to a Tudor window. Only fragments of the parapet survive against the stair tower where a single plain loop is visible in a crenellation.

The D-shaped tower was entered at ground floor through a doorway at the centre of the rear

*Fig. 50 The east curtain wall of the Middle Bailey*

66

elevation, later blocked by a two-light Tudor window (Fig. 52). The level of the adjacent curtain wall-walks is marked by the survival of the limestone quoins on the tower, with the first and second floor of the tower accessed through a doorway on the southern side leading to a staircase faced in ashlar limestone. A similar doorway, now hidden by Tudor walling but whose relieving arch can be seen, gave access to the wall-walk over the gateway. Another type of arrowloop this time with a rectangular rather than a circular basal oillet survives at first-floor level (Fig. 51.4). The wall top is marked by a projecting course and weathered coping.

The eastern stretch of curtain wall was extensively remodelled in the Tudor period. However at either end at ground level next to the two

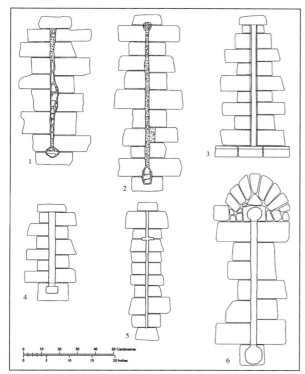

*Fig. 51 Comparative drawings of arrowloops in the Middle Bailey and elsewhere*
*1. Ground floor, corner and D-shaped tower*
*2. Ground floor, east curtain wall*
*3. First floor, D-shaped tower*
*4. First floor rear, D-shaped tower*
*5. South-west tower, Upper Barbican*
*5. Rear elevation, Marten's Tower, Lower Bailey*

towers, tall arrowloops with basal oillets—the same type as in the ground floor of the towers—survive (Fig. 51.2). Both are now blocked, but part of the plain, ashlar rear arch survives alongside the D-shaped tower (Fig. 52). This may have been semi-circular, as just inside the Tudor doorway is a chamfered jamb with a pyramidal stop which may indicate the other side of the reveal. The form of these loops is unusual as the archer could walk in from ground level at the rear. Any others in this stretch of wall have been lost to the Tudor alterations.

The circular corner tower of the Middle Bailey shares many similarities with the D-shaped tower, but there are important differences. Where the tower projects over the Dell it required a more massive raking plinth. Within its south-western side are two ashlar limestone-dressed latrine shutes and it has a chamfered limestone band at ground-, first- and second-floor levels. The tower included a basement level with now blocked arrowloops covering the face of the exterior curtain walls and one where the Tudor doorway survives viewing along the east curtain wall. Access into this basement was from a now blocked doorway in the south-east corner of the Middle Bailey. The 'ground' floor has one arrowloop with a basal oillet viewing into the Lower Bailey and three viewing across the Dell. At first floor, the arrowloops are plain and again command both the Lower Bailey and the Dell. The second floor is really the parapet level. Traces of the wall-walk and a single reveal which survived the later 17th-century adaptations can be seen internally.

The medieval access arrangements around the upper floors of this tower is confused by later alterations. There is the remains of a semi-circular headed doorcase and a rubble-vaulted passage from the wall-walk along the east curtain wall-walk (Fig. 167). This opens alongside a spiral staircase which went down to 'ground' floor and up to the second floor or parapet level. There does not appear to have been any original access onto the south curtain wall or the Lower Bailey curtain wall. In the absence of any evidence for an open set of steps, the puzzle remains as to how you reached the east curtain wall from ground level, except via the two towers.

## South Curtain Wall and Interval Tower

The south curtain wall is bonded into the corner tower, showing that they were contemporary. The length running to the D-shaped interval tower must be close to its original height though areas seem to have been patched following Civil War damage and the parapet level was extensively remodelled later in the 17th century to accommodate four musket loops. However two incomplete arrowloops survive within what must have been crenellations. These are very narrow with Dundry Limestone surrounds, the one to the west having a flared basal oillet. The mixture of stone used in this length of curtain wall is different to the east curtain wall and its towers, in using larger blocks of Carboniferous Limestone, with some yellow and pink sandstones mixed in, laid in quite regular courses. However this contrasts with the D-shaped interval tower and the lengths of curtain wall to either side, which are made of angular Carboniferous Limestone rubble with a softly eroding face.

This interval tower divides the south curtain wall in half. Whilst similar to the two towers of the east curtain wall, it uses Dundry Limestone dressings much more sparingly. The flared plinth has no ashlar capping and the three ground-floor arrowloops have only the round basal oillet cut out of a block of Dundry. The four rectangular arrowloops at first-floor level are entirely framed by rubble stone. The top floor or parapet level was completely remodelled to create late 17th-century gunports. The ground-floor entrance is hidden by the later thickening of the curtain wall and the interior is filled with rubble. The first floor was entered directly from the wall-walk through a chamfered semi-circular arched Dundry Limestone doorcase of a type seen in the Main Gatehouse. There is a rectangular slot window alongside. The reveals of the three

*Fig. 52 Rear of the D-shaped tower in the Middle Bailey*

arrowloops remain open. They have pointed, rubble-stone rear arches and high sills, and the loops are orientated to fire down to the adjacent ground levels. A similar but smaller doorway leads from the wall-walk into a spiral staircase up to the parapet level.

The length of curtain wall from the interval tower to the Great Tower is complicated. About 3.5m west of the interval tower there is a vertical joint which runs to a point about 1m above present ground level, where it becomes less distinct. From this point west, a low, flared plinth of angular limestone continues to the point where the wall turns to meet the Great Tower. East of the vertical joint, the wall is made of the soft grey Carboniferous Limestone used in the interval tower. West of this joint, the wall includes a mixture of yellow, red and brown sandstones and some porcellanized limestone. Some patching took place following Civil War damage and the remodelling of the parapet to create musket loops is evident.

The only medieval feature in this length of curtain wall is a low, segmentally-arched doorway inserted into the flared plinth. It uses blocks of dark, red sandstone for the arch and a mixture of stones for the jambs. The doorway is 0.7m wide and now stands only 1m high, the remainder being buried. It is rebated internally with traces of holes for latches and bolts but no drawbar socket. The doorway opens into a rubble-vaulted passage through the curtain wall, which is blocked by rubble walling 0.8m back from the wall face.

The curtain wall turns at an oblique angle to meet the Main Tower. The character of the walling of this face and its quoins to the main curtain wall is consistent to its full height.

**Conclusions**

The terracing and parchmarks in the Middle Bailey may provide sufficient evidence to suggest that the Norman or earlier 12th-century Chepstow Castle had a ward east of the Great Tower. However this was superseded when William Marshal extended the castle to the east by building the Main Gatehouse and the Lower Bailey (see chapter V).

The entrance through the Main Gatehouse and its barbican began a processional route through the castle. Though now interrupted by Roger Bigod's domestic range[3] this would have led to the Middle Bailey gateway and given the first, clear sight of the Norman Great Tower through its pointed archway (Fig. 48). The disposition of the arrowloops in the corner tower also respects the position of the Lower Bailey curtain wall (Fig. 49) implying that the two baileys were planned together. Work may have moved from east to west, especially in the construction of the south curtain wall of the Middle Bailey. Here the interval tower and adjacent short lengths of curtain wall may have been raised independently and the vertical joint west of the interval tower suggests that the remainder of the curtain wall was completed as a second phase. This might be explained if William Marshal's mason retained any pre-existing defences on the upper terrace of the Middle Bailey, until the new walls and towers of the Lower and Middle Baileys had been raised sufficiently to be effective. The pre-existing walls could then be demolished and the stone re-used to help complete the curtain wall up to the Great Tower.

There are considerable similarities in architectural detail between the Main Gatehouse and the Middle Bailey defences. The widespread—but not absolutely exclusive—use of the Dundry Limestone for the dressed stonework and local angular Carboniferous Limestone rubble for the walling is consistent. The chamfered, semicircular-headed doorcases are found in the Main Gatehouse, the corner and the interval towers. The plain, segmental rear arch of the Main Gatehouse and Middle Bailey gateway are similar even though the entrance arches are very different. The greatest variation is in the form of the arrowloops, first discussed some years ago by Jeremy Knight.[4] The basic form in the Main Gatehouse is an arrowloop with a round basal oillet and a cross slit. However in the D-shaped tower, there are examples with round and rectangular basal oillets and many just plain rectangular slots, none having cross slits. No chronological typology of arrowloops can be proposed for the

Marshal period at Chepstow or at his other castles at Usk, Caerleon and Pembroke.

The towers in the Middle Bailey were entirely defensive in character, though the latrine shutes in the corner tower and at the north end of the curtain wall overlooking the cliff suggests they had some basic facilities. Access into the basement or ground floors of the towers was independent from that to the first and upper floors.[5] These could only be reached from the wall-walk implying that there are lost flights of stairs from the rear of the curtain walls. This would allow defenders to isolate themselves within the towers if an attacker had managed to enter the Middle Bailey.

The sophisticated character of the Middle Bailey defences can be added to the revolutionary design of the Main Gatehouse. Further refinements will be seen in the Upper Bailey before William Marshal's development of Chepstow Castle is put into its wider military context in chapter VIII.

# CHAPTER VII

# The Upper Bailey

*by* Rick Turner

The Upper Bailey forms a long, narrow, rectangular area measuring 40m by 14m to the west of the Great Tower (Fig. 53). It formed part of the original Norman Castle. The visible fabric from this early castle can be seen in the exterior of the south curtain wall. This consists of a length of convex plinth similar in form, but smaller in scale, to that beneath the south wall of the Great Tower. Above the plinth is a panel of masonry made of rectangular blocks contained within the later, angular rubble limestone. The geology of this masonry is very varied and distinctively different to the range of stones used in the Great Tower, suggesting that the two were not built at the same time.[1]

The defences of the Upper Bailey were almost completely rebuilt by William Marshal, probably quite late on in his life, and after the completion

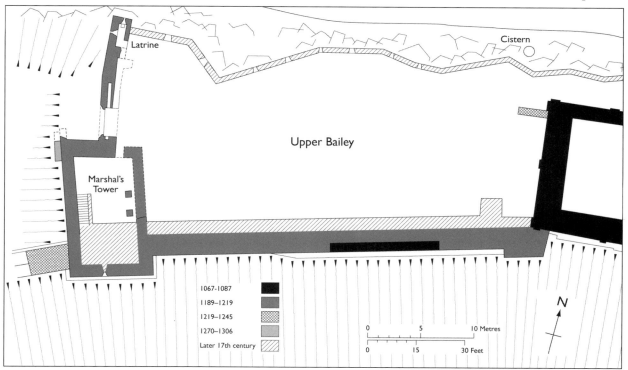

*Fig. 53 Plan of the castle showing the Upper Bailey to the west of the Great Tower*

of the work on the Lower and Middle Baileys. The Upper Bailey was the westernmost defence of the castle and the west wall incorporated the rectangular south-west tower. This tower will be called Marshal's Tower to differentiate it from the South-West Tower in the Upper Barbican. It contains an important, well-lit and well-decorated room at first-floor level and what was probably a kitchen in the ground floor. The defensive circuit is quite cleverly taken up onto and around the roof of this tower, so connecting with the south curtain wall. In the opposite corner of these western defences, a latrine chamber has been incorporated into the curtain wall, which discharged directly into the river.

There are hints in a short length of wall foundation, and sockets for roof timbers in the west wall of the Great Tower, of a building added within the Upper Bailey (Fig. 54). One of the inventories of the castle taken during Edward II's reign lists a bakehouse after the Great Tower.[2] If the inventory was taken sequentially then this may have been the function of this added building.[3]

A rectangular platform 14m by 6m near the centre of the ward suggests a free-standing building in this area.

There are very few visible alterations to the Upper Bailey from the later Middle Ages and Tudor period. A broad buttress with four tiers of weathered coping was built beneath the north-west corner of Marshal's Tower. This provided some support to a small barbican added in front of the main gates (Fig. 54) and what survives from this structure includes the reveal of an arrow loop overlooking the bridge across the ditch. The style of this buttress is repeated in Marten's Tower suggesting that this addition is of Roger Bigod's time.[4] The surviving doors in the gateway have been dendrochonologically dated to the first half of the 16th century and are described in chapter XX.

A much more fundamental remodelling of the Upper Bailey defences, which was undertaken in the later 17th century, is described in more detail in chapter XXII. Most dramatically, the tall, south, curtain wall, built by William Marshal, was reduced in height by up to 5m, and an inner wall was constructed to create a rubble-filled sandwich. Marshal's Tower was partly demolished to allow for the thickening of this wall and openings modified to take guns. The west curtain wall was breached to give direct access to the Upper Barbican and a wall with musket loops was built along the cliff edge.

## The surviving fabric from William Marshal's Upper Bailey

*The West Exterior Wall*
This elevation is dominated by the rectangular Marshal's Tower (Fig. 55). It was built directly off the bedrock and has angular Carboniferous Limestone rubble walls and Dundry Limestone dressings. The elevation is blank except for two, tall, rectangular windows, lighting the main first-floor room. These are slightly recessed behind a chamfered semi-circular-headed surround. The windows are also chamfered and retain sockets for one vertical and three horizontal glazing bars.

The wall top has four tall crenellations 1.8m high and 0.6m wide with a brownstone flag forming each of the sills. Below the line of crenellations are five rectangular sockets, 0.25m wide and 0.4m high, passing through the parapet wall. These must have contained the wooden beams to support a hourd that ran across this face of the tower and turned onto the south wall. Below the central socket is a drain hole with a short spout carved from a single block of sandstone.

The northern return wall of Marshal's Tower contains one window at first-floor level of the type already described. The wall top has a single

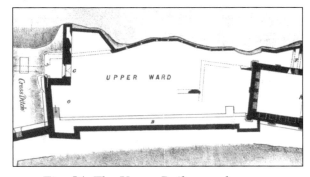

*Fig. 54 The Upper Bailey as shown on Ellis and Frame's plan of 1865*

*Fig. 55 The exterior of the west wall of the Upper Bailey with the Marshal's Tower on the right*

crenellation. This contains an inner panel reducing its depth. To the left and slightly below is a rectangular arrow loop with a basal oillet and a triangular head. This is orientated to fire downwards on anyone attacking the main gates.

The remainder of the elevation is protected by a thick curtain wall on two planes, keyed into Marshal's Tower. The main gateway formed the west entrance into William Marshal's castle, and consists of a two-centred arch of two chamfered orders of neatly-dressed Dundry Limestone. The doorway is 3.9m high at its apex and 2.36m wide. There are square sockets to support the centring at each springing point. The doors are Tudor in date. The original doors were secured by a stout drawbar, whose socket survives in the north wall. About 1m up the joints of the inner order are two shallow sockets, 0.13m square, which must have received the handrails of a bridge from a later period.

The plane of walling running to the cliff edge is angled slightly backwards and is lower than the rest. It ends as a broad buttress with plain Dundry limestone quoins and a single weathered step part way up. The only feature, apart from the putlog holes, is a small chamfered, rectangular window, cut out of a single block of limestone. This lights the latrine chamber within the curtain wall.

### *The Exterior of the South Curtain Wall*

The western end of these defences is formed by the south wall of Marshal's Tower (Fig. 54). This stands on exposed bedrock and projects forward from the remainder of the south curtain wall, and the later wall of the Upper Barbican. Some brownstone flags were used in a relieving arch and a narrow band, and larger sandstone blocks were used for quoins and a window sill.

The tower stands on a plinth which projects slightly on all sides. The ground floor has one opening. This is a tall rectangular slot made of rubble stone with some Dundry ashlar in the reveal, a blue lias flag lintel and a long sandstone flag projecting forwards as a sill. The sandstone flag had a semi-circular channel, 0.1m wide, on its upper surface, and it is long enough to throw water or waste over the plinth. It would seem to act as a drain from the ground-floor room, but the inside is now hidden by 17th-century rubble masonry.

The first-floor windows are of slightly different forms. The one to the left is identical to those described on the west and north walls of this tower. It was blocked in the 17th century to make a gun loop. That to the right has a similar semi-circular-headed outer order but it is taller and narrower than that to the left. The recessed window is also chamfered, but has a semi-circular rather than a flat head.

The wall top is crenellated to the same pattern as the west wall. There are three sockets to receive timbers to hold the hourd, which must have extended across this face. This side differs in having arrowloops in the two central merlons. These have Dundry limestone dressings with a basal oillet and short cross-piece to the top. They would have been redundant if the hourd had been a permanent structure.

The east return of Marshal's Tower has a rectangular gunport at first-floor level punched through in the 17th century. It has plain limestone jambs. Within the parapet wall is a single, plain arrowloop with a basal oillet.

The south curtain wall is of three basic builds. The first consists of a heavy convex plinth of large blocks of stone survives for half the length of wall, and the scar of where it has been robbed away is visible along the remainder. It is similar to but less massive than the plinth of the Norman Great Tower. Associated with this plinth are patches of curtain walling of large blocks of a variety of stone.

The second phase consists of angular Carboniferous Limestone in which there are lines of putlog holes. This walling is bonded into Marshal's Tower. At its east end is a rectangular turret of a similar build, which involved the cutting away of part of the plinth of the Norman Great Tower. The present parapet walls of this turret are modern. It provided a view and line of fire along the Upper Bailey curtain wall and the unprotected south wall of the Great Tower.

The upper part of the curtain wall was reduced by about 5m and then a new parapet wall was added in the 17th century (Fig. 56). It is not easy to see the junction on the outer face, though it is

*Fig. 56 The south curtain wall of the Upper Barbican and Upper Bailey.*
*The South-West Tower is to the left, Marshal's Tower in the centre and the Great Tower to the right*

clear on the inner face. The original height of Marshal's curtain wall is marked by the toothing against the corner tower, and a weathered capping isolated high up on the south-west corner of the Great Tower. The new parapet contained a line of eight musket loops made of Dundry Limestone with a green sandstone flag lintel. Each loop is a tall rectangular slot, recessed behind a splayed reveal. The wall top is ragged and incomplete. The extraordinary height of the Marshal curtain wall was to provide protection from the elevated area immediately across the Dell, just inside the town or Port Wall. This location always commanded the otherwise largely impregnable castle.

*The Rear of the Defences of the Upper Bailey*
These defences are treated as one, as the parapets over Marshal's Tower were incorporated into the defensive circuit and were entirely independent of the rooms below. Access to these defences was gained by a flight of stairs rising over the plain limestone rear arch of the main gateway (Fig. 57).

To the right is a latrine built within the curtain wall, reached by an external flight of steps, as its floor is 1.6m above present ground level. The chamber is roofed by slabs of blue lias and is lit by two rectangular, chamfered, unglazed slot windows. The position of the wooden latrine seat shows as ragged sockets in the wall. The chute is made of a dressed Dundry block, running at an angle to vent directly into the river.

Lying between the rear of the main gateway and the latrine chamber is the flight of steps that gave access to the wall tops. The bedrock has been cut away removing the evidence for the lowest part of the stairs. Remains of the first tread rise directly off the rock and run at an angle of just greater than 45° directly over the rear arch of the gateway, through an opening onto the wall-walk above Marshal's Tower. Close to the top, these steps give access to the wall-walk over the west curtain wall. The parapet wall angles to follow these changes in height and turns across the end of the wall on the cliff side.

The wall-walk around the top of the tower must have been at the height of the projecting stone band and made use of the near-flat lead

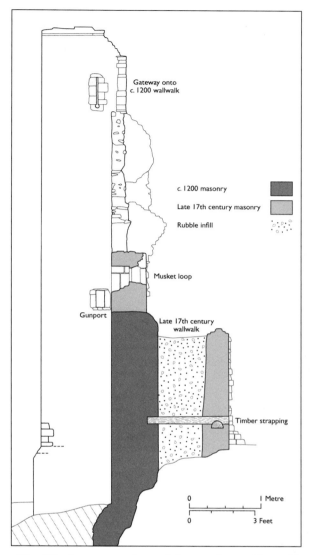

*Fig. 57 A cross-section of the south curtain wall against Marshal's Tower of the Upper Bailey*

roof. The first arrow loop and its reveal were angled down to allow a crossbow man to fire on anyone in front of the castle doors. The sockets for the hourd are also above the roof line to allow the timbers to be inserted and project over the roof. Access to the hourd must have involved climbing through the crenels. The drain for the roof is below the projecting stone band; the lead work of the roof must have been modified to allow the rainwater to drain away.

The three sockets in the south wall show that the hourd turned around the south-west corner of

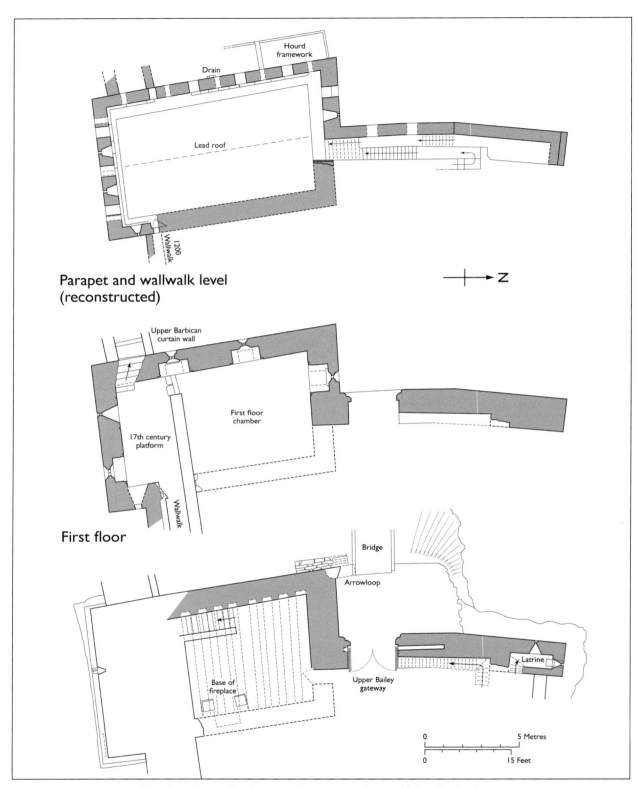

**Parapet and wallwalk level (reconstructed)**

Hourd framework

Drain

Lead roof

1200 Wallwalk

Z

**First floor**

Upper Barbican curtain wall

First floor chamber

17th century platform

Wallwalk

Bridge

Arrowloop

Base of fireplace

Upper Bailey gateway

Latrine

0                     5 Metres

0                     15 Feet

*Fig. 58  Ground-, first- and parapet plans of Marshal's Tower*

the tower. Each of the next two merlons has an arrow loop giving fire across the Dell when the hourd was dismantled. The east wall also contains an arrow loop providing a field of fire along the outer face of the curtain wall.

Opening off the wall-walk around Marshal's Tower is a gateway opening onto the south curtain wall running towards the Great Tower (Figs. 57 and 59). The scar of the south curtain wall rises to the base of this gateway. The scar is quite narrow at 0.6m wide and is keyed into the fabric of the tower. Behind, the wall of the tower is fair faced and has no evidence of a wall-walk, though some toothing projects across the fair face of the tower wall. This may imply that the rear portion of the curtain wall carrying the wall-walk was not bonded into the tower. There are two possibilities, either a timber platform was carried on beams set in sockets through the wall or the wall-walk was carried on a tall arcade of masonry arches only lightly keyed into the tower (Fig. 59). When the town walls of Tenby in Pembrokeshire

were widened following a petition of 1457, an arcade was built against the rear of the wall to carry the wall-walk, considerably saving on the volume of masonry required.[5]

The curtain wall continues in its reduced Civil War form to a small, rectangular turret built against the south-west corner of the Great Tower. By the time the curtain wall reaches the tower it has become 1.9m thick, easily wide enough to carry a wallwalk. The present junction with the rectangular turret is awkward and it has narrow parapet walls, only 0.4m wide, which may be recent in date.

*The interior of Marshal's Tower*

Much of this important building has been demolished or obscured by 17th-century alterations and therefore some of its original form can only be a matter for speculation. The ground-floor room was entered in its north-east corner by a short, rubble-vaulted passage, leading to a door hanging on an inner rebate of Dundry Limestone (Fig. 58);

*Fig. 59 A reconstruction of Marshal's Tower*

the socket for one of the pintles is present. No windows survive in this room, though a tall slot and drain are visible in the south exterior wall. However the bases of the two jambs of a fireplace do survive on the inside of the now partially demolished rear wall. The fireplace is 1.14m wide and the limestone bases were chamfered. The room had a ceiling of massive, closely-spaced joists varying between 0.4 and 0.5m wide and 0.4m high spanning the full 5.4m width.

Access to the first-floor room must have been via an external staircase built against the rear wall (Fig. 59). Its location is not certain but the plain quoins of what appears to be a doorway opening onto the existing curtain wall-walk suggests it was here. These quoins, however, are later and partly infill an earlier, angled reveal which was modified to create the 17th-century gunport alongside. Within the wall is part of a blue lias limestone lintel, which must have spanned the passageway formed by this reveal. Access at this point would have brought one out alongside the window with the semi-circular rear arch. This window is distinctively different from the four other windows surviving in the room. There is an inner and outer roll moulding to the rear arch, neither with the nib that characterises the other windows. The window itself sits eccentrically within the reveal, and has a semi-circular head and a brownstone sill. There are glazing bars and a rear shutter rebate. The window is also remarkable for the extent of the survival of the painted plasterwork in the reveal, which has a white ground with red, single ashlar lining forming a network of small blocks. Above the window and alongside the centre of the left-hand jambs are patterns of red lines overlying the ashlar work, which might be starbursts or floral motifs.

Why this window is distinctively different to the other four is not clear. It could have lit an internal porch behind the main entrance but there is no evidence for any timber fittings. The plaster is intact above the window head and no trace of any porch ceiling is visible. This window, with its rounded-headed rear arch and round-headed light, seems slightly anachronistic and compares with similar forms particularly in the Main Gatehouse. It seems unlikely that the design was changed during construction to the more pointed rear arches as this building must have been raised as one as it forms such an important part of the castle's defences.

The other four windows are of the same type and are regularly disposed in the western half of the first-floor room. Their rear arches have a bold roll moulding with a slight nib. The arch is two-centred with the centres set well below the springing point. Each has a window seat with a boldly chamfered sill. A slab of blue lias limestone is used in the north window, but otherwise all the dressed stone is Dundry Limestone. The window reveals are rectangular in section and the rectangular window stands 0.45m above the window seat. There is a shutter rebate, with sockets for the shutter bolts on the right-hand side. There is one vertical and three horizontal glazing bars but no glazing slot. Very little plasterwork survives within the reveals and no wall painting has been traced. The window in the south wall was blocked in the 17th century. The window seat seems to have been removed and the dressed stone was used in the blocking, which contains a musket loop. In the right-hand jambs of the rear arch are four small, square sockets, two containing iron pins fixed in lead. These are secondary and may have held some form of door to close the breach created through the west wall at this later date.

The remainder of the first-floor room consists of plastered rubble. The plaster is lichen-covered but a close inspection from scaffolding has revealed that traces of the same painted red ashlar pattern seen in the round-headed window still survive. The roof had a very low pitch and sat on the wall top. There is one small, quarter-round corbel in the north wall and a disturbed area at the same height in the centre of the west wall, which may indicate the position of another. Nothing similar occurs on the south wall. This may suggest that there was a central truss with brackets to support the ridge piece. A roof of this pitch could only have had a lead covering.

It is assumed that the demolished east wall would have contained a fireplace above that in the ground floor and perhaps another window to balance the entrance. There must have been an unusual arrangement in the north-east corner as there is what appears to be a stepped roof crease built into the rear wall above the gateway. The wall of the tower below is substantial, but masonry toothing survives above showing that the tower wall continued above the line of the roof crease to support the roof. What this represents is unknown.

Though relatively small, the two rectangular rooms within Marshal's Tower provide well-decorated and useful accommodation (Fig. 58). The presence of a fireplace and a drain in the ground-floor room suggest it was a small kitchen. The floor above had an independent external access and appears to have been a single room, probably with an internal porch in the south-east corner. It was heated but with no integral latrine, there being one over the river. It was well lit with five windows, four of an architecturally-advanced type. The windows were glazed and shuttered and their seats offered fine views to the south over the town and to the west over what was then the castle ditch, looking towards the river gorge. The room was plastered throughout and decorated with a red single-line ashlar pattern with motifs in at least one window. The main approach into William Marshal's castle was from the east through the Lower and Middle Bailey gatehouses, making this tower the most remote and therefore potentially most private part of the castle, yet it was ingeniously incorporated into the western defences.

The architectural style of the windows in the main, first-floor room demonstrate the transition from Romanesque to Early English. They must represent an innovation introduced towards the

*Fig. 60 The* domus regis *at Corfe Castle, Dorset, built by King John, which has parallels for the apartments built in the Marshal's Tower at Chepstow*

end of William Marshal's life, for only round-headed arches occur in the Main Gatehouse. The combination of round-headed lights and two-centred arches surrounds can be seen in a slightly different combination in the two main windows of the great Round Tower of Pembroke Castle.[6] This tower was probably begun by William Marshal after he was made earl of Pembroke in 1199 or more likely following his first visit to the castle in 1204.[7]

Other parallels to the Marshal's Tower at Chepstow can be found in the *domus regis* built by King John in the inner ward of Corfe Castle, Dorset, during the middle years of the first decade of the 13th century (Fig. 60). This rectangular suite of rooms lay beyond the Great Tower in the remotest part of that castle. It was entered by a castellated and defendable porch, lit by tall rectangular windows, then across a bridge and through a doorway into the King's Hall. To the left was what is conventionally known as the presence chamber, but which documents suggest was a chapel. Leading at right angles from the opposite end of the hall was the long chamber. These first-floor rooms have very fine ashlar dressings including chamfered, two-centred arches with a roll-moulded outer order. Some Purbeck marble detailing survives. Earlier plans show that the barrel-vaulted, ground-floor rooms included a kitchen and a staircase rising to the king's rooms above.[8] From 1280, the building accounts kept for Edward I refer to this group of buildings as the 'Gloriette'. This term also appears in the building accounts for Chepstow under Roger Bigod, fifth earl of Norfolk. Although the references after 1282 to the Gloriette at Chepstow can be shown to refer to the domestic quarters built by the earl along the cliff edge of the Lower Bailey (chapter XIV), the first building account for the period 29 September 1271–29 September 1272[9] describes repairs to buildings already in existence:

For roofing and repairing the chamber next to the 'Gloriette'…

For masons, making a tablement above the 'Gloriette' and repairing the prison door, for lime bought with the wages of the same (masons) making a wall behind the Countess's chamber, and for the repair of the steps to the Gloriette and other repairs in the castle …

Marshal's Tower in the Upper Bailey may be the Gloriette referred to in this account. It did have steps leading up to it, but there is no ancillary chamber next to it, nor does any tablement (a decorative stone band) survive. It may prove to have been the Countess's chamber, but this is the only reference to the room of this name. It has also been suggested from an analysis of a series of inventories, that by the early 14th century, the main room may have become the Steward's Hall.[10] All of these attributions are speculative making the name used here, Marshal's Tower, distinctive and non-controversial.

In conclusion, this tower would seem to belong to the first decade of the 13th century. The high-quality dressed stone work and wall painting of the first-floor chamber has parallels in the more elaborate *domus regis* at Corfe Castle. It shares the remote position of the building at Corfe in being sited in the uppermost ward of the time, and beyond the Great Tower. Where it differs is in being made part of the defensive circuit, which must have reduced the practical size of the windows. It must have functioned as a private chamber with what was probably its own kitchen beneath. Access to a latrine involved a walk in the open to the chamber carried over the cliff, which may suggest that the tower was not used as a bedroom. Given its remoteness and high quality of decoration it could only have been for the use of the earl and the countess and was probably a retreat from the, as yet little altered, Norman audience chamber in the Great Tower.

# CHAPTER VIII

# William Marshal's castle at Chepstow & its place in military architecture *by* Richard Avent

During the last two decades of the 12th and in the opening years of the 13th centuries major changes were taking place in castle design and William Marshal's building work here at Chepstow and at his other castles, most notably Pembroke, was at the forefront of these. Two factors were paramount: the introduction of the crossbow as a weapon of castle defence and the adoption of rounded towers.

The crossbow was a weapon of antiquity but considered too cruel for use against Christians and, therefore, forbidden by the Church at the Fourth Lateran Council in 1139. Although used against the Infidels in the East, it does not appear to have become widespread until the later 12th century in the West when it was used extensively by King Richard I before, somewhat ironically, he was to meet his death at the hands of a cross-bowman before the castle of Chaluz in 1199.[1] While other forms of bow can also be used to fire through arrowloops, the crossbow was the specialist weapon for this purpose, being more manoeuverable and capable of use in confined spaces.[2]

The introduction of arrowloops brought with it the ability to use flanking and enfilading fire along the line of castle curtain walls from strategically-positioned mural towers. This concept was taken up with enthusiasm by King Henry II in his major building works in the 1180s on the defences of the inner ward at Dover, Kent, and the upper ward at Windsor, Berkshire. At Dover,

Henry constructed a great square keep surrounded by an inner bailey with regularly-spaced rectangular mural towers, two of which were paired to form the gates (Fig. 61). His outer defences on the north-eastern side of the castle included two towers of the same form and, at the eastern angle, the polygonal Avranches Tower with its formidable battery of arrowloops.[3]

At about the same time Roger Bigod, second earl of Norfolk, was re-building in stone his castle at Framlingham in Suffolk. He, too, employed regularly-spaced rectangular mural towers but, in contrast to Dover, the gate took the much simpler form of a defended passageway through one of the towers.[4] Here it has been demonstrated that a combination of fire from fighting galleries on the top of the towers and from the parapet and lower levels of the inter-vening lengths of curtain would have been highly effective over the entire area in front of the curtain.[5] Henry II's work at Dover is also an early example of the use of concentric defence in Britain.

The move from angular to rounded towers is seen as a means of both strengthening towers by rendering them less vulnerable to undermining (and, incidentally, more capable of deflecting missiles launched against their outer face) and improving the all-round view, particularly for use of the crossbow. A convergence of the two forms can be seen in France as early as the first half of the 12th century.[6]

Fig. 61 *Reconstruction of the 12th-century keep and inner ward at Dover Castle with King John's north gatehouse in the foreground*

Fig. 62 *Conisbrough Castle, Yorkshire, with the 12th-century keep on the right and rounded mural tower on the left*

Some towers in England have been interpreted as being at a 'transitional' point between the two forms. Henry II built three such towers at Chilham, Kent, (1171–75), Tickhill, Yorkshire (1179–82) and Orford, Suffolk (1165–73). Another, at Conisbrough, Yorkshire, was probably built during the 1180s, by Henry's illegitimate half-brother, Hamelin Plantagenet. In plan the Chilham and Tickhill towers are polygonal on both their interior and exterior faces. The other two towers have circular interiors, with the exterior of Orford consisting of three projecting square turrets, while Conisbrough has six angular buttresses (Fig. 62). At both Orford and Conisbrough the towers on the surrounding curtains appear to have been constructed following completion of the principal towers.[7] Those at Orford no longer survive, but an illustration of 1600[8] shows them to have been similar to the towers at Dover and Windsor, while at Conisbrough they are of a solid rounded form rising above the height of the adjoining curtain wall-walk (Fig. 62).[9]

The fact that the king, whose buildings would have been in the forefront of castle design, was still constructing a traditional square keep at Dover while experimenting with something rather different elsewhere in England should not be seen as reflecting any technical limitations on his part, for he was soon to be found building round towers at his castles in France. In the closing years of his reign, Henry strengthened the outer curtain at Gisors, Eure, introducing up-to-date towers including the D-shaped Tour du Diable, fully equipped with arrowslits and every bit a match for the Avranches Tower at Dover.[10] On the Loire he built a round tower (Tour du Moulin), along with rounded flanking towers, at the western end of his castle at Chinon, Indre-et-Loire (Fig. 63).[11] None of this should come as a surprise for there is nothing new in the use of rounded towers—they have a long history and Roman examples were still around for all to see. Indeed, the Norman invaders probably spent their first night in England within the old Roman fort of Pevensey, Sussex, with its rounded mural and

widely-spaced gate towers.[12] Elsewhere in Europe, at the end of the 11th century Raymond of Burgundy constructed a magnificent town wall at Avila in Spain—probably making use of an existing Roman town wall—with no less than 88 rounded towers including those paired to make the Alcázar and San Vicente gates.[13] The changes that were taking place in castle design in the later 12th century should, therefore, be seen as a response to military developments and functional change rather than, necessarily, a progressive improvement in the building skills of the day. After all, whilst a rounded tower is a much more effective military structure, it is a decidedly less convenient living space.

To obtain the most complete impression of the dynamics of change towards the end of the 12th century, one has to turn to Richard I's great castle

*Fig. 63 Twelfth-century Tour du Moulin at Chinon, Indre-et-Loir, France*

at Château Gaillard high above the River Seine at Les Andelys (Fig. 64). Built by one of the leading military men of the age at breathtaking speed between 1196 and 1198, the castle and new town cost more than all of Henry II's work at Dover. The concentric design made full use of the rounded tower to gain maximum effect in the use of flanking and enfilading fire. The great tower lies behind an inner bailey curtain composed of a whole series of rounded projections, while rounded towers are disposed at regular intervals along the middle and outer bailey walls with a particularly strong tower at the southern end guarding the main approach.[14] All of these architectural changes would have been very familiar to William Marshal who had distinguished himself, particularly in France, through his skill on the tournament field and unswerving loyalty to the English monarchy.[15]

It is against this background that the Marshal's work at Chepstow needs to be viewed, starting with the construction of the Main Gatehouse almost certainly during the 1190s. This was followed by the Middle Bailey towers which must have been going up at about the same time

as Marshal was building his great cylindrical tower at Pembroke with the Horseshoe Gate and probably the Dungeon Tower on the surrounding inner ward curtain (Fig. 65). This work at Pembroke dates from about 1200 after Marshal was able to take possession of his lands in Pembroke and Leinster.[16] A decade later Marshal rebuilt Kilkenny Castle on his Irish estates with round corner towers and a twin-towered gatehouse. Also in Ireland, Dunamase Castle, Co. Laois, has traditionally been attributed to Marshal but he was only in a position to carry out building works there between 1208–10 or after 1215.[17] His remarkable round-towered lighthouse on the Hook Peninsula, Co. Wexford, also dates to the early 13th century.[18] Returning to Wales, the Marshal's work at Usk, Monmouthshire, which includes the circular Garrison Tower sitting astride the south-west curtain, probably dates to his final years between 1212 and 1219 (Fig. 66).[19] Apart from at Dunamase, all these castles feature the use of round towers. Paired together these can form gatehouses, or they can be spaced along the line of the curtain, or act as corner towers. Many adopt a distinctive circular form, sometimes

*Fig. 64  King Richard I's castle at Château Gaillard, Les Andelys, France*

standing proud of the curtain. Occasionally, one of these towers is larger than its companions, perhaps signifying a more important function.

Philip Augustus' ruinous castle at the Louvre in Paris provides a good starting point from which to seek comparisons for Marshal's work at Chepstow and elsewhere (Fig. 67).[20] Built between 1190 and 1202, it had a square plan with round towers at each corner and D-shaped towers midway along each side, two of which were paired together to form the main gatehouse. At the heart of the castle lay a great round tower, *tour philippien*, pre-dating Marshal's great keep at Pembroke by just a few years. Another French castle of square plan with round corner towers and short D-shaped gate towers was built at Dordives, Loiret, by Henri le Maréchal in the opening years of the 13th century.[21]

In England, probably towards the end of the 12th century and in the early years of the 13th, Robert de Roos adopted the same general plan form for the north gatehouse and corner towers at

*Fig. 66 The Garrison Tower at Usk Castle, Monmouthshire*

*Fig. 65 Aerial view of Pembroke Castle. William Marshal's great Keep is in the foreground with the foundations of the Horseshoe Gate below and to its right*

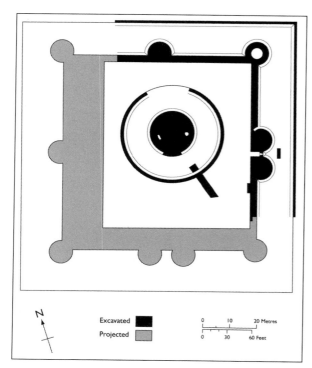

*Fig. 67 Plan of Philip Augustus's castle at the Louvre, Paris, France*

Helmsley Castle in Yorkshire (Fig. 147). As at the Louvre, the structures are ruined to ground level but the D-shaped western gate-tower still has a ground-floor arrowloop facing out to the field while the interior of the other tower contrasts with the exterior by being angular in plan.[22] The nearest comparison in England to the north gate at Helmsley is to be found in the inner gatehouse at Skipton, also in Yorkshire. This may be the work of William de Fors I, who inherited the castle in 1190 but died just five years later, or of his son, William de Fors II, sometime before 1220. If the former, this would be another very early gatehouse. Later work has partially obscured the rounded front of the gatehouse. The entrance passageway over a long pit may have included a drawbridge; at its inner end a portcullis protected the main doorway.[23]

A re-assessment of the dating of the north gatehouse at Dover Castle suggests that it could have been constructed within a decade of that at Chepstow. Built by King John, it was certainly in existence at the time of the Great Siege of 1216

forming part of a powerful defensive system at the northern end of the castle with towers, with inter-linking passages, flanking the gatehouse, an external ditch and beyond that a substantial barbican (Fig. 68). As part of his subsequent rebuilding of this end of the castle, Henry III blocked the gate and added new towers. Little of the original gatehouse survives, although it

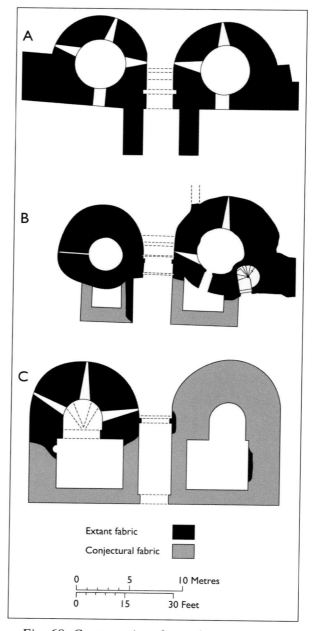

*Fig. 68 Comparative plans of gatehouses at Limerick (A), Chepstow (B) and Dover (C)*

clearly consisted of two elongated drum-shaped towers (Fig. 69).[24]

In all the above examples the gate towers have been of D-shaped plan. In contrast the northern gate tower of the main gatehouse at Chepstow is round (Fig. 68) and, therefore, more analogous to the corner towers at the Louvre, Dordives and Helmsley. While the southern tower adopts a more traditional external plan it, too, is round on the interior. For comparisons, one needs to cross the Irish Sea.

The gatehouse at Limerick Castle on the western side of Ireland may have formed part of King John's building works recorded in the Pipe Roll for 1211–12. While its gate towers project forward as two D-shaped towers, they are circular internally (Fig. 68). Furthermore, as at Chepstow, the gate passage extended on into the castle but, in this case, excavations in 1993 demonstrated that this extension took the form of a vaulted rectangular building to the rear of the gate.[25] The three contemporary corner towers were round and significantly larger than the gate towers. On the other side of the country, in 1204 John issued a mandate for the building of a castle in Dublin, although it appears that only the round south-west tower (Bermingham Tower) was constructed at that time. The other building works probably did not begin until about 1213, coming to an end around 1230. The gatehouse no longer survives but, from a plan dated to 1673, it appears to have consisted of a pair of elongated D-shaped towers and the castle's overall plan is similar to Limerick in also eventually having drum towers at each corner.[26]

Of particular interest to Chepstow is the evidence for the now lost gatehouse at William Marshal's castle at Kilkenny in Ireland. Two 18th-century plans show the gate to have consisted of two round towers located midway along the south curtain of the castle.[27] The more sketchy of these, dating to 1767,[28] seems to suggest that the western gate tower was larger than its companion; an impression reversed in an earlier distant view of the gate dating to 1699 in which the eastern tower appears to be the larger of the two.[29] It is clear from the 1699 view that the gatehouse had been altered over time and a recent reconstruction of the castle as it might have appeared in the 13th century has opted for two round gatehouse towers of equal size and, on balance, this seems the most probable.[30] Although the castle has undergone substantial alteration, the three remaining corner towers and parts of the intervening curtain walls contain varying degrees of medieval fabric and distinctive arrowloops. The south tower at Kilkenny (and probably the now lost north tower) along with the south-east tower (Record Tower) at Dublin are more substantial than their companions and resemble in many ways the great circular towers or keeps being built elsewhere in south Wales (Pembroke) and in France. At both castles these were, strategically, the most exposed towers perhaps necessitating greater strength.[31]

The other possible Marshal castle in Ireland with a twin-towered gatehouse was that built at Dunamase, Co. Laois.[32] The front of the gatehouse leading into the lower bailey is badly ruined, but it is of a quite different form to those at Chepstow and Kilkenny and, on a smaller

*Fig. 69 Artist's impression of Dover Castle during the siege of 1216 with King John's North Gatehouse under attack*

*Fig. 70 Artist's impression of Pembroke Castle in the 14th century with William Marshal's keep and Horseshoe Gate below and to its left*

scale, may have looked more like the contemporary structure at Warkworth in Northumberland.[33] Both consisted of a pair of narrow towers of sub-rectangular form and were well equipped with arrowloops.

The closest gatehouse to Chepstow, in terms of sophistication if not in design, is that leading to the inner ward at the royal castle of Pevensey which may date to around 1200. The present structure is in a ruinous state but much of the original arrangement can be reconstructed. Two drum-shaped towers, with timber backs, flanked a vaulted entrance passage. Each tower had three tiers of arrowloops although the detail of these has been lost. There must have been a drawbridge and the chase for a portcullis can still be seen on one side of the entrance passage from which doors entered each ground-floor room.[34]

Two other English castles feature rounded towers, in both cases built by King John.

Throughout his reign over £1,400 was spent on building operations at Corfe Castle with construction of the 'gloriette' in the inner ward (Fig. 60), and the towers and curtain wall of the west bailey almost certainly date to the early part of his reign. Little survives of the westernmost octagonal, Butavant Tower, built between 1202 and 1204 and the south tower has also collapsed. However, the northern tower has survived and is semi-circular outside with a polygonal interior and four arrowloops.[35] John's earliest work at Scarborough on the curtain of the inner bailey, completed by 1206, includes three solid, rounded, mural towers similar in form to the slightly earlier ones on the inner ward curtain at Conisbrough Castle. The second phase of John's work at Scarborough, dating to before 1212, involved rebuilding the rest of the western curtain overlooking the town and equipping it with a series of D-shaped towers of similar form to the northern tower on the eastern curtain of the Middle Bailey at Chepstow.[36]

No consideration of the Marshal's building works during this period would be complete without some further discussion of his work at Pembroke Castle, the gateway to his newly-acquired lands in Ireland. There are different views over the dating of the outer ward defences at Pembroke and the Dungeon Tower on the inner curtain but there is general agreement that the great cylindrical tower at the castle and the Horseshoe Gate leading into the inner ward form part of Marshal's earliest work (Figs. 65 & 70).[37] A comparison between the cross-form of arrowloop used in the Dungeon Tower with the very early use of this form in the upper levels of the Chepstow gatehouse may tip the balance in favour of this tower also forming part of these early works and, therefore, being contemporary with the construction of the middle bailey towers at Chepstow.

Marshal is clearly adopting the latest fashion in round towers at Pembroke, the earliest development of which has already been discussed. From the 1190s onwards, the king of France, Philip Augustus started to construct a very particular type of massive tower of cylindrical form harking back to the formidable structure built by Thibaud V, Comte de Blois, between 1170 and 1190, at Châteaudun, Eure-et-Loir (Fig. 71).[38] The earliest of Philip Augustus' towers is probably that now only surviving to its lowermost courses at the Louvre in Paris (see above). Known as *tours philipiennes*, these were soon appearing at a number of French royal castles with notable examples at Gisors (Tour du Prisonnier) and Chinon (Tour du Coudray).[39] It seems probable that the Pembroke tower is modelled on these, although Marshal would have also been aware of Henry II's similar but slightly earlier cylindrical tower at Chinon (Fig. 63).

Marshal's round towers at Usk and Kilkenny have already been mentioned but he built another, free-standing, cylindrical tower although not as a military structure. On the Irish coast Marshal appears to have constructed the remarkable Tower of Hook as a lighthouse to aid navigation by ships into his new port of Ross. It compares well with other round towers of the period and is stone vaulted to avoid fire (a very real hazard for a structure with a fire burning on its roof as a navigation light for much of its life). Although the top of the tower has been modified, it still stands largely unaltered for most of its height.[40]

The other novel Marshal structure at Pembroke is the Horseshoe Gate at the entrance to the inner ward (Figs. 70 & 72) As its name implies, this takes the form of a horseshoe-shaped tower with entry through one side with a right-angled passage leading to an exit into the inner ward via a door in the rear of the tower. The antecedents for this type of entrance can be found in Muslim and Byzantine gates and similar bent

*Fig. 71 Twelfth-century cylindrical tower at Châteaudun, Eure-et-Loire*

entrances were also used by the Crusaders, although the towers were rectangular.[41] However, an exactly comparable plan involving another horseshoe-shaped tower can be found at the Frankish castle of Saranda Kolones at Paphos on Cyprus (Fig. 72). King Richard I sold Cyprus to the Knights Templar in 1192 who, in turn, passed the island on to Guy de Lusignan, sovereign of the Crusader kingdom of Jerusalem. This concentric castle was probably built in about 1200 and subsequently destroyed by an earthquake in 1222. Like that at Pembroke, the horseshoe-shaped gatehouse tower has been reduced to its lower-most courses but it appears to have originally been vaulted, possibly with a chapel in its upper storey.[42] Finally, a similar side entrance was used to enter the barbican at Pembroke although there is uncertainty over whether this was the work of the Earl Marshal or half a century later.

It is now clear from the dendrochronological dating of its doors and from comparison with similar structures elsewhere that the round-towered main gatehouse at Chepstow is one of the earliest examples of this type. Furthermore, the now-lost gatehouse at Kilkenny suggests that Chepstow may not have been a one-off. If the sequencing of building construction at Chepstow is correct, then the inclusion of rounded towers on the Middle Bailey curtain also represents the early use of this type of tower which was also to be seen, in its grandest form, in the keep at Pembroke, where Marshal's design was probably inspired by contemporary developments in France. Marshal went on to employ round towers elsewhere and they were soon to be adopted by Marcher lords throughout south Wales. Finally, the Horseshoe Gate at Pembroke may well have drawn inspiration from Crusader castles. In all of this, the Marshal's building works were at the cutting edge of developments in military architecture at this time, precisely what one would expect of a man with such extensive military experience, political standing and, by the end of the 12th century, financial wealth.

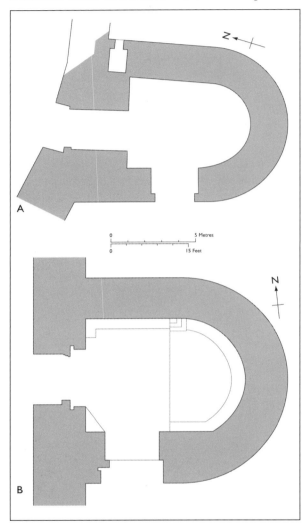

*Fig. 72 Comparative plans of the Horseshoe Gates at the castles of Pembroke (A) and Saranda Kolones, Paphos, Cyprus (B)*

# CHAPTER IX

# The Marshals' use of the Great Tower

*by* Rick Turner, Stephen Priestley *and* Chris Jones-Jenkins

The Norman Great Tower seems to have remained largely unaltered for about 150 years after it was built, although there is a reference in the Pipe Roll of 1185 of repairs to the tower and castle of Striguil at the cost of £10 13s. by order of the king.[1] Despite William Marshal's transformation of Chepstow Castle into a fortress incorporating the most sophisticated military engineering of the day, very little evidence for his development of the domestic accommodation survives,[2] apart from the rectangular Marshal's Tower in the Upper Bailey. As has been shown in chapter VII, this contained a large, heated first-floor chamber with elegantly moulded window reveals and painted decoration.[3]

Minor alterations to the Norman Great Tower appear to have included the insertion of a lancet window in the south elevation, which has similarities with the windows in Marshal's Tower, and the possible remodelling of the entrance into the first floor.

## The Documentary Evidence
*by* Stephen Priestley

Upon the death of William Marshal in 1219, his castle and estates at Chepstow were inherited in turn by his five sons. With the death of Anselm in 1245, the male line of inheritance became extinct and Chepstow Castle was part of the estates which passed to the Marshal's eldest daughter, Maud or Mathilda, an ageing and sickly woman who died in 1248, and

whose eldest son, Roger Bigod, fourth Earl of Norfolk, then inherited (Fig. 73).[4]

There are three entries in the Close Rolls recording grants by the king of oaks to the sons of William Marshal, for works to Chepstow Castle. The first, to the eldest son, William Marshall II, reads:

> *28 Mar 1228. De quercubus datis. Mandatum est Rogero de Clifford quod habere faciat comiti W. Marescallo x quercus in foresta de Dene de dono domini Regis sparsim per loca ubi minus appareat ad minus nocumentum foreste cepi possint, ad operationem turris de Striguil.*[5]

> 12 Mar 1228. Concerning a gift of oaks. Roger de Clifford is ordered that he is to let William Earl Marshal have 10 oaks in the part of Dean of the King's gift to be taken from the place where it is least damaging to the forest, for the work of the tower of Striguil.

Work may have been interrupted after William Marshal II's death, for his brother Richard quarrelled with the king and after what almost amounted to a minor civil war, Richard withdrew to Ireland where he was killed in 1234.

However, when Gilbert inherited the lordship he seems to have very rapidly regained the king's favour, for in August 1234 he received a grant of fifty good oaks for joisting his tower at Chepstow.

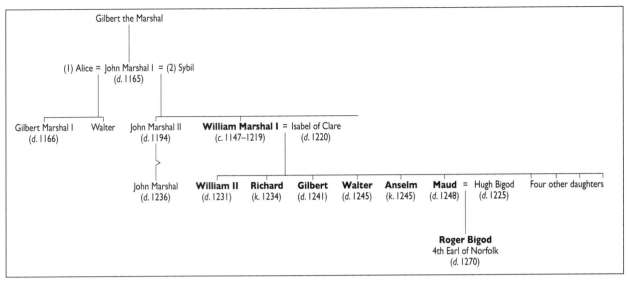

*Fig. 73 The Marshal family tree*

Gilbert received another grant, this time of twenty-five oaks, in December 1234, but this was for the repair of the '*jarruyllium castri*' rather than work on the Great Tower.[7] *Jarruyllium* can have a number of translations, and was taken by Perks[8] to mean a 'gallery' and so date the feature along the north side of the Great Tower to this period. However, 'jarruyllium' more commonly means a brattishing or palisade and, as the timber was for repairs rather than new construction, this reference may have no relevance to the development of the Great Tower.

## The surviving fabric

*West external elevation* (Figs. 14 and 74)
The fabric of the Marshal phase is almost entirely built on top of the Norman wall tops and any remnant gable containing the two circular windows. The building was raised by at least 9m, almost doubling the height of the Norman work. The rubble walling is made of irregular courses of angular Carboniferous Limestone with the quoins and dressed stonework being of Dundry Limestone.

Though the right-hand angle buttress has been robbed away in its upper half, there are remains of a weathered cap made of small but finely-dressed Dundry Limestone blocks, which turn to continue onto the south face. This marks the junction of the Great Tower with the 13th-century curtain wall of the Upper Bailey. This ran from the top of Marshal's Tower to a small rectangular turret, constructed against the corner of the Great Tower.[9]

The top of the elevation includes part of the crenellations. The three, large square holes are drains from the wall walk, between which are two arrow loops, the one to the right being complete. This is very tall with a small cross slit and circular base and allows the archer to fire down to ground level. The form of the arrow loop is the same as used in the South-West Tower of the Upper Barbican, whose present stone defences are considered to have been added to the castle by one of the Marshal's sons.[10]

There is evidence of a building being added to this side of the Great Tower at this period. A short length of rubble limestone footings butts against the left-hand angle buttress. The position of the roof timbers may be indicated by a square socket in the central pilaster, a more blundered socket in the right-hand angle buttress, and a neat square block of red sandstone set into the left-hand angle buttress. The implication, from a number of inventories of the castle, made in Edward II's reign, is that this was the bakehouse with two ovens, which lay beyond the Great Tower,[11] and this may have been the original function for this building.

*Fig. 74 The west external elevation of the Great Tower*

*South external elevation* (Fig. 15)
The details visible on the west elevation turn and partly survive above the first bay of the south elevation. Rubble limestone walling is built directly onto the Norman eaves courses and the weathered capping and quoins in Dundry Limestone rise to just above the wall-walk level. The Norman eaves course continues to just beyond the second pilaster to the point where the double archway spanned the interior. The east wall of the second floor must have been built directly above this arcade. Beyond that point the wall top has been raised by about 1.1m marked by the difference in height between the Norman eaves band and the moulded string course of this phase, which survives above the fourth pilaster. New stonework to raise the third and fourth pilasters is quite easily identified, though the break between the two phases of rubble walling is not so clear.

The other substantial modification is the insertion of a two-centred, arched, outer window frame through the third pilaster. This has small, neatly-chamfered Dundry Limestone dressings but the window opening itself is rectangular and recessed, suggesting it was similar in form to those surviving in Marshal's Tower, so may predate the major changes in this phase.

*East external elevation* (Figs. 16 and 75)
Much of the ground floor and plinth of this elevation appears to be unchanged from the Norman period except for the butting up of the Middle Bailey curtain wall. What has emerged only recently is that the tympanum was blocked and the Norman chip carving rendered over (Fig. 76. This was most likely carried out by the Marshals as part of their remodelling of the Great Tower, so obscuring what had become anachronistic decoration.

However, the first floor was quite extensively remodelled. The central pilaster was truncated and given a weathered cap in Dundry Limestone. To the right, a rectangular panel of angular rubble limestone above the main doorcase implies the removal and blocking of a Norman window. At a higher level are two lancet windows with neatly chamfered Dundry Limestone surrounds. Further

Fig. 76 *The tympanum of the east doorway photographed* c.1948 *before the blocking was removed by the Ministry of Works*

to the left is a very neat, rectangular, slot window lighting the spiral staircase rising from the first-floor doorway.

The tops of both the angle buttresses have been remodelled with stonework of a different character for a height of about 1.2m and the moulded string course appears to have been reset beneath the right-hand corner turret and for a short length across the centre of the elevation. A rectangular socket above the staircase window may be a drain from the wall walk.

Within the bays of this elevation are traces of external render with a coarse dark aggregate. As this occurs on both the Norman fabric and the alterations of this phase, it must belong to the latter date. More extensive patches of this render survive on the north elevation.

Fig. 75 *The east external elevation of the Great Tower*

Fig. 77 *The north external elevation of the Great Tower, rising above the limestone cliff*

*North external elevation* (Figs. 18 and 77)

This elevation shows extensive remodelling of the Norman Great Tower. The ground floor remained unaltered but the first floor was transformed by the insertion of four new windows. Two new windows and a doorway were added within the heightened portion above the right-hand two bays, which formed the second floor.

The left-hand angle buttress and first pilaster were raised about 1m in height to meet the moulded string course which runs across the elevation, to where it was neatly truncated just before the position of the third pilaster, which had been reduced and a neat weathered capping added. Though the Norman window in the first bay is now open, it is likely to have been blocked and rendered over in this phase. The second and third bays contain three mullioned and transomed two-light windows with trefoil-headed upper lights and a quatrefoil light in the apex. The windows are contained within an outer, chamfered, two-centred, arched frame with a hood-mould with simply carved stops. The upper lights and quatrefoils of these windows have external glazing rebates.

The fourth and fifth bays are dominated by a larger opening inserted above the fourth pilaster. It consists of a pair of windows similar to those in the second and third bays but given an outer order of a roll-moulding. These are set within an outer chamfered arch with a hood mould and carved head stops. Piercing the rubble stone tympanum is a large quatrefoil within a roll-moulded frame. The rubble relieving arch above this window rises higher than the Norman eaves course.

The second floor must have been added upon the completion of the great window below. It has two mullioned and transomed windows of the same form as those surviving in the second and third bays, but with much meaner dressings, and no outer frame. Also at this level, and slightly offset above the third pilaster, is a chamfered, two-centred, arched doorcase. There are no sockets, corbels or mortar fillets surviving to show how this doorway, standing 11m above the floor of the Gallery, was reached.

The rubble stone of this phase must have extended across the third bay to provide support for an external staircase to the wall walk above the second floor. Though the masonry in the right-hand corner rises above the wall-walk, no details of the crenellations or arrowloops survive.

Larger areas of render with the dark, coarse aggregate survive on this elevation. This render covers the blocking of the Norman windows and is drawn up to the dressings of the new windows. It also passes across the line of the roof of the Gallery. It can be assumed that all the rubble stonework of the Great Tower was rendered at this date.

*West internal elevation* (Fig. 19 and Plate 2)

This elevation is more complex than it might superficially appear. The four Norman niches were retained open but the sills and the walling immediately below were patched and made up with angular limestone. This, and other evidence from the south elevation, suggest that the floor level was lowered 0.7m to the tops of the boards running above the joists, by the removal of the flagging and bedding layers. By making up the sills of the niches to a level incorporating the bases of the piers, the niches are converted into seats rather than walk-in recesses.

The building break between the panel of brownstone blocks and the limestone walling containing the two circular windows is at the level at which the massive, chamfered, two-centred, blind arch is sprung. This archway widens the upper part of the wall by 0.9m, probably to allow for the wall-walk to pass behind the crenellations. Part of the rear arch of the right-hand circular window is hidden behind the masonry of the blind arch. These two windows would have been crossed by the line of the second floor and so must have become redundant and almost certainly filled in during these alterations.

Above the apex of the blind arch is a moulded corbel at the base of an angled slot with dressed quoins. This slot must have carried an angle brace to the ridge beam of the roof. There is no other evidence of the roofline or pitch in this area. A similar but more crudely executed corbel and slot survives just above the centre of the arcade of niches. It is set within a panel of rough rubble masonry that straddles the building break. This probably contained another angled brace, this time to a ceiling beam, which ran along the length of the room and into the rear of the double archway spanning the interior. The height of the floor is marked by a deep socket just above the string course.

*South internal elevation* (Fig. 20)
The most obvious remains of the alterations on this elevation are the moulded pilaster and springing point of one of the two arches which were inserted into the Great Tower to create rooms, one 16m long and the other 10m long. The full details and reconstructed form of this double archway are discussed in chapter X.

The archway was bedded into the blocked niche behind and the dressed stone rises from the reduced floor level observed on the west elevation. This once again converted the five open niches in this elevation into seats rather than floor-level recesses. To the left of the archway are the remains of what was postulated in the Norman period to be a large central niche. The rubble-stone arch and the two short lengths of vertical joints rising from the lowered floor level are perhaps most easily explained as the conversion of the central niche into a fireplace. With the floor reduced to wooden boarding, a central hearth would have been impossible. There is some modification to the joist holes below this fireplace, which implies that a heavy hearthstone had to be supported. Unfortunately a fireplace cannot be proven at this point as no flue is visible in the wall top above; later capping of the wall tops have probably hidden the evidence.

To the left of the proposed fireplace is a window. Its rear arch is made of small, rather crudely-dressed stones with a semi-circular head. The sill rises from the reduced floor level through the deep reveal to a rectangular window measuring 2m high and 0.7m wide. Its rear arch is similar to the relieving arch of the doorway in the south-east corner, implying that they may have been contemporary and probably of William

Marshal's time. Within the doorway, good ashlar Dundry Limestone is used to form the spiral staircase walls rising to the wall-walk, in contrast with the mixture of rubble stone used in the staircase down to the main entrance.

Between the window and the doorway the walling must have been reconstructed to remove two of the niches. On the wall top above is the blundered remains of the moulded string course (a single complete stone from this course survives in the south-west corner). The height of this corresponds with a line of four rough corbels or toothing stones above the archway.

*East internal elevation* (Fig. 22)
The ground floor of this elevation is unaltered in this phase, but at first-floor level there are two, finely-wrought reveals for the lancet windows. The two-centred rear arches have a roll and fillet moulding with a similar hood mould with stops carved in the form of tight balls of foliage. The sills of the reveals are stepped and the lancet to the left is not symmetrically placed within its reveal, being offset to the right. The construction of the window reveals led to the blocking of earlier Norman features.

Between the two windows, there is a tall, rectangular slot rising from a moulded corbel. The slot is framed by dressed limestone blocks and is similar if larger than the slot surviving above the blind arch on the west elevation. This must have contained the support for the ridge beam of the roof running over the eastern room. Given its height in relation to the moulded string course on the long walls, it implies that this end of the roof was hipped. None of the original wall top of this phase survives unaltered.

*North internal elevation* (Fig. 23)
As with the other internal elevations, the ground floor was unaltered in this phase. There were fundamental changes to the first floor and the addition of a second floor, and this elevation demonstrates these changes more completely than elsewhere in the building.

The Norman wall top does not show as a hard horizontal line, but there is evidence of a building break between the mixture of stones which make up the Norman walling, and the angular limestone rubble between 1.2 and 1.3m below the moulded sandstone string course, which marks the first-floor wall top in this Marshal phase. The Norman windows were blocked and new windows were punched through the existing walls. The western room was framed by the large, blind arch against the west wall and the northern jamb of the double archway. Between these two features is a large, double window. It has a semi-circular, roll and fillet moulded rear arch with a hood mould and carved head stops. The jambs run down to the plain, chamfered window seats. There is a deep, rubble stone relieving arch, which had to be truncated to fit below the first-floor band.

Within the rear arch are the remains of a pair of two-light, mullioned and transomed windows. These windows had their own rear arches, which consisted of now-lost colonnettes (probably in Purbeck Marble), stiff-leaf capitals and moulded arches above. The lower lights were shuttered whilst the upper lights and the quatrefoil were both glazed and shuttered. To the right, the Norman doorway seems to have remained in use and been unaltered, though the reduction in the floor level may explain why its threshold was cut away.

The northern jamb of the double archway must have been set into a slot cut into the Norman walling, and it is only keyed in above the line of the building break. The outer mouldings of the arch are brought down to form the sides of the flat Dundry Limestone jamb, and they die onto a sloping stop just above the lowered floor level. The stones at the base of the jamb are fire-reddened, perhaps through the burning of the wooden floor at some date.

Careful observation of the corbels and the abacus suggest that they were inserted into the jamb after it, and probably the outer ring of the arch, were in place. The joints of the components of the lower corbel do not respect the joints of the jamb, and some of the corbel stones have diagonal edges. The upper corbel and its cluster of Purbeck Marble shafts also seem to have been

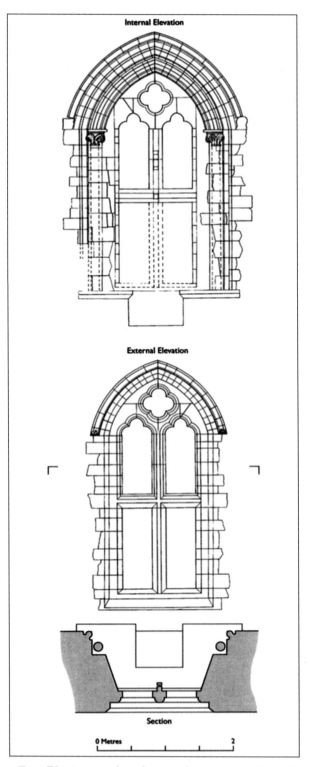

*Fig. 78 A record and partial reconstruction of the new windows inserted into the first floor of the Great Tower*

built *in situ*, with the component parts slid into place, rather than laid one of the top of the other. The lowest courses of the relieving arch of flaggy Brownstone survive on this elevation.

Within the eastern room created at first-floor level in this phase, there are three two-light mullioned and transomed windows. They were of the same form as the individual windows which made up the double window in the western room, except in their pointed, rear arches. These three windows vary in the details of the carving of the hood-mould stops, the stiff-leafed capitals and the rear projections on the upper mullion, which received the shutter bolts (Fig. 78).

The second floor was built over the western chamber of the first floor. It was created by building a solid party wall over the double archway, pierced by a passage and doorway against the north wall. This doorway opened out onto the wall-walk over the eastern first-floor room.

The floor of this upper chamber was carried on a massive square beam, whose socket (about 0.4m square), survives against the blind arch in the north-west corner. The ragged masonry in the opposite corner might have contained a socket for a similar beam, but there does not seem to have been any intermediates. The moulded string course is not strong enough to have carried any of the floor timbers, so there must have been joists, 9.2m long, spanning these two beams. This would have made for a very massive and rather unstable floor, which contrasts markedly with the quality of the stonework.

The upper chamber is lit by a pair of windows, similar in form, but plainer in detailing than those on the first floor. The rear arches have plain chamfers and no carved detail. The chamber was entered by a door in the north-east corner. This too has a simply-chamfered rear arch. The wall top of the upper chamber is marked by a single stone from a moulded band of the same profile as that above the first floor. This created a room 4.6m high compared to the 6.4m height of the room beneath. There is no evidence for the form of the roof trusses above this chamber or elsewhere in this phase.

## The Plan and Function of the Marshal Great Tower

At ground floor, the plan is almost unaltered except that the central pier of the double archway introduced into the first floor must have passed through the wooden ceiling and down to the bedrock floor (Fig. 79 and Plate 5). Much more radical changes occurred at first-floor level. The entrance remained in the south-east corner of the building, but the erection of the twin arches changed the orientation of the building. Upon entering, there must have been the sense of walking down the aisle of a great cathedral or abbey church. The line of mullioned and transomed windows in the north wall was closed by the double archway (Fig. 81). This provided a division, if not a solid one, with the smaller room beyond. If the lord's table was placed in front of the arches, then a more conventional hall may have been created, with side tables down the south wall, flanking the newly-created fireplace and hearth. The stops on the jambs of the twin arches are in a position, which shows that the floor level of the Norman period was lowered. This may have followed a collapse, fire or other catastrophe because the grant of timber in 1234 was specifically for joisting.

The two lancet windows erected in the east wall provided some top lighting into this room and their position is typical, though their style is plainer, to other entrance gable windows.[12] The lowering of the floor probably led to the remodelling of the doorcase in the south-east corner, and by this date this doorway could have been the main entrance for visitors to the Great Tower rather than just for the lord, as argued in the Norman phase. The roofing was also heightened by almost 0.8m and closed with a string course down each long wall. A paired rafter roof, perhaps with a barrel ceiling, is the most likely form to heighten the effect created by the double archway whose apexes rose to about 4m above the floor level. Putting this evidence together the eastern room of the Marshals' Great Hall would have been orientated east-west, been entered from the south-east corner, lit by large windows in the north wall (Plate 5) and heated by a fire-

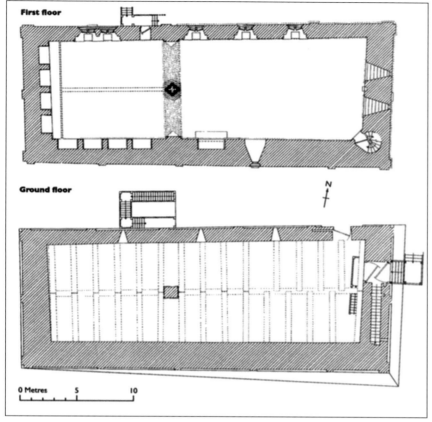

**First floor**

**Ground floor**

N

0 Metres    5         10

*Fig. 79 The reconstructed ground-and first-floor plans of the Marshals' Great Tower*

place in the south wall. Nevertheless it remained a highly unconventional hall.

There is no evidence for any timber screen or partition closing off the double archway. Indeed their elaborate corbels and any similar embellishments on the central column were intended to be seen in the round. The upper clusters of capitals are just above normal head height. Looking up to them from floor level would have allowed an appreciation of the stiff-leaf details which were carved inside the cluster. So anyone entering the eastern room from the doorway in the south-east corner would have been able to see through the arcade into the western room beyond. This room is almost square in plan and would seem to be arranged south to north to look through the magnificent double mullioned and transomed window towards the river gorge. The doorway alongside this window is assumed to have

remained in operation, but its function may have changed, as it would have led directly into what is assumed to have been a more private room than that to the east. It would have opened out onto a wooden staircase leading up to the doorway of the newly-created room above and down to the ground floor. It is in this period that the building at the west end of the Great Tower seems to have been added. This may have been a kitchen or even a suite of service rooms that was apparently so singly missing from the Norman period.

The western room was odd in other ways too. It seems to have retained four open niches within its south and west walls, which in the latter case perhaps even retained their Norman decoration. These niches were no longer at floor level but now 0.75m above it making them more convenient to sit rather than stand in. The room was unheated and had a flat, wooden ceiling divided by a braced ceiling beam running west to east. Though most easily explained as a withdrawing or great chamber, set behind the dais of the presumed hall, it remained open to public gaze and without its own fireplace or latrine.

The device of incorporating an arcade or single great arch across the main room in a castle keep is known in two surviving examples from the first half of the 12th century. The first is in the keep at Rochester Castle where the central spine wall is pierced by two twin arches allowing free circulation around the second floor where Archbishop Corbeil's hall was presumed to be sited. A simpler, but no less impressive device, was the great single arch built across the hall in the keep at Castle Hedingham for Aubrey, earl of Oxford.[13] Both these sites are of one phase but the

99

*Fig. 80 A reconstruction of the exterior of the Marshals' Great Tower*

central arcades or arch were required to carry the spine wall to the upper levels of the keep. The same is true at Chepstow even though the arcade is an insertion, for it supports the east wall of the second-floor chamber, whilst allowing for free circulation around the first floor.

This second-floor chamber was much more private as access was via the wooden tower staircase against the north wall. This was just a single chamber with two mullioned and transomed windows looking north (Fig. 80). These windows were plainer in detail and without any Purbeck shafts like those on the first floor. So, perhaps unusually for the period, the most private room

for the lord seems to have been the plainest. There may have been a fireplace and even a garderobe in the now lost south wall making this more comfortable than the one below.

A doorway in the second-floor chamber led out onto the wall-walk above the eastern end of the Great Tower. This part of the wall-walk could also be reached from the spiral staircase in the south-east corner. Another flight of steps was necessary to climb onto the wall-walk above the second floor, and this must have followed the position later used by Roger Bigod in his re-modelling of the Great Tower.

# CHAPTER X

# The Architecture and Decoration of the Marshals' Great Tower

*by* Nicola Coldstream *and* Richard K. Morris

The remodelling of the Great Tower for William Marshal's sons is a work of exceptionally high quality for a secular building in its period. Its architectural details are paralleled only in the most ornate features of contemporary great churches, especially in processional portals, and its sculptural ornament is precocious in relation to court works of the 1240s and 1250s at Windsor and Westminster. The justification for this assessment is the subject of this chapter, setting the remodelling in the context of the Early English style of Gothic architecture in the south of England, south Wales and Ireland. The sites to be examined for comparative architecture and sculpture include Wells Cathedral (which is of particular relevance), Gloucester Cathedral, Tintern Abbey and Winchester Castle. The evidence for dating and patronage is reviewed, as well as that for possible attribution to particular masons' workshops and named 'architects'.[1]

By the second quarter of the 13th century, the old-fashioned interior of the Great Tower no longer met the needs of the patron and the first floor was refurbished essentially to create two formal reception rooms. By this time, the Marshal earls of Pembroke were well landed and locally very powerful, despite some ruptures in their relations with the court. Gilbert Marshal, earl 1234–41, was in effect the ruler of the southern March. As well as his own lordships he held Carmarthen and Cardigan from the king, and was given custody of Glamorgan and the Braose family estates in the central March.[2] The family also had extensive holdings in Ireland: William Marshal I (d.1219) held Leinster through his wife, an inheritance passed to their son, William II (d.1231), in 1220. William II became Justiciar of Ireland in 1224, the year he married King Henry III's younger sister Eleanor. In Leinster he was an active building patron, founding boroughs and castles and nurturing religious houses.[3] In view of their status, it is not surprising to find that the decorative scheme of the Great Tower is related to the more modern halls that were being built by their peers.

The outstanding feature of the first floor is the former double archway which divided the hall from the chamber (Fig. 81). Its quality can be judged and its form reconstructed from the surviving corbels, which are made up of two tiers of multiple capitals carved with stiff-leaf foliage, supported on figure corbels. The other features of note are the two-light windows with a quatrefoil of plate tracery in the head (Fig. 78), and especially the double window of the eastern room. The rear arches of the window apertures were enriched formerly by detached colonnettes, with water-holding bases and stiff-leaf foliage capitals. The hood moulds terminate in stops carved with human heads.

Sources and parallels for the above characteristics are to be found in four outstanding palace-building projects of the first half of the 13th century: at Canterbury, Winchester, Wells and Clarendon. At Canterbury, the great hall of the archbishop's palace (*c*.1200–20) had two-light windows doubled into four-light compositions with a large foiled figure in the head.[4] The window apertures were provided with built-in stone seats, as at Chepstow, and Purbeck marble was used extensively for colonnettes in the window apertures and for the arcade piers. It is clear that the archbishop's hall set a very high architectural standard for details and materials for all subsequent 13th-century great halls and great chambers.

At the royal castle of Winchester, the great hall (1222–35) has window lights with cusped heads, like those at Chepstow and an advance on Canterbury. In other respects, however, the architecture at Winchester is simpler than Chepstow. The arcade arches are much plainer in their mouldings and the corbels at each end lack the

playful elaboration of the Chepstow corbels. There is no stiff-leaf foliage, and the windows are framed by attached colonnettes of coursed masonry rather than detached ones of Purbeck. These contrasts could suggest that Chepstow is later than Winchester, but they might equally reflect the differing purposes and scale of the two spaces—the multiple arcades of a great hall compared with a two-bay arcade dividing hall and chamber.

The closest surviving parallels for details at Chepstow are found in the bishop's palace at Wells. The relevant work of Bishop Jocelyn (bishop 1219–42; building from *c*.1230) is the first-floor hall or great chamber, leading to an inner chamber: a plan not unlike that of Chepstow but without arcades. Some significant similarities appear in the mouldings, for example in the window rear arches. In the inner chamber, the composition of a pair of two-light windows with a large quatrefoil as a separate element above, as pioneered at Canterbury, gives a reasonable idea of how the large double window at Chepstow

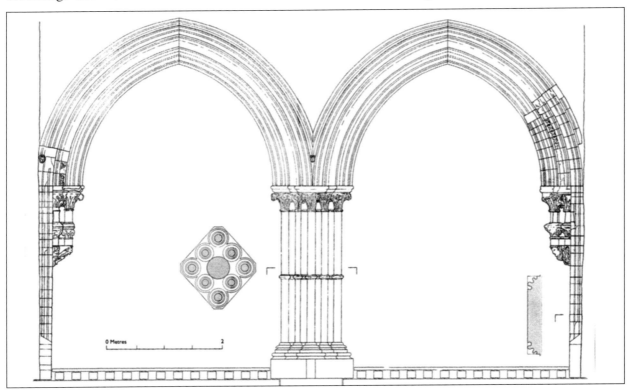

*Fig. 81  A reconstruction of the double archway in the Great Tower*

must have looked. The Wells window shares with Chepstow the use of a mullion carved entirely with mouldings, rather than the more usual design with a detached colonnette (Figs. 82.4, 82.5), thus anticipating a form of mullion that became standard in England for bar-tracery windows in the later 13th century.

The lost royal palace of Clarendon, near Salisbury, is known only from excavations. King Henry III took an interest in Clarendon, his favoured country residence, from about 1227, but most construction probably took place in the 1230s and later.[5] Fragments of worked stones dating to the 13th century abound in the records of the 1930s excavations. They can provide only general clues about the nature of the extensive works there, but much use was evidently made of Purbeck marble for piers, and mouldings share some profiles with those at Chepstow.

The physical evidence for dating the architectural details at Chepstow can also be assessed in relation to the styles (or stylistic preferences) found in contemporary ecclesiastical architecture in southern England and south Wales. First is the regional style of Early English Gothic, the so-called 'West Country school of masons'.[6] The buildings identified with their production extend from south-west England through south Wales and into the West Midlands over a period from c.1175 to c.1240. The school's main creative force was centred on the masons' workshops at Wells, from c.1175, and Glastonbury from 1184, and fruitful comparisons can be made between them and Chepstow. Second, a later development is a more regulated and metropolitan style of Gothic, more French in inspiration, for which the term 'the southern manner' of Early English has been proposed.[7] It is represented by a number of buildings in the southern counties, from Kent to as far west as Wells. Its most distinctive output in the years c.1215–1240 includes such works as the palace halls mentioned above as well as Salisbury Cathedral (begun 1220) and the choir of the Temple Church, London (c.1220–40). The light-weight structures, use of Purbeck and other coloured stones, and wide segmental arches to doors and windows are particularly significant

for Chepstow. A third development combines the taste for elaborate mouldings shared by the West Country school with the stylistic sophistication of churches in 'the southern manner'. The retrochoir of Winchester Cathedral, built c.1200–20, is an important early exemplar of this trend.

Influences from all three stylistic trends can be detected at Chepstow. The continuous orders of mouldings framing the windows and outer order of the double archway are typical of the West Country school, whereas the overall design of the arch and its corbels appears closer to the general principles of 'the southern manner'. However, some mouldings of the archway are specifically indebted to developments in the third stylistic trend, and to appreciate this a closer description of the archway is required. It is made up of three orders of mouldings (Figs. 82.1, 82.4), of which the outer order is standard West Country work (as above), but the middle and inner orders are much more distinctive. The profile of the middle order is a masterpiece of craftsmanship, focusing on a large central hollow housing a row of carvings in the form of pyramidal foliage bosses (Fig. 82.1, ABC; Fig. 84.1). The quality is maintained in the inner order, which is notable for its lateral canted fillets and lateral bead mouldings (Fig. 82.1, DE).[8] Moreover, the upper corbels supporting the arch represent a virtuoso performance of cutting and assembly skills. The four Purbeck colonnettes are grouped in depth in a lozenge formation, and the freestone matrix for the rear colonnette is hollowed out to form three-quarters of a circle, thus almost entirely concealing the colonnette (Fig. 82.2; Fig. 83).

The mouldings of the inner order of the arch are particularly indebted to the new elaboration of detail associated with the third style. The use of the lateral fillet is anticipated in the retrochoir of Winchester Cathedral, an outstanding work of the turn of the century for display of wealth in rich materials—notably Purbeck marble—and of quality of craftsmanship. The lateral bead moulding also developed in the south of England in the early 13th century. It was used notably in the Galilee of Glastonbury Abbey (c.1225–35), a building influenced by the retrochoir of

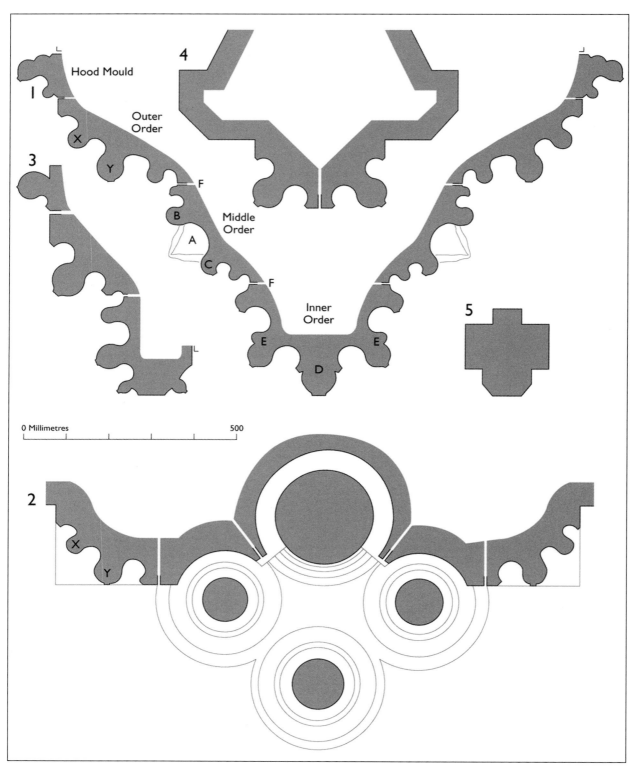

*Fig. 82 Moulding profiles in the Marshals' Great Tower at Chepstow. 1 the double archway, arch;*
*2 the double archway, upper level of arch springer; 3 two-light windows, rear arch;*
*4 four-light window, main mullion, exterior profile; 5 two-light windows, mullion. Scale 1:10*

Winchester, and a version became particularly popular with the masons at Wells from *c*.1220 onwards.

However, an arcade arch design which comes closer than any other to the mouldings of the inner order at Chepstow is that employed in the five east bays of the nave of Christ Church Cathedral, Dublin, 'the most distinguished piece of Gothic architecture in Ireland.'[9] These arcades are constructed of imported Dundry stone like Chepstow, and were probably executed after 1234, perhaps *c*.1234–40. The close links of Christ Church with works in Worcestershire have been long established,[10] and the discovery now of its affiliation with Chepstow suggests that the Marshal family interests in Ireland could be significant in this connection. Their patronage there was established initially during the six years when William Marshal I had lived there, while out of favour with King John.

The middle order of the arches at Chepstow are the most distinctive and helpful for dating and attribution (Fig. 83). Its general form, with mouldings overlaid with carved foliate decoration, takes their lead from such sumptuously decorated works of the early 13th centuries as the dado of the retrochoir at Winchester Cathedral and the processional door from the cloister to the Martyrdom transept at Canterbury Cathedral. The specific pedigree of Chepstow is, however, a series of portals in the area of the West Country school—four doorways at Wells Cathedral, spanning the years *c*.1185 to *c*.1230; the transept portals at Lichfield Cathedral (1220s or 1230s),[11] and the former refectory portal at Gloucester Cathedral (*c*.1246). They all share with Chepstow the profile of a deep hollow moulding returned into roll-type mouldings (Fig. 82.1, ABC), with the hollow spanned by a row of pyramidal foliate bosses in all cases except at Gloucester. The Wells portals are closest in their moulding details to Chepstow, but the fact that this distinctive profile also occurs at Gloucester hints at a potential exchange of craftsmen with Chepstow, in conjunction with further evidence to be presented below.

*Fig. 83 The surviving fabric on the north side of the double archway in the Great Tower, after conservation*

The motif of pyramidal foliate bosses, which presumably derives from dogtooth, consists of four long, undercut leaves or petals, meeting in a small round boss. A simple form is quite widespread in the arches of such great churches as the nave of Lincoln Cathedral and the choirs of Worcester and Durham Cathedrals, but the Chepstow examples are more complicated. They resemble fat little filigree cushions, domed up and decoratively carved with berries and lanceolate leaves (Fig. 84.1). The bosses in the Lichfield portals have the little tuft of foliage at the apex, of which there are only traces at Chepstow, but it is the examples from the Wells Cathedral workshop that are most significant for Chepstow (Fig. 84.2; Fig. 85). Of the Wells doors, all situated in the cloister and the west front, the portal at the south end of the east cloister walk is closest of all. Its foliate carving shares all the characteristics of Chepstow, and of all the parallels it is the only one in which the bosses are constrained within a geometrical pyramidal shape (Fig. 84.2). This door belongs to the works of Bishop Jocelyn, probably in the 1220s.[12]

Also to be associated particularly with the Wells workshop is the design and craftsmanship of the corbels for the Chepstow archway. The skilful grouping of the colonnettes in depth in the upper corbel (Fig. 82.2; Fig. 83) is indebted to early surviving examples like the arcade responds of the retrochoir at Winchester. However it is at Wells that the potential of the idea is exploited, as in the central door of the west front (Fig. 86). The same door also includes the other virtuoso feature of the upper corbels at Chepstow, the amazingly deep three-quarter hollow which almost envelops the rear colonnette (Fig. 82.2). Other Somerset examples of deep recesses housing colonnettes include the first-floor windows of the Wells Bishop's Palace and the east door of the Galilee at Glastonbury.

*Fig. 84*
*1 (top) Pyramidal foliate bosses on the double archway in the Great Tower at Chepstow Castle*
*2 (lower) Detail of south door arch in the east cloister walk at Wells Cathedral*

*Fig. 85 Arch and capitals on the central doorway in the west front at Wells Cathedral*

*Fig. 86  Jamb and bases of the central doorway on the west front at Wells Cathedral*

It is worth mentioning at this point that complex arrangements of detached colonnettes and deep hollows are a feature of the monastic buildings at Tintern Abbey, the other major architectural work under way in the vicinity of Chepstow in the second quarter of the 13th century (Fig. 87). Exchanges of masons between these two sites are to be expected, as they are barely four miles apart. Moreover, the interest of the Marshal family in Tintern is documented, including family burials.[13] The relevant works are the chapter house, parlour, warming house and refectory, but unfortunately very little survives intact and no other specific parallels can be made with the architectural and sculptural details at Chepstow. This might be explained by the losses of fabric, or by the different building requirements for a great aristocrat and for Cistercian monks. Alternatively, however, the works may be of different dates or by different architects. The works at Tintern are not firmly dated, but a grant of 1224 included the right to quarry building stone, and it has been suggested that Abbot Ralph (*c.*1232–45) could be a prime mover in the rebuilding.[14]

The foliate carving of the capitals and the figure sculpture at Chepstow was of outstanding quality, and is related both to local buildings and influential on those much further afield. The stiff-leaf foliage on the capitals of the arch corbels and the windows is of two main designs attached to two types of stalk. The stalks are either single,

*Fig. 87  The refectory interior, Tintern Abbey*

107

*Fig. 88 Upper and lower corbels on the south wall of the double archway in the Great Tower at Chepstow Castle*

separate stems or formed by two converging ribs separated by deep troughs (Figs 88, 89.1). Both kinds are found on the multiple capitals of the archway corbels, with a preference for the double-ribbed variety. The foliage consists of single, fist-like bunches of rounded leaves, with marked rims, some with bulbous centres, others with central veins and looser, elongated stems and leaves that swirl and overlap. Minor differences in the profiles of the abaci may indicate that two sculptors worked on the capitals. It appears that all the foliage on the multiple capitals was of the bunched type. The right-hand capital on the centre window of the eastern room has a feature

unique at Chepstow: a small, trifoliate spray at the base of each set of stalks (Fig. 89.2).

The rounded leaves appear in numerous buildings from the 1220s onwards, notably at the level of the narrative quatrefoils on the west front of Wells Cathedral. Of more interest are the capitals with convergent double stalks and bunched or loosely curling leaves. These are highly characteristic and rare, but significantly the inside of the west front at Wells has one capital with these stalks, and both types of foliage and the double stalks appear on the screen-like structure in the north transept of Gloucester Cathedral (Fig. 90).

The Gloucester screen is valuable in providing evidence for a reasonably local context for the Chepstow foliage and figure styles. It is a work of fine quality and has much else in common with the decoration at Chepstow—three arched openings with two lights and a quatrefoil of plate tracery; foliage capitals on Purbeck colonnettes, hood moulds with head stops, and intricate mouldings employing fillets and beads. It will be recalled as well that the refectory door at Gloucester was one of the few parallels for the middle order profile of the double archway at Chepstow. The capitals of the Gloucester screen have double stalks leading to bunched leaves, whilst on the spandrels of the arches loose, curling leaves are carved in undercut relief. Sprays of foliage adorn the bases of the arch mouldings. The monk's head stop at the west end (Fig. 91) has carefully detailed ears similar to the surviving ear at Chepstow (Fig. 89.4), and his cowl is draped with the same ample grace as the drapes of material on the double capitals and the head stop west of the arch on the south wall (Figs. 89, 89.1, 89.3). Now bearing a crenellated top, there are hints in the masonry of the Gloucester screen that the structure may originally have had gables and pinnacles, giving it the appearance of a miniature hall. Welander argues that this structure was some sort of reliquary, in place when the cathedral was rededicated in 1239,[15] but in fact it has no known function and is not reliably dated.

No match has been found, however, for the double capitals of the Chepstow corbels, set in front of the deeply carved hollow moulding

*Plate 1  An aerial view of Chepstow Castle showing the New or Marten's Tower bottom left, the Main Gatehouse bottom right with the Gloriette and service rooms above the river on the north side of the Lower Bailey. Above this is the Middle Bailey, then the Great Tower, the Upper Bailey and finally the Upper Barbican beyond. The Dell runs along the southern side of the castle*

Plate 2  *A cutaway reconstruction showing the interior of the Norman Great Tower*

*Plate 3*
*The plaster*
*decoration in*
*Bay 2 of the*
*Great Tower*
*before*
*conservation*

*Plate 4 A cutaway reconstruction of William Marshal's Main Gatehouse*

*Plate 5 A cutaway reconstruction of the Marshals' Great Tower*

*Plate 6*
*A cutaway reconstruction of the Gloriette in its heyday. From right to left, there is a feast in the hall, servants wintling up wine barrels into the cellar, a small balcony garden between the buttresses, and servants at work in the buttery, pantry and kitchen. A corner of the earl's chamber is shown with a chevron decoration copied from Chinon Castle, France. The two chambers alongside the kitchen have two-light windows. The Main Gatehouse is shown with its hourd and barbican reconstructed*

Plate 7  The east interior (on the left) of the Great Tower showing the rubble Carboniferous Limestone walling and the Dundry Limestone windows of the Marshal period

Plate 10  Cutaway reconstruction of the Inner East Gatehouse at Caerphilly Castle. This building is similar in plan and date to the New or Marten's Tower, though even greater in scale

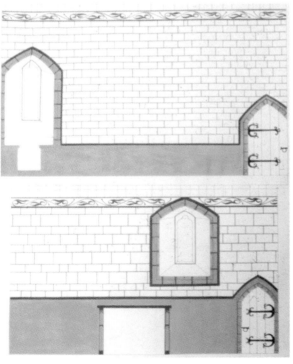

Plate 8 [14.5]  Reconstruction of the entrance into the hall within the Gloriette

Plate 9  Reconstruction of the painted decoration in the first- and second-floor chambers of the New or Marten's Tower

*Plate 11 Chepstow Castle, interior. Watercolour from nature by J. West showing the pump by the entrance to Marten's Tower and the adjacent range of buildings*

*Plate 12 Chepstow Castle by Philip James de Loutherbourg published in* Romantic and Picturesque Scenery of England and Wales, *1805, showing rustic lean-to buildings against Marten's Tower and the north tower of the Main Gatehouse. The latter is sometimes shown as totally open-sided, or at least open-fronted and was perhaps a small pavilion to take advantage of the view*

*Plate 13  The Procession Picture showing Queen Elizabeth I under the canopy and her master of horse, Edward, 4th earl of Worcester, in the foreground. To the rear are possible representations of Chepstow Castle (left) and Raglan Castle (centre)*

*Plate 14  A view of Chepstow Castle from across the river, with the Main Gatehouse on the far left, the Gloriette and service rooms, the Great Tower and the buildings of the Upper Barbican (far right)*

*Fig. 89  Decorative features of the Great Tower
at Chepstow Castle*
*1 (top left)  Figurative corbel on the double archway on the north wall; 2 (lower left)  Stiff-leaf capital
of the central window in the eastern room; 3 (top right)  Head stop in the eastern room;
4 (lower right)  Head stop of the central window in the eastern room*

adorned with stiff-leaf decoration in relief (Figs. 88, 89.1). If the two figure forms on the corbels are to be interpreted as the upper (north) and lower (south) parts of the same individual, we should perhaps conclude that the central column between the arches had purely foliate ornament, presumably a cluster of capitals over multiple colonnettes (Fig. 81). The north corbel, with its two clutching hands, suggests possible relationships. A number of 12th-century halls have wooden corbels with foliage arranged like clutching fingers,[16] and the motif continued into the 13th century. A head stop on the nave vault at Gloucester Cathedral clutches sprays of foliage, a

motif found also in Winchester Castle hall, where two of the figured corbels that carry the shafted responds of the arcades, hold objects in their hands—a female figure holds sprays of foliage and a bearded man holds a fish. The swathes of drapery round these figures and those of Gloucester give them some stylistic affinity with the Chepstow corbels. On the south side of the nave of Llandaff Cathedral (probably 1220s) the fourth pier from the west has a small figure clutching foliage.[17] Llandaff is interesting also for the capitals on the west door, which are cones with twisted stiff-leaf and berries; they also contain a man (left) and a bird (right), which

109

*Fig. 91 Monk's head stop on the north transept screen at Gloucester Cathedral*

invites the suggestion that the lost capitals of the central pier of the double archway at Chepstow may also have been inhabited (Fig. 92).

The evidence assembled above suggests that the sculptural decoration fits best into the regional context in the 1230s. This western group of buildings, including possibly Llandaff, subsequently appear be a source of motifs for royal and London buildings of the 1240s and later. The only other valid comparisons for the distinctive stiff-leaf are with the royal works of the 1240s and 1250s, notably the Dean's Cloister at Windsor, completed by 1250–51,[18] and work at Westminster Abbey. At Westminster, the looser, curling leaves appear in relief, in the same manner as the Gloucester screen, in the spandrels of the wall arcade in the ambulatory chapels of St. John the Baptist and St. Edmund, built between 1246 and *c*.1250.[19] Trifoliate sprays sprout from the stems surrounding the busts of

*Fig. 90 The 'screen' in the north transept at Gloucester Cathedral*

*Fig. 92 The south capital on the west door of Llandaff Cathedral*

angels in the soffits of the lancets in the north wall of the north transept, of a similar date. A crowned female head in the choir triforium has the characteristically pointed chin of the head stop on the south wall at Chepstow, and a drape more like a modern head-scarf than a wimple. The appearance of a crown on the Westminster head suggests that the Chepstow head was also originally crowned (Fig. 89.3).

It is fairly evident that local craftsmen were employed to execute the mouldings and sculpture of the new work in the Great Tower, with the workshop at Wells as the most fundamental source for their ideas. But who was the designer, especially of the double archway?

An association has been suggested by some authorities between Elias of Dereham and several of the works mentioned here, including the palaces at Canterbury, Winchester, Clarendon and Wells, and especially Clarendon with its close links with neighbouring Salisbury. The case for Elias as architect of the new cathedral and settlement at Salisbury has recently been revived,

arguing that he was more than simply an administrator and clerk of the works.[20] Yet his role still appears to be one of an architectural facilitator and interior designer, and there is no evidence that his training included the craft of designing mouldings.

Given the high regard in which Elias was held in royal circles, he was very likely known to William Marshal II and Gilbert Marshal and, as executor of the will of their father, William Marshal I, he would have had to work with them.[21] Elias was evidently a significant figure with a taste for contemporary architecture, albeit 'the southern manner'. Had he been consulted about the refurbishment of the Great Tower at Chepstow he would have brought an awareness of smart metropolitan architecture to the local workforce. He could have harnessed their undoubted carving skills to produce a work of more than regional quality that, in its turn, influenced the metropolis. Yet without firm evidence, speculation about Elias' possible involvement at Chepstow is tendentious.

If a specific attribution cannot be made to Master Elias, the possibility should be entertained that the architect is more likely to have been a master mason trained in a workshop of the West Country school, and with an acquired knowledge of buildings in the 'southern manner'. By the time of the remodelling of the Great Tower, the traits of both 'styles' could have been absorbed in the work of a single designer. A potential candidate would be Thomas Norreys, master mason of Wells Cathedral *c.*1229–49, but nothing is known about his career beyond Wells. He may have been the deputy to the previous master at Wells, Adam Lock (d.1229), and if so would have been familiar with the series of portals at the cathedral which have been shown to be so influential on the design of the double archway in the Great Tower. The known dates of his career also permit the possibility that he was the designer of the nave arcades of Christ Church Cathedral, Dublin (after 1234), perhaps a commission directly following that in the Great Tower. However, the Dublin work is anonymous and so this hypothesis is as speculative as that regarding Elias of Dereham, except that in principle it is more likely that the actual 'architect' of the works at Chepstow was a professional master mason.

In conclusion, it has been demonstrated that, to the nearest decade, the 1230s was the most probable time for the remodelling of the Great Tower. Works undertaken at Wells during the episcopacy of Bishop Jocelyn (1219–42) provide the most parallels for the mouldings and some other details at one site, where the dates are generally agreed to span the 1220s and 1230s. The architectural sculpture also finds comparisons in works at Lichfield, Gloucester and Llandaff, but their dates are speculative. On the other hand, there are no parallels for the distinctive details of Chepstow at the Elder Lady Chapel of Bristol Cathedral (1218–22), a well-dated regional work in Dundry stone. This difference is

*Fig. 93 Double arcade in the solar at Goodrich Castle*

best explained by placing the remodelling of the Great Tower later than the Lady Chapel, whereas it may precede the nave of Christ Church, Dublin (probably begun after *c*.1234). The moulding profiles of the Dublin nave arcade arches look more developed than those of the double archway at Chepstow.

Thus, the comparative evidence tallies well with the documented gift in August 1234 of timber for joisting the tower at Chepstow (see p.92), which suggests that the remodelling may date to *c*.1234–35. Gilbert Marshal (1234–41) emerges as the most likely patron, though the work might have been started by his older brother, William II. His grand-daughter, Joan de Valence, erected an arcade similar to that in Chepstow in her solar at Goodrich Castle, Herefordshire, perhaps in homage to it (Fig. 93).[22] As effective ruler of the southern March, Gilbert would have been immensely wealthy and occupied a position at court similar to that held by Hubert de Burgh and Peter des Roches before their downfalls earlier in Henry III's reign.

A relative place has been established for Chepstow in the development of palatial architecture of the period. The new work is clearly indebted to the halls of the archbishop's palace at Canterbury and Winchester Castle, but its details are grander than either. It is most likely to be the contemporary of Bishop Jocelyn's palace at Wells and Henry III's work at Clarendon Palace. The apparent links with Clarendon are potentially of great interest because they raise the possibility that we may be able to gain insights into its lost splendours through the surviving work at Chepstow.

In both craftsmanship and richness of materials this phase of the Great Tower is a work of great ambition, intended to vie with the finest architecture of the period. The playful disposition of details in the double arch appears to be intended to entertain the viewer, appropriately in a space designed for entertainment. The Marshals' remodelling is a precocious work, placing the Great Tower in the front rank of buildings in the decades before 1240.

# CHAPTER XI

# The Upper Barbican

*by* Rick Turner

The Upper Barbican extended the stone defences of Chepstow Castle westwards of the line chosen by the Normans and improved by William Marshal, early in the 13th century. It replaced the massive rock-cut, dry ditch, over 8m wide and 4m deep, which ran across the narrow limestone ridge between the cliff edge and the Dell on which the castle was first built, as the outermost defence.

This is another area of the castle for which there is little direct documentary evidence. On 13 December 1234, Gilbert Marshal was granted 25 oaks from the Forest of Dean to repair the '*jarryllium*' (palisade or brattise) of the castle.[1] The grant implies that there may have been wooden defences at the castle, which were perhaps damaged during Richard Marshal's dispute with the king. If so then there may have been wooden defences enclosing the Upper Barbican, which were later replaced by the present stone walls. The Upper Barbican extended the castle by 24m to the west and overlooked a very broad rock-cut ditch about 18m wide with straight sides. This probably acted as the quarry for most of the stone used in the new defences (Fig. 94). There does not appear to have been any substantial buildings within the walls and the area seems to have been used exclusively for defensive purposes.

Two references to the Upper Gatehouse appear in the Bigod building accounts. The first was for 1298/9. Here carpenters were being paid for making and repairing the bridges, and for making anew the drawbridge at the upper gate of the castle. Iron was purchased and made into new fittings for the drawbridge. The following year, masons rebuilt a pillar located under the outer gate.[2] These references imply that there was a drawbridge immediately outside the Upper Gatehouse, resting on a masonry pillar, with one or more bridges beyond to cross the remainder of the rock-cut ditch. As late as 1679, this part of the castle was known as the Drawbridge Tower.[3]

The south curtain wall butts up against Marshal's Tower of the Upper Bailey. Where it crosses the ditch it stands on a wider base, which contains a sallyport passing through the curtain wall in the bottom of the ditch. There are plainly dressed, Old Red Sandstone, semi-circular arched doorcases on the inner and outer faces. That on the inner face is 1.25m wide and now stands 1.35m high and is rebated to allow for a door to open into the barbican. There is a rubble-vaulted passageway, whose mortar bed fossilizes the layout of the wooden formwork. The outer door is narrower, only 1m wide, as it was built within the passageway, and was rebated internally. Details of the door hanging are hidden by later blocking.

The curtain wall is massive at 2.1m wide and rises close to its original height. It is made entirely of angular Carboniferous Limestone rubble and the only feature is a line of putlog holes. The present wall-walk is lower than the medieval level, which is marked by the threshold

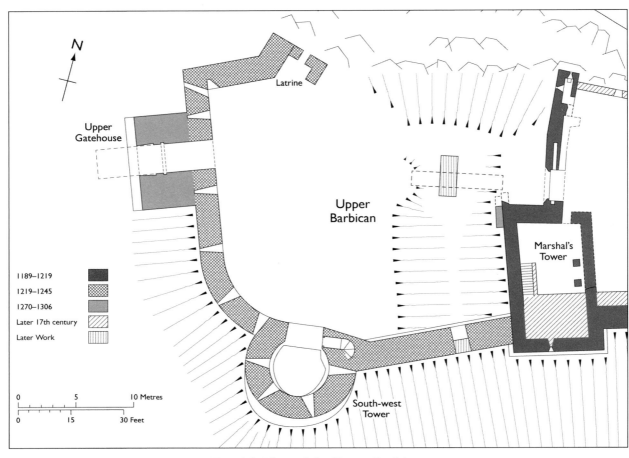

*Fig. 94  Plan of the Upper Barbican*

of the doorway into the South-West Tower—the only access in the Middle Ages. Any crenellations or other wall top features have been removed.

The South-West Tower is D-shaped and stands three storeys high over an unlit basement sunk within its plinth (Fig. 95). All the floors were reached by a spiral stone staircase in the north-east corner of the tower with semi-circular arched doorcases opening into each level. The floors were carried on massive timber beams. The tower seems to have been open-backed, with the square sockets of the rear floor beam visible in the reveals of the main opening.[4] Each level of the tower had four arrowloops, disposed in different patterns on each floor (Fig. 96). The rear arches of these arrowloops are semi-circular and made of a mixture of Dundry Limestone and Old Red Sandstone at ground floor, and exclusively Old

Red Sandstone at higher levels. The sills of the loops are raised and the tapering rubble-vaulted reveals angle down towards the arrowloops. These are best viewed from the outside, where a number have been carefully restored in recent years (Fig. 95). Only traces of the parapet have survived the 17th-century alterations, with the bases of the arrowloops in the crenellations just visible in places. The walltops are too altered to say whether it was roofed or floored at this level.

The tower has a weakly-flared base and there are four arrowloops on each floor. At the ground floor they are tall, plain and with a cross-slit. At first-floor level they are shorter with a small, basal rectangular oillet and at second-floor level shorter still and plain. They are not regularly placed around the tower but provide a comprehensive field of fire along the curtain walls and across the Dell. Restoration has demonstrated that the loops were originally only 40mm wide (Fig. 95).

One of the arrowloops on the ground floor is alongside a vertical line of rubble toothing, patched up near ground level with modern stonework. This would seem to represent the end of a wall, 4m high and 1m wide running diagonally across the rock-cut ditch, to be built into the base of the tower. This area has other features including a short length of vaulted passage, but these structures may belong to a pair of limekilns shown on an 1865 plan of the castle in this immediate area.[5] This rubble stone scar may represent the original end of the town or Port Wall.

A short length of curtain wall runs from the South-West Tower to the Upper Gatehouse. This west curtain wall differs in its details from that to the south, but is equally massive and high. It looks artificially high on the inside as the ground level was subsequently lowered by up to 1.2m.

This must have been to generate soil and rubble to fill the South-West Tower when it was converted into a gun platform in the later 17th century.[6] It has left four, originally ground-level arrowloops apparently stranded part way up the curtain wall. These have rubble-stone rear arches, one of which is blocked by alterations to the Upper Gatehouse, so only three, narrow, plain rubble-stone arrowloops show on the outside. Between the third and fourth rear arches, there are large patches of pinkish pebbly mortar and a broken brick fragment implying that some structure was built against this part of the wall in the 17th century.

Below the wall-walk level, externally, there is a line of large square sockets for the beams of a hourd. They have been filled with sawn-off, oak timbers. Internally, the sockets are blocked though one contains a projecting stone corbel. Immediately above this line of blocked holes is a projecting chamfered Old Red Sandstone band

*Fig. 95 External view of the South-West Tower in the Upper Barbican*

*Fig. 96 Reconstruction drawing of the rear of the South-West Tower*

115

*Fig. 97 Photogrammetric elevations of the Upper Gatehouse: west elevation (top) and south elevation (below)*

below a corbel table of roughly-dressed, quarter-round sandstone blocks. A plain rubble stone parados is carried on this corbel table. Access to the wall-walk is from the second floor of the South-West Tower. Three wooden steps rise up to a semi-circular arched doorcase, where a flight of ten stone steps passes through the tower wall and under a short, rubble-vaulted passageway up to the medieval wall-walk. The external, castellated parapet has broad crenels (1.8m wide) and two of the merlons contain a plain sandstone-dressed arrowloop. The wall-walk ends with a flight of shallow steps up into the second-floor of the later Upper Gatehouse.

The gatehouse is of two periods. It began as a simple gateway through the curtain wall. This had a plain, segmentally-arched Dundry Limestone rear arch, whose threshold was about 1m above the present path. Within the gate passage there is a clear junction between the original outer wall face and the later work. This obscures remains of a semi-circular arch from the original outer gateway. The inner order of this gateway and its door rebates were cut away in the later period, leaving only a deep drawbar hole surviving in the northern jamb. The west curtain wall-walk would have run over this gateway and connected with the short length now isolated in the north-west corner. However the corbel table and chamfered band were removed when the gateway was remodelled.

In the second phase of the Upper Gatehouse, the gate passage was extended within a building constructed against the side of the rock-cut ditch. The roof of the passage contains two murder slots opening from the first-floor room and a portcullis slot rising from where the present doors are hung.

The exterior of this new gatehouse is striking, though rarely clearly seen because of the adjacent trees (Fig. 97). It is built of rubble-stone and has a flared base on three sides. The external archway is very tall and only weakly pointed with two orders of slabs making up the voussoirs. The original entrance level of the gatehouse is marked by the lowest stone in the jambs of this outer opening. There are two square murder holes in the soffit of the arch. The inner arch is lower and has just a single order of slab voussoirs. The stonework has fallen away above this arch so evidence of how the drawbridge was lifted is missing. Two massive sockets in the jambs of the outer arch suggest there was a massive timber crossbeam to act as a buffer to the raised drawbridge. In the northern jamb there is an angled line in the rubble masonry, which resembles the angled sockets seen in the gatehouses at Caerphilly Castle, though at Caerphilly the slot angles down rather than up.[7] These seem to have received the metal pivots of the bridge. The base of a rubble-stone pier in the ditch shows the length of the bridge, meaning that when the bridge was raised it would have been contained within the outer arch, though there is no counter-weight pit.

The top floors have broad arrowslits with flared cross-slits and top and basal oillets, and a corbel table runs around the wall-top. Access to the upper floors was only possible from the west curtain wall-walk into a doorway into the second floor. A trapdoor and wooden ladder must have led down to first floor. There is a small latrine in the north-east corner of both rooms and the two-light, round-arched limestone window looking back into the Upper Barbican must have been re-used from elsewhere in the site.

The original curtain wall continued to the cliff edge and contains a pattern of arrowloops at ground level to fire on anyone seeking to climb around the rock face. A lower length of wall with a slight outward kick (Fig. 94) provides a further obstacle to those trying to enter the castle. The base of a latrine shute has been recently consolidated against the end of this wall and the remainder of the cliff-edge was protected by a narrower wall to stop anyone falling over.

The Upper Barbican is later than William Marshal's rebuilding of the Upper Bailey defences, which may be stylistically attributed to the first decade of the 13th century. The curtain walls were much thicker than those built by William Marshal and did not require re-enforcement in the 17th century. The South-West Tower develops the defensive capabilities of the towers built by William Marshal in the Middle and Lower Baileys. The use of elongated arrowloops with cross-slits is paralleled by the form of the loops in the top of the west wall of the Great Tower, built as part of Gilbert Marshal's remodelling of that building. Semi-circular and segmental arches are used extensively and though Dundry Limestone is used in the ground- and first-floor openings, it is completely replaced by Old Red Sandstone dressings at higher level. Taking this evidence together, it is likely that the Upper Barbican defences were added to the castle after 1234 and probably completed before Gilbert Marshal's death in 1241. The second phase of the Upper Gatehouse must belong to the later-13th century, by comparison with such sites as Caerphilly Castle, and so fall in Roger Bigod's lordship. The references in the building accounts for 1298–1300 are for replacing the drawbridge and its support. This implies that the gatehouse was earlier and may date to the period 1272–1282 for which no building accounts survive.

Though the use of semi-circular arches for doorways is anachronistic by that date, the design of the South-West Tower and its comprehensive field of fire is at the forefront of military engineering. The earliest open-backed mural tower in England was the Avranche Tower, Dover Castle, built for Henry II in the 1180s. It was polygonal, rather than D-shaped and commanded a causeway across the eastern moat with batteries of arrowloops.[8] Similar towers, but rectangular in plan, were built on the new curtain wall of Framlingham Castle, Suffolk, by Roger Bigod II, in the late 12th century.[9] However, it was not until after the South-West Tower at Chepstow was finished in the 1230s, that open-backed, D-shaped towers became widespread. They can be seen for example in the Outer Bailey of Corfe Castle, Dorset, and a little later as mural towers at White Castle, Monmouthshire and Kidwelly Castle, Carmarthenshire in the third quarter of the thirteenth centuries. The interval towers on the Port (or town) Wall of Chepstow are also D-shaped and open backed. As this wall is bonded into the South-West Tower, it opens the possibility that the two are contemporary.[10]

The original Upper Gatehouse was simply designed and detailed when compared to the earlier Main Gatehouse. Outside the west end of the castle were its gardens and the Barton, the main estate farm. So the Upper Gatehouse acted as a functional rather than ceremonial entrance into the castle, yet it occupied a potentially vulnerable defensive position as the land rises to the west.

# CHAPTER XII

# The Sub-tidal Cistern

*by* Rick Turner

At the base of the limestone cliff below the Great Tower is a stone, water cistern where a limited excavation and recording has taken place (Fig. 98). The surviving stone structure is set into the estuarine silts below high water mark and was built to capture a vigorous fresh water spring which emerges at about 2m below the present high tide mark at the foot of the cliff. Originally, the cistern must have risen well above the high water mark to allow uncontaminated fresh water to be raised to the castle above. This beautifully-made stone structure may have provided the water source during the early phases of the castle's history.

The castle stands on a cliff of Carboniferous Limestone, rising up to 30m above the river at low water, which contains a number of natural fissures and small caves. The site is therefore very free draining and the only known well is in the Lower Bailey just outside the entrance to Marten's Tower. Here the water level is 7m below the surface. As the Lower Bailey was only added to the castle at the end of the 12th century (see chapter V), the problem remains of how was the earlier castle supplied with water? Lack of water was the greatest threat to the defenders of a castle facing a siege.

## The Discovery of the Cistern

The presence of a well-like structure at the base of the cliff below the north-west corner of the Great Tower has been known for around a century (Fig. 99). It can be seen from high vantage points in the castle and from across the river as a nearly complete circle of well-dressed stones poking out of the top of the inter-tidal mud. The site has been investigated on three occasions.

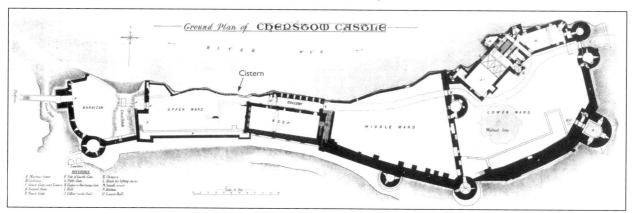

*Fig. 98  Plan of Chepstow Castle showing the location of the cistern*

*Fig. 99 The Great Tower perched on the cliff above the Wye. The position of the cistern is marked with an X*

*Fig. 100 Dr Orville Owen standing in front of the steampipe boiler used to pump out water during his excavations in 1911*

The first excavation of the cistern formed part of a bigger and quite bizarre campaign of work within the river below Chepstow Castle (see pp.260-61). This project was led by Dr Orville Owen of Detroit, Michigan (Fig. 100), in partnership with Dr Prescott of Boston. Dr Owen had undertaken a long study of Shakespeare's plays and works by other Elizabethan dramatists and poets such as Christopher Marlowe and Sir Philip Sidney. He believed that all these works were written by Sir Francis Bacon, whom he argued was an illegitimate child of Queen Elizabeth I and Robert Dudley, earl of Leicester. Claiming some spiritual guidance from Sir Francis Bacon himself, Dr Owen believed that the plays and other poetic works contained a cipher. He devel-

oped a machine on which all the texts were cut up and pasted onto a 1,000ft (300m) length of calico, which could be rotated to throw up juxtapositions of letters and words giving Bacon's true message. The publication of the decodings of this cipher was eventually to fill six volumes.[1]

To cut a long story short, one reading of the cipher led Drs Owen and Prescott to come to Chepstow firstly in September 1909, and for a more concerted campaign in 1911. Somewhere in the river below the castle, they believed that they would find the original manuscripts of Shakespeare's plays hidden in a cave in 66 lead-lined, iron-bound boxes sealed within a masonry and concrete chamber. The Duke of Beaufort (the owner of the castle and holder of the

*Fig. 101 Hammond's photograph of the 1911 excavation showing the courses of ashlar exposed at the top of the cistern*

*Fig. 102 Hammond's photograph of the 1911 excavation showing six courses of ashlar that were excavated clear of the mud*

riparian rights) employed a local engineer, Fred Hammond, to oversee the proceedings, to ensure that his interests were not damaged and to make plans of the excavations. After working in a cave below the castle and in the river bed by the Roman bridge, Dr Owen's workforce seem to have excavated the cistern. Two of Hammond's photographs survive in Chepstow Museum.[2] The first shows the top of the excavated cistern shaft with a complete ring of inner ashlar stones at the level of the top of the inter-tidal mud (Fig. 101). The second shows that the outside of the ring of ashlar stones was excavated out of the mud for at least six courses (Fig. 102). There is an indication that the top course was chamfered to form a plinth for a less massive superstruc-

ture, perhaps a narrower cylinder rising above the tidal limit. This masonry has now fallen away.[3]

The second excavation was undertaken by a group of local men led by Bill Whatton, over three days in August 1998. They were able to empty out much of the interior and excavate around the outside of the masonry structure, to reveal a platform of wooden beams upon which it was constructed. The timbers were massive, tightly packed and supported on piles driven into the mud. This raft foundation extended well out from the cliff and the masonry was built directly upon it. One large outer baulk of timber had slots cut into it, which one of the excavators, Jan Cernik, felt may have held braces to give additional support to the structure. No proper record of this work was undertaken though some colour prints of the top of the stonework survive, and a single block from the cistern lining was recovered and is now in Chepstow Museum.

*Fig. 103  General view of the excavated site*

*Fig. 105  Detail of the ashlar masonry*

## The recent recording of the Cistern

With the help of the local inshore lifeboat crew, a team of four were marooned at the base of the cliff on a favourable tide on 22 July 2001.[4] It was a spring tide and the top of the stonework was not revealed until one and a half hours after high tide. There is a refuge above an ash tree growing out of the foot of the cliff, but access to the cistern involved quite a treacherous walk through the thick estuarine mud.

The upper course of the ashlar stonework was revealed at about 1.6m below the high-tide mark on the cliff. The structure was filled with estuarine mud to a depth of 0.8m and contained a short aluminium ladder and other debris from the 1998 excavation. The area around the cistern had been partly buried by angular lumps of rock, which had fallen from the cliff during stabilisation works undertaken in 2000.

Only three and a half hours of excavation were undertaken. The site was arranged to leave a section running perpendicular to the cliff and leave the western half of the structure unexcavated (Fig. 103). This allowed the estuarine mud that had accumulated since 1998 and the debris of that excavation to be removed. In the end a total of six courses of fine, ashlar masonry standing 1.5m high was revealed with a seventh course visible in the water below. Digging below that level proved impossible because of the constant flow of fresh water from the spring in the cliff which filled the cistern and ran away around its eastern side.

The structure was built within an irregular 'chimney', about 1.5m wide and up to 0.4m deep, cut into the face of the limestone cliff (Fig. 104). This 'chimney' can be traced for at least 5.2m above the top of the surviving ashlar stonework and could easily have continued even higher into what becomes a natural cleft in the rock. A Distomat reading—a laser measuring device—suggests that the cliff face is 27m high above the top of the surving cistern. Within the rock-cut chimney, mortar can be seen adhering to the rock-face for a height of at least 2.2m above the top of the surviving stonework—that is above the high-

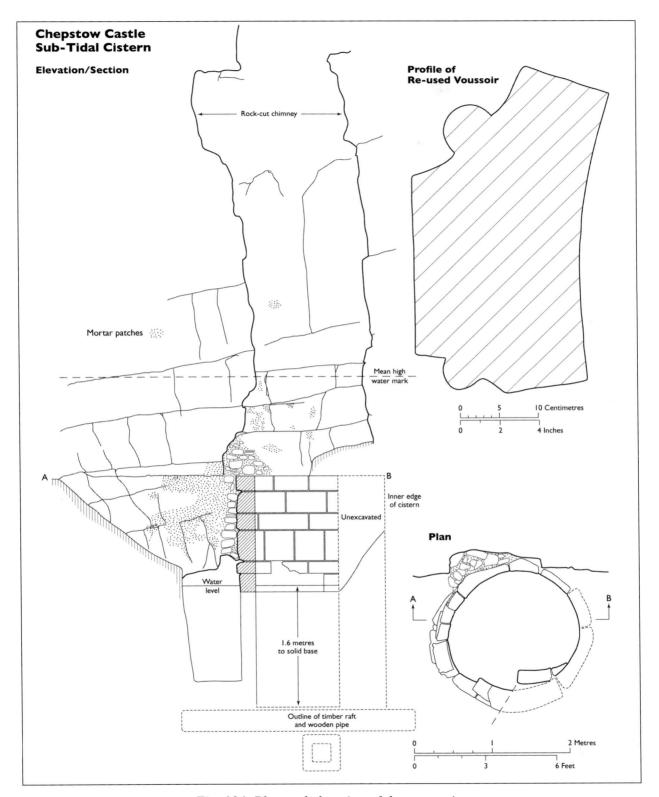

## Chepstow Castle
## Sub-Tidal Cistern

**Elevation/Section**

Rock-cut chimney

Mortar patches

Mean high water mark

**Profile of Re-used Voussoir**

0 ... 5 ... 10 Centimetres

0 ... 2 ... 4 Inches

A

B

Inner edge of cistern

Unexcavated

**Plan**

A

B

Water level

1.6 metres to solid base

Outline of timber raft and wooden pipe

0 ... 1 ... 2 Metres

0 ... 3 ... 6 Feet

*Fig. 104  Plan and elevation of the excavation*

tide mark—and the masonry is quite likely to have risen at least as high as the rock cutting.

The cistern has an internal diameter of 1.50m, but the pressure of the water has caused the north-eastern quadrant to bow out, and the weight of the estuarine mud has caused the north-western quadrant to collapse inwards. The inner ring of stone is made of the finest ashlar and most blocks are made of fine-grained, buff-brown sandstone. Each block was carefully cut to form sectors of a tightly-jointed circle, with the horizontal courses varying between 0.18 and 0.39m in height. The longest stone measured 0.68m. The inner faces have neat diagonal tooling (Fig. 105) and the joints are very narrow—no more than 5mm originally—and some are packed with very thin pieces of green slate to further improve the water-proofing. The back faces of these ashlar blocks were left only roughly dressed to bond in with the outer rubble masonry.

Two of the blocks found during the excavation were re-used. One was fully revealed (Fig. 104). It was a Jurassic Limestone voussoir from a large window or doorway with the outer moulding surviving on each edge but with the central mouldings chiselled away. The second block was of a similar type, but had had all of its mouldings cut away before re-use. Finally, the block recovered in 1998 and now in the museum also shows evidence of re-use. It is of Old Red Sandstone and formed part of a chamfered plinth or window opening. The stonework had collapsed between the two re-used blocks allowing the fresh water to flow out, but water pressure had also blown out two blocks from the lowest course, allowing most of the water to flow out around the eastern side.

The ashlar stonework was held within a mass of limestone rubble and mortar. This was only one stone thick against the cliff face, but the mortar patches visible on the eastern part of the cliff (Fig. 104) suggest that it may have been over 1m thick as it curved around the river side of the cistern. Sockets framed by the rubble-work adhering to the cliff show that the ashlar lining rose for at least three more courses originally.

Probing with a ranging pole showed that there was a soft fill to the depth of 1.2m below the ambient water level outside the eastern part of the structure and between 1.4 and 1.6m on the inside. Jan Cernik, one of the 1998 excavators, visited during the course of this excavation and confirmed that this was the likely depth of the wooden platform described above. He also explained that the water gushes out of a small cave whose mouth is about 0.5m square and spills into the base of the cistern.

This elaborate and beautifully made structure was designed to capture the pure spring water gushing from the cave at the base of the cliff. The masonry would have to have risen high enough to ensure that there was no contamination by the tidal waters, requiring a column of stonework at least 5m high. If the water pressure was sufficient to fill this column, then it would have contained a volume of 23.5m$^3$, about 23.5 metric tonnes in weight. Twice a day this structure would have to withstand the tide rising and falling and travelling at speeds of up to 13 knots (25km/h). This explains why it needed to be so robust, finely made and secured on massive wooden foundations.

**The Hammond Photograph Album**

Since writing the initial excavation report,[5] a photo album entitled *Dr Owen's Search in the River Wye near Chepstow 1911*, put together by Fred Hammond of Chepstow has turned up.[6] Most of the photographs trace the investigation of the river bed and the remains of the Roman bridge upstream of the castle. This began in January 1911, and continued into June of that year. The last four photos show work on the cistern and don't include either of the two photographs now in Chepstow Museum. The first is inscribed, *6 June 1911 Well found under Chepstow Castle Rocks by Dr Owen*, and is a distant view of the top ring of stonework from the refuge by the modern ash tree. The second photo is a close up of the top ring with piles of timber and tools alongside in readiness for the excavation.

The most exciting are the last two photographs. These show a small group of men working below the wooden raft on which the stone cistern was built. The more distant view is captioned: *The square wood pipe drains the bottom of the WELL. The topman stands on the foundation platform.* This shows a wooden platform carried on two squared baulks of timber running perpendicular to the cliff face (Fig. 106). The ends of the baulks are carried on roundwood props, which were inserted by Owen's men as they undermined the foundations. The baulks carry thick planks of wood to form a floor on which one man stands. Between the two baulks and below the floor is the square wooden pipe mentioned in the caption, which one can estimate as at least 0.4m square, with the neatly fashioned hole about 0.2m square. It projects about 0.3m

*Fig. 106 Hammond's photo of the cistern showing 'The Square Wood Pipe'*

forward from the neat edge of the foundation. Built up from the platform, behind the standing figure, is a flat wall of over eight courses of ashlar running parallel to the cliff side. This implies that the rubble core surrounding the cylinder of ashlar, was itself contained within a rectangular ashlar surround. The return is visible on the right-hand side.

The second photo is closer up and is entitled: *Man is examining the rock foundation.* This shows a man standing below the square wooden pipe cleaning below the platform and revealing the steeply shelving rock face beneath. It is not clear how the forward edge of the platform would have been supported in the Middle Ages.

Owen's excavations revealed and undermined the front face of the cistern, as well as emptying out the interior. This may have left the structure vulnerable to rapid erosion, and the loss of the outer ashlar face and the falling away of part of the inner cylinder may have followed quite quickly. The excavators in 1998 reported both the survival of the wooden platform and the props, though they did not specifically mention the square drain pipe. These structures may therefore have survived and be capable of re-investigation at some future date.

**The Operation and Date of the Cistern**
The natural spring is very vigorous and was well capable of supplying the needs of the castle's garrison. The practical difficulties of constructing the massive timber raft and the very fine stonework within the inter-tidal zone must have been very considerable. However, they were possibly far less demanding than the effort required to excavate a well, which would have needed to have been at least 30m deep, into the limestone bedrock.

Whilst the masonry cylinder can be realistically reconstructed to 5m in height, it may have risen to the top of the rock-cut chimney at about 8m high. The square wooden pipe must have acted to relieve the water pressure inside the cylinder when the tide was out, but would have required a very effective non-return valve when the tide was in. Whether the stone cylinder carried a lighter stone or wooden superstructure up to the cliff top or whether buckets were lowered into the cistern with the help of a rope or chain guide is not clear. A winding house with a pulley arm operating the buckets could have stood directly above the cistern a few metres from the north-west corner of the Great Tower, where railings enclose a modern viewing point (Fig. 80). Whether the bucket was raised by a simple hand winch or a more sophisticated machine, (such as the donkey wheel which survives at Carisbrooke Castle, Isle of Wight), is unknown. There is no mention of a well, well-house or the water supply in the very extensive documentation now assembled for the castle.

The only date that can be offered comes from the stonework. The re-used limestone voussoir provides a *terminus ante quem* but its moulding profile is incomplete and only the outer orders remain (Fig. 104). Richard Morris cannot yet assign a date other than broader 13th or early 14th century.[7] The chamfered plinth in Old Red Sandstone now in the museum cannot be directly compared with a surviving structure in the castle, though this type of stone most commonly occurs in the work of William Marshal's sons. The form of construction, which uses a very accurately-dressed ashlar cylinder clasped within rubble masonry, does occur elsewhere in the castle. It is present in the Main Gatehouse, where two circular shafts run vertically down in front of the forward portcullis and may have housed the counterweights to operate this device.[8] The ashlar limestone ring set within the Carboniferous Limestone rubble is best seen on top of the gatehouse, though the diameter (0.3m) is far smaller than that of the cistern.

Taking this rather inconclusive evidence together suggests the cistern dates to the very end of the 12th century at the earliest but a more likely date falls within the 13th century. It could belong to the remodelling of the nearby Norman Great Tower, probably undertaken by Gilbert Marshal in the 1230s (chapter VIII). If so then it does not solve the question originally posed—how was the Norman castle supplied with water? It therefore seems likely that the present stone cistern is not the original, and that the timber raft may belong to an earlier structure used to raise the water above high-tide level. Only full excavation and dendrochronological dating could provide the answers to the origins of this unique structure. For the moment this lies beyond the resources of the present research programme.

# CHAPTER XIII

# The Life of Roger Bigod, Fifth Earl of Norfolk *by* Marc Morris

Roger Bigod, fifth earl of Norfolk and marshal of England, is generally remembered—if he is remembered at all—for one of two things. Most famously, perhaps, he was the man who, in the course of the parliament of February 1297, confronted Edward I and refused a royal order to fight in Gascony. In the four-year period that followed, the earl became the king's principal political opponent, and the last man until the 17th century to take a stand in defence of Magna Carta. Sadly, by assuring his place in posterity in this way, Roger found he had compromised his own future. In 1302, the earl performed his second celebrated act when he surrendered his estates to Edward I and effectively made the king his heir. Both these episodes, however, occurred only towards the end of a long and varied career. As this chapter sets out to show, there was considerably more to the last Bigod earl of Norfolk—not least his extensive building work at Chepstow Castle.[1]

Roger was born in 1245, a year of momentous political change, and one which (conveniently) explains how, twenty-five years later, he came to be lord of Chepstow.[2] In the closing weeks of that year, Walter and Anselm Marshal, the last of the five sons of the great William Marshal, died in quick succession. This was a political shockwave of the first order; none of William's sons had left any children, so their estate—the greatest private estate in the British Isles—was set to be divided amongst the numerous descendants of his

five daughters.[3] Chief among these beneficiaries were the Bigods, earls of Norfolk since the mid-12th century (Fig. 107). They had been close friends and allies of the Marshals since 1206, when Hugh Bigod (earl from 1221 to 1225) had married Maud, the eldest of the five Marshal girls.[4] In 1245, Maud was still living, and so personally inherited a fifth share of her brothers' estate. But as an old lady, twice widowed, she was only the heir in a temporary sense: the important question was who would reap these rewards in the future? The immediate answer was Maud's eldest son, Roger Bigod, fourth earl of Norfolk, but he, despite twenty years of marriage, had fathered no children of his own, and was clearly becoming rather agitated on this score. It was at precisely this juncture that he began divorce proceedings against his countess, no doubt in the hope of avoiding the kind of dynastic disaster that had befallen his Marshal uncles. This tactic, however, ultimately failed when the pope declared that the marriage should stand.[5] As it turned out, the future of the Bigod family lay with the far more fruitful union of the earl's younger brother Hugh and his wife Joanna. In 1245 they celebrated the birth of the first of their eight children—a boy, who, in the best family tradition, was also named Roger. It must have been some consolation for the old earl to know that both his names would live on after he was gone. Roger junior appears to have been a member of his uncle's household during his

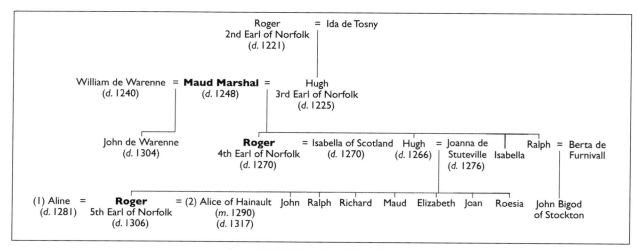

*Fig. 107  The Bigod family tree*

adolescence, and eventually succeeded him in 1270.[6]

The new earl celebrated his accession by holding a tournament at Chepstow, which was one of the properties that had descended to him from his grandmother's share of the Marshal inheritance.[7] The fact remains, however, that the lordship was a small one, and represented only a fraction of the total estate that Roger had acquired.[8] The bulk of his fortune lay in East Anglia, and came to him from his Bigod ancestors. In Norfolk, Suffolk and Essex, he acquired twenty-six demesne manors, including two with large castles at Bungay and Framlingham, and was overlord to scores of under-tenants.[9] From the Marshal inheritance, his greatest assets were not in Wales but in Ireland: principally, these were the town, county and castle of Carlow, and the thriving port of New Ross, but he was also the owner of several smaller manors in Ireland and overlord of many more.[10] Finally, the earl inherited a scattering of other properties across England, smaller in scale but still far from negligible. His father Hugh had developed lordships centred on the Bigod manor of Settrington in Yorkshire and the Marshal manor of Bosham in Sussex. Finally, there was Hamstead Marshall in Berkshire, also (as its name indicates) a former Marshal property.[11]

Putting a precise value on this vast estate is impossible. One set of contemporary estimates—the figures used to calculate widows' dowers in 1249 and 1307—suggests that Roger's inheritance from his uncle was worth around £1,650 a year.[12] This seems far too low (as is normally the case with dower valuations). Another estimate made towards the end of the earl's life, by assessors working for the Crown, suggests he was worth £4,000 a year and is probably closer to the truth.[13] But whatever his real income was, the importance of these figures is where they place Roger in relative terms. It has been said that the 'average' earl in the 13th century had an annual income of around £1,600; clearly if this is the case then the earldom of Norfolk was by either estimate above average.[14] In fact, of the ten to twelve earldoms that existed during the reign of Edward I, Roger's was one of the richest. He was not as supremely well-off as the Marshals had once been—measured by the same yardstick of dower values, they were worth twice as much—nor as wealthy as the earls of Lancaster and Cornwall, respectively the king's brother and cousin.[15] But of the non-royal earls, Roger probably ranked number two after the earl of Gloucester who, in the early 14th century, was reckoned to be half as rich again.[16] At the start of their careers, however, the two men's incomes were much closer. By his first marriage to Lady Aline la Despenser, celebrated at some point between 1265 and 1270, Roger controlled an additional twenty-one manors spread across southern England.[17] This was always destined to be an impermanent acquisition; Aline had a son by an earlier marriage who would one day lay claim to it, a day that came rather sooner than expected when she died in 1281.[18] Down to this point, however, there was probably not much to chose between Norfolk and Gloucester. Moreover, Roger had one further financial advantage over his near neighbour. As the descendants of the senior Marshal daughter, the Bigods had inherited the title 'marshal of England', and this brought not only additional prestige but also further opportunities for profit.[19] Again, the precise extent to which this enhanced their income is incalculable, but the office of marshal probably accounted for several hundred pounds of extra income each year.[20]

As this very brief survey shows, Roger Bigod was one of the richest individuals of his age, with estates scattered from the Yorkshire moors to the Sussex coast, from Ireland to East Anglia. As such, he was naturally an important political figure, and it is to his political career—or, more specifically, his relationship with Edward I—that we now turn. By reading backwards from their confrontation in 1297, historians have in the past often assumed that the two men did not get on.[21] In actual fact, for most of the time, they seem to have got on well enough. Inevitably there were occasional disputes, as there were between the king and his other magnates. It is, however, hard to see their final confrontation as the climax of a long-running feud. Admittedly, though, things did get off to a shaky start. In 1273, Roger, like many others, took the trouble to cross to Gascony and greet Edward as the king returned from his crusade, and the following year he officiated as marshal at the coronation.[22] Nevertheless, the earl still managed to misread the change in mood which had accompanied the accession of a new monarch; in particular, he clung to the notion, developed by his uncle, that he could ignore indefinitely demands for repayment of debt issued by the king's exchequer. Edward had come to the throne determined to reassert the Crown's authority on such issues, and compelled (one has to assume) Roger to surrender four of his manors

in order to raise the money.[23] It was not long, however, before matters between the two men improved, largely as a consequence of the king's wars in Wales. Edward needed the military support of his magnates for these adventures, and so began to soften his stance on Roger's debts. Demands for satisfaction were for a time suspended, and ultimately the earl was allowed (like his uncle) to pay at terms.[24] The king seems to have been especially impressed by the service Roger rendered during the war of 1282–83, when the earl went to considerable effort in shipping supplies to north Wales from his Irish estates.[25] Consequently, when Edward embarked on a victory tour of the conquered principality in 1284, he elected to stop at Chepstow for a few days in December, and, in the New Year, Roger received 1,000 marks (£667) from the king in recognition of his wartime services. This, arguably, was the highest point in their relationship.[26]

Thereafter there were occasional tensions and strains: arguments over Roger's rights as marshal in 1287 and 1294, disputes over the size of his debts to the Crown, and probably some friction—as was the case with most magnates—over the *Quo Warranto* inquiries.[27] All of this, however, can be regarded as little more than the normal cut and thrust of politics. In the same period, there is also continued evidence of successful collaboration. Roger actively supported Edward in Scotland, first by acting as an auditor in the hearings to determine the Scottish succession (the so-called 'Great Cause' proceedings), and later by participating in the military campaigns north of the border.[28] Similarly in 1294 he was making preparations to support the king's planned invasion of Gascony, and fought in Wales when the rising of that year demanded that the army be diverted westwards.[29] It was only really in the year 1297 itself that the relationship between the two men began to deteriorate, as Edward for the first time parted company with mainstream political opinion in pursuit of his war with France.[30] In February of that year came the Salisbury parliament at which Roger famously refused the king's demand to lead an army to Gascony. According to a rather inventive chronicler, Edward angrily threatened to hang the earl for his opposition, prompting Roger to respond 'By God, O King, I shall neither go nor hang!' (notice the improbable pun on his surname). Whatever words were really spoken, the earl certainly quit the court and made ready to resist.[31] His reasons for doing so were of fairly recent origin: the excessive financial demands being made on him and his supporters; the belief that, with Wales and Scotland only recently pacified, going to Gascony was a mistake; also possibly a certain sympathy with the plight of the Church, which Edward was punishing for its failure to vote him war funds.[32] As the crisis worsened, other factors came into play—Roger made an issue over the marshalship, and Edward resurrected the spectre of the unpaid Bigod debts.[33] After three years of playing cat-and-mouse with the opposition, the king was obliged to make major concessions in 1300 and 1301, concessions he bitterly resented.[34] By this stage, however, his principal opponent was also physically and financially exhausted. The two men therefore came to an arrangement of a kind favoured by Edward, by which Roger, childless despite two marriages, effectively made the king his heir.[35] As had been the case at the start of their careers, there was probably some degree of compulsion involved in this agreement, although the contemporary evidence which explicitly states that this was the case looks highly unreliable.[36] Another contemporary story has it that Roger acted deliberately to spite his grasping brother, who was set to inherit the earldom.[37] There was also some consolation for the earl in the form of an enhanced income; while he lived Edward was bound to pay him an extra £1,000 a year.[38] Roger died in December 1306 at Framlingham Castle (Fig. 108), and was buried six months later at Thetford Priory alongside his Bigod ancestors. Edward died a few weeks later at Burgh by Sands, in Cumbria, preparing to lead an army into Scotland.[39]

On the basis of the latter part of his political career, historians have usually judged Roger Bigod a failure and concluded that he was not a

*Fig. 108  Framlingham Castle*

particularly capable man.[40] This is probably somewhat unfair—as we have seen, Edward was pleased enough with Roger's service in Wales, and their argument in 1297 was partly brought on because the king *wanted* the earl to lead an army into Gascony. The truth is that, as the 13th century progresses, it becomes increasingly difficult to form an impression of what individuals were really like, even if they were earls and kings. We have a much less rounded view of Edward I than we do of his father, Henry III, because, as time wears on, the quality and quantity of the chronicle material diminishes.[41] In the same way, Roger Bigod is less well defined than his namesake uncle, who is variously described by contemporaries as *strenuus*, *bellicosus* and *praeclarus*.[42] Matthew Paris, the gossipy chronicler who provides so much of our information about the royal court down to his death in 1259, offers several entertaining and illuminating episodes that help characterize the fourth earl (he was, for example, a great tourneyer).[43] With the fifth earl, however, we have no such anecdotes or descriptive adjectives. His only notable chronicle appearances occur as a result of his clash with Edward in 1297 and his deal with the king in 1302. Both episodes are recorded by a north-country writer called Walter of Guisborough, whose testimony is often less reliable and more inventive than one could wish.[44]

Even when these allowances for the evidence are made, however, it must also be admitted that there is little in Roger's conduct that suggests he was a truly distinguished individual. There are the barest hints that he may have possessed the same kind of legalistic ability for which his father, Hugh Bigod, had once been famous. Roger was one of only two earls selected for the panel of twenty-four which deliberated the question of the Scottish succession in 1291–92 and in 1299 he appealed to Edward I to act in accordance with 'human and divine reason'. His second wife, Alice de Hainault, possessed a French translation of a Justinian law code—though of course it does not automatically follow that she discussed its contents with her husband.[45] Roger was not, however, sent on any diplomatic

missions, as his uncle and father had been, and as was the case with several of his contemporaries.[46] The only occasion when the earl was employed as a government agent was during his trip to Ireland in 1280, and this was at the request of the Irish justiciar rather than the king himself.[47] Moreover, it is also possible that Roger lacked some of the lordly skills which were essential for a successful political (or for that matter personal) career. His affinity appears to have had no strong geographical centre, and was characterized by a high degree of desertion.[48] In the same way, an analysis of his estates in Norfolk suggests he may have been a less-than-exacting landlord.[49] Even when the earl took centre-stage in February 1297, there is the suspicion that he did so only for want of other candidates; once he had been joined in opposition by Humphrey de Bohun, earl of Hereford, he was apparently content to let this new associate do most of the talking.[50] Overall, it seems fair to say that Roger, for all his vast wealth, did not strike contemporaries as a particularly important or imposing figure, and his biographer has to face the strong possibility that the lack of chronicle interest in the earl and his affairs may be due to the simple fact that neither was especially interesting.

Luckily, however, for those who would wish to know more about the man and his apparently unexceptional life, there is one major saving grace. As a consequence of his decision in 1302 to make the king his heir, a huge amount of documentary material from Roger's estate found its way into Crown custody and, remarkably, much of this material has survived. Now kept in the National Archives at Kew, there are some 670 parchment rolls covering over fifty manors.[51] They are financial records, created for the earl's auditors to scrutinise the workings of his estate, and therefore most useful for those seeking answers to economic questions.[52] Occasionally, however, they afford brief but revealing glimpses of the everyday lives of the earl and his household. In the early rolls, for example, there are numerous expenses for tournaments, mostly involving Roger's younger brother, Ralph.[53] In later rolls more space is devoted to gardening—in

1296, for instance, £4 was spent on laying out a new garden at Bosham. There are also indications of the kind of indoor entertainments the Bigod household was wont to enjoy from time to time. In 1292 they were entertained by the players of Edmund of Cornwall, who were collectively rewarded £3 for their histrionics. In the same year, the receiver of Chepstow noted without comment that he had given Roger 30s. to play at 'griesche', which would appear to be a gambling game, though not necessarily one at which the earl excelled; the next entry reveals that he had cadged a further 25s. from his knight Thomas de Berkeley for the same match.[54]

By far the most important aspect of the earl's life that these rolls document, however, is his building work. Indeed, it is through this work that we can best imagine what Roger's world was like and also, perhaps, come closest to apprehending his personality. The large amount of surviving documentation is matched by a correspondingly impressive quantity of standing masonry, and it seems reasonable to conclude from this that the earl was preoccupied to an uncommon degree with the need to reshape and re-order the world around him in stone (he certainly built far more than his uncle and probably most of his contemporaries). As well as his best-known work at Chepstow, the earl commissioned new buildings at almost all his properties. At Bungay he added a new twin-towered gatehouse to the existing 12th-century castle (Fig. 109).[55] At Walton in Suffolk he constructed a new hall, parts of which remained standing until the 19th century.[56] It is known from the record evidence that the earl invested at least £83 in a new castle in Ireland, and the result may well be the mysterious, unfinished structure now known as Ballymoon.[57] At Hamstead Marshal, Bosham, Halvergate, Hanworth, and Framlingham there are expenses for brand new buildings which are now lost, as are the new quays built in Ipswich and London.[58]

*Fig. 109 The twin-towered gatehouse added to Bungay Castle, Suffolk, by Roger Bigod*

Furthermore, to this list must surely be added the new abbey church at Tintern (Fig. 110). While there is little direct evidence of the earl's financial support, it is inconceivable that the monks of Tintern would have embarked on such a costly project without substantial outside funding. That their principal benefactor lived a few miles downstream at Chepstow is strongly suggested by the fact that the new church was begun at the time of his accession, and was finished with a great east window decorated with the Bigod coat of arms.[59]

From Roger's sponsorship of the new church at Tintern his ambitions and aspirations for the afterlife can de discerned.[60] How closely his other building work can be correlated to his life on earth is a more open question. For instance, it may well be that the 'new tower' at Chepstow, now known as Marten's Tower, was inspired by Edward's brief stay at the castle in 1284, and built in anticipation of future royal visits.[61] At the same time, Roger could well have required the tower's suite of new chambers to meet his more normal hospitality obligations. As one of the greatest magnates in the country he was regularly accompanied by a household which could swell to seventy men or more, and which often included high-ranking individuals—for instance, Hugh Despenser, Thomas de Berkeley and John de Seagrave—who would have expected accommodation built to just such a high standard.[62] Moreover, for all the additional domestic luxury it afforded, Marten's Tower remains a mighty bulwark to the castle's south-eastern flank; it may not therefore be entirely coincidental that it was begun in 1287, a year which witnessed a major revolt in south Wales.[63] On a similar military note, what should one make of the earl's decision in the late 1290s to mount springalds—giant crossbows—on the four corners of Chepstow's newly enlarged Great Tower? It was no doubt an act of defiance, but it surely must have been only an act and nothing more. Roger, after all, had seen at first hand the kind of assault that Edward I could unleash, and cannot have been seriously considering using his beautiful castle to offer armed resistance to a royal army.[64]

If we cannot be entirely confident in our interpretation of the earl's motives for undertaking individual parts of his building programme, we can nevertheless make one statement which seems far more certain. The scale of Roger's investment at Chepstow, both in the fabric of the castle itself, and also throughout the lordship as a whole, indicates that it was probably the favourite of his many properties.[65] As the new interpretative work presented in this volume shows, hardly a year of the earl's career went by in which some major new construction project was not in progress. If one was to seek a reason for this preference, it would probably lie in the fact that, of all his estates, it was Chepstow that offered Roger the greatest freedom. In the March of Wales, as Bigod bailiffs were only too happy to point out when challenged, the king's writ did not run.[66] Indeed, in the March it was possible to behave rather like a king oneself. Here a lord could hunt in his own forests, hold his own court, and dine on dishes normally reserved for royalty.[67] It was a

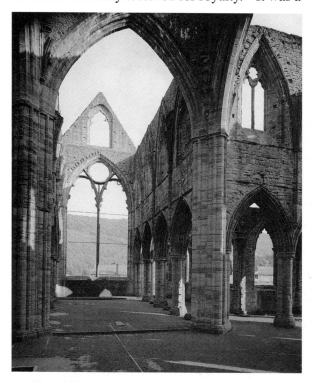

*Fig. 110 Tintern Abbey church which was presumably funded by Roger Bigod as principal benefactor*

place for escapism, and perhaps it was escape that Roger Bigod sought most. It seems very significant that his final building project was a new, whimsical little castle in a remote corner of Wentwood Forest. Begun after his surrender to Edward I, Cas Troggy can only have been built for the earl's personal enjoyment.[68] In his last years, perhaps rather humiliated and in failing health, Roger forsook the king's court.[69] Tired from the recent political struggle and from constant campaigning, it is nice to think of him retreating to his Welsh estates and indulging his private passions. And if the deal he had struck gave him any cause for regret, it was surely in Chepstow, the lordship that he had transformed so dramatically throughout his long career, that he would have found the greatest solace.

# CHAPTER XIV

# The 'Gloriette' in the Lower Bailey

*by* Rick Turner, Stephen Priestley, Nicola Coldstream *and* Bevis Sale

The north side of the Lower Bailey was closed by an extensive range of buildings running from the outer face of the Middle Bailey curtain wall to the rear of the Main Gatehouse (Fig. 111). These buildings provided new private apartments for Roger Bigod, fifth earl of Norfolk. Their designer, Bigod's master mason Ralph Gogun of London, showed great ingenuity in using the changes in height and the different projections of the limestone cliff to produce a visually dramatic range of buildings. The rooms for the earl and his family were cleverly integrated with the main service rooms and the chambers of his principal servants. Indeed the building demonstrates a level of sophistication in domestic planning not seen by this date in the castles of the Welsh Marches and perhaps even in royal palaces of the 13th century.

Roger Bigod inherited Chepstow Castle in 1270. The earliest set of manorial accounts date from September 1271 to September 1272.[1] This records a series of repairs and purchases that seem to have been undertaken in preparation for what may have been the earl's first visit to the castle. For example the kitchen pots were repaired, canvas bought for tablecloths and firewood boated down from Tintern. Significant repairs were made to the 'Gloriette'. This was reached by steps, had a chamber alongside and had a *tabula* or decorative band of stonework added to its roofline. At the same time masons were building a wall behind the *cameram Comitesse* or Countess' chamber. The value of

these works does not suggest that much new building was taking place. So Roger must have inherited these suites of rooms from an earlier lord of Chepstow. One or other may be what is now called Marshal's Tower in the Upper Bailey (see p.77-79). More likely, they may have been buildings already standing in the Lower Bailey.

There is then a gap in the annual receiver's accounts for Striguil (Chepstow) until 1282. There is mention of masons and plumbers working in the castle in 1279/80 but no specific buildings are mentioned.[2] In 1282, masons and carpenters were busy building the new kitchen,[3] and for the first time Master Ralph the mason is named. He had been building a castle in county Carlow, Ireland for Roger Bigod in 1280/1 and during 1282 he was lent to Roger's accountant and attorney, Thomas Weyland, to help build the new church at Chipping Sodbury, Gloucestershire.[4] Ralph was to work at Chepstow until his death, recorded in the account for 1293/4.[5] He was also active at the earl's manor of Bosham, Sussex, where he is referred to as Ralph Gogun, the earl's mason, and later Ralph, mason of London.[6] Given the unity of design and planning seen in the buildings in the Lower Bailey, their design must be credited to Ralph, who perhaps brought the latest ideas from London. Whilst working at Chepstow Castle he may also have had some role in the building of the new church at Tintern Abbey for which Roger Bigod would become the principal patron.[7] (Fig. 110]).

*Fig. 111 The cliffside elevation of the 'Gloriette' running from the Main Gatehouse to the left to the Middle Bailey curtain wall to the right*

The masons continued work on the kitchen and the chambers adjoining into 1283, when Master Ralph received 40s. for his two robes.[8] Repairs were made to the roof of the Chamber of the Gloriette. Work continued into the autumn of 1284, with the masons finishing the stonework, all the carpentry for the kitchen being undertaken and a lead roof laid over the kitchen and the neighbouring chambers. A new oven was also built in the kitchen.[9] The total recorded expenditure on the new kitchen and chambers was £55 7s. 8d., the building taking about two and a half

*Fig. 112 The courtyard view of the 'Gloriette' with the ruins to the left with its castellated porch intact. The earl's chamber is at the centre with the kitchen and pair of chambers beyond*

years to complete. Master Ralph was paid 2s. per week to supervise the work.

This suite of buildings was ready in time for the visit of King Edward I and Queen Eleanor and their households from 17–21 December 1284, a visit that marked the end of the king's triumphal tour through Wales following his victory in the second Welsh War. Nearly £7 was paid to some carpenters to prepare the castle for the visit, whilst £5 was spent on firewood.[10] Bigod's steward even had to travel as far as Bosham to gather provisions for the feasts. Bigod moved on with the king and queen to Bristol, where on New Year's Day the king gave him 1,000 marks in recognition of his service in Wales.[11]

Later accounts do not throw much light on the changes or improvements to this group of buildings. In 1286, the chamber of the earl between the hall and kitchen was roofed with old lead,[12] and in 1291/2 timber was cut and planed to make tables for the kitchen.[13] More significantly the accounts for 1292/3 refer to repairs to the roof of the 'Gloriette', the chamber of 'la Gloriette', the earl's chamber and the roof of the earl's chamber 'la Gloriette'.[14] Together these references show that the earl's chamber was part of or equivalent to the specially named Gloriette. The same account refers to the daubing and painting of the new hall (Plate 6).

To understand how this new range of buildings was used and to reconstruct what they would have looked like, it is easiest to divide them into two: the earl's accommodation and the service rooms.

## The Earl's Accommodation

The main entrance into the hall was through the projecting castellated porch whose doorway faces west, as if to receive people coming down from the Great Tower (Fig. 112). As they passed through the Middle Bailey gateway, they would have been faced with the blank rear gable of the hall and then walked in front of the three main courtyard windows divided by buttresses. Recent excavations have shown that there was a deep stone-lined pit in front of the porch doorway

(2.6m by 1.6m and over 1.3m deep), the western and northern sides of which have sloping sides. This resembles a counterweight pit for a drawbridge, so perhaps access into the porch was controlled in this way. Given the many other points of access into these buildings, such a drawbridge would have been more a conceit than a defensive measure.

The porch is ceiled by a two-bay quadripartite vault. This is sprung from conical fluted corbels and has heavy moulded ribs (Fig. 113). A large two-light window overlooks the courtyard and a small window looks down towards the gatehouse passage. There is a substantial, chamfered and stopped doorway into the main hall. This is rebated and there is a blocked drawbar socket behind. Over the doorway there are two shields painted onto what may be the plaster referred to in 1292/3 (Plate 8). The shields are long and pointed in the style of those on the rolls of arms of the 13th century.[15] They are outlined in black and painted as if hanging by a ribbon from a

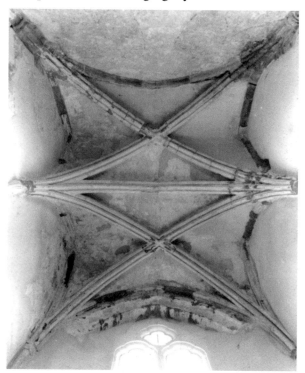

*Fig. 113 The ceiling of the porch to Roger Bigod's hall*

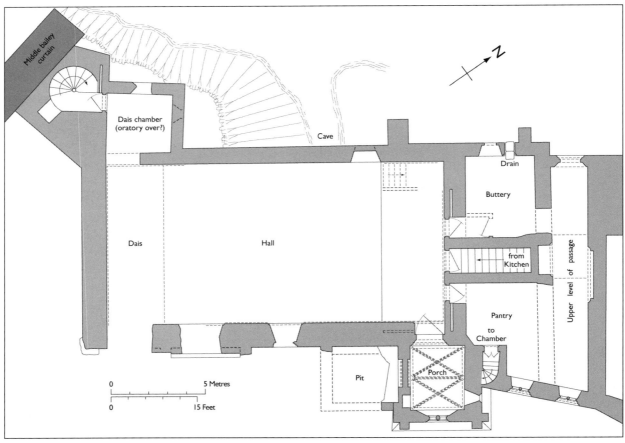

*Fig. 114  Plan of the hall block*

*Fig. 115  View of the east end of the hall showing the doorway on the left at intermediary floor level to the earl's chamber*

hook. A third hook shows in the centre. The left-hand shield has a red ochre ground with traces of a black outline, but is too fragmentary to identify. The right-hand shield has a single red chevron on a plain ground, and within the shield 12 horizontal lines have been carefully scribed into the plaster. This may refer to the Clare family whose arms were three red chevrons on a white ground.

The hall measures 18m by 8.9m internally (a 2:1 ratio). Within the east wall, alongside the entrance, were the three service doorways. Each has a pointed, hollow-chamfered arch with a bar stop and a hood mould with carved head stops. Traces of double, red-lined ashlar wall painting can be seen in this area. The larger central doorway opened onto the stairs leading down to the kitchen, the nearer, right-hand doorway into the pantry and the far doorway into the buttery. The doorways are not central to the elevation as

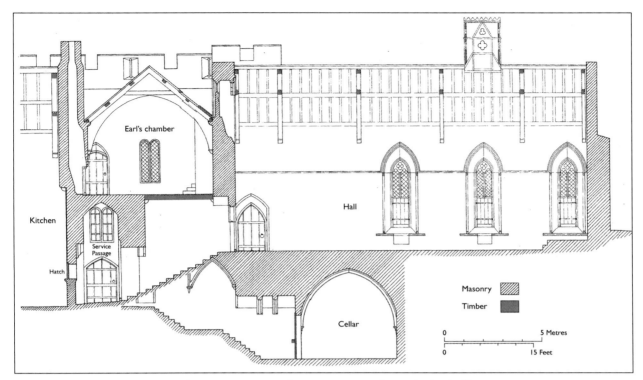

*Fig. 116 A reconstructed cross-section through the hall range*

they had to respect a wooden staircase rising to the doorway into the earl's chamber above (Fig. 115). A moulded band runs around the hall and rises to respect this doorway. In the apex of the gable was an elaborate window, allowing light in from over the roof of the earl's chamber. The rear arch was decorated with drop tracery and a hood mould. It may have contained stained or armorial glass which would have thrown a pool of coloured light into the centre of the hall.

The main body of the hall is less well-preserved. Some modifications were made in the Tudor period; more damaging was the construction of a glass retort in the 1760s and later the construction of part of the custodian's house at the eastern end. There is a slight step in the modern floor which marks the wall of the cellar beneath. At the far end was a raised dais, standing 0.7m above the present floor, whose irregular footings can still be seen at the base of the west wall. This was where the earl's high table was set. A succession of inventories taken in the early 14th century record two fixed tables, two demountable trestle tables and seven benches as the permanent furniture within this room.[16] The room was lit by three, tall, narrow windows overlooking the courtyard (Fig. 116). Clark wrote in his description of the hall in 1882, that it then had 'two large windows of two lights, trefoiled and with a quatrefoil in the head, one looking into the ward, and one upon the river'.[17] Only parts of two rear arches now survive. Both have finely-carved motifs of four elongated leaves meeting at a central boss, some fully undercut (Fig. 117). In the window nearest the porch, the boss is small and the leaves concave, their centre lines marked by ridges. In the other, the boss is more pronounced and the convex leaves are marked by grooves. The arches themselves are carried on fine cone-shaped corbels with twisted tails. With its painted decoration and full complement of architectural ornament, the hall was highly decorated. The ornament that survives is very delicate and seems to suit the description of this suite of rooms as 'la Gloriette'. However the bar tracery of the windows and some of the decorative motifs

*Fig. 117  Carved details from the rear arches of the hall windows*

seem to hark back to the style of the Marshal's sons' Great Tower (see chapter X) and may be a blatant evocation of that earlier building. Whilst many great 13th-century buildings have foliate decoration on vaults and window dressings,[18] none matches the four-leafed versions at Chepstow. Here the comparisons are in metal-work or in such buildings as the Sainte-Chapelle, Paris, heavily influenced by or intended to evoke work in precious materials.[19]

The hall has no fireplace, so a large central hearth must have been used with the smoke rising through a louvre in the roof. The floor was prob-ably laid with decorated tiles, 'ornamented with birds and flowers'.[20] Alongside the dais, is a small tower built out on a projection of the cliff (Fig. 114). Lit by two, tall, pointed arched windows, it provided a small chamber or oriel into which the occupants of the high table could retreat from the noise of the hall.[21] A door leads to a wide spiral staircase to a similar room above which may have been a small chapel or oratory.

The earl and his principal guests would have sat at the high table to eat. The permanent

wooden furniture would have been covered with white linen tablecloths and set with silver and gilt dishes, carried in the earl's baggage train. The food would have been brought on serving dishes carried up the stairs from the kitchen. The earl's steward in his livery and holding his ceremonial staff would have met them at the central doorway and led them in procession past the fireplace to the high table.[22] Wine and beer would have been brought out of the buttery and bread from the pantry. The earl would have been served with some of each dish by the carver and his elaborate cup filled by the butler. Others sat at the high table would have been served, then the dishes were passed to lower members of the household sitting at the tables ranged along the sides of the hall. Groups of dishes, both savoury and sweet were served in messes, two or three for regular meals, more for special feasts. Lighter delicacies or *entremets* were served between messes. The formality of these meals, and the rituals which surrounded them, meant that up to a third of the day could be spent seated at table.[23]

On finishing the meal, the earl would have risen and walked down the hall to the steps up to his private chamber (Fig. 116). Like many aspects of this hall, this arrangement was becoming anachronistic. The last quarter of the 13th century saw a change where the lord's private rooms were placed behind the dais end of the hall, the plan familiar from the remainder of the Middle Ages.[24] Here the earl's chamber occupied the whole of the first floor over the service rooms of the hall (Figs. 116 & 118). It has an irregular plan but its maximum dimensions were 12.1m by 6.5m.

The focus of the room is the fireplace central to the east wall. It now has a massive stone lintel supported by corbels and engaged, filleted colonettes, but this may be an alteration as hooded fireplaces were more common at this date.[25] There is a broad two-light window in the north wall overlooking the gorge of the Lower Wye Valley and a smaller window looking over the courtyard. Servants could enter via a narrow spiral staircase from the pantry below. A doorway in the north-east corner leads to a well-appointed closet and latrine oversailing the river, and a now blocked

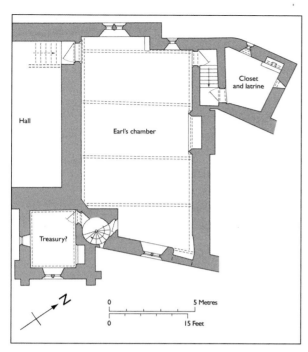

*Fig. 118 Plan of the earl's chamber*

From this evidence, coupled with that gleaned from medieval romances, some idea can be gained of what presumably has been lost from the earl's chamber at Chepstow. It may have been painted with biblical or Arthurian scenes, hung with Italian silk, decorated with gold and semi-precious stones or contained remarkable objects such as the fake tree with carved birds which squirted water on visitors to Count Robert of Artois' gloriette at Hesdin, northern France.[28]

The final part of the earl's accommodation is a small square room over the porch, reached by the spiral staircase from the pantry. It has a fireplace and good windows. It may once have been a private closet for the earl or countess to retreat to (or could have acted as a treasury or record office for use by the earl's receiver).

### The Service Rooms

The main axis for the service rooms is a cross-passage which separates the hall and kitchen ranges (Fig. 119). It was entered from the court-yard through a broad doorway secured by a drawbar. The passage was much higher (at 5.65m), than it appears today, for originally the wooden floors of the buttery and pantry would not have been carried across. The two-light window above the courtyard doorway acted like a giant fanlight, and a window of similar proportions lit the far end of the passage overlooking the river.

On entering the passage from the courtyard, the door into the kitchen was immediately on the right. Further on was the serving hatch, spanned by a very broad, low two-centred arch with a complex moulding. The serving hatch was probably divided into three, with the shelf set into a recess, and the hatches rebated on the kitchen side to take wooden shutters. On the left hand side of the passage is an L-shaped room measuring 3.7m by 5.7m. It is lit by a small glazed and shuttered window of two rectangular lights. There are two large cupboards in the north wall, contained below the stairs up to the hall and a third below the stairs rising from the pantry. The building accounts refer to a number of service rooms not yet identified in the present building. These include a saucery, laundry house and

doorway in the south-east corner opened onto the Great Pentice (see p.148). The wall plates for the roof ran along the continuous, quarter-round corbel table along each long wall, with the position of the roof trusses marked by corbels at a lower level. The roof was low-pitched, covered in lead which needed regular repair[26] and may have had a wooden ceiling similar to the modern reconstruction. The chamber has been stripped of all its plaster and paintwork, but must have been highly decorated originally.

To be given the title 'Gloriette', this was no ordinary earl's chamber—it must have been very special and exotic in character. Only two other 13th-century castles in Britain had rooms or complexes referred to as gloriettes. The first is the *domus regis*, built by King John at Corfe Castle (Fig. 60) in the early 13th century and called 'gloriette' during Edward I's reign. The second is a suite of apartments built on an island within the moat at Leeds Castle, Kent by Queen Eleanor for her husband, Edward I. Ashbee has drawn together the evidence for all these sites and tried to compare them with those from continental Europe, Sicily and Moorish Spain.[27]

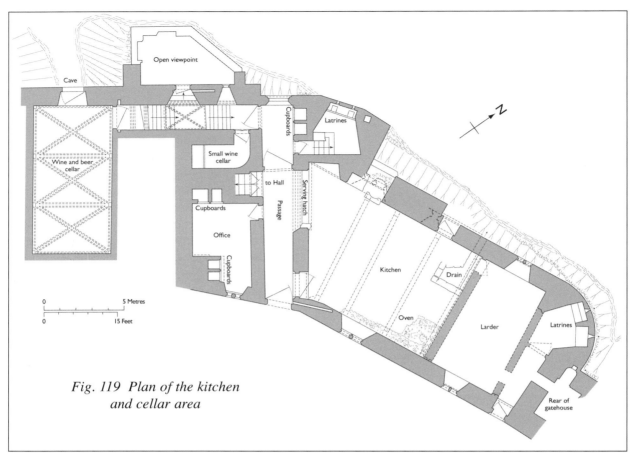

Cave

Open viewpoint

Wine and beer cellar

Small wine cellar

Cupboards

Latrines

to Hall

Serving hatch

Passage

Cupboards

Office

Cupboards

Kitchen

Drain

0    5 Metres

0    15 Feet

Oven

Larder

Latrines

Rear of gatehouse

*Fig. 119  Plan of the kitchen and cellar area*

wardrobe house. Peter Brears has reviewed the documentary and physical evidence for the service rooms at Chepstow Castle[29] and considers that this room may have been the 'office' for the cofferer or receiver. It would have been their job to receive the coffers or records, cask, plate etc., which came with the earl's baggage train, when he came to stay.[30] In addition, they would account for the deliveries of food and drink to the service areas, and supervise the supply of food, wine and ale to the hall and chamber. The cupboards would provide suitable storage for records and other valuable items.

Beyond the office are the stairs up to the hall which had a pair of doors at their lower end, lockable from the kitchen side. Another doorway divides the kitchen half of the passage from the entrance to the cellars. Beyond this door is the access to a pair of latrines. This rather dark, stone-vaulted polygonal room, has two stone seats above open chutes, projecting on stone corbels beyond the cliff face. These garderobes were the most convenient for those eating in the lower end of the hall and more senior officers of the household. The final feature of the passageway is another pair of stone cupboards set within the thickness of the wall and rebated to receive wooden doors.

Running perpendicular from the north-west corner of the main passageway is a long flight of steps, with an intermediate landing, descending into the cellar beneath the hall. The first room on the left has a narrow doorway leading into an L-shaped room beneath the buttery floor. (see Fig. 116). The doorcase has two horizontal slots suggesting that a wooden board could be pushed in to form a shelf. Brears believes this to be either the wine cellar, or more likely a room where wine could be held in smaller barrels for measuring out and carrying up to the buttery.

Above the intermediate landing, there is a single bay of quadripartite vaulting sprung from cushion capitals with facetted sides (Fg. 120.1). This vault helps support the massive east wall of the hall above (Fig. 116) but it also provides emphasis to the doorway that opens through the external wall onto a platform of rock. This lies immediately below the earl's chamber and is framed by two massive buttresses. The other walls running around the cliff edge are Tudor, but the space may have just had a light fence originally. The architectural treatment of the doorway and vaulting suggests this was a view-point, or even a small garden for use by the earl and his guests. It provides fine views up the Wye Gorge and down to the bridge and would have been a cool spot on a hot day.

The staircase continues down a second flight with the last step cut on the skew to allow the cellar door to open. The doorcase has a rounded rather than chamfered moulding on the face within the cellar, and there is a drawbar to lock the door from the staircase side.

The cellar is a magnificent room measuring 9.6m by 4.95m, close to a 2:1 ratio. It had to be built over a fissure in the limestone rock. Access to this area has been recently obtained to allow for conservation work. This showed that a plat-form of wooden beams was laid across the top of the fissure. This supported the centring for a pitched rubble vault made of large slabs of Sudbrook Sandstone. The vault tapers back to 2.5m wide and is closed by a wall 5.5m back from the wall face. The imprint of the wooden planks from the centring of this vault is preserved in the mortar. On the riverside, the vault is closed with two dressed, Old Red Sandstone arches with the rounded moulding of the cellar doorcase. One supports the inner face, and one—now collapsed—supported the outer face of the outer wall of the buildings above.

The cellar is divided into three equal bays, each with a quadripartite vault of boldly cham-fered ribs (Fig. 121). These are carried on water-holding, semi-circular capitals on delicate conical corbels, with delightful dog-tooth detailing and

  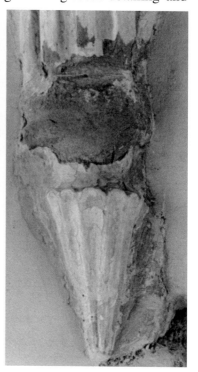

*Fig. 120 Detail of vaulting capitals:*
*1 (left): stairway; 2 (centre): cellar; 3 (right): porch*

*Fig. 121 A view of the cellar vaulting*

The size of the cellar reflects the demand for ale, wine and cider when the earl's household was in residence. Buried below the hall and with only north facing openings it would have remained permanently cool. In 1284, the account records a payment for hoistage and ullage of six barrels of wine bought at Bristol.[31] In 1287, it was recorded that there were two barrels and one cask of wine, and one barrel and one cask of cider remaining in the cellar.[32] An inventory taken in 1310, gives the contents of the cellar as three barrels, four tankards, two casks and eight goblets.[33]

There is no brewhouse in Chepstow Castle as the earl had a prise, a proportionary tax, of all the

carved points (Fig. 120.2). The floor is partly flagged/partly native rock.

The external wall has two openings framed by a series of Sudbrook Sandstone relieving arches (Fig. 122). The lower opening is treated like a doorway with the rear arch and reveal within the cellar. The doorway no longer reaches the ground and is blocked to waist level, probably in the Tudor period. Immediately above the doorway, is a squat, arched window in a deep reveal, providing light into the cellar when the door below was closed. A mid-19th-century lithograph shows the original situation, with the door surviving *in situ* and a big iron loop set into the floor (Fig. 123). The loop must have been the anchor point for a crane or winch, whose arm projected out of the doorway or window above. This was used to hoist the barrels from boats beached or temporarily moored in the fissure below.

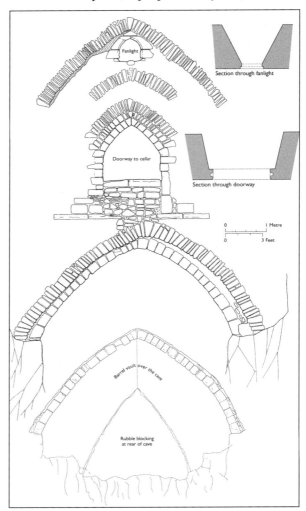

*Fig. 122 Part of the cliffside elevation of the cellar*

144

*Fig. 123 Nineteenth-century lithograph of the cellar*

have been done on open hearths or charcoal braziers nearer the centre of the room. A large ashlar, catch-pit drain set into the north-east corner of the kitchen provided a waste disposal system. The roof of the kitchen was carried on four tall wooden trusses whose corbels and sockets can be traced on the side walls. Into the middle of the 19th century these carried an elaborate louvre drawn by Buckler in 1815 (Fig. 124) and again by Parker, some 25 years later.[35] The louvre may have been made of pottery rather than stone, as in 1801 Coxe writes:

> Not less than twenty-four ancient chimnies still remain; the principal one of the inhabited part [the louvre] is handsomely decorated on the outside, and the inside is glazed, which prevents the accumulation of the soot, and it was never swept during the memory of Mrs Williams, which must have been nearly eighty years.[36]

ale brewed in the borough. This could be commuted for cash if there was no demand for the ale.[34] The beer would have been boated around from the Back or quay in Chepstow for hoisting into the cellar.

The eastern half of the 'Gloriette' is dominated by the kitchen. Slightly irregular in shape it measures on average 10.5m long and 7.5m wide and rises through the whole building. The size of the kitchen not only reflects the amount of food that would have been produced when the earl and household were in residence, but also emphasises the importance of hospitality and conspicuous consumption to a great magnate. The room was originally lit by three large, two-light windows (Fig. 112 and 168). These were set high in the walls to throw light down onto the working surfaces and draw heat and fumes out through their unglazed but shuttered lights.

The stone footings for a large oven remain in the south-east corner, perhaps that built in 1284 (see p.136 above). Otherwise the cooking would

*Fig. 124 The kitchen louvre drawn by J. Buckler in 1815*

The inventories of 1309/10 record the contents of the kitchen as one oven, two dressers —tables on which the food was prepared, 24 dishes, 20 platters and 24 salt cellars.

In the north wall of the kitchen is a doorway that opens onto a small projection of the cliff. On the external wall is a dressed stone roofline, designed to receive an open timber porch. This seems to provide a point from where foodstuffs could be winched up from boats moored below, directly into the kitchen and the larder which lay alongside (Plate 6 and Fig. 20.4). Also against the north wall, a large Tudor fireplace was added (now blocked), partly hiding one of the medieval windows. Beneath the other window is a circular stone-setting perhaps to mount a boiler, which again seems to be a later alteration.

To the east of the kitchen, where the shop is now sited, was the larder. There is a door from the kitchen and from a passage to the rear of the gate-house which allowed for the free flow of goods in and out of the store. The room is cellar-like and

| | Bread | Ale | Eggs | Beef | Great meat | Poultry | Fish |
|---|---|---|---|---|---|---|---|
| Sat | 1 bushel flour $9^3/_4$d. | 1 measure 4d. | 6d. | | | | |
| Sun | 7 bushels corn 5s. $8^3/_4$d. | 3 measures 12d. | | 1 + offal & suet 5s. | 1s. 4d. | + a pottage 10d. | |
| Mon | 5 bushels corn 4s. $^3/_4$d. | | | 2 beefs 2s. 4d. | | | |
| Tues | 3 bushels corn 2s. 5d. | | | | | | 13s. $10^1/_2$d. |
| Wed | 3 bushels corn 3s. 4d. | | | | | 1s. | 3s. $3^1/_2$d. |
| Thurs | 4 bushels corn 3s. 3d. | | | | 2s. 5d. | $10^1/_2$d. | |
| Fri | 3 bushels corn 2s. $5^3/_4$d. | | | | | | |
| Fri | 1 bushel corn $9^3/_4$d. | | | | | $2^1/_2$d. | 1s. 7d. |
| Sat | 1 bushel corn 7s. $3^3/_4$d. | | | | | 8d. | 2s. 4d. |
| Sun | 4 bushels corn 3s. 3d. | 18 barrels 10s. | | | 3s. 8d. | $8^1/_4$d. | |
| Mon | 6 bushels corn 4s. $10^1/_2$d. | 1 measure 4d. | | | 4s. $10^1/_2$d. | $8^1/_4$d. | |
| Tues | 6 bushels corn 4s. $10^1/_2$d. | | | | 2s. $5^1/_4$d. | $10^3/_4$d. | |
| Wed | 1 quarter corn 6s. 6d. | 1 measure 4d. | | | 2s. 10d. | 6d. | |

*Account of Countess of Norfolk for provisioning the castle of Striguil on account of the Welsh War, 28 Jan to 8 Feb 1295. For comparison a skilled craftsman earned 3d. per day*

has opposed high set windows to allow for a cooling cross-draught, in which the raw and any preserved meat could be hung.

One remarkable document survives that describes the provisioning of the castle during the period 28 January to 8 February 1295.[37] Alice de Hainault, the countess of Norfolk, was placed with her household in Chepstow Castle for safekeeping whilst her husband was helping suppress the Welsh uprising of that winter.[38] Roger had established a separate household for his wife to be managed by Sir Goscelin, his chaplain. The goods purchased by Goscelin have been tabulated by Peter Brears (see table opposite).

This volume of food was dwarfed when, in 1326, Chepstow and Bristol Castles were provisioned to receive King Edward II, Hugh Despenser and their followers in expectation of a long siege. The wardrobe purchased 43 oxen, 40 pigs, 80 sheep, 180 salmon, 40 quarters of oats, 20 quarters of beans and 80 waggon loads of hay.[39]

Beyond the larder was a passage and a pair of latrines for use by the kitchen staff, one of whom scratched a graffito of a soldier as he sat in contemplation (Fig. 125). Above the larder were two well-appointed chambers, both having an irregular plan (Fig. 126). Each had a window looking over the river and the courtyard, and

*Fig. 125  Graffito of a soldier in the larder latrines*

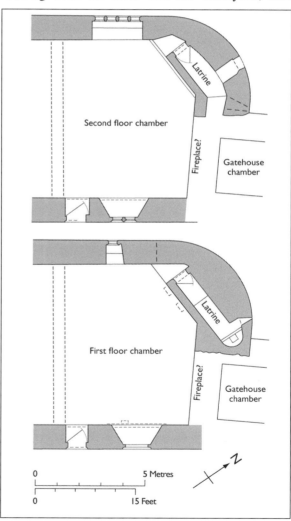

*Fig. 126  Plans of the kitchen chambers*

private latrines set into intra-mural passages. They may also have had fireplaces within the now-collapsed wall at the rear of the gatehouse. Access into the chambers was via external wooden stairs which formed part of the Great Pentice.

The Great Pentice itself was perhaps the most remarkable part of the 'Gloriette', though as yet it has defied accurate reconstruction.[40] Pentices or alleys were common in medieval great houses and abbeys, providing covered walkways between buildings or within lean-tos against buildings, so that people could go dryshod. They were roofed open timber structures, normally at ground level such as around the inner courtyard at Goodrich Castle, Herefordshire, but in the case of Marlborough Castle in 1245, the constable was required to make 'an alley of two storeys between the King's Chamber and the Queen's Chamber'.[41] The best idea of what these pentices were like can still be experienced in the medieval Rows of Chester.[42] At Chepstow Castle, the pentice had three storeys and was up to 12m high. It extended from the rear of the main gatehouse, across the face of the chambers and kitchen, to cover the door into the cross passage and the blocked doorway into the earl's chamber (Fig. 127). The pentice would have been carried on tall wooden posts and the roof ridge beam would have sat in the line of hooked corbels below the battlements. There is a pattern of quarter-round corbels and sockets across the remainder of the wall face, which must have supported a staircase up to the first and second floor chambers and a platform running across the main kitchen window somehow leading to the earl's chamber.

What the pentice achieved was to allow the principal servants of the household, probably the chamberlain, steward, chaplain and constable to gain access to their earl's chamber from their chambers alongside the kitchen and in the gatehouse undercover and without passing through any other rooms. Whilst this was an ingenious idea, the pentice must have severely compromised the architectural unity of this range of buildings. Master Ralph had used a consistent style of windows throughout, capped by battlements with arrowloops, running level across the whole elevation. It would have been interesting to have heard his reaction when Robert Stake, the master carpenter, started to erect his elaborate timber lean-to across the front of the building.

## Conclusion

The 'Gloriette' at Chepstow Castle demonstrates Roger Bigod's passion for new building. With his master mason, Ralph Gogun, he seems to have swept away any earlier buildings within the Lower Bailey. They then took the opportunities and the challenges presented by a sloping, uneven cliffside location to construct a brilliantly-planned, highly-integrated set of apartments for the earl. This is more than a traditional hall, chamber and service rooms. What survives of its decoration shows that it was exquisitely detailed. However much more exotic decoration must have been lost from this group of buildings, for the earl's chamber at its centre to have earned the title 'Gloriette'.

Roger Bigod was earl Marshal of England. Though by his time the title involved fulfilling a mixture of ceremonial and legal responsibilities, its origins were as the 'marshal of the royal household'. He would have been responsible for policing the area around the king—the verge—and disciplining the household. Roger Bigod fulfilled his duties through a deputy, an example being Fulk de Vaux one of his closest companion knights. Nevertheless, who was better placed than the earl of Norfolk to bring order to his own household, to provide working spaces with a clear division of labour and create patterns of circulation which policed the area immediately around his own person.[43]

If work began on the hall of the castle in the late 1270s, then it was started after the first of Edward I's Welsh Wars (1276–7). With this victory, Roger Bigod was encouraged to invest heavily in the highest quality domestic accommodation, rather than to elaborate the defences of the Marshal's castle in a relatively safe corner of Wales. A similar pattern can be seen in other

Marcher castles. At Caerphilly Castle, Gilbert de Clare, earl of Gloucester began to build one of the most elaborately-defended castles ever seen in the late 1260s and early 1270s.[44] Initially he built a great hall block against the inner south curtain wall. This consisted of the great hall, with a chamber and chapel over a buttery and pantry at the end away from the dais. Other accommodation was provided separately in the gatehouses and towers. The kitchen must have stood isolated, somewhere in the inner ward. Later in the 1270s —no building accounts survive for Caerphilly— a large chamber block was added to the west end of the hall behind the dais. This had a latrine tower projecting outside the inner curtain wall. It also involved vaulting the original wallwalks along the south and part of the west inner curtain walls which allowed the occupants of the south-east and south-west towers, and the inner West Gatehouse to have private, covered access to the earl and countess' chambers. This is reminiscent of the pattern of circulation produced by the Great Pentice at Chepstow. In addition a D-shaped tower and Watergate were built outside the inner curtain wall containing an elaborate brewhouse, kitchen, larder and other service rooms for the earl's use. Finally, as part of third work, a large new kitchen was added alongside the D-shaped tower to provide for the rest of the household.

Gilbert de Clare may have been consciously competing with Roger Bigod to maintain his higher status. He was only one of two magnates richer and with a larger household than the earl Marshal.[45] However at Caerphilly the domestic accommodation developed incrementally. Similar patterns of development can be seen at Kidwelly Castle, Carmarthenshire[46] and Ludlow Castle, Shropshire,[47] for example. Perhaps the only rival to the work at Chepstow Castle was the redevelopment of Goodrich Castle, Herefordshire by the de Valences, earls and countesses of

*Fig. 127 The courtyard elevation of the 'Gloriette' with the porch to the left and large kitchen window at its centre. The Great Pentice contained the service passage doorway and blocked door to the earl's chamber above and ran to the back of the Main Gatehouse*

Pembroke.[48] Respecting the Norman keep, the accommodation was built around a square courtyard, with covered walkways, and wrapped in a series of towers with spur buttresses. William de Valence (d.1296) was well known to Roger Bigod, as they had both connections by marriage to the Marshal heiress, been involved in some disputes over property and were co-leaders of the force which suppressed the rebellion in south Wales in 1294–5.[49] They were men of equal status and wealth. They had also along with Gilbert de Clare received the king on his triumphant tour of Wales in 1284. It is perhaps not surprising that they should try to out do each other with the sophistication and grandeur of their domestic accommodation.

# CHAPTER XV

# The New or Marten's Tower

*by* Rick Turner, Stephen Priestley, Nicola Coldstream *and* Bevis Sale

Marten's Tower has been called 'the mural tower to end all mural towers'.[1] It stands in a very dominating position in the Lower Bailey of the castle, forming the south-eastern corner of the defensive circuit. The historic and modern approach to the castle was from Castle Street along a causeway around what was known as the Castle Pool. Marten's Tower dominated this approach and was the first part of the castle to be seen (Fig. 128), indeed Castle Pool may have acted as a mirror increasing the apparent size of the structure.

The building accounts refer to this building as the New Tower. Its present name comes from Henry Marten, one of those who signed King Charles I's death warrant, who was imprisoned in this tower by King Charles II from 1668 until his death in 1680.[2] However there must have been a tower in this position since the construction of the Lower Bailey defences under William Marshal, presumably similar to the two towers which make up the Main Gatehouse. It may have been called the Red Tower, where minor works were undertaken in 1282/3.[3] The first reference to the New Tower as such is in 1287/8, when a modest advance payment of 15s. for carpentry work was made to Robert Stake.[4] This may provide the date when the preliminary work for building this tower was undertaken. The next set of detailed accounts date to 1291/2, where there are specific references to the collection and laying of freestones, the cutting and raising of joists and the laying of a lead roof on the tower. The total expenditure for works and materials on the 'nova turris' in that year was £43 19s. 8¾d.[5]

Work continued into the following years account — 1292/3 — on the chapel which projects from the tower, north-east over the curtain wall. Payments were made to masons and carpenters, and the main tower had to be re-roofed. The total expenditure in this year was £6 3s. 4½d.[6] The same account includes for daubing and painting both the new hall and new tower, and this scheme of decoration still survives (see below). The final reference occurs in 1299/1300 when further repairs were required to the roof.[7] The accounts imply that the New Tower may have taken up to five years to complete, with the bulk of the work being undertaken in 1290–3. It was therefore started after the Gloriette had been finished, itself probably in readiness for the visit of King Edward I and Queen Eleanor in December 1284. The work on the New Tower was completed before the death of the master mason, Ralph Gogun, in 1293/4,[8] and immediately preceded Roger Bigod's re-modelling of the Great Tower.

## Architectural Description

The main tower is D-shaped in plan, measuring 16m by 12.8m externally with turrets to each side to provide access to the curtain walls. The rear wall is 4.5m thick and the external walls are 3.5m

*Fig. 128 The New or Marten's Tower from the approach to the castle*

thick. It contains five storeys, including a basement and a room at wall-walk level contrived within the roof space. In addition the chapel is carried out over the east curtain wall and is entered from the main staircase at a point between the top two storeys. The tower was built of porcellanized Carboniferous Limestone rubble, from the Tidenham quarry and the dressed stone is a mixture of Oolitic Limestone, from across the Severn Estuary, and Devonian Sandstone from the Tintern quarry.

The tower has a formidable and brooding exterior (Fig. 128). The semi-circular front rises from flaring spur buttresses with the junction between the buttresses and main tower made by skillfully-masoned quoins respecting the planes of both faces. The lower part of the rubble masonry of the tower was refaced in red sandstone by Eric Francis for the Lysaght family, early in the 20th century. In the ground floor, there are three arrowloops symmetrically placed. These have circular oillets. The other circular openings in the slits were a 17th-century adaptation for musketry.

The first floor has two loops with circular terminals placed directly above the apexes of the spur buttresses. There is a third opening on the north-east side of the tower whose original form does not survive as it has been replaced by a two-light Tudor window. On the opposite side there is a blocked window in a similar position.

The second storey has two, single trefoil-headed windows, which are not symmetrically placed. At the level of the heads of these windows, the form of the rubble masonry changes markedly, with much smaller pieces of limestone being used. This led Perks and later Knight[9] to suggest that the tower was not completed until after Bigod's death, though the building accounts clearly contradict this. The level of the parapet walkway is marked by a plain, projecting ashlar band with a semi-circular section, which continues onto the projecting turret to the west but not onto the turret containing the chapel. There are three drain holes marked by lion's mask spouts contained within the band.

The parapet has five broad merlons each with an arrowloop with circular terminals and a steeply-stepped and weathered coping with a roll moulding along the top. At the centre of each length of this coping are the torsos of large figures

*Fig. 129  The internal elevation of the New Tower*

looking out from the castle. These are described in more detail below. The crenels between the merlons have plain rectangular loops.

The projecting turret on the north-east side rises from ground level and is neatly quoined where it stands separate from the earlier curtain wall. It is not quite rectangular in plan. There is an arrowloop in the small room leading onto the wall-walk and a trefoil-headed light with a hood mould into the chapel. The crenellations rise higher than those around the main tower, where they were finished with the same coping detail. The exit onto the curtain wall is concealed behind a wall raised above the level of the curtain wall parapet. It is corbelled out from the curtain wall and has the same coping detail as elsewhere.

The projecting turret on the opposite side is much shallower and rises directly from what is a rebuilt stretch of curtain wall. It was designed to form a defendable access onto the adjacent curtain wall protected by a portcullis that was raised at the level of the wall-walk. There are small lights in the angle with the main tower and overlooking the wall-walk. The turret is finished with a solid parapet wall rising to the same height and with the same coping detail as that above the chapel.

The internal elevation of the tower is on a similarly monumental scale as the exterior (Fig. 129). The main face rises four storeys with the parapet walls at the corners raised to the level of the turrets which are set back from the main face. Present ground level is perhaps 0.6–0.9m higher than the 13th-century level, so the path ramps down towards the main doorway. This is centrally placed to the main face and has plain jambs and a low-pitched, hollow-chamfered, two-centred arch of five orders. The windows to the first and second floors have been changed in the Tudor period, though their internal reveals show that these were a modification of the late 13th-century originals. Above the second-floor window, the revealing arch of the 13th-century window survives. Its size implies that it contained a two-light, mullioned and transomed window, probably of the type used in the domestic range opposite. To the left hand side are two, tall arrowloops

with circular terminals lighting the staircase, and a smaller similar loop on the right-hand side lights the small room leading onto the curtain wall.

The semi-circular projecting band marks the level of the parapet walkway and the smaller rubble masonry appears at that level. The parapet has two broad merlons with central loops and a simpler weathered coping detail than elsewhere. However, the corners of the building are raised 2m higher and have the full coping detail to match the tops of the turrets to either side.

On the inside of the parapet walkway, the inner wall continued upwards to form a low triangular gable whose apex rose to the height of the coping of the raised corners. It contained a single lancet window. This gable stood until the late 19th century and is shown on prints and early photographs. This shows that the tower had a half-hipped roof of low pitch, originally covered in lead.

The turret on the right-hand side continues the features of the main face and there is a carved corbel spout at the junction in the form of a male head. The base of this turret and its relationship to the earlier curtain wall is obscured by later masonry.

The turret on the left-hand side is raised off the earlier curtain wall. It does not have the plain band at parapet walkway level, but it does repeat the parapet detail. There is a trefoil-headed, single-light window to the room leading onto the curtain wall-walk. This has a double-hollow chamfered and rebated moulding. Above is a lancet window to the chapel with a hood mould and head corbels. A coped buttress has been formed projecting from the wall corner at the level of the curtain wall-walk. The large north-east window of the chapel has lost its tracery, but its size suggests that it was of three lights. Only the hood mould survives externally.

As part of the building of the New Tower, the curtain wall running eastwards to the Main Gatehouse was raised by about 2.5m with a new crenellated wall added to both inner and outer wall faces using the same arrowloop design as in the parapets of the New Tower. It must have also involved raising the stair tower within the Main Gatehouse and some modifications to the parapet walkway. The curtain wall running west from the New Tower has a very complex history. The portion against the tower is a modern reconstruction following a collapse recorded about 1873/4. Clark implies that the collapsed curtain walling was contemporary with the New Tower and had 'a visually high parapet and rear wall'.[10]

The tower was entered through the main doorway from the courtyard. Immediately in front of the main doorcase is a portcullis slot, the portcullis being lifted originally into the window reveal above, a feature blocked during the Tudor remodelling. The chamfered doorcase has a Tudor door surviving, with the original being secured by a drawbar in the socket to the right (Fig. 130). The passage continues through the thickness of the wall, with a doorcase to the left with a drawbar securing the rear of the door

*Fig. 130 The main entrance into the New Tower*

leading to the base of the spiral staircase. Immediately in front is another chamfered doorcase leading into the ground-floor room, which was again secured to the rear with a drawbar.

The ground-floor room provides a very elegantly designed and symmetrical space (Fig. 131). The room is raised over a D-shaped basement, with a pitched cobble floor. There are three sockets in the left-hand side wall, suggesting the position of a wooden staircase down into this basement. A massive wooden floor would have rested on the stone ledges formed by the wall tops of the basement. This floor seems to have been taken into the inner half of the reveals of the arrowloops. These three loops do not provide a comprehensive field of fire around the exterior of the tower and along the curtain wall, as typified by the earlier South-West Tower in the Upper Barbican of the castle, suggesting that this floor was as much an exercise in geometry as defence.

The spiral staircase of 1.2m radius provides access to all the upper floors and wall-walks. It is lit by three arrowloops. Entry into the first-floor room is via a half landing, set at 45° to the main wall face. This accommodated the door, which opened into the landing rather than the room beyond. The first-floor room is D-shaped in plan, measuring 9.9m by 6.7m and 5.1m high with the north-east corner cut off by the entrance. The floor is paved above the entrance lobby beneath and the remainder had a wooden floor supported on the stone ledges formed by the inner walls of the ground-floor room. As a result the wall thickness is reduced to 3m at this level. There were originally five window openings to this first-floor room. Of these only the two arrowsloops over the apexes of the buttress beneath survive as built. These have low arched heads with plastered, pitched stone vaults beyond. Just beyond half way through the wall a substantial stone fills the narrowing reveals and this drops away, to allow for downward fire through the loop. The windows on the side walls may have been of the same form, but the one which remains open now has a two-light Tudor window replacing the loop. There is a blocked window on the opposite wall above the main fireplace. All these loops were unglazed and may have been closed by push-fit, wooden shutters. The reveal of the courtyard window is a small step up from the main floor level. The lower blocks of Tintern sandstone of the inner arch are original, and are chamfered with a bar stop. However, the remainder of the opening has been remodelled in Oolitic Limestone in the Tudor period to form a reveal with a ribbed vault, containing a four-light, wooden, mullioned and transomed window.

The first-floor room contains two fireplaces (Fig. 132). The original is the larger with its massive stone lintel and jambs with two tiers of a trefoil-headed, hollow-chamfered detail. The smaller fireplace belongs to the Tudor remodelling. In the north-east corner of the room a latrine is contrived within the thickness of the wall with a slit-window which would have overlooked the courtyard but is now hidden by the inner curtain wall. Quite extensive areas of original plaster

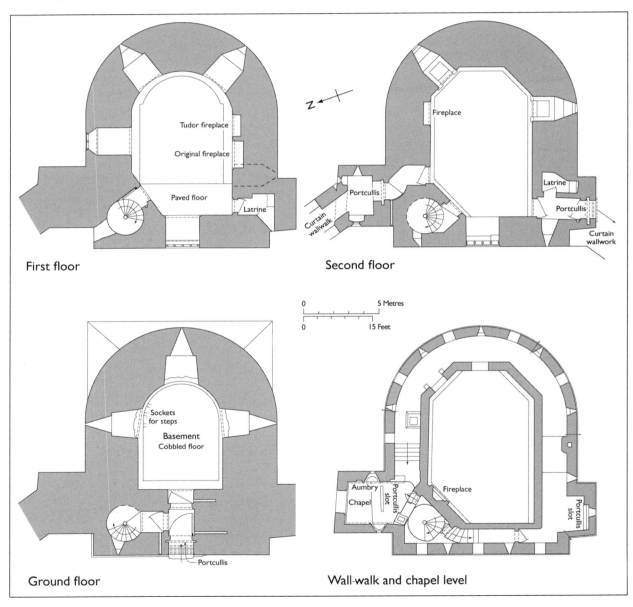

*Fig. 131 Plans of the New Tower*

156

remain in this first-floor room, with sufficient traces of the painted decoration surviving to allow a scheme to be reconstructed (see below). The wooden ceiling was carried upon a continuous quarter-round and filleted stone corbel table, which runs around the whole room, except on the courtyard wall. The flat ceiling and its supporting beams would have offered another surface for ornamentation.

The staircase continues to rise to the second-floor room (Fig. 133), which was also entered off a landing laid out to receive the door opening into the staircase. The room is rectangular with a semi-hexagonal end and one angle lost to the staircase. It measures 10.5m by 6.8m, and was 5.4m high. There was a wooden floor measuring 0.3m thick including the depth of the ceiling beams beneath.

The room was lit by three windows, of which two looking out from the tower are intact. The reveals contain window seats whose chamfered sills turn around onto the wall-face. The rear arches are chamfered and have the bar and ball stop typical of the doorcases all around Bigod's building. The trefoil-headed light is rebated to receive a shutter and glazed panel. The courtyard window is similar to that in the room below in that the lower blocks of the rear arch are original though the remainder of the opening has been remodelled in the Tudor period to form a four-light, stone mullioned and transomed window in a rib-vaulted reveal. A fireplace with a monolithic lintel and chamfered jambs is in the east wall. There are doors leading into passageways through the thickness of each side wall and so onto the curtain wall-walks. In front of the doorway opening out onto the east curtain wall is a portcullis slot, with the portcullis being lifted up into the chapel above. Beyond the portcullis is a small rectangular chamber, 2.7m by 1.5m, which had a wooden ceiling. This has a small window in each wall and then opens through an archway directly onto the curtain

*Fig. 132 The first-floor room in the New Tower*

157

wall-walk. The archway is partly concealed by flanking walls projecting on either side. The other passageway leads from the north-west corner with a door at either end. A single light illuminated the passage, but the intra-mural latrine appears to have been unlit. The outer doorway is protected by another portcullis, this time operated from a room contrived over the parapet walkway.

As with the first-floor chamber, the wooden ceiling was carried on a continuous corbel table running down the long and canted sides of the room. Again there are extensive areas of original plaster surviving and on these are sufficient traces of the painted decoration to suggest a reconstruction of the original scheme (see below).

From the staircase between the second floor and the parapet walkway a small landing with an additional step up led into the chapel in the turret which stands over the curtain wall. The room has a trapezoidal plan and measures up to 4.5m by 2.6m, and stands 4m high. The floor is partly formed above a stone vault including a portcullis slot and was partly in timber. The chapel is dominated by a window which looks north-eastwards and must have stood above the altar. Only the hollow-chamfered outer order survives, decorated by a pattern of richly-carved and undercut flower motifs with a narrow projecting moulding outside. The inner orders have fallen away, though traces show on a view of 1815 by Buckler.[11]

Near the east window is a small aumbry with a finely-moulded, trefoil-headed surround, used for storing the holy vessels. On each side wall, there is a trefoil-headed window. Within the window reveal is a semi-circular backed window seat, sufficient for one person. Standing above the back wall of the chapel is a square chimney. This served a small Tudor fireplace in the back wall, described by Parker[12] as 'perfect'. The roof of the chapel was supported by a continuous corbel table down each side wall, and the low pitch is

*Fig. 133 The second-floor room in the New Tower*

marked by a stone seating for the rafters over the gable window.

The spiral staircase rises a few steps further up from the chapel level onto a tiny landing and through the present doorway up towards the wall-walk. This doorway is very narrow at 0.65m wide and the door opens across the treads of the staircase, which continues four steps higher. This leads across the courtyard face of the tower and through another narrow doorway into a flat-roofed area over the portcullis above the entrance onto the south curtain wall, closed by a wall against the chimney. This was a dead end in the 13th century. The spiral staircase must have risen into a stone-vaulted vice with a door opening onto the wall-top between the chapel and main tower and from there down a broad flight of five steps onto the main wall-walk which looks out from the castle.

The walls on the inside of the wall-walk are now about 0.8m high. Their tops are ragged and they probably rose perhaps to 1.2m or more and then carried the roof timbers of the half-hipped roof. The roof would have projected over these inner walls so that rainwater fell onto the wall-walk where it was channelled through the three drain holes and out of the lion's mask spouts. This created a substantial room in the roof space of the same plan as that on the floor below. It should not be considered as a low attic, for the height of the ridge beam in the roof was probably 4.5m above floor level. There are two possible doorways in the semi-hexagonal wall faces, though neither is rebated for a door, implying the use of wooden doorcases. The floor of this room was formed by the wooden ceiling of the room beneath. A single lancet window is recorded in the gable wall and the other windows must have been dormers in the roof. A fireplace was constructed within the wall against the staircase.

The wall-walk on the east side has the plinth of the chimney of the second-floor fireplace. Old prints of Marten's Tower, when it was still roofed in the early 19th century, show a tall, square chimney with a cap rising above the level of the parapet walls.

*Fig. 134 Carved head spout in the north-west corner of the New Tower*

**Sculptural ornament**

The New Tower has sculptural decoration in the form of hood moulds, waterspouts, parapet figures and a decorated window in the chapel. The east and north windows of the chapel have exterior hood moulds with weathered stops of male and female heads. The male heads have short hair and the females have wimples, but they are otherwise unsurprising and more cannot usefully be said about them. Of the three waterspouts on the string course below the parapet, the two facing out from the tower are weathered lion's masks. The spout on the north-west corner (Fig. 134), facing into the Lower Bailey is a fine, *faux-naif* human head, with a large, round stylised face. It has drilled eyes and nostrils, sculpted eye sockets and strongly-marked, continuous eyebrows. Its forehead is furrowed and its hair *en brosse*.

The inner tracery of the chapel windows is lost, but the inner embrasure of the main east window is decorated with large rosettes in relief (Fig. 135). On each side, corresponding to the base of the hood mould, a carved eagle was substituted for a rosette. Each of the ashlar

*Fig. 135 Details of the rosettes on the east chapel window*

blocks, which form the voussoirs, carries through from the hood mould and has two carved rosettes. Below the level of the hood mould, they are more spaced out with only one rosette to each block. The rosettes differ in detail, suggesting that more than one hand may have been at work, but they essentially consist of two rings of seven or eight petals radiating out from a deep central core.

Such window decoration is unique in surviving architecture from the period, but as in the hall, reference to the precious arts may be relevant. A group of Parisian ivories, dated towards 1300, divides the scenes with bands of roses (simpler than the Chepstow rosettes); it would be reasonable to suggest the former existence of similar ivories.[13] Yet the Chepstow rosettes are far more emphatic and monumental, and an architectural source would be preferable. They seem to be an evolved form of the double diaper that adorns the south wall of the south

transept of Westminster Abbey (1253–9), where square versions are deeply cut around the gallery windows. Closest of all are the circular rosettes in the blind arcades of the dado of the same wall. Some of the bosses of the high vault have double rings of foliage, although it is much more naturalistic, but a capital in the Muniment Room above the west aisle of the same transept combines birds and leaves.[14]

As with the hall windows, parallels for the decoration of the new tower are apparent in the late 13th-century work at Tintern Abbey.[15] The lower west front of the abbey church, probably dating from the early 1280s, has a rosette of exactly the same type as those in the Chepstow chapel window, and the dense, bold nature of the carving on the north-east cloister door, although using different motifs, nevertheless owes much to the spirit (Fig. 136). It is evident that there was a continuous architectural dialogue between Tintern and Chepstow at this date.

*Fig. 136 The north-east cloister door at Tintern Abbey showing a similar spirit of work to that at the New Tower*

*Fig. 137 The five parapet figures on the New Tower.*
*Figure I to V as mentioned in the text are from left to right*

The figure sculpture in the New Tower, however, has no such connections. The eagles in the chapel window embrasure may be a reference to the kingship of Edward I. More simply they may represent Roger Bigod's claim to power. This question of interpretation arises again with the line of five figures adorning the parapet. They are perched on the coping stones, gazing outwards to any approaching visitors, so people on the wall-walk only see their backs. The figures are badly weathered and have been repaired in the past and were conserved in the mid-1990s. The heads of two have been destroyed, and the three remaining are eroded; yet enough survives to show that they are all male figures and each one is differentiated by details including pose, dress and attributes (Fig. 137). All are carved in Oolitic Limestone.

Moving in an anti-clockwise direction, Figure I is headless and the arms have been destroyed above the elbows. He is seated on the coping stone, his legs crossed at the knee and he wears finely-pointed shoes. The remains of his arms show that the right was raised and there is evidence that his left hand rested on his left knee. He wears a short, belted tunic with lively folds, and the cowling at the neck suggests a hood.

The other four figures have a more upright stance; their buttocks and the hems of their robes merge with the coping stone, so their legs and feet are not shown. The pose of Figure II, tilted slightly to the right, is halfway between sitting and standing. His eroded head survives, his right arm, held at his side, is cut off at the elbow; but his left holds a viol against his shoulder. He probably therefore held a bow in his right hand. He has an elegantly slim waist, shown off by the long, belted gown with vertical folds.

Figure III is headless but wears a similar belted gown with long folds, perhaps this time representing a surcoat, since his left arm holds a shield. His right arm is bent upwards against his chest. If it is not due to erosion, the rough texture at the shoulders and the base of the neck could represent a mail coif, and a projection below the shield could be the remains of a scabbard.

Figure IV wears an unbelted gown with a pointed hood on the back. The back of the gown falls in graceful folds down and over the edge of the coping stone. The eroded remains of the head survive. His right arm is bent high across his upper chest touching his collar, and his left hand holds a scroll. The folds of his dress hang down vertically to the rear where a pointed hood falls down the back. A hollow container runs diagonally from the waistband under his right hand.

Figure V looks more youthful, but this may reflect his more alert pose. Enough of his head survives to show that he had short hair curled just below the ears.[16] His gown is tightly belted. He holds his left arm across his chest; his right arm is cut off at the elbow, but the angle suggests he may have been making a gesture.

Figures were placed on the parapets of several secular and ecclesiastical buildings from the late 13th to the mid-14th centuries, and longer on castles, where examples survive from the 15th.[17] The earliest reference to such figures is to work on St Thomas' Tower at the Tower of London in 1276, when painters were paid for colouring the stone images seated over the Great Chamber. These have been interpreted by Jeremy Ashbee as parapet figures. They may have already disappeared in 1313, when works were done to the battlements of St Thomas' Tower, but they were certainly in existence when the New Tower was being built.[18] Apart from the eagles on the Eagle Tower, which are dated 1317, Caernarfon has the remains of carved heads on the parapets of several of the mural towers, including the Queen's, Chamberlain, North-east and the Granary Towers.[19] The indications are, however, that none of these towers were crenellated until after the Welsh Revolt of 1294. In the present state of knowledge, the figures on the New Tower, unless they were an afterthought, chronologically follow the figures in London.

Parapet figures and heads are difficult to identify, but the set at Chepstow offers more clues than most. The five men are distinct and distinctive. They include a musician, a knight and a scholar (or perhaps a lawyer) holding a scroll. They could represent different people or different aspects of one person. These aspects might be aristocratic virtues. Aristocratic boys' education in the late 13th century was formalized and based on a tradition associated with Aristotle.[20] They would learn letters and music, which went with military skill and helped in the formation of character and virtue. They learned to dance and play chess indoors, did military training, archery,

athletics, hunting and hawking outdoors. These attributes fit well with the New Tower figures. Figure II, the viol player, represents music; Figure III, the shield bearer, stands for the military arts; Figure IV, the hooded scroll bearer, for literacy; whilst Figure V could have held a hawk on his wrist, representing the skills of the chase.

Since dancers were often depicted in a lively cross-legged stance, Figure I could represent a dancer, another aristocratic accomplishment. Yet there is an alternative, and more persuasive interpretation of this figure and its cross-legged pose may provide the key to this suite of sculptures. This pose is often identified with David and Solomon, as for example in a psalter in the Fitzwilliam Museum, Cambridge, depicting the Judgement of Solomon.[21] The crossed legs could, therefore, indicate a judicial role, part of Roger Bigod's role as a Marcher lord. Yet the pose is not associated with aristocrats, it is reserved for royalty. If the New Tower was built in anticipation of a visit by the king, the figures could symbolise the virtues not of just an aristrocrat but of a monarch, with Figure I representing the king as a source of justice.

**Painted Decoration**

Extensive, but fragmentary, schemes of painted decoration survive in the main rooms of the first and second floors of the New Tower. The decoration is painted on the primary layer of plaster applied to the rubble stone walls and almost certainly dates to 1292/3, when the accounts refer to the daubing and painting of the new hall and New Tower for the cost of 55s. 2d.[22] The Tudor remodelling of the tower seems to have led to a skim coat of plaster being applied over the original scheme. The tower remained in use until the end of the 17th century, and visitors to the castle record the tower being roofed and floored into the early decades of the 19th century. So these schemes of decoration have only been exposed to the weather for about 170 years. However in that time most of the Tudor shelter coat has become lost, and large areas of the 1290s scheme have fallen away at an increasing rate over recent years. This has led Cadw to undertake the conservation of the plaster work and to re-introduce a roof onto Marten's Tower to ensure the long-term survival of this rare example of aristocratic domestic decoration.

The recording of these paint schemes was undertaken in 2000. As access was limited to the two walkways crossing the inside of the tower, and much of the inspection was carried out with binoculars and the record drawings made of the west and north walls of the two rooms were made from hand measurements. Since that date more of the decorated plaster has fallen away. Nevertheless it has proved possible to recreate the original form of the decoration to a great extent.

The basis of the decoration in both rooms is a pattern of ashlar masonry marked by single lines of red ochre on a pale yellow ochre ground. The course and block sizes vary. In the first-floor room the ashlar pattern is found above a broad dado band with a red ochre line at the top and bottom, infilled with a less intense block of red paint. The height of this band seems to have been chosen to pass above the fireplace and below the now blocked window. Below the red band the plaster is painted a deeper shade of yellow ochre. The dado band and block yellow colour beneath rise to frame the door and probably the window openings. The doorway in the west wall has a line inscribed in the plaster around its chamfered surround. This line is picked out in red ochre and faux voussoirs are created by double-line, red ashlar painting. It was impossible to gain access to either of the original window reveals, so it cannot be certain how the pattern may have been taken into these spaces beyond the red lines in the junctions of the wall planes, visible through binoculars.

The second-floor room shows some variation in the detail. The dado band is thinner and set lower, and evidence for the yellow ochre dado is much more fugitive. The band does rise to frame the doorcase, which has similar voussoir detailing. Small fragments of a red-ochre frieze are visible immediately below the corbel table. This seems to be a running foliage pattern within two horizontal lines. By taking details from one

room and applying them in another a full reconstruction of the decoration on the west and part of the north walls has been attempted (Plate 9).

The use of red-line ashlar decoration on the walls of important medieval buildings must have been widespread, and is a common if normally fragmentary survival in many types of buildings. The style varies in whether there are single or double lines on the horizontal or vertical axes. The ashlar masonry patterning can be the most dominant motif or provide a backdrop for more complex patterns or decorative scenes. It can be found in churches, monastic buildings, castles and houses. The most immediate parallels for the work in the New Tower are at Chepstow Castle itself.

Traces of red, single-line, ashlar decoration survive in the upper room of Marshal's Tower in the Upper Bailey. Best seen in the window reveal looking over the Dell, it also has some additional sunbursts within the small panels. Ashlar line decoration also covered the hall in the Gloriette. What survives is double-lined, marking the rear arch of the main door and traces of the jambs around the service doorways. This type of decoration seems to have been very widespread in high-status buildings; in some cases it provides a framework for simple stencilled ornament, usually five or six-petalled flowers. In the Western Hall, Lamphey Bishop's Palace, Pembrokeshire, the ashlar blockwork is treated as trellis in which the roses are entwined in the window reveals.[23] In other cases, the decoration is overlain by decorative schemes, such as Capel Church in Kent and the more fragmentary scheme in the chapel of Manorbier Castle, Pembrokeshire.[24] So the schemes in the New Tower are relatively plain except for the frieze. Nevertheless they are rare, dated survivors in a domestic context, for many of the better examples, such as in the Leadenhall, Salisbury Cathedral Close have now been lost.[25]

## What was the New Tower for?

There is no doubt that the New Tower added considerably to the formidable appearance of Chepstow Castle as it was approached from the east. The ground-floor was designed to defend the base of the tower and the adjacent curtain walls. However, when compared with the South-West Tower of the Upper Barbican, which occupies the equivalent position when approaching from the west, it lacks the same comprehensive field of fire at each storey of this earlier tower. The South-West Tower had no domestic details or ornate decoration; it was solely for defence.

The New Tower provided a heated, plastered and decorated room at first and second floor, both with a private latrine (Fig. 131). The rooms were well-lit from within the courtyard and at second-floor level. Climbing higher, a small chapel was built over the curtain wall with no room for more than the occupants of the tower and their chaplain. Continuing up the spiral staircase to the top, it opened out onto a broad wall-walk, where the merlons were topped by sculptures displaying lordly or even royal attributes.

Though the tower is linked to the curtain walls to its east and west, these routes, and the main doorway, could be barred by portcullises. However, these were not substantial and were raised in odd locations. The portcullis in front of the main door rose into the main first-floor window reveal. The one closing access from the east curtain wall emerged into the chapel in front of the altar, and that from the west curtain wall into a roofed area at wall-walk level. None of these locations had room for a winch, so the portcullises must have been lifted by hand or using a pulley hanging from the roof. This implies that they were not heavy and that they would normally have been lowered when the tower was occupied.

Roger Bigod had recently completed his Gloriette across the Lower Bailey when he started work on the New Tower. This had provided him with a comprehensive suite of apartments, themselves lavishly decorated, one of which was specifically referred to as the earl's chamber or Gloriette. Associated with these apartments were the full range of service rooms and chambers for the key members of the household, with private access to the earl's chamber via the Great Pentice. This would suggest that the

New Tower was not for the earl's personal use but provided accommodation for important guests.

There were towers being built elsewhere in Wales and the Marches with similar plans and ambition during Edward I's reign. The most prominent of these was the Eagle Tower at Caernarfon Castle. This is the largest of the mural towers, placed in full view for those arriving by sea (Fig. 138), and standing alongside but a little remote from the great hall.[26] It has three storeys

*Fig. 15.11 The Eagle Tower at Caernarfon Castle which has similarities with the New Tower at Chepstow in its plan and use of parapet figures*

over a basement, and an elaborate roofscape with carved heads on the crenels of the main battlements and eagles on the attenuated turrets, which provide for elevated viewpoints. There are large, good-quality chambers at first and second floor, well-lit and with access to private latrines. Given the position, size and architectural emphasis of this tower, Mathieu has suggested that it provided private quarters for Edward I.[27]

This pattern repeats itself in two towers in the Marches. The first, the Great Tower at Clun Castle, Shropshire, was added by the earl of Arundel to his hunting lodge around 1300.[28] It is a three-storey tower over a basement. It has large, well-appointed rooms at first and second floor, entered from the top of the motte. These rooms had large windows overlooking the elaborate water gardens in the valley below.

*Fig 139 The South Tower at Stokesay Castle, a close parallel to the New Tower at Chepstow Castle*

A more exact parallel to the New Tower is the South Tower at Stokesay Castle, Shropshire. This large corner tower was added following the completion of the main domestic range (Fig. 139). The patron was Laurence of Ludlow, the greatest wool merchant of Edward I's reign, who died in 1294 in a shipwreck during an expedition to the Low Countries on behalf of the king, aimed at raising monies for the French wars.[29] In 1291, Laurence received a licence to crenellate[30] and presumably built the South Tower. It stands slightly separate from the domestic range and is the most prominent point on the curtain wall. The ground floor is entered from the courtyard, but access to the two principal rooms involved crossing a flimsy drawbridge from the top of the solar stairs. Each room has windows with shutters and seats, a large fireplace and a private latrine. The intra-mural staircase rises to a battlemented rooftop with an additional battlemented turret, affording fine views over the adjacent countryside.

Similar arrangements were also expressed not in a mural tower but as a gatehouse. Local to Chepstow, this was most spectacularly achieved at the Inner East Gatehouse, Caerphilly Castle, built by Gilbert de Clare, earl of Gloucester in the 1270s. This has very large chambers at first and second floors over the gate passage, each with a private latrine and including a small chapel off one of the spiral staircases (Plate 10). There is an elaborate roofscape with spectacular views. This gatehouse is separated, except for a length of open curtain wallwalk, from the earl's hall, chambers and service rooms, which form the south range, elaborated over three phases in the last quarter of the 13th century.[31]

Edward I built himself a similar gatehouse, or more accurately a water gate, at the Tower of London from 1275.[32] Here the hall, chamber and oratory were all at first floor and linked to the remainder of the Tower by a covered bridge to the Wakefield Tower. The same form of building, but freestanding, is found at Acton Burnell Castle, Shropshire. Given a licence to crenellate in 1284, this compact fortified house was built by Robert Burnell, Edward I's chancellor and bishop of

Bath and Wells.[33] It stands a little distance away from the manorial complex at Acton Burnell, but adjacent to the new church. The extensive and well-lit accommodation was at first floor with latrines in the turrets.

These structures, and others like them, were imposing and expensive. They consistently contained two finely-appointed chambers with access to private latrines, and in some cases to a small chapel. They had elaborated roofscapes and panoramic views, often over water. They stood apart from the main domestic ranges of the castles in which they were built and were added after these ranges were completed. Sometimes this separation was emphasized by barred doors, portcullises or drawbridges. They were built by the king, his great earls or his most trusted servants, made wealthy by his patronage.

The conclusion must be that each of these buildings was intended to act as the king's lodgings should he come and stay. This was true even at his own castles, as with the Eagle Tower, Caernarfon and St Thomas' Tower, Tower of London.[34] Following the second Welsh war, Edward I and Queen Eleanor spent much of 1284 in a celebratory tour of Wales, overseeing the royal works and exacting tribute from their new conquests.[35] Whilst travelling around, he stayed at his new castles and those of his trusted supporters, such as Robert Burnell. He ended the tour with a stay at Chepstow Castle from 17 to 21 December. Edward I was not to return to Wales until 1291 and it was during this gap that the New Tower and some of its equivalents were built. It must have been essential to have been able to offer accommodation of a quality to receive the king, even it never came to be used. This type of building is well known from the late Middle Ages and Tudor period, with examples in the Little Keep, Warkworth Castle, Northumberland, from the late 14th century, the tower at South Wingfield Manor, Derbyshire in the 15th century, the range at Acton Court, Somerset visited by Henry VIII, and the enormous house built by Sir Christopher Hatton at Holdenby, Northamptonshire, which was ignored by Elizabeth I. It was perhaps unimportant that the king never returned to Chepstow Castle and used the New Tower. It was built when Roger Bigod still had the king's trust, and was an appropriate structure for a great Marcher lord to build as a symbol of that trust.

# CHAPTER XVI

# Roger Bigod's Great Tower

*by* Rick Turner, Chris Jones-Jenkins *and* Stephen Priestley

Roger Bigod, fifth earl of Norfolk, had spent up to twenty years in creating a new range of private domestic quarters, with the potentially exotic '*Gloriette*' at its centre, and then a magnificent corner tower—the New Tower—containing a set of fine lodgings with its own private chapel (Fig. 140). At this point the Great Tower had received no attention, and could have only retained a ceremonial function for the focus of the earl's accommodation was now in the Lower Bailey.

The first reference to Roger Bigod's work on the Great Tower appears in the account for September 1292–September 1293 when stones were being split and lime burned.[1] The following year work must have proceeded apace for the account records: 'Expense of the Great Tower. For the whole cost of making the Great Tower as appears in the roll of particulars £91 12s 7½d'.[2] In that year Master Ralph Gogun, the master mason, died, suggesting that though he probably

*Fig. 140  A reconstruction of Roger Bigod's castle at Chepstow*

designed the modifications to the Great Tower he did not see the work completed. The earl was in residence at Chepstow Castle in July and August 1294.

On 30 September 1294, the Welsh rose in revolt, led by Madog ap Llywelyn in the north and Morgan ap Maredudd in the south-east.[3] Roger Bigod and William de Valence, earl of Pembroke, were put in charge of the military response in south Wales. Accounts show that Roger's household contributed 33 knights, 25 esquires, seven clerks and five valets to the army. However Roger's involvement was not without complaint, for on 21 November, at the final council of war at Worcester, the earl protested that his rights as Marshal were being overlooked by the king. Over the next six months, Roger moved between Chepstow and the front-line, eventually surpressing the uprising.[4] As a result work may have had to have been abandoned on the Great Tower during the war and whilst emergency improvements were made to the castle's defences. During that winter palisades and hurdles were made for the castle 'on account of the War'.[5] The countess and her household stayed at the castle in January and February 1295 for safekeeping, at the same time that the Welsh had pinned down Edward I at Conwy Castle.[6]

The receivers' accounts are missing from September 1294 to September 1298. However, the account of 1298–9 contains a long passage which describes the building of four springalds (giant crossbows) by Master Reginald the Engineer (Fig. 141) and the building of a crane to raise them onto the roof of the Great Tower.[7] This account also records that the earl and his household were present at Chepstow from the Sunday after the feast of St Augustine to the Sunday on the eve of St Margaret.[8] Work was completed on the Great Tower in 1299/1300 when the account records it as being roofed in lead.[9]

**Description of the surviving fabric**

*East external elevation* (Figs. 16 and 75)
In this phase, the second floor was extended across the eastern end of the Great Tower, but fabric only survives on the east and north elevations. The Gallery (Fig. 142) was added running along the north side, its entrance on the east elevation, whilst a turret, now standing 6.6m high, was created at the north-east corner of the east elevation by carrying part of the second floor 0.4m forward on an inserted, continuous corbel table with a quarter-round and filleted profile. This form of corbel table occurs throughout Roger Bigod's work in the Lower Bailey.

*Fig. 141 A reconstructed springald at Caerphilly Castle, such as erected at Chepstow in 1298–9*

*Fig. 142 The Gallery added to the north elevation of the Great Tower*

The fragment of wall at the centre of the second floor rises up from the unaltered moulded band to a height of 4.7m. The masonry stops just before the position of a window whose reveal survives on the inside. A fragment of another moulded band above the window head implies that this marks the base of the wall-walk and castellated parapet, which can be seen in profile on the return of the turret wall.

*North external elevation* (Figs, 18 and 78)
The Gallery provided a defended eastern entranceway, and a covered walkway with a crenellated platform on the roof. It also provided a covered area in front of the Norman doorway into the undercroft and a more substantial exit from the Norman doorway at first floor. The Gallery is entered by a double-chamfered, two-centred arched doorway, 2.6m high and 1.4m wide. There is a drawbar socket on the river side. The threshold of this doorway is 0.5m above the present pathway. The top of the east wall is stepped to provide the seating for a lead roof, with a narrow wall walk, and a castellated parapet. Two arrow loops with cross-slits and circular oillets survive, of the same form used above Bigod's domestic range in the Lower Bailey.

The north wall of the Gallery was built directly on the cliff edge and rises irregularly to follow the line of the bedrock. The wall is pierced by seven, regularly-spaced, semi-circular-headed openings now partly blocked. Internally their thresholds are at ground level and they are framed by a single chamfered order with bar stops using Tintern Sandstone. They formed an open arcade set very dangerously above the cliff edge. On Ellis and Frame's plan of 1865 (Fig. 26),[10] there are traces of three cross walls or arches running across the west end of the Gallery, thought by Clark to be parts of an upper gateway, and a recess which may be the base of a spiral staircase leading up to the platform formed by the Gallery roof.

The roof beams of the Gallery show as three square sockets cut into the first three pilasters just above the line of the heads of the undercroft

*Fig. 143 The bovine spout on the north elevation of the Great Tower*

windows. In the first bay of the Great Tower just above the line of the Gallery roof a chamfered rectangular window has been inserted. It is directly in line with the joists and ceiling of the undercroft and was probably intended to act as a fanlight to the undercroft, to compensate for the loss of light when the windows were hidden below the Gallery roof.

A corbel was added to the north-east corner to assist in forming the projecting turret on the east elevation. The angle buttresses and the first pilaster were raised as plain pilasters to articulate the second floor, which was closed by a distinctive horizontal band. This consists of lengths of quarter-round and filleted corbel table alternating with lengths of concave mouldings. Against the first pilaster is a spout carved in the form of a bovine animal head with rounded ears, a broad brow and a wide open circular mouth, broadly similar to the animal waterspouts on Marten's Tower in the Lower Bailey (Fig. 143).

At second-floor level, the junction with the earlier fabric of the Marshal work is not clear. Both openings in the Bigod second-floor level are two-light mullioned windows with Caernarfon or

*Fig. 144  A reconstruction of the exterior of Roger Bigod's Great Tower*

shouldered-arched heads. The stonework is all in ashlar Tintern Sandstone. A small, rectangular, slit window with a chamfered surround lights the intra-mural staircase.

Above the corbel table, running across the top of the second floor, the masonry rises another 2.9m to form a corner turret reached by a flight of steps rising from a wall walk. This turret could have supported a platform no greater than 2.5m square surrounded by narrow parapet walls (Fig. 144).

*East internal elevation* (Fig. 22)
A horizontal band, which runs above the first floor, is of the quarter-round and filleted type typical of the Bigod work. Above this band, all

the masonry belongs to this final phase. The fragmentary reveal of one window survives with a plain jamb rising from the moulded end of a window seat. Stubs of the rear arch of this window survive and consist of two deeply-chamfered orders, both on the inner and outer faces. Nothing of the window dressings survives, but a projection of the rear arch would allow for a two-light mullioned window with Caernarfon-arched heads as seen in the north elevation.

Above the window head the width of the masonry was reduced to form the corner turret with plain quoins and the line of the roof crease passing across it. The outer face has the remains of the reveal for the first arrowloop of the parapet, with a quarter-round and filleted corbel to carry a shouldered rear arch behind the loop. The same detail is apparent on the wall-walk of Marten's Tower.

*North internal elevation* (Fig. 23)
The string course marking the top of the first floor belongs to the Marshal phase, but it is disrupted in two places by later work. Close to the stump of the crossing arch, there are six crudely dressed corbels laid in a line. A little further along a more substantial projection is created by three tiers of quarter-round and filleted corbels. This carries the southern jamb of a shoul-dered doorcase giving access to the intra-mural staircase rising to the wall-walk. The other part of this doorcase is contrived within the reveal of the adjacent window. The staircase is supported by a massive segmental arch, formed by two courses of Tintern Sandstone blocks, carved with two, large, double ogee mouldings. Given the docu-mented date range of this work (1292–1294), this constitutes a very early and large-scale example of this distinctive profile.[11]

The two window reveals are similar in form except that the one to the left has a low threshold to allow access into the staircase and the one to the right has moulded window seats. The rear arches have a roll and fillet moulding.

Above, most of the second floor contains a corbel table of quarter-round and filleted profile. This was broken through where the feet of the roof trusses passed. The roof was of four bays, each 4m wide, with the trusses springing from corbels set at mid-wall height. There are three moulded corbels whilst in the corner is a finely-carved bearded head (Fig. 145). Details that can be made out include a long face, with hair waving down the neck and curling beside the jaw; bold round eyes with frowning brows; and a short nose and open mouth. The chin seems to jut, but this may be the effect of decaying stone. The style of this head looks forward to the 14th rather than back to the more rounded heads of the 13th century. The position of the corbels indicates that the trusses were either arched-brace cruck or collar trusses.

*Fig. 145 The bearded head corbel in the north-east corner of the Great Tower*

**Reconstruction of Roger Bigod's Great Tower**
The addition of the Gallery provided a covered and defendable walkway along the north side of the Great Tower (Fig. 146). The eastern doorway could be closed with a drawbar and Clark records evidence of a gateway or tower at the western end. The Gallery had the effect either of sealing off the Great Tower from both directions, or of dividing the upper and lower parts of the castle from each other. The function of the open arcade overlooking the cliff top is puzzling. It could have commanded boats passing up and down river, but with no form of closing the arches it would have been extremely dangerous.

At first-floor level, the nearly flat roof of the Gallery provided a potential fighting platform. Access was either from steps down out of the

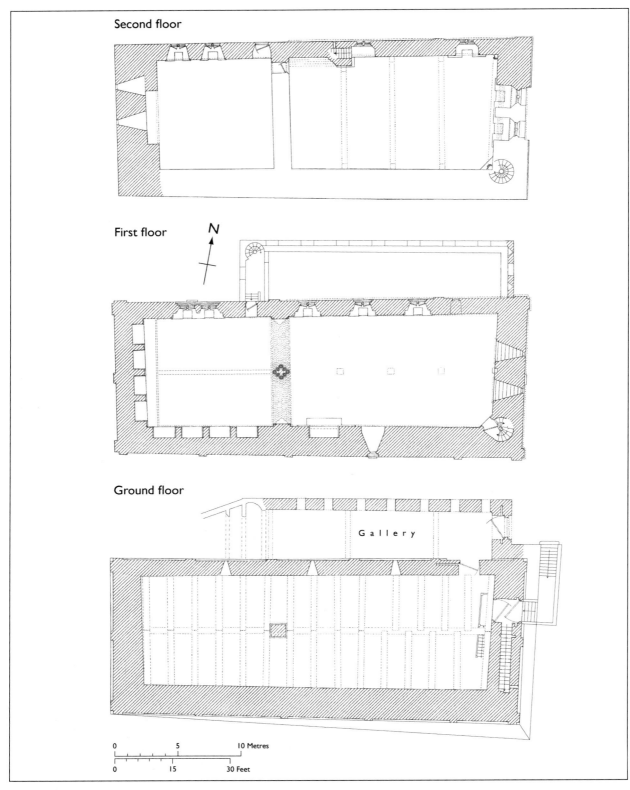

Second floor

First floor

N

Ground floor

Gallery

0        5        10 Metres

0        15        30 Feet

*Fig. 146  A reconstruction of the ground-, first- and second floor plans of Roger Bigod's Great Tower*

Norman doorway at the first floor or via a spiral staircase from below. This phase of work saw the removal of any earlier staircases or staircase towers, which have proved so difficult to reconstruct in the earlier periods. A castellated parapet with arrowloops can be reconstructed around the Gallery.

The principal approach through the great east doorway and up the intra-mural staircase to the first floor must have been reinforced during this phase. The plan of the first floor remained the same as in the Marshal Great Tower yet the imposing height of the eastern room and the appearance of the twin arches was much diminished by the insertion of the new floor. This room is just over 9m wide. Any joists must have required intermediate supports to span those distances and a line of posts running down the centre of the room has been postulated.

The second-floor plan was dominated by the new room created in the eastern half of the building (Fig. 146) to the same plan as that immediately below. Access was via a continuation of the spiral staircase rising from the first floor. Two windows survive in the north elevation and two can be inferred in the east elevation. One of the windows in the north elevation contained access to an intra-mural staircase through a Caernarfon-arched doorway leading up to the wall-walk. This arrangement can be paralleled at Bishop Burnell's contemporary Great Hall at Wells, where a similar staircase to the wall-walk is entered from the reveal of the solar window.[12] Access to the western chamber was now via the former external doorway through the partition wall, removing the need for any staircase to the elevated doorway in the north wall.

An attempt to reconstruct the wall-walk level can only be made in outline. There must have been a vice and doorway at the top of the intra-mural staircase to stop the rain running down the steps. The two corner turrets on the east wall are obvious locations for two of the springalds mentioned in the account of 1298/99, which were craned up onto the Great Tower. Platforms may have been contrived in the north-west and south-west corners to mount the other two springalds

through the reference to 'hauling it [timber] up onto the towers' may suggest other locations in the castle were used. The account refers to joists and planks needed for 'raising, setting up and covering the said engines', implying that they were protected by roofed timber structures with open or demountable sides (Figs. 141 and 145).

**The function of Roger Bigod's Great Tower**
The completion of Roger Bigod's Great Tower sees the building at its most imposing. The eastern elevation with its additional storey, its corner turrets and possibly its springalds in place stood at least 23m high and would have looked very dominating for those crossing Chepstow bridge and walking up to and through the main entrance into the castle. Was this its main function, to impress and re-emphasize Roger Bigod's inheritance from the distinguished men who had been lords of Chepstow in the past and built the earlier phases of this tower?

Because the documentary evidence for this period is so good, the work to the Great Tower can be put at the end of a sequence of building undertaken by Roger Bigod. He first completed an entirely new suite of domestic accommodation for himself, his family and the senior members of his household along the cliff side of the Lower Bailey, which integrated with pre-existing chambers in the gatehouse. He continued by building the New (or Marten's) Tower, which, it has been argued, was designed as lodgings for very high status guests if not the king himself.[13] It can be assumed that the Great Tower retained some of the functions that it had fulfilled in earlier phases. This could include the armoury and other valuables stored in the undercroft, and ceremonial and other major administrative functions of the lordship in the first-floor rooms. However the main eastern room was made less impressive than in the preceding phase, by the insertion of a floor and almost certainly a timber arcade to support it, when the room was added above. Bigod's work had the effect of raising the main room within the Great Tower to the second floor.

The one room missing from the plan of Bigod's castle is a chapel. There was potentially a small oratory above the dais chamber in the lower bailey hall and a small, if finely-decorated, chapel for the occupants of the New Tower. The inventories taken early in Edward II's reign describe a chapel with quite extensive contents.[14] Did this new second-floor room in the Great Tower provide a chapel for the full household and those attending ceremonies in the rooms beneath? It is orientated east to west, and it is at the top of the tallest building on the site. Yet the architectural detail, which survives on the interior is not specific to a chapel and no undue emphasis seems to have been given to the east window.

There are two buildings from the later part of Edward I's reign which provide some parallels to the modified east front of the Great Tower. The first is the D-shaped keep at Helmsley Castle, Yorkshire (Fig. 147). Here the inner face was raised by the addition of two flat but highly ornamented turrets and crenellations as part of a wider remodelling of the interior of the early 13th-century keep by William Lord Ros (1285–1316).[15] The second was another building with both the height and narrow base of the Bigod Great Tower, the similarly named Great Tower at Clun Castle, Shropshire. Munby says the building 'was probably built in about 1300 and was deliberately designed to echo the great Norman keeps of the 12th century'.[16] This tower may have provided some high status lodgings as it has a similar plan to Marten's Tower. Its eastern face is given emphasis by the application of broad plain corner buttresses rising from a flared base.

Marc Morris in chapter XIII has described Roger Bigod's role on the national stage whilst he was extending the Great Tower. His political fortunes were to change quite dramatically. In the 1280s and early 1290s, Roger was one of the main supporters of King Edward I in his Welsh and Scottish campaigns, and he was a frequent witness to royal charters.[17] However in 1293, the king increased the pressure on Roger to pay outstanding debts to the crown, and also began to usurp Bigod's rights as earl Marshal. In 1294, whilst Edward and his leading magnates were preparing for war with France, rebellion flared up across Wales. Bigod and the earl of Pembroke were put in command of the armies in the south of Wales and seemed to be on campaign until the spring of the following year. Despite raids by French pirates, Edward mounted another campaign against Scotland where again Roger Bigod served loyally. However in 1297, the king's ever-increasing demands for taxes to pay for these wars saw the political consensus between Edward, his magnates and the senior clergy break down. Roger Bigod, earl of Norfolk and Humphrey de Bohun, earl of Hereford were to lead the opposition against the king's demands. Civil war between the two factions seemed imminent until William Wallace's successes in

*Fig. 147 The inner face of the remodelled keep at Helmsley Castle, Yorkshire*

Scotland and northern England saw the two sides temporarily unite to put down the rebellion. In 1298, the king wanted to lead another campaign in Scotland but the two earls again led the opposition and these tensions were to continue into 1299.[18] By 1300, royal finances were in such a poor state that the king had to accede to the demands of parliament to have a say in the collection of taxes. Bigod had been successful, but it was to be short lived as his mounting debts to the Crown saw him enter an agreement with the king to surrender his earldom on his death in exchange for an annual payment of £1,000.

The extension of the second floor of the Great Tower pre-dated the rebellion in Wales and so does not seem to be involved with strengthening the castle. The work may have been a continuation of the planned redevelopment of the castle drawn up by Roger Bigod's master mason, Ralph Gogun. It may have been a way of re-asserting Roger's title of earl Marshal by extending the tower of earlier Marshals, at a time that the king had begun to undermine the office. If it was to add a new large chapel, then it presaged the addition of chapels to earlier keeps at castles such as

Oystermouth, near Swansea (Fig. 148), and Beverston in Gloucestershire in the early 14th century.[19]

## Conclusion

Throughout its history, the Great Tower has been the dominating presence at the centre of Chepstow Castle. Its massive walls to the south and west were largely devoid of openings. Crenellations were added to the wall tops in its second and third phases. Finally in 1299, springalds were craned onto the corners of the building. This gave the building a passive military strength. However from William Marshal's time the increasingly elaborate defences of the castle were concentrated on the gatehouses, towers and curtain walls. The Great Tower never provided a satisfactory place to withstand a protracted attack.

At no time during its three phases did the Great Tower provide a complete and comfortable suite of domestic accommodation. If successive lords of Chepstow used it as their great hall, it never provided latrines, easy access for food and drink, or small, well-heated and lit private cham-

*Fig. 148 The early 14th-century chapel added to the second floor of the keep at Oystermouth Castle, near Swansea, is clearly visible as a result of its large Gothic window*

bers in which to retreat. Later accounts suggest that the undercroft of the Great Tower served as the castle's granary and armoury,[20] which may have been its role throughout its history.

Much has been made in this book of the potential ceremonial function of the different phases of the Great Tower. The large size of the first-floor rooms and their elaborate form and decoration would certainly have provided an appropriate setting for courts, the receiving of important guests, or the acceptance of homage and tribute from tenants and vassals. Roger Bigod may have created a chapel large enough to take his whole household. If ceremony was the main function then the Great Tower can only have been used very intermittently, for throughout most of its history Chepstow Castle was visited only briefly by its lords.

The Great Tower must have symbolised the presence and magnificence of the lord of Chepstow. Prominent from the land and river, it grew larger and increasingly elaborate as the rest of the castle grew around it. In the Norman period, the transport of Roman building materials from Caerwent to Chepstow may have been as much symbolic as expedient. The retention of the core of what has been argued as King William's

foundation into the later phases may have indicated a desire by later lords to acknowledge its royal origins.

The upper echelons of medieval society were entranced by the grail romances.[21] In Chrétien de Troyes' *Le Conte du Grael*, the earliest surviving of this group of tales we travel with Perceval.[22]

> In this way he travelled on the nag through wild, desolate forests until he reached flat country with a deep river so broad that no cast from a sling, mangonel or catapult could have reached the other side, and no crossbow could have shot across it.
>
> Above the water on the opposite bank was situated a very skilfully constructed fortress, exceedingly strong and powerful … The castle was so splendidly founded on a cliff that no man alive ever set eyes on so mighty a stronghold; for on a rocky outcrop was set a vast palatial hall built entirely of dark marble.[31]

When we visit Chepstow Castle having passed through the Forest of Dean and see the Great Tower from across the River Wye, are we still seeing the image that the lords of Chepstow were intending to create (Plate 14)?

# CHAPTER XVII

# From Edward II to the Later Middle Ages

*by* Stephen Priestley

The death of Roger Bigod, earl of Norfolk in December 1306 is usually regarded, with some justification, as inaugurating a period of decay and decline both for the castle and the borough of Chepstow. Little structural evidence of building works at the castle has survived for the 14th and 15th centuries, with the possible exception of the masonry at the top of Marten's Tower, which was tentatively assigned by J.C. Perks to the early fourteenth century.[1]

However, while there may be an almost complete lack of architectural evidence for this period, a considerable body of documentary evidence has survived, particularly for the years 1306–12, when the castle and lordship of Striguil were in the hands of the Crown. This includes the detailed *inquisition post mortem* concerning the estates of Roger Bigod,[2] the annual accounts of the receivers of the lordship of Chepstow while it was in royal hands (many of which were enrolled in the Pipe Rolls of the Exchequer),[3] files of letters and inquisitions relating to the activities of the various royal custodians, and numerous royal letters entered on the Chancery Close and Patent Rolls.[4]

Of especial interest is a series of inventories of the contents of the castle. These, taken when a departing custodian delivered custody of the castle to his successor, supply exact details of all the arms, armour, furniture, victuals and other provisions stored in particular buildings. The vestments, books and ornaments of the castle chapel are specified, as are the furnishings of the Earl's Hall, the Gatekeeper's Chamber, and the contents of the kitchen, larder, pantry, bakehouse and other domestic departments. All these documents, taken together, provide a fascinating and remarkably detailed snapshot of the state of Chepstow Castle in the period immediately after the death of Earl Roger, which was by no means an uneventful period in the castle's history.

## Edward II's Reign

After Bigod's death in December 1306, the earldom of Norfolk, including the castle and honour of Chepstow, came into the hands of the king, in whose hands it remained for six years. It would appear that Edward I had made plans, several months before Bigod actually died, to transform the earldom of Norfolk into a royal appanage, to provide an inheritance for either or both of his sons by his second marriage to Margaret of France, namely Thomas of Brotherton and Edmund of Woodstock. On 31 August 1306, Edward made an agreement with his brother-in-law, King Philip IV of France, by which he bound himself to provide a suitably large endowment from the estates of Roger Bigod, amounting to 10,000 marks a year to Thomas, and 7,000 marks annually to Edmund.[5]

However Edward's intentions were not realised until several years after his death.

Between 1306 and 1310, the estates of the earldom were placed in the hands of various royal custodians. During the last two years, Striguil was committed to the custody of Walter of Gloucester, the king's escheator (6 Dec 1306 to 2 June 1307) then Elias Pouger (2 June to 29 Sep 1307) and finally John de Crumbwell (29 Sep 1307 to 24 April 1308). It is likely that these custodians spent little time at the castle; all three were royal servants employed on many other duties for the Crown. Of these three the most interesting is John de Crumbwell, a Lincolnshire knight who subsequently became one of Edward II's leading household officials, being appointed constable of the Tower of London in 1308 and holding the post of steward of the royal household between 1314 and 1316.[6]

The accounts of Walter de Gloucester and Elias Pouger for the lordship of Chepstow (enrolled in the Pipe Rolls) supply no evidence of any building work or repairs to the castle, and no account has survived for John de Crumbwell's keepership. However there is a later reference, in a receivers' account for 1308, to the sale of the branches and loppings of 218 oaks 'felled for timber for carrying out the works of the castle of Striguil by letters patent of the King's father [Edward I]'.[7] In spite of this solitary piece of evidence, there is good reason to believe that the castle (and the town of Chepstow) fell into a state of decay and dilapidation during this period.

In March 1308, the castle and honour were placed in the custody of Edward II's favourite, Hugh le Despenser the younger, who appointed one John de Tany as his deputy to take charge in his absence. The castle appears to have fallen into a state of significant decay prior to 1308, for an inquest taken in 1311 regarding the condition of the castle when John de Tany took charge noted that 'it was in a poor state, all the lodgings within and without were ruinous and uncovered, so that none of them could be inhabited because of the falling rain'.[8]

In his pioneering article written in 1947 on the architectural history of Chepstow Castle, Perks suggested that the lack of roofing over the lodg-ings of the castle might be an indication that Bigod's work in the lower bailey was well advanced, but was not all completed at the time of his death.[9] However, in view of the evidence of the Bigod receivers' accounts (of which Perks was unaware until several years later) clearly showing substantial expenditure on the roofing with lead of the chambers and towers at Chepstow during the 1280s–90s, this suggestion has to be discarded. This leaves the question— when exactly were the lodgings of the bailey stripped of their lead roofing, and by whom? It seems unlikely that it would have occurred during Bigod's lifetime; he continued to reside quite frequently at Chepstow, and spent money on its maintenance almost to the end of his life.

More plausibly, the removal of the lead roofing took place after the castle came into the hands of the Crown, probably between December 1306 and March 1308. This is not a unique case, other examples can be quoted of baronial castles in royal custody, which were, for want of a better word, despoiled of building materials, arms and armour, furniture and victuals by an unscrupulous custodian. Indeed, in 1415, an inquest held concerning goods removed from Chepstow Castle, while it was in royal custody (owing to the forfeiture of the estates of Thomas Mowbray, earl of Norfolk), shows that the castle had again been ransacked, goods amounting to £54 having been removed.[10]

Further evidence of decay and disrepair at Chepstow Castle is supplied by an inventory of weapons, furniture and victuals when it was formally delivered by John de Crumbwell to Hugh le Despenser in April 1308. This inventory, originally in the form of an indenture or deed, is enrolled in the accounts of John de Tany (contained in the Pipe Roll for 1310–11).[11] In comparison with an inventory compiled two years later (at the end of the Despenser/Tany keepership), when the castle was abundantly stocked with munitions, furniture and food, it is clear that, by March 1308, the castle had been stripped of many of its arms, furnishings and goods, others being allowed to fall into a state of decay, virtually beyond repair. The chapel vestments are described as decrepit; three of the springalds which had been provided for the defence of the castle only ten years earlier were broken and stored in the great tower; most of the arms and armour in the castle (including 10 old broken crossbows) are described as being old and decrepit.

The three enrolled accounts of John de Tany for 1308–10 show that he instituted a programme of repairs to the castle costing some £356 8s. 6d.[12] Unfortunately, there is little detailed knowledge of the repairs actually carried out, owing to the lack of surviving particulars of account, but the inquest of 1311 asserts that de Tany 'much amended the castle', suggesting that the repairs must have been extensive.[13] De Tany's first account for the period from 24 March to 29 September 1308 shows that 189 oaks were felled between May and August 1308 for the work on the castle, plus another 40 oaks felled out of season, because of the haste of the work. His second account, for 1308–9 mentions the felling of 114 oaks for building works, while the third and final account, for 1309–10, refers to another 227 oaks felled for work on the castle.

Unfortunately the enrolled accounts do not specify how and where all these oaks were used in the repairs. However, it seems likely that they would have been used in making new beams, joists and rafters for repairing the roofs and floors of the various lodgings. A later description of repairs in 1311 mentions the completion of a new stable, which may also have been begun by John de Tany. The fact that no reference is made to the purchase of lead for repairs to the roofs may imply that some of the roofs were covered with tile instead of lead. The accounts certainly refer to tiles being manufactured at the Barton manor, adjoining the castle, during de Tany's keepership.

In addition to carrying out wholesale repairs, de Tany also fully re-provisioned the castle with arms, armour, furniture and victuals. In 1308, 34s. was spent on the purchase of four crossbows, 1500 quarrels, rope and canvas and other items for its defence, while in 1309–10, the sum of 36s.

$11^3/_4$d was paid for one quarter of salt, 80 salted morrice (fish), a barrel for storing bread and two tankards. An inventory of stores in the castle taken on 8 September 1310, when custody of the castle was delivered by John de Tany to his successor, reveals the extent to which the castle had been refurbished and re-provisioned during the previous two years.

In the Earl's Hall, there were now four tables instead of three, while the kitchen had been completely refurbished with a new oven, three lamps, 24 dishes, 20 platters and 24 salt-cellars. The cellar, where wine, ale and drinking vessels were stored, was supplied with three barrels, four tankards and eight goblets. Two of the castle springalds appear to have been either repaired or replaced with a petrary (stone throwing engine) and a springald with three ropes and brass fittings. Large numbers of new quarrels (bolts) fledged with brass and iron were provided for the springalds. Nine new crossbows were supplied, along with 2,400 quarrels with iron heads.

During this year, the castle served as a prison for a Scottish knight, Sir John de Lyndesay, who was captured during the Scottish wars and held as a hostage at Chepstow from 1307 to 14 November 1308, when it appears he was released from imprisonment. He was evidently a prisoner of some importance, receiving a daily stipend of 4d. for his expenses while at Chepstow.

In October 1310, Edward II finally assigned the estates of Roger Bigod to his half brothers, Thomas and Edmund. They seemed to have had a junior household in which the offices were held by boys of their own age. On 6 December 1311, at Striguil Castle, they witnessed a boy bishop and his 'accomplices' hold the religious offices and sing a canticle in the chapel.[14] As they were not yet of full age, Edward placed the estates in the custody of various royal officials. The castle and honour of Striguil were granted to Sir Robert Darcy, another absentee constable, to hold in the name of Thomas and Edmund, presumably till they came of age. Darcy, like a previous custodian John de Cromwell, hailed from Lincolnshire (Great Sturton), and had risen to become one of

Edward II's most trusted household knights, as had his father, Norman Darcy, during the reign of Edward I. He entrusted the castle and honour to his lieutenant, John de Pateshull, while he was away campaigning with the king against the Scots.

The period of Darcy's constableship is very well documented. Although there are no enrolled accounts in the Pipe Rolls as before (the reason for which will be explained shortly), a very interesting file of documents has survived relating to the repair, garrisoning and provisioning of Chepstow Castle during the years 1310–12, as well as two account rolls of John de Pateshull, described as Robert Darcy's lieutenant, for the month of September 1310 and for the year 1311–12.[15] The second account is usually identified as dating from 1312–13, but this must be an error, as Darcy formally handed over custody of the lordship of Chepstow to the attorney of the Duke of Norfolk in February 1313.

These documents show that John de Pateshull carried out further repairs to the castle, spending 108s 5¼d on repairing various lodgings and mending the drawbridge towards the Barton. This may well have been motivated by the need to provide suitable accommodation for Edmund of Woodstock and Thomas of Brotherton, who resided there on several occasions between 1310–12. Chepstow Castle was also provided with a very substantial garrison during this period, with as many as 20 knights and 60 foot soldiers (who are listed by name) residing in the castle from 12 July–23 August 1311, and supplies and equipment were speedily dispatched by the king (carried by two royal carters from London to Chepstow) in October 1311, for the making of a springald. This strengthening of the garrison and the castle defences may well be connected with the political crisis caused by Edward II's favourite, Piers Gaveston, earl of Cornwall, which eventually came to a head with Gaveston's murder in 1312. It is worth noticing that similarly hasty measures were taken by the king to strengthen the defences of nearby St. Briavels Castle at around the same time.

In about January 1313, a rather startling incident occurred at Chepstow, when John de Pateshull absconded with goods from the castle estimated to value no less than £1,000.[16] Moreover, he is said to have gathered together a band of local tenants (many of whom are listed as members of the castle garrison during the stay of Thomas and Edmund), by gifts of robes and money, with the intention of conspiring against Thomas, who was granted the earldom of Norfolk, including Chepstow, in December 1312 (though he did not take full possession of the castle and honour of Striguil until 13 February 1313).[17]

Why would Pateshull (who otherwise appears to have been a complete nonentity) have attempted to stage an apparent insurrection against the king's half-brother? This is very puzzling indeed. One can only speculate, but it seems improbable that John de Pateshull could have been acting on his own, possibly he was acting with the tacit support of one or more neighbouring Marcher lords, who saw the grant of Striguil to Thomas de Brotherton, still only thirteen years of age, as an opportunity to make encroachments upon the lordship of Chepstow.

All that is known is that Pateshull fled, first to Llanfihangel, within the Marcher estates of Humphrey de Bohun, earl of Hereford, and then to Gilbert de Clare's lordship of Usk, evidently taking advantage of the special status of the Marcher lordships (which were immune from royal jurisdiction) to seek sanctuary from the sheriff of Gloucester and other royal officials ordered by the king to apprehend him. Indeed, Pateshull may well have escaped justice entirely, since a person of the same name received letters of protection from the king in February 1316, for going with Humphrey de Bohun to Wales on the king's service (presumably at the time of the Llywelyn Bren revolt in Glamorgan).

A comparison of the 1310 inventory with another list of stores at Chepstow Castle taken on 13 February 1313, when custody of the castle was handed over by Sir Robert Darcy to the attorney of Thomas de Brotherton, shows that several items were missing from the chapel, including a silver chalice and a psalter. The kitchen seems to have been emptied of most of its contents; the 3 lamps, 24 dishes, 20 platters and 24 salt cellars mentioned in the 1310 survey had disappeared three years later, while four of the nine crossbows listed in the earlier inventory had also disappeared.

The subsequent history of the castle and honour of Striguil is extremely sketchy and poorly documented. J.C. Perks commented that 'there is no evidence that Thomas de Brotherton regarded the castle and lordship as anything more than a source of revenue'. Certainly, it is true that no receivers' accounts have survived for the period of de Brotherton's lordship. However, the evidence of the Pipe Roll accounts and a number of household accounts shows that Thomas resided frequently in the castle during the years 1310–12. Moreover, it should not be assumed, in the absence of documentary evidence, that the castle was neglected by Earl Thomas. The fact that Thomas complained to King Edward III in 1331 about the holding of a royal inquiry concerning the raising of weirs on the River Wye within the lordship of Striguil, claiming it was an infringement of his rights as a Marcher lord, suggests that he was not entirely unconcerned with the affairs of Chepstow.

The next significant event in Chepstow's history occurs on 17 August 1323, when Thomas de Brotherton granted the castle and honour to Hugh le Despenser the younger for the term of his life.[18] Chepstow was only one of a group of important lordships in south Wales and the Marches acquired by the avaricious, unscrupulous Despenser (memorably described by a contemporary chronicler as 'homo cupidissimus'),[19] who appears to have been intent on creating a semi-autonomous principality in the Welsh March, building upon the lordship of Glamorgan which he had acquired by right of his wife on the partition of the estates of Gilbert de Clare, earl of Gloucester in 1317.

Already, his aggressive territorial acquisitions in south Wales and the March had provoked most of the Marcher lords (with the apparent exception of Thomas of Brotherton) to rise up in revolt during 1320–21, laying waste to many of Despenser's castles in Glamorgan and elsewhere. However, although the baronial opposition briefly scored a victory, forcing Edward II to banish Despenser, the success was short lived.

Edward II decisively defeated the rebellious barons, led by Thomas of Lancaster and Humphrey de Bohun, at Boroughbridge on 16 March 1322, and shortly afterwards Despenser regained possession of his vast estates in south Wales and the March, which he continued to enlarge, building up an empire in south Wales stretching from Milford Haven and Cilgerran in the west, to Chepstow and Abergavenny in the east.

Despenser was in a position of seemingly unassailable power, and it may well be that, with the king's backing, he cajoled Thomas de Brotherton into giving him the lordship of Chepstow in return for the somewhat small annual sum of £200. It is not unlikely that Brotherton entered into this transaction with some reluctance, and it could have influenced his subsequent support for Mortimer and Edward's queen's, Isabella, revolt against the king (and the Despensers) in 1326.

Unlike at Caerphilly Castle, where the younger Despenser carried out substantial works, there is no evidence of building activity at Chepstow during his tenure of the castle. However, it is unlikely that Despenser would have allowed such a strategically important fortress to fall into disrepair. In early 1326, as the threat of a French-backed invasion by Queen Isabella and Roger Mortimer grew ever larger, it appears that Despenser, with the assent of the king (perhaps at his own initiative), took measures to replenish his Welsh castles, Chepstow included, with arms, victuals and other provisions. The account book of the King's Chamber (the revenues of which Despenser virtually controlled as King's Chamberlain) for 1324–26, contain a payment of 20s. to John de Thyngdon, king's clerk, for going from

*Fig. 149  Roger Mortimer greeting Isabella, wife of Edward II, in front of Hereford in 1326
with the younger Despenser being led off for execution by the gateway into the city after his and
Edward II's capture at Neath*

Kenilworth to Yarmouth after weapons, and carrying them to Striguil in Wales by the king's order.

In October 1326, when faced with defeat by the rebel forces led by Queen Isabella and Roger Mortimer, Edward II, along with the younger Despenser, his chancellor Robert de Baldock, and other members of his household, fled from London to Wales via Gloucester, taking refuge at Chepstow Castle from Thursday 16 to Sunday 19 October. Shortly before his arrival, the king ordered the sheriff of Gloucester to 'purvey hay, oats, beans, beeves and swine for the munition of the castles of Strogoill and Bristol'.[20]

From the size of the provisions sent to Chepstow and Bristol castles, it would initially appear as if Edward was preparing to rally

supporters and make his stand there against the opposition forces. However, neither the Chamber account book, nor an account roll of expenses incurred during Edward's flight from London to Chepstow, supply any evidence suggesting that temporary wooden fortifications were erected at Chepstow in anticipation of a siege (as one would expect).[21]

Instead it would seem that Edward, taken aback at the magnitude of support for Mortimer and Isabella's revolt (including that of Thomas de Brotherton, who defected to the rebel cause almost immediately) and despairing at his own failure to rally supporters among the Marcher lords (not surprising, in view of the hatred generated by Despenser's territorial aggrandisement), fled by boat from Chepstow on 20 October, planning either to go to Ireland or the island fortress of Lundy in the Bristol Channel.[22] Bad weather forced Edward II and his dwindling band of supporters to return to Wales, landing at Cardiff on 25 October. Thereafter, the king went to Caerphilly Castle, where he briefly established his headquarters between late October and early November, before being captured at Llantrisant, near Neath on 11 November (Fig. 149).

Chepstow Castle was left with probably little more than a skeleton garrison, and apparently surrendered to the rebel forces without a fight, unlike other Despenser castles, such as Caerphilly, which held out against the forces of Mortimer and Isabella in a protracted siege which carried on till March 1327, some five months after the king's capture.

## The late Middle Ages
After the fall of Edward II (Fig. 150), Thomas of Brotherton immediately resumed possession of the castle, which he held until his death in 1338. Thomas's widow, Mary, continued to hold the

*Fig. 150 The alabaster head of Edward II on his effigy in Gloucester Cathedral*

earldom in dower until her death in 1362, at which time it devolved to the eldest daughter, Margaret, who died in 1399. It is unlikely that either the Countess Mary or her daughter spent much time at Chepstow.[23] The few receivers' accounts surviving for this period make no reference to works in the castle.[24] The only noteworthy event during this period occurred in 1340, when a number of local landowners, 'assembling a multitude of Welsh and English in the marches', burned the palings of the New Park of Chepstow, hunted therein, carried away deer and killed the parker.[25]

On the death of Margaret, countess of Norfolk in 1399, her grandson Thomas Mowbray, duke of Norfolk, briefly inherited the earldom, but was banished from the realm and died in the same year, his estates passing to his eldest son, also named Thomas. The rising of Owain Glyndwr in the early 1400s once more revived Chepstow's military importance, and in 1403 the duke of Norfolk was ordered to provide the castle with a sizeable garrison of 20 men at arms and 60 archers. However, Chepstow was not besieged by Glyndwr's forces.

In 1405, the estates of the earldom of Norfolk, including Chepstow came into royal hands, after Thomas Mowbray was executed for conspiring against King Henry IV. Chepstow remained in royal custody for eight years. The castle again seems to have fallen into a state of decay and neglect during this period, as shown by the inquest held in 1415 concerning arms and provisions unlawfully taken from the castle, two years after John Mowbray, Thomas's brother, regained the earldom of Norfolk.[26]

The 15th-century history of Chepstow remains shrouded in obscurity. The castle and lordship continued to be held by the earls of Norfolk until 1468, when they granted it to William Herbert, earl of Pembroke in exchange for considerable estates in Norfolk, Suffolk and Lincolnshire amounting to £1,000.[27] William Herbert, a prominent Yorkist supporter and lord of nearby Raglan Castle, had recently acquired a large part of the Usk and Trellech estates (formerly part of the Striguil lordship), which had been granted to him by Edward IV. However, the lord of Raglan did not live long to enjoy the honours bestowed upon him; he was captured at the battle of Edgecote in July 1469 and killed shortly afterwards. Shortly after Herbert's death, the earl of Warwick and George, duke of Clarence, who had defected to the Lancastrian cause, led an army to Chepstow Castle, demanding that the garrison hand over Richard Woodville, Lord Rivers and his son, who had earlier taken refuge there under the protection of the Herberts. According to the contemporary chronicler, Jean Waurin, the garrison capitulated without a struggle, handing over custody of Woodville and Rivers who were executed shortly afterwards.[28]

The lordship of Chepstow was inherited by William Herbert's son, also named William, who was married to Mary Woodville, sister of Elizabeth Woodville, Edward IV's queen. It is highly likely that William would have entertained members of the royal family at the castle, possibly even King Edward himself.

# CHAPTER XVIII

# The Hunting Preserves

*by* Rick Turner *and* Stephen Priestley

Hunting was the most favoured pastime of medieval kings, their great lords and households. It had a number of functions both practical and intangible. The skills of horsemanship and the use of arms were both training and a rehearsal for war. It provided game for the aristocratic table; it allowed for the display in the quality of the horses, hounds and falcons in their finery; it also enabled courtly skills and grace to be displayed as well as providing excitement and diversion.[1]

Whilst there will have been centuries of earlier practices,[2] it was the Normans who established hunting preserves governed by strict laws into England and Wales. The idea had already been developed in continental Europe before its adoption in Normandy.[3] Hunting preserves took the form of forests, chases and parks. Royal forests, such as the New Forest, were large tracts of unenclosed land, not necessarily heavily wooded, where wild game was protected by laws and courts for the king's pleasure. They remained a royal prerogative until the issue of the Forest Charter by Henry III in 1217 which extended the right to create forests to the nobility. The right of chase, granted by the king, involved the transfer of forest law to a lord, so in effect creating a private forest. The park was an area of land enclosed under royal licence in which game could be kept and hunting undertaken under more controlled conditions.

The medieval documentation assembled for Chepstow Castle shows that the lordship of Chepstow had examples of all three of these hunting preserves as part of its appurtenances. These were the Forest of Wentwood, Tidenham Chase, Tidenham Park and the New Park (Fig. 151). Remarkably, these four areas of land still remain largely undeveloped and unenclosed. They retain evidence of the medieval and later structures built to maintain and enjoy them, which can be compared with the rather dry evidence from the medieval accounts.

However to understand how significant hunting was to a medieval magnate and what role it played in his and his household's daily life, extracts from some contemporary descriptions are helpful. There were manuals which describe not only the practicalities of the hunt, but also the customs and manners which surrounded the event. The most famous, *The Master of Game*, was written by Edward, duke of York between 1406–13, which was a translation and adaptation of the French '*Le Livre de Chasse*'.[4] It was not only a practical but also a moral guide. The hunter was a vigorous and active man in tune with nature and the works of God, who was too busy to stray into the seven deadly sins which were believed to be brought on by idleness.

A more specialised form of hunting was falconry which could be enjoyed by both men and women. The best known medieval manual on falconry is the *Boke of St. Albans* written by Dame Juliana Berners in 1486.[5] There is some evidence for falconry from Chepstow.

More vivid are the descriptions of hunting in the medieval romances which so captivated the aristocracy.[6] An early example is Chrétian de Troyes' *Erec and Enide* from the late 12th century. It opens with King Arthur setting out with his knights from his court at Cardigan.

Tomorrow morning we shall all derive great enjoyment from going to hunt the white stag in the forest where adventures abound. It will be a truly marvellous hunt.[7]

Later the Lord Guivret provides Enide with a palfrey, a hunting horse, whose breast cloth was full of gold and emeralds, the saddle covered with a precious purple cloth and the saddle bows made of carved ivory. The lord brought with them 'many tawny and mewed goshawks, many tercels and sparrowhawks, many tracking dogs and greyhounds'.[8]

*Sir Gawain and the Green Knight* is an English romance written for a lordly household in the West Midlands in the late 14th century. Its third episode revolves around Sir Gawain's stay at the castle of Sir Bertilak de Hautdesert over Christmas.[9] The castle is described as being 'surrounded by a park, set about by a palisade of close-set spikes, which enclosed many trees in its circuit of more than two miles'.[10] For three days, Sir Bertilak, his guests and their servants rode out before dawn to a more distant forest, to hunt all day for deer, wild boar and the fox. 'Keepers of hounds went to their hunting stations, huntsmen cast off their leashes; at their splendid sounding there arose a great commotion in the forest'.[11] Each prey exhibits its qualities of speed, bravery and trickery. The beauty of the scene when they ride out is described; 'for the frost clinged to the ground; the sun rose red against the drifting rack, and in full radiance sailed amidst the clouds in the heaven'.[12]

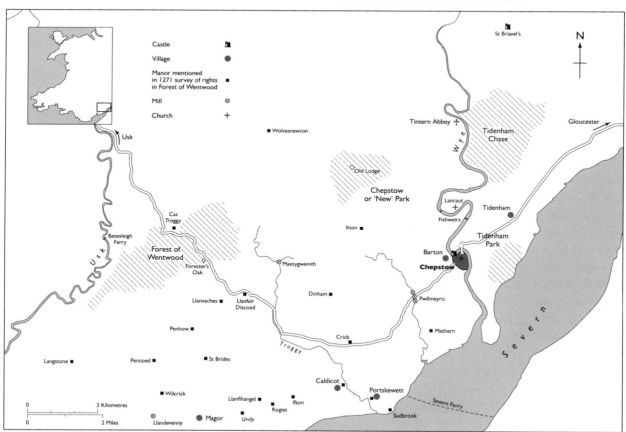

*Fig. 151 Map showing the hunting preserves of Chepstow Castle*

Whilst there is a comprehensive study of hunting preserves in Scotland,[13] no similar work has been carried out in England and Wales. Woolgar has collected the extensive documentary evidence for the earls and countesses of Pembroke at Goodrich, Herefordshire,[14] but the survival of the hunting preserves associated with Chepstow makes the documentary evidence come to life.

The comprehensive set of transcribed accounts relating to Chepstow Castle have frequent references to the forest of Wentwood, the New Park in the manor of the Barton, and the chase and park of Tidenham on the Gloucestershire side of the river. These references occur particularly in the receiver's accounts and the reeve's accounts from the time of Roger Bigod, from which a detailed picture of the management, use and products of these four parcels of land can be built up.

## Forest of Wentwood

This is an extensive tract of rolling hills covering an estimated 11 sq km, east of the lower Usk Valley, some 16kms from Chepstow Castle. It survives today as a series of Forestry Commission and private plantations, but in the Middle Ages it was an area of common land and was quite densely wooded. The tenants of the lord of Chepstow, who held land adjacent to the Wentwood, had various rights in the forest, which included estover, the right to take a reasonable amount of firewood for their own use (Fig. 151). The earl's steward held an inquisition in the Great Tower of the castle in 1271 to establish exactly who held what rights soon after Roger Bigod became lord of Chepstow.[15]

However the main products of the forest, particularly timber and the right to hunt and trap game remained the privilege of the lord. These rights were overseen by the forester, John de Newent for part of Roger Bigod's time, who also oversaw work in the chase and two parks. He was paid 2s. $^{1}/_{2}$d. per week (3$^{1}/_{2}$d. per day) and, in 1283, 20s. per annum for his livery.[16]

The product most frequently recorded was firewood, felled and cut, then delivered to the castle; according to two references, by water. This activity was normally supervised by the Gatekeeper or Janitor of the castle and undertaken by the lord's tenants of the manor of the Barton as part of their labour dues or works. If the quantity demanded was high, cash payments were also made.[17] The castle was always well stocked with firewood in advance of a visit by the earl or countess, and particularly for the four-day visit of Edward I and Eleanor in December 1284.[18]

Only a limited amount of wood from the forest were deemed suitable for building work or even the making of large kitchen tables.[19] However the forest did supply timber for roofing shingles, casks, wagon wheels and axles.[20]

There is no direct reference to hunting, but in 1302/3 seven men worked day and night for seven days in the winter and seven in the summer 'keeping and putting right the nets in the Chase and Wentwood for catching deer'. Also, there is one payment for the carriage of venison from Striguil to Bosham in Sussex in 1290/1.[21] Other products seem more limited. In 1283 wages were paid to Ralph the Miner and his two fellows, and in 1287/8 five gallons of honey from the forest were sold.[22]

## Cas Troggy

Just to the north-west of the Wentwood, in the medieval manor of Plateland, are the ruins of Cas Troggy on the line of the ancient road from Chepstow to Usk and just below the famous summit viewpoint of Pen-y-cae mawr.

The site of Cas Troggy is in a slight hollow within the plateau. From ground level one does not enjoy the magnificent views to the north over the Vale of Usk, though these would probably have been visible from rooms at the top of the towers. There is a natural spring line in the field to the west and the waters from these springs are gathered together in ditches around the west and north of the castle and together form the source of the River Troggy or Nedern Brook as it is known lower down. The castle does not occupy a dominating position, though it is supplied with natural spring water and is close to an ancient routeway through the forest.

This ruined castle is little known and relatively unrecorded, with ancient beech, wild cherry and oak trees growing out of the walls. The interior is partly covered by scrub, and in the summer it is an almost impenetrable thicket of bramble and bracken.

Roger Bigod, fifth earl of Norfolk (1270–1306) acquired the manor on 28 October 1302 when he granted to the abbey of Tintern his manor of Alvington, Gloucestershire in exchange for the manor of 'Platalanda'.[23] Building work must have started almost immediately, for the Chepstow receivers account for 1303–4 records:

> Expense of the New Castle: For the expense of the New Castle per annum as appears in the roll of particulars by weeks £112 4s. 1³/4d. by one tally against Master William the Mason.[24]

As there is no building work known for this date at Chepstow, this reference must be to the building of Cas Troggy. In the same year two barrels of wine were stored in the 'New Castle',[25] the identity of which is confirmed in Roger Bigod's *inquisition post mortem* taken on his death in 1306, which includes the following:

> Toroggy and Plateland. Also they state that there is at Toroggy a certain tower newly built which is worth nothing after its maintenance per annum. And they say that there is at Plateland pertaining to the said tower a messuage with a curtilage and garden which is valued at 2s. per annum ...[26]

On Roger's death, the castle of Troggy and the manor of Plateland with the rest of the earl's land were forfeited to the crown, and there follow a number of references to the two properties in the records from Edward II's reign. The land itself seems to have been rented back to the abbey of Tintern, whilst an account for the period 1308–10[27] records the wages of a man 'keeping the castle of Taroggy and the Plateland', references which continued into 1311. After this the documents are silent, suggesting the castle may in effect have been abandoned soon after it was built.

In 1536–9, the antiquarian John Leland, made a series of long journeys through England and Wales. He wrote:

> There appear at v or vi English miles from Chepstow in a great wood side under a hill very notable ruins of a castel called Trogy, whereby runneth a little broke of the same name. The name of this castle somewhat cometh to the name of Strigulia, but it standeth, as they say there, in Middle Venceland.[28]

In 1587 Thomas Churchyard wrote in his poem *The Worthines of Wales* the following verse about Cas Troggy:

> Upon the side, of woodie hill fayre,
> This castle stands, full sore decayed and broke:
> Yet builded once, in fresh and wholesome ayre,
> Full neere great woods, and many a mightie oke.[29]

The confusion over the name of the castle was continued by William Camden in his *Britannia*,[30] where he takes the Domesday reference to Striguil Castle to refer to Cas Troggy rather than Chepstow. Chepstow Castle is usually referred to as Striguil Castle in documents into the 14th century, but by the early 15th century it is consistently referred to by its modern name. The transfer of the name to Cas Troggy must have occurred after that date.

Later references are very sparse. Ogilvy's road map of 1675, showing the route from London to St. Davids, indicates the ruins of Striguil Castle as a landmark alongside the road as it passes out of the Wentwood.[31] The Badminton Estate Maps. assembled in 1764,[32] show a multi-towered building in ruins in the Manor of Plateland entitled 'The Ruins of Struggle Castle'. Coxe's *Tour of Monmouthshire* of 1801, includes a detailed plan of the site and a tree-covered engraving of the south-east tower.[33] A more detailed engraving of this tower was published in J.S. Prout's *Castles and Abbeys of Monmouthshire*, published in 1838, and there is an undated watercolour painting in the Bagnell-Oakeley's album in Monmouth Museum.

The only other attempt to prepare a description and large-scale plan was undertaken by Octavius Morgan and Thomas Wakeman and published in 1863 (Fig. 152).[34] They faced the same problem as today of trying to piece the evidence together within dense undergrowth and their plan concentrates on the south range. They concluded that the building was of two periods with the south-east tower forming the earlier build, with the hall range and octagonal south-west tower — more of whose plan was visible than today — being later and possibly dating from Edward II's reign rather than Edward I's.

*The Exterior of the South Range*

The ruins of the castle are contained within an area roughly 70m square (*c*.0.5 ha). The most prominent remains are of the south range, where masonry is still standing over 7m high. This overlooks an irregular L-shaped pond fed by the spring water. However there are no earthworks suggesting a moat on the other three sides, nor would the levels allow for any buried moat to have been water filled. Yet the pond would seem to be an original medieval feature, more for ornament than defence.

The south range consists of a long rectangular central block flanked by the bases of two large towers at each end (Fig. 153). In the angle between the towers and the main curtain walls are smaller projections which seem to have contained

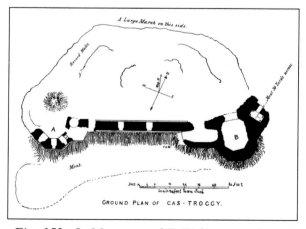

*Fig. 152 O. Morgan and T. Wakeman's plan of Cas Troggy of 1863*

stair towers. The external wall of the central block has a flat 1m-wide berm on the side of the pond. The masonry rises from a slightly offset foundation course to form a tall, battered plinth rising 2.5m high and set back 0.9m at its top. The external facework is made of coursed, roughly-dressed Old Red Sandstone blocks varying in height between 0.14 and 0.2m with occasional, thin, levelling courses. A lot of the blocks still show their diagonal tooling marks.

The main features of the south wall are the two tall window reveals rising above the main body of the masonry, which are picturesquely clasped by ivy. No dressed stonework from the openings survives, but they are not wide and may have had lancet rather than two-light windows. A large beech tree growing from the wall top to the east of the right-hand opening may occupy the position of a third window.

Immediately west of the left-hand window is the toothing of a wall 1.3m wide rising the full height of the surviving masonry. This is part of a small turret, projecting forward from the main wall face. Its external shape is no longer clear but it may have been rectangular like the equivalent projection at the east end of the central block. It cannot have projected more than 2.8m from the main wall face and would almost certainly have needed a battered plinth as it stands high over the pond below. This projection contained a small room, whose rear wall face survives along with the remains of a spiral staircase.

There was a large corner tower at the west end of the south range. Both the plans published in Coxe's and Morgan's books (Fig. 152) show it was octagonal. However, in its present tumble-down and overgrown condition no true sense of its original size or plan can be gained. The interior is dominated by two massive beech trees clasping lumps of masonry. There is a large, still articulated lump of masonry fallen towards the pond. This seems to consist of the top of a window reveal similar to the two that survive. A short length of wall face marks the eastern wall of any first-floor chamber, but no more can be said of the internal arrangements.

A similar, and possibly symmetrical arrangement, survives at the east end of the central range. The main wall has lost its dressed wall face to reveal the sandstone rubble behind. The junction between the rectangular projection and the central block is not visible, but sufficient of the footings of the projection survive to show that they came forward 4.2m from the base of the plinth. It does not stand above the pond and so would have not required the massive foundations of the west end of the range. A large proportion of the external wall face and rubble core have fallen away from this part of the castle and there are no features visible on the external face of this projection or for most of the massive corner tower.

There are only two courses of external, dressed stone facework, measuring c.4m long. This is the only definite evidence that the plan of

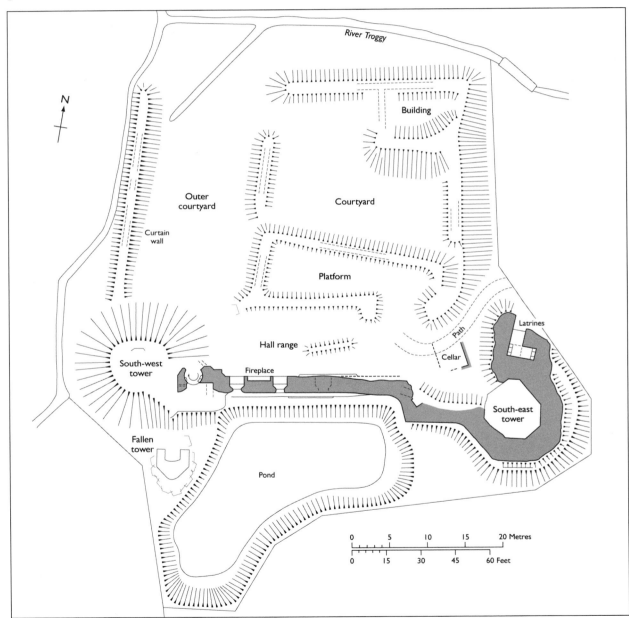

*Fig. 153  A modern plan of Cas Troggy*

190

this tower was polygonal rather than circular as implied by earlier authors (Fig. 154). The ruins of the tower stand 4-5m above the general ground level. The main feature is the huge doorway into the latrine pit, which survives on the north side of the tower. The latrines are in a projection from the main tower and the tall, two-centred arched entrance is flanked by what were probably flared buttresses.

The entrance is 1.8m wide and currently stands 3.6m high. There is no evidence for a door or grating, but lines of three rectangular sockets at the springing point along the passageway probably held the centring needed during the construction of the vaulting. The quoins and voussoirs are simply dressed with external tooling on which traces of render survive. The entrance passage leads into an even higher barrel-vaulted rectangular latrine pit. This is unevenly divided by a lower rubble arch. Emptying through the vaulting on each side of this arch are a pair of slightly-tapering, rectangular-sectioned shafts which all rise to the top of the surviving masonry. These must have served upper chambers, which no longer exist.

### The Interior of the South Range
The internal plan of the south range can only be recovered in parts and the position of the west, north and east walls can only be intimated from the surviving earthworks. The east corner tower retains the plan of its basement, but nothing significant of the internal arrangements of the west corner tower can be traced.

What is clear is that the principal accommodation was at first-floor level and above, with the ground floor consisting of undercrofts, basements and cellars. The central block contained the hall and short lengths of facework on the south side suggest that it was up to 16m long and possibly 9m wide. Its floor was up to 3m above the present ground level. The rubble stonework and projecting footing against the south wall suggests that it was raised above a longitudinal, barrel-vaulted undercroft.

Two window reveals, 1.8m wide, survive in the south wall. These have window seats and the

*Fig. 154  A romantic view of the ruins of Cas Troggy in 1838*

heads are made of dressed slabs of rubble stone. Between the two reveals is a fireplace 2.6m wide and 1.4m deep with a splayed back. Just enough stonework survives to suggest that it was probably hooded. In the south-west corner of the hall the wall face splays, which may indicate the position of a doorway behind the dais leading to the chambers in the tower beyond. Immediately below is a similar splay containing at its base part of an arch near the present ground level, which may have been a doorway from the undercroft. This area to the rear of the dais leads to a spiral staircase mainly contained within the rectangular projection. The staircase is 2.3m in diameter and the ends of five sandstone treads are visible originally rising to the upper storeys. Leading south out of the staircase is an opening into a small, barrel-vaulted room (a latrine?) within the rectangular projection. A drawbar hole in the masonry to the west suggests it could be locked on the inside.

The rectangular projection at the east end of the central block contains the only visible, dressed stonework on site (Fig. 155). This consists of a chamfered, stone door jamb. The angle of the dressed stone and a corresponding block on the inner wall face suggest that this doorway may have been approached along a 1m wide intra-mural passage from the central block. The doorway opened into a small triangular space with a flagged floor which turns to what seems to have been a straight flight of steps leading up to the main first-floor rooms of the south-east corner tower. The floor level of this triangular space is below the floor level of the hall.

What appears to be the basement level of the east corner tower survives. It may have been entered up a ramp of stone as it is today. The plan is an irregular, seven-sided polygon, which can be traced intact except on its south-western side. This room has no windows. The irregularities in plan may have been to accommodate the latrine shafts on the northern side, which can all be seen in the wall top. The upper chambers may have been more symmetrical and contained tall windows as shown in the 19th-century views.

### The Northern Half of the Site

The northern half of the site consists of earthworks in the top of which wall faces can be seen in places. The east side is formed by an earthwork standing over 2m above the external ground level. There is a gap alongside what may be the north-east corner of the south range, but the earthwork continues and returns to the north. A rubble sandstone wall, 1.2m wide is visible in the northern arm. Contained within the flatter, northern part of the side is a rather shapeless mass of masonry, whose west wall is formed by a narrower less prominent earthwork. This runs up to the corner of a triangular platform against the north wall of the south range. This platform was contained by a masonry wall, still visible within part of the earthworks.

Another wall/earthwork forms the western edge of the site. It runs from the base of the outer face of the west corner tower and is truncated by modern ditches at its northern end.

These walled enclosures may have provided the service court for the castle. It would have needed to include a kitchen, stable, storeroom

*Fig. 155 The dressed door jamb and flagged passage at Cas Troggy*

and accommodation for lesser members of the household. It will also have contained the main gateway or gatehouse into the castle, but no obvious location has been identified.

*Conclusions*

Cas Troggy was the last building that Roger Bigod, fifth earl of Norfolk produced on his vast estates across England, Wales and Ireland. He was close to the end of his life, once widowed and childless. In 1302, he had reached an agreement with King Edward I to forfeit his estates to the Crown on his death, to clear his debts and to guarantee an annual income of £1,000 during the rest of his lifetime. However, in that same year he had exchanged with the abbey of Tintern one of his manors in Gloucestershire for the manor of Plateland. This exchange must have been with the express purpose of building Cas Troggy. At this date, the Welsh were not rebellious. Whilst Cas Troggy stands alongside an ancient roadway, its position is not particularly strong and the large windows in the south wall do not make it easy to defend. Cas Troggy is more of a fortified manor house than a castle.

As such Cas Troggy formed one of five castles or fortified manors which ring the Forest of Wentwood (Fig. 151). The others are Llanfair Discoed, Dinham, Penhow and Pencoed Castles. All the owners of these other castles had long-standing rights in the Forest of Wentwood. Even though Roger Bigod held the forest from the king, perhaps he needed to have an adjacent manor to claim full rights. Also given his advancing years, Cas Troggy could have acted as a hunting lodge adjacent to the Wentwood, or even a retreat from his principal castle at Chepstow. The pairing of a large, lordly castle with a smaller castle with more compact living quarters in an architecturally distinctive form can be found elsewhere in south Wales. The relationship of Caerphilly Castle and Castell Coch in Glamorgan, and Usk and Llangibby Castles in Monmouthshire[35] show that the even more powerful Clare family may have established a pattern into which Roger Bigod's work at Cas Troggy can be fitted.

## The later history of the Wentwood

On Roger Bigod's death, the lordship and hence the Wentwood reverted to the Crown. The office of forester was maintained and firewood and blown trees were still taken from the woods.[36] Following the Glyndwr Rebellion, David Smith was hanged at Chepstow for harbouring Madog Comcarsan, Thomas ap Howell ap Llewelyn and other unnamed felons and outlaws in Wentwood Forest in 1414 and supplying them with victuals and weapons.[37] It is only in the 16th century that records of the forest begin to increase and in 1584 the forester was charged with keeping his speech court at the Forester's Seat beneath the great Forester's Oak. The ancient rights held by the owners of the manors around the forest were threatened about 1630, when Henry Somerset, fifth earl of Worcester, was given permission by the king to enclose about a third of the Wentwood.[38] This was to lead to a generation of disputes between the earls and later marquis of Worcester and the manorial tenants over the infringement of their rights. It culminated in 1678, when the marquis felled timber to the value of £60,000.[39] The core of the Wentwood is now maintained by the Forestry Commission and has largely been replanted with coniferous species, parcels of which are being felled as they reach commercial size. The Commission's present plan is to evolve the woodland into a continuous cover forest with a mixture of deciduous and coniferous species of different ages.[40]

## The New or Chepstow Park

This medieval park covering approximately 3,300ha survives intact as the Forestry Commission's Chepstow Park Wood, 6.5km north-west of the castle. It is first referred to in an account of 1283 as the New Park, implying that it has been established earlier in Roger Bigod's lordship.[41]

It was enclosed by a tall fence of wooden palings which ran for about 7.8km. This fence required constant renewal and mending, and payments or labour dues for this work occur annually. The cost of erecting new fencing varied between 6d. and 8d. per perch (4.95m) from summer to winter. This gives an estimated cost of £26 for the initial erection of the park fence with additional sums for any ditching and other works. The park was entered via a gate, which was fitted in 1288/9 and given a new lock in 1299/1300.[42] In the latter year, a hut was built with twigs, daubing, mortared walling and roofing;[43] this sounds too ephemeral to equate to the structure within the circular moat later known as the Old Lodge (see below).

In the 1280s, there were up to three parkers paid 2d. or 1½d. per day who supervised the work. They were overseen by the forester who received an additional 1d. per day for his troubles.[44] Later a single parker and a warrener were employed during Edward II's reign.[45] Roger Bigod's *inquisition post mortem* stated that the park contained deer and that the abbot of Tintern also grazed 60 oxen there.[46] This mixture of wild and large domestic animals is recorded at other medieval parks, such as that maintained by the bishop of St. Davids at Lamphey, Pembrokeshire.[47]

Small quantities of wood were taken or sold from the park rather than the Wentwood and there is a single record of Wrennok King, keeper of the charcoal pit, selling £7 19s. 10½d. of charcoal in 1286/7.[48] Apart from some rushes, the park is not documented as producing other commodities and the considerable cost of establishing and maintaining it was for the pleasure of the earl, his guests and his household.

The park was maintained during the first part of the 14th century, but was probably rendered useless and abandoned after events in 1340, when:

> William de Derneford, Robert his son, Howel Martel and Robert ap Yevore, outlawed for felonies and misdeeds whereof they are suspected in the parts of Strogull and Newport in Wales, assembling a multitude of Welsh and English in the marches of that land and bringing an armed force, entered a park of Mary, late wife of Thomas, earl of Norfolk ..., called 'le Newpark' in Wales, burned the palings of that park, hunted therein, carried away deer and killed the parker, and that they are now vagabond in these parts day and night,

> craftily striving to enter the castle of Strogull and the Town of Chepstow, and perpetuate other crimes ...[49]

The later history of Chepstow Park is similar to that of the Wentwood in that the earls of Worcester tried to exploit its resources and re-enclose the ground. In 1581, a suit was brought over the felling of 20,000 trees in a three to four year period, in woods including what was then known as the Old Park to make five to six tons of iron a week in local furnaces.[50] The park may have been re-enclosed about 1630 when a high, dry-stone boundary wall was constructed on or close to the line of the medieval pale. This wall, of angular, pebbly sandstone blocks, can still be followed today for much of its length, varying from the survival of a foundation 1.2m wide rising in parts to form a wall over 1.5m high tapering in to a thickness of 0.5m. The best-preserved sections are on the south-east and in the north-west corner of Chepstow Park Wood. A keeper of Chepstow Park was included in a 17th-century list of the earl of Worcester's household officers.[51]

**The Old Lodge**

The Old Lodge lies in the northern half of Chepstow Park Wood (NGR ST 490 979). It consists of a circular, moated site with the ruins of a long rectangular stone building on the central platform (Fig. 157). It sits on a gentle slope, just below the highest point in the park at a height of 270m AOD. It is orientated to view to the south-east, towards Chepstow and the castle some 6.5km away. However the densely planted conifers of modern times obscure that view and whether the two sites were truly intervisible is not proven.

There is very little historical evidence for the site. Superficially it resembles a medieval moated site, though these are very rarely circular in form. The Badminton Estate maps of 1764 in the National Library of Wales describe it as 'The Ruins of an Old Lodge', set in a landscape that appears more open than today (Fig. 156). The earthworks are depicted on the various additions of the Ordnance Survey Maps, and are noted by antiquarians and archaeologists. However no large-scale plan or accurate description of the site has been produced until now. It remains little known as it is hidden within the trees even though it is only a few metres north of the main east to west forest road which runs through the present plantation.

The site consists of an outer, nearly circular earthwork bank whose maximum external diameter is 48m. There is a slight, outer counterscarp bank, a flat central berm and steeply sloping sides into the main ditch. The north-western half of the site seems to have been just an earthwork originally. At its maximum, it probably stood c.3m above the base of the ditch. In the south-eastern half, the earthworks are lower. Along various stretches of the inner face, a battered drystone wall shows through the leaf litter, which may have stood up to 1.5m above the base of the ditch. It is built of rough, angular blocks of a pebbly, Old Red Sandstone. The same stone is also used in the central building and in the visible lengths of the park wall. The revetment wall is built in straight lengths giving a polygonal plan to this part of the site. There may have been ten sides originally. The berm above this revetment is flat and feels gravelly when survey

pegs were driven in. This may imply that a pathway ran around this part of the site. The outer bank and revetment walls are disturbed in places where trees have blown over and root balls have been lifted. A more substantial disruption is where a track or drain has been driven from the modern forest road to the south-east side of the ditch breaching the outer bank. This work may relate to the planting alongside the ditch of a number of cypress trees. Where they have recently been felled they have a ring count of 62 years implying that they were planted during the Second World War.

In the south-west part of the ditch is a small, stone-vaulted chamber built over what is probably a natural spring. The chamber measures 2m deep and 1.3m wide (Fig. 157). It has a low, segmental vault and the floor appears to be flagged. Outside the entrance there are two large flags placed over a stone with modern drilled holes. These may cover an original chamber or culvert.

The internal platform measures 30m in diameter. The north–western half rises steeply up to 2.5m above the ditch and has a small counterscarp bank on the interior. The slope on the south-eastern side is lower and more gently shelving though it is badly disrupted by tree throw. Across the middle of the platform are the ruins of a two-phase building. The larger and older— Building 1—is 16.8m long. It consists of three bays, which are sunk into the earthwork platform to form a basement, still visible in the central bay. The south-western room is wider at 7m, and a projection suggests a bay window looking south east. The rubble stonework is well constructed and mortared but no dressed stonework is visible. The end rooms are partly rubble filled and their plans cannot easily be made out. However, the central bay has been re-excavated and a later building— Building 2—created inside. This is nearly 5m square and 2.6m high. It is made of drystone and is partly built over

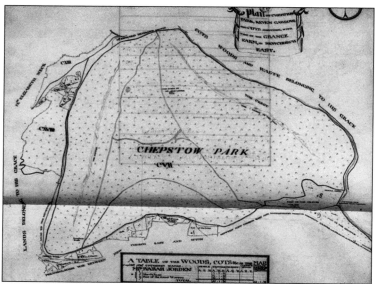

*Fig. 156 Chepstow Park from the Badminton Estate maps, Vol 1, of 1764*

the walls of the earlier building. These show a slight offset internally. There is a simple doorway driven through the walls of Building 1 to form a lobby. The rubble blocking of an internal doorway to the north-east is apparent. The main room is entered through a simple doorway. There is no roofing material, but pieces of a modern iron grate and clay chimney pots suggest that this building is not old. It may be contemporary with the track and cypress trees described earlier and the slight hollow way in the central platform which leads to the main door. If so it could be a Second World War lookout.

The site retains a number of mature Scots pine trees, which were perhaps planted in the 19th century as a decorative clump. Otherwise there is

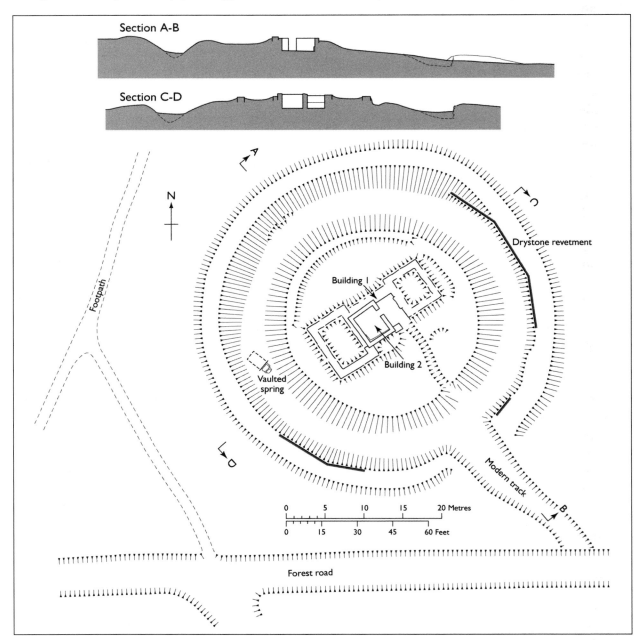

*Fig. 157  Plan of the Old Lodge, Chepstow Park Wood*

a mixture of mature beech and oak trees with an understorey of holly and hazel. Some sycamore saplings are invading the site.

## The Date and Function of the Old Lodge

The site has generally been taken to be a medieval moated site. However, its circular form, its elevated position and its location within a late 13th-century hunting park makes this explanation unlikely. The building accounts refer to a timber and wattle and daub hut being built. However these earthworks represent a much more elaborate and robust site.

Probably by the 15th century the hunting park had fallen out of use and the area reverted to common land. In the 1630s, the earl of Worcester re-enclosed Chepstow Park and a number of other woodlands. The present park wall probably dates from this period, as the medieval park was known to have been enclosed by a wooden pale. Given that the stonework in the park wall is similar in character to the revetment walls and Building 1, then it points to the work being contemporary.

16th- and 17th-century parks and gardens often included geometrical buildings and earthworks. Lodges were described by Randle Holme in 1688 as 'Houses built in Forest Chases and Parks for preservation of the Deere; also for recreation, and to see the game hunted.'[52] Sir Thomas Tresham's late Elizabethan, Triangular and Cross-Shaped lodges in Northamptonshire are well known.[53] The earls of Worcester had developed a geometrical water parterre with pavilions below Raglan Castle in the 16th century, and out in the deer park to the south he had a rectangular complex of buildings identified in Smythe's map of 1652 as the 'Lower Lodge'.[54] So the Old Lodge was probably built when Chepstow Park was re-enclosed in the 1630s, to provide an ornamental building in a moated setting for visitors to the park and orientated to view back to the castle from where they had set out. The hunting of deer remained an important pastime for great nobles in the 17th century, as it had for Roger Bigod in the 13th century. The vaulted spring provided a natural water supply

and may have even been a cold plunge for the hunters to enjoy after a hard day's riding.

Following the sieges of Chepstow and Raglan Castles in the Civil War, the earls of Worcester (later dukes of Beaufort) abandoned both as residences and built Troy House near Monmouth and Badminton House in Gloucestershire as alternatives. Both were to be provided with fine gardens and parks.[55] It is likely that the Old Lodge was abandoned soon after it was built for it to be ruinous in 1764. It was later to be the subject of ornamental planting in the 19th century and re-used. probably during the Second World War, as a look out or informal shooting box.

## Tidenham Chase and Park

Tidenham Chase is an area of open heathland 6km north-east of Chepstow, which is being restored back to its natural state (Fig. 151). Tidenham Park lies over the limestone hill on the east bank of the River Wye and runs down to the Severn Estuary, 2.5km east of Chepstow. References to these two sites are fewer than to the Wentwood and the New Park, but they imply that they were used slightly differently.

The Chase produced heather for bedding animals, probably in the castle stables, rushes for the chamber floors, furze for kindling and some firewood.[56] Withies were also cut to make palisades and hurdles for temporary defences at the castle during the Welsh uprising of 1294/5.[57] There must have been deer in the Chase because of the reference to netting there in 1302/3.[58]

Tidenham Park was first mentioned in 1279/80 and its paling fence seemed easier to maintain, with far fewer payments and labour dues recorded.[59] As well as deer, this park also seems to have provided temporary grazing for the earl's warhorses and draught animals.[60] A limited amount of firewood and structural timber is recorded being taken from the park. A payment of £4 3s. 2d. was made in 1293/4 for the building of a 'santor' or shrine within the park suggesting it may have been a place of retreat as well as hunting.[61] In the following year, a channel was constructed down to the sea, perhaps to facilitate the shipping of timber to the castle.[62]

## Overview

In addition to the site specific records there are one or two references to hunting in the accounts. In 1283/4 the earl's hounds were kept at Striguil for five weeks and bought new collars[63] and in 1291/2 his falcons were being fed for over 12 weeks at the cost of 1d. per day.[64] A year earlier, there is a payment for taking the falcons and hounds to the earl from Striguil to Norfolk.[65] These are only glimpses of what must have been one of the main attractions of coming to Chepstow. Hunting and falconry were options in four different sites, two of which were provided with buildings to rest and and in one case to pray. Up to four members of staff were employed to oversee these appurtenances and though they produced commodities for use in the castle or for sale it seems unlikely that the income they generated in any way met the cost of establishing and maintaining the four sites.

The forest, chase and parks also contributed to the earl's table. There is little direct reference in the Chepstow accounts, but an example of the Christmas feast held at Usk Castle in 1326 by Elizabeth de Burgh can be taken.[66] Here the kitchen supplied 5½ beasts of the chase and two heads and another portion of boar. Poultry included three swans, two herons, two bittens, two egrets, thirteen partridges and woodcock.

A great lord like Roger Bigod, fifth earl of Norfolk could display his great wealth, his hospitality and his courtly manners in several ways. It certainly would have included: the extent and variety of his hunting grounds, the quality of his horses, hounds and falcons and their apparel, and the diversity and elegance of the great feasts to be held in his new hall following the hunt. In this way he was no different to the other great Marcher lords of Wales and the borders. However, it is the survival of the documentary evidence and the almost-undeveloped character of the four hunting preserves, that allows us to visualize this most-loved aspect of a medieval magnate's life.

# CHAPTER XIX

# Chepstow Town, Priory and Port Wall

*by* Ron Shoesmith

*The river Wye flows ... past Hay Castle and Clifford, through the city of Hereford, past the castle of Wilton and Goodrich Castle, also piercing through the forest of Dean with its abundance of iron and venison, and thence to the castle of Striguil, below which it opens into the sea, and here today marks the border separating England and Wales.[1]*

It has already been shown (chapter I) that the early Norman settlement probably grew alongside the road that joined the priory to the castle, but sufficiently far from the latter to preserve its defensive capabilities. Upper Church Street is considered to be the remaining part of this road and the breaks in alignment of the several streets (Middle Street, St. Mary Street and Nelson Street), leading down the peninsular site towards the river bank, at this street line tend to confirm this hypothesis (Fig. 159).

It has also been suggested that the line of Nelson Street and Lower Church Street could reflect the line of a Roman road which may have been used to delimit the boundary of the monastic precinct. Excavations in 1973–4 have certainly shown that the alignment followed by Nelson Street was apparent; that buildings were lined up with it during the earliest phase of monastic activity; and that the priory boundary apparently followed a line parallel to this street at least during the latter part of the monastic use of the site.[2]

One of the most noticeable features of the town plan of Chepstow is the series of roads which run, roughly parallel with one another, from the Town Gate and Port Wall area down the central part of the peninsula towards the river. It is these streets which have led to Chepstow being described as a typical Norman planned town. Certainly, apart from the inner relief road, there has been little change in the street pattern since the latter part of the 17th century. However, the original design of the Norman borough may have suffered substantial changes in the period between the 11th and 17th centuries as a result of late medieval features such as the construction of the Port Wall, the various extensions on the north-west of the castle and the possible changes in the position of the river crossing, either as a ferry or as a bridge.

The earliest part of the castle is the Great Tower. This would have soon been protected by baileys on both the east and west. The main entrance was probably through the easternmost bailey which led directly to the entrance to the Tower. Thus, for perhaps 100 years the entrance to the castle would have been from the inner bailey. Following William Marshal's restoration of the Middle and Lower Baileys in the late 12th century (chapters V and VI), the new entrance was some 60m to the east of the earlier one.[3] This would have left the postulated road from the priory incongruously crossing Castle Dell and arriving at a blank wall. It would seem probable that the remaining traces of any such road would have been totally destroyed as the north side of Castle Dell was scarped to form a more efficient defence for the new extension of the castle.

If Upper Church Street indeed follows the line of one of the earliest roads to be built in Chepstow after the Conquest, then the roads at right angles to this line, Hocker Hill Street, St. Mary Street and Nelson Street to the south-west, and Church Road to the north-east, would have provided a small grid system commensurate with the size of the Domesday borough. Extensions to some of these streets could have led out from the town centre, either along the peninsula or down to a crossing of the river.

There may have been no need for defences for this small settlement during the late 11th and 12th centuries. During this period Hereford, in a similar position on the Welsh border, was apparently undefended until a gravel bank and accompanying ditch were constructed at the end of the 12th century,[4] and at Richards Castle, also a Norman foundation, the town bank was not built until about 1200.[5] It would appear that the earliest post-Conquest defence in many of the Welsh border towns at the end of the 12th century consisted simply of a ditch with an internal bank, probably surmounted with a fence of brushwood and thorn palings.[6]

At Chepstow, the 1973–4 excavations did not produce any evidence for a pre-stone phase of the defences along the line of the present Port Wall. Although a slight bank was observed behind the wall in the 1971 excavation[7] this was not considered to be defensive and may have been simply used for marking out purposes.[8]

Indeed, had there been any necessity for an earlier defensive work, the circuit may well have been on a completely different line to that of the late 13th-century Port Wall, including only the medieval town within its perimeter. Assuming that the earliest part of the town was between the castle and the church, possibly extending into the

relatively safe area towards the river and a little way to the south, any late 12th-century defensive line would have been somewhere between Upper Church Street and the Port Wall. One possible alignment, which is still apparent on the modern plan (Fig. 159) and is also evident on Millerd's map of 1686 (Fig. 3), is the line of Station Road. Continuing this alignment to the north-west across Beaufort Square, leads to the curious re-entrant on the Port Wall at the top of the castle ditch, where there is now a square tower. Traces of a small 'spur' wall or bank continue this alignment further to the north-west across Castle Dell to a point on the western side of the ditch in front of the early 13th-century barbican gate of the castle.

A bank and ditch following the line described above would have provided additional protection for the castle and, on the south-east, could have joined up with the precinct wall of the priory. The priory precinct wall, if it existed at this time, may have provided sufficient defence on the south and east, or alternatively a further defence may have linked the priory precinct with the river to the east of Lower Church Street. The most likely position for a gate in this postulated defensive circuit would appear to be in the Beaufort Square area, although the junction of Nelson Street and Station Road is also a possibility.

The several streets which run from Upper Church Street towards the Town Gate may originally have been an open market area. Gradual infilling, in the areas between Hocker Hill Street and Bank Street on the north-west and St. Mary Street and High Street on the south-east, would have created the present situation. This is very similar to the market infilling which can be seen in Ludlow[9] and has been postulated in Hereford outside the Saxon defensive line.[10]

As has already been suggested, much of the growth of Chepstow during the period immediately after the Norman Conquest would probably have been towards the river and the ferry or bridge crossing. There was certainly a bridge in the early 13th century[11] and one may have existed at a much earlier date or, alternatively, a ferry would have been in use. Certainly development down Bridge Street, and possibly Lower Church Street, leading towards the river bank, must have taken place at an early period in the town's history. All this, however, is conjecture which can only be tested by planned archaeological excavation.

The town had grown substantially by the end of the 13th century and in 1294 was granted the right to hold an annual fair and weekly market. The *Inquisition Post Mortem* of Roger Bigod in 1306 provides much additional information. At that time he held 308$\frac{1}{3}$ burgages in the town which yielded £15 8s. 4d. per annum payable quarterly. In addition there were several 'free' tenants who paid less. This was not all, for the shops in the market place were worth 60s. per year and the *prise* of ale from the whole borough was worth £20 per annum—the lord receiving 'from every tavern of a burgess so often as he brews, 32 gallons of good ale for 4d. from the lord' or various alternatives if some cash was taken in the prise. The market tolls with the customs of those passing through the borough were also worth £20 per annum. The lord even received one good fresh fish from each boat entering the borough! The total value of the borough at that time was calculated to be £61 12d. per annum of which the prior received annually £3 13s. in tithes.[12]

However, all was not well, and when Edward II asked the burgesses to provide one ship for the war against the Scots in 1311, they replied that 'for the last seven years only four ships belonged to the town, and of these three were wrecked ... . They are in such poverty by the death of their liege lord Roger le Bygot Earl Marshall ... Pray the king to have regard to their poverty, until God mends their condition'. The *dorse* (rear) of the letter mentions that the three ships were lost with all hands and goods and the fourth had not returned. The burgesses state that they have been 'so impoverished that they have nothing except the roofs over their heads'.[13]

## The Priory

Following the revival of monastic life in Normandy during the first half of the 11th century,[14] the Norman lords had an obligation to provide funds for their home abbeys by allocating lands in their new territories. Thus, William fitz Osbern set up a dependent cell at Chepstow to his great abbey of Cormeilles. In the first instance this small establishment was probably staffed by two or three French monks whose principal duty was to collect the rents from the lands between the Wye and the Usk that had been granted to Cormeilles before 1071.[15]

However, it would not have been long before the cell acquired conventual status, then having a minimum of 12 monks and a prior in residence.[16] In 1163 it was confirmed to the abbey at Cormeilles by a bull of Pope Alexander III and, about the same time, by a charter granted by Henry II.

As with many Benedictine monasteries, the nave of the priory church was used by the townspeople as their parish church,[17] and the vicar had his own room at the priory, being treated as one of the monks.[18] After the loss of his French territories by King John in 1204, relations between the great French abbeys and their dependent cells became more difficult and the number of monks probably fell, although there was some local recruitment of novices.[19] In 1291 the priory had an estate of 126 hectares and an assessed value of £35 19s. 11d. including both spiritualities and temporalities.[20]

In Roger Bigod's *Inquisition* of 1306 the priory, 'of the foundation of the earl's ancestors', was valued at £20 per annum, the prior having to provide a monk to celebrate divine service in the castle three times a week. During the reign of Edward III (1327–77) the value of Chepstow priory was £45 6s. 8d.[21] and by 1370, the earliest date for which figures of the number of monks are available for Chepstow, there were only four listed including the prior.[22] This was at the time when stringent measures were brought out against 'alien' priories, and in 1387 the Chepstow house was put into the hands of commissioners until the prior paid a fine for custody incurred since the beginning of the war with France.[23] The result was rather inevitable and the house had neither monks nor a prior from 1394 until 1398.[24] The buildings became dilapidated and hospitality and almsgiving ceased, so in 1399 Parliament agreed that Englishmen could be admitted to these alien priories providing they paid the *apport* (the yearly payment due to the abbey of Cormeilles) to the king.[25] Although this resulted in a temporary revival of fortunes, the worsening national relations resulted in a fundamental change, the priory becoming attached to Bermondsey Abbey,[26] a relationship that continued until the priory was suppressed in 1536.

At the time of the dissolution there were three 'religious' in residence and the total value was £32 3s.[27] The property was leased to Morgan Wolfe, excepting the rectory and priory buildings 'which the said Lord King [Henry VIII] will have ordered to be demolished and removed'.[28] Leland, visiting shortly afterwards, noted 'The town now hath but one paroche chirche. The celle of a Blake Monke or two of Bermondsey by London was lately there suppressed'. The demolition apparently took place, for in the early 17th century Camden noted that the greater part of the priory had been demolished with the remainder converted to a parish church.[29]

The parish church is one of the few buildings in Chepstow that can be compared in terms of size and stature with the castle. The Norman church was designed on a large scale with choir, choir aisles, a crossing with transepts and a central tower, and a long nave with both north and south aisles. The choir was demolished at the reformation and the central tower, shown on Millerd's map (Fig. 3), fell down about 1700, to be replaced by one above the Norman west front in 1706. In 1841 the nave aisles were removed and the eastern end, crossing and transepts were rebuilt.[30] The magnificent west doorway, the massive squared piers and the triforium and probably the clerestorey on the south side, still give a vivid impression of the aspirations of the Norman founder and his builders.

But what of the priory buildings and its extensive grounds in Chepstow? The archaeological excavations in 1973–4 provide some of the picture.[31] Although the church was built on a west-east alignment, the earliest buildings (apart from a putative chapter house) were built to the south of the church and were lined up with Nelson Street. They may have been used as accommodation for the builders themselves as well as by the original monks from Cormeilles.

It was during the late 11th and early 12th centuries that there was a period of monastic expansionism in England,[32] and it is likely that the new conventual buildings were built during the first few years of the new century. Oddly, they were not built to align with either the church or Nelson Street, being at an angle between the two. In the first instance a new chapter house and parlour, probably with a dorter above, were built as an eastern range to the cloister with a slype separating them from the south transept. The cellarer's range formed the western side of the cloister, possibly with the prior's lodging on the first floor. The kitchen was apparently a separate building as there was no southern range, just a wall sealing off the cloister.

By the early 13th century the parlour had been demolished and that and the wall replaced by a frater which properly enclosed the cloister on the south. This was presumably the period when there was a full complement of monks.

At this time an indication of the use of the area around the church and cloistral buildings can be suggested. The kitchen was still a separate building with its own well, standing to the south of the cellarer's range, and a large buttressed stone barn, some 10m wide and 22.5m long, was built further to the south-west, presumably to store grain and other produce from the priory holdings.

The excavations only covered a limited area, but there would doubtless have been other buildings. To the west, and probably fronting onto the end of Upper Church Street, would have been the gatehouse, with a boundary wall running south towards the barn. The area immediately to the east of the church would probably have been reserved for monastic burials, other areas around the church being used for burial by the towns-people. Also, and again most probably to the east, would have been the infirmary for the sick and aged monks. Somewhere there was also a dovecot and there were doubtless many other buildings for animals and general storage.

The extent of the priory grounds in Chepstow is uncertain—there would have been kitchen gardens, herb gardens, orchards, probably a vine-yard, and possibly arable and pasture land. Millerd's map suggests that this was probably to the south and east of the conventual buildings and Waters considered that the precinct wall ran up the south-east side of Nelson Street and crossed the School Hill as far as the Port Wall.[33] However, the archaeological evidence seems to indicate that the boundary was to the east of Nelson Street, at the rear of properties facing the street. On the north, the precinct may have only included the present graveyard, with a boundary curving to the south to exclude the river frontage and its associated buildings. Even so, this would have meant that over half the area within the Port Wall was under the control of the priory. However, there must have been some open ground near the priory, for in the summer of 1307 the castle had a garden 'next to the priory' which returned an income of 20s. from 'the sale of fruit and herbage'.[34]

By the 15th century the barn was in ruins, but the frater had been improved by the installation of a fireplace, and a reredorter or latrine block had been added to its eastern end. Was this due to the arrival of monks from Bermondsey who appreci-ated their home comforts? During the final 50 years the frater was apparently again improved with a new fireplace in the northern wall and a dias built for the high table. It may have had a first-floor inserted into what was probably origi-nally an open medieval hall, suggesting more accommodation was needed.

The alterations to the western range were apparently much greater. Although the archaeo-logical evidence is slight, it is suggested that the whole of the early 12th century western range was demolished and that a new range was built slightly further to the west. This new range may have included a cellar, which was later to be used as a bonded wine store. The monastic barn was refurbished, probably as a stable with an open front on the west side.

Although Chepstow Priory was rather poor as compared with other Benedictine houses in South Wales, it had a great influence on the evolving growth of the town, an influence that can still be seen today.

**The Market Place**

Beaufort Square is the remaining open part of the market area of Chepstow which originally stretched from the Town Gate north-eastwards to the line of Upper Church Street. It is on the sides of this square that some of the most important medieval secular buildings in Chepstow must have stood (Fig. 159). On the south-east side, gardens would have stretched behind the build-ings, perhaps as far as Nelson Street (originally Back Lane), as appeared to be the case at the rear of the Beaufort Hotel.[35] On the other side of the Square, gardens could have stretched well back towards The Dell.

An impression of the buildings that once surrounded the Square is provided by Coxe who visited at the end of the 18th century:

> Near the Beaufort Arms are two stone build-ings, which are now used for a barn and coach house; the one has a gothic, and the other a rounded arched doorway; the windows are ancient, and both bear the appearance of having been used as chapels. Opposite to the Beaufort Arms a small vault, under Fydell's long room, probably the crypt of a chapel, deserves to be visited on account of the stone roof, which is vaulted and engroined, and similar to the roofs of the subterraneous cellars in Chepstow castle. Within the memory of some of the inhabitants, part of the wall of the chapel with the east window was standing.

He goes on to mention the chapel of St. Anne, near the bridge, then used as a bark house (for tanning), whilst another chapel adjoined Powis's Almshouse and was dedicated to St. Owen.[36]

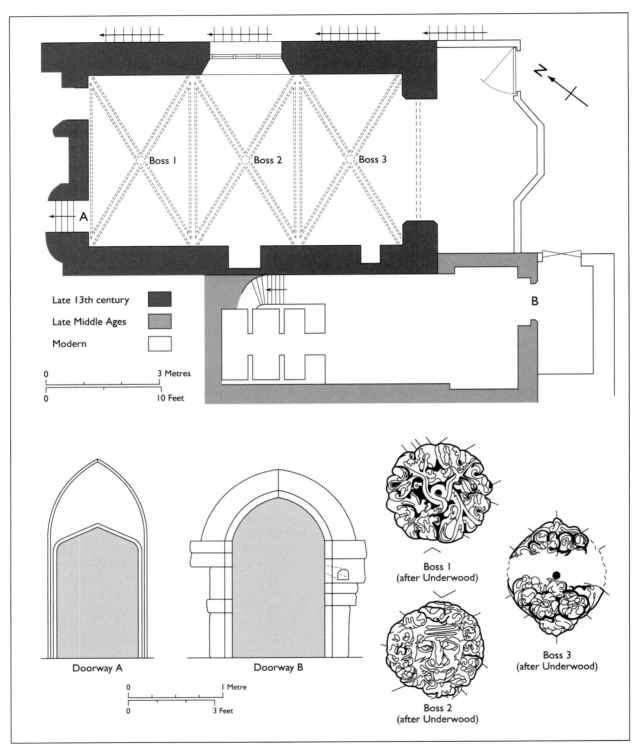

*Fig. 158 Plan and details of the vaulted medieval cellar of Raglan Lodge, Beaufort Square,
and the late medieval cellar of the building to the south-west.
The carved bosses are at the centre of each bay of the vaulting*

Late 13th century

Late Middle Ages

Modern

0     3 Metres

0     10 Feet

Boss 1

Boss 2

Boss 3

A

B

Doorway A

Doorway B

0     1 Metre

0     3 Feet

Boss 1
(after Underwood)

Boss 3
(after Underwood)

Boss 2
(after Underwood)

Of the buildings that Coxe observed, only the vault remains. This is underneath Raglan Lodge, No. 13 Beaufort Square, on the north-west side close to the present war memorial, now the home of the British Legion. Most of the cellar is used for beer storage by the Legion who occupy the upper levels of what is apparently an early 19th-century building.[37] The beer cellar has false walls and an inserted ceiling, making access to the medieval fabric difficult. The front part, which includes an early 19th-century forward extension, is entered at street level and is used as a needlework shop. Stubs of the medieval front wall some 0.9m thick, with part of the rear arch of the medieval opening, still survive.

A plan drawn by Hammond and a contemporary photograph (Chepstow Museum) provide some extra detail. The main body of the cellar, which contains three symmetrical bays of quadripartite vaulting, measures c.9m by 4.4m internally. The ribs, of a fine sandstone, rise from the rubble, carboniferous limestone walls; where they meet, in the centre of each bay, is a flat carved boss.

Boss 1 is decorated by tightly curled vine tendrils, which wrap up over the rubs. Boss 2 has a green man with a heavily furrowed brow and his tounge sticking out of a wide grin. His hair and beard is made of leaves, and he has been identified as Oceanus—the father of all rivers—or Bacchus—the god of wine. More simply,he is more likely to be a pagan symbol of a type often found in medieval buildings. Boss 3 is partly obscured but seems to consist of six five-petalled flowers around a central motif with a ring of leaves turning onto the rib chamfers.

There is a window opening in the central bay of the north-east wall which, although altered, is probably original with a steeply-sloping cill and an undressed rear arch following the shape of the vaulting. A doorway at the rear of the cellar (doorway A), leading to a staircase, may also be original, although again altered.[38]

There is a similar cellar with ribbed vaulting in the lower bailey of Chepstow Castle. Cellars with rib-vaulting and bosses occur widely in buildings of status and are often either associated with the wine trade or used as taverns. They are usually dated from the 13th to the 15th centuries. It has been suggested that, for a building of this quality and date it is likely that Roger Bigod may have been the patron. This could equally apply to the remains of the two other buildings in Beaufort Square described by Coxe over 200 years ago.

One possibility is that the cellar was associated with the Bothall or Boothall, which is mentioned several times in documentary sources and could well have been in this area. Accounts in 1279–80 include 'For making the foundations of the bothall, carrying stone for the partition walls, earth for making mortar, and making mortar and carrying out other tasks ...'.[39] However, the Bothall was apparently not a single building for in 1279–80 the carpentry of the houses in Bothall required minor repairs.[40] Additions also took place, and the receiver's account for 1287–8 mentions a payment to Robert Stake, carpenter, for making new stables in the Bothall by order of the Seneschal.[41]

The account of Walter de Gloucester, who was escheator to Roger Bigod, made after his master's death in 1306, mentions the sum of £1 16s. 9d. 'for the rent of divers shops in the Bothall for the Christmas and Easter terms 1306–7'. A later account for the period up to 29 September 1307 included a rent of 40s. for the shops in the Bothall.

Further details are given in Hugh le Despenser's account during the latter half of 1308 where there is mention of a fixed rent of 61s. 1 1/2d. for 'certain fixed stalls ... in a certain place called the Bothehall'. By 1310 repairs were necessary and John de Patishull, keeper of the castle, spent 27s. 3 1/4d. on repairs to the Bothall 'being near to ruin'.[42]

Waters believed the Bothall stood on the corner next to the Beaufort Arms to be replaced by a later market hall. Its remains may have been the first building described by Coxe.

Waters suggested that the cellar of Raglan Lodge could have been part of the 14th-century Moot Hall—the meeting place of the freemen of the borough. In the latter part of the 17th century it was described as 'The Old Chappell'.[43]

It is perhaps more likely that the cellar was originally part of the House of St. John. The accounts of the beadles of Chepstow have not been examined in detail but those of Nicholas Clecar from 1285–90 contain frequent references to the 'house of St. John' (*domus Sancti Johannis*) where there were three burgage plots, which were 'in the Earl's hand'. [44] However, this

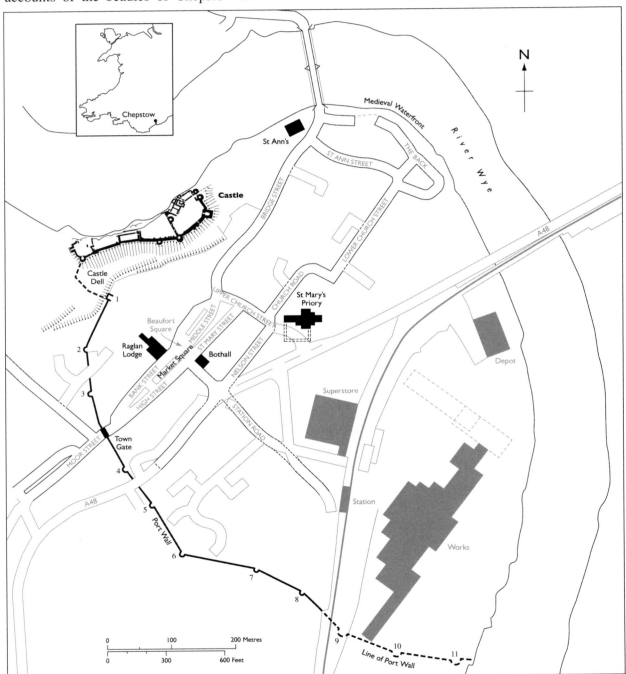

*Fig. 159 Plan of Chepstow showing the original street pattern superimposed on that prevailing today, together with the towers on the Port Wall*

206

description could equally well apply to the other buildings mentioned by Coxe at the end of the 18th century and since lost.

The cellar of Raglan Lodge, with its fine ceiling, was designed to be seen and is thus unlikely to have been a simple store. Its date is somewhat uncertain, but similar cellars occur in various towns such as Chester,[45] London[46] and Hereford.[47] They could be part of merchants' houses, particularly those associated with the wine trade, where prospective purchasers would be invited to sample the wares, perhaps leading to their use as taverns at a later stage in their life.

## The Port of Chepstow and the Wine Trade

The growth of Chepstow in the late 11th and 12th centuries was due to its position, not just as a port, but because of its situation at the mouth of the Wye. By the time of the Domesday survey 'Earl William built the castle of *Striguil* and in his time paid only 40s. from the ships going into the woodland'.[48] Chepstow was not just a growing port, it was also an important source of revenue from vessels arriving from abroad.

Throughout the 12th century and later, one of the chief imports into England was wine from the Aquitaine region of France—at that time an English possession. Wine arriving at Chepstow and other ports were subject to *prisage,* whereby the king took two tuns from each English ship importing more than 20 tuns. It would appear that William Marshal, as a marcher lord, considered his port of Chepstow to be exempt from such dues; doubtless to his own benefit!

In the 13th and 14th centuries trade began to expand, with taxes now levied on such diverse items as wool and hides. However, the Lords of Chepstow were still independently minded, and it would seem that the Collector of Taxes, based in Bristol, had a hard time in collecting the dues from ships arriving at and leaving Chepstow. By the 15th century diversification had continued with dried fish arriving from Iceland and manufactured goods and grain being sent by return. Throughout the period Chepstow flourished as Englishmen used the port to try and evade customs duty.[49]

The authority of the Lords of the Marches was abolished in 1536, about the time when Leland wrote 'to Chepstow may cum great shyppes'.[50] By 1573 there was a Customs House at Chepstow, and gradually the local merchants realised that they had lost their ancient privileges and would, in future, have to pay the same rates of duty as other ports in England and Wales.[51]

## The Port Wall

The wall that defended the medieval town of Chepstow has been called the Port Wall for many years. It encloses the 53 hectare (130 acre) peninsula site on which the town is built. When complete the wall was 1,123m (1,217 yards) long, following the shortest possible route commensurate with the defensive requirements of the town, castle and priory and the local topography (Fig. 159).

Much of the wall still survives, and from the Town Gate at the top of High Street it stretches in a northerly direction past a semicircular tower to a recent breach, which allows access from Welsh Street to the large car park overlooking Castle Dell. It then curves around the car park, past another semi-circular tower, to a square tower on the southern side of Castle Dell, opposite the western end of the castle. The possible courses from this point are discussed later.

To the south of the Town Gate the Port Wall originally continued in a gentle south-easterly curve as far as the river bank (Fig. 160). Five semicircular bastions survive on this stretch, but the wall has been breached several times. The first cut was for the railway in 1846; a second for a minor road to allow access to the school from Hardwick and Bulwark, and finally a larger breach for the inner relief road. On School Hill the wall veers to the east and perches precariously on the southern edge of a quarry that opens from Station Yard. The stretch of Port Wall between the railway and the river together with its three mural towers were demolished in 1916 to make way for the shortlived National Shipyard No. 1.[52]

The Port Wall was apparently planned as a whole and excavation has shown that the mural tower examined at the car park breach, was

*Fig. 160 Looking along the Port Wall and Tower 5, just south of the inner relief road*

bonded into the wall, both wall and tower therefore being built at the same time. The other semicircular towers appear to be of a similar construction to the one examined, so it may be assumed that, with the exception of the square tower near Castle Dell, the whole defensive work is initially of one constructional period. The rectangular tower (no. 1) is some 4.3m wide and 2.25m deep internally.

The wall originally had eleven towers, of which eight survive in various stages of completeness. Apart from the rectangular tower they are all open-backed, half-round, projecting towers and have been described as having an average external diameter of about 8.2m (27ft) standing up to 7.6m (25ft) high. The wall itself is about 2.1m (7ft) thick and stands up to 6.1m (20ft) high with the remains of a wall-walk and crenellations along the top (Fig.161). The wall-walk continued around the inside of each of the semicircular towers.

Some of the towers have been measured internally and show quite large divergences, which may well make them worthy of further detailed study. Tower no. 2 is about 5m wide and 3m deep, whilst the one partially excavated in 1972 (no. 3) was slightly larger being some 5.4m across and 2.6m deep internally. The next tower that could

be measured (no. 4) behind the George Hotel was even larger, being 6.8m wide and 4.1m deep internally. Continuing southwards, the tower on Castle Hill, south of the inner relief road was 4.1m wide and 4.75m deep whilst the tower on the bend in the wall (no. 6) was of smaller dimensions being 4m wide and 4m deep. The ones at the top of the quarry (nos. 7 and 8) are inaccessible and nos. 9–11 have been demolished.

Assuming that the wall and towers were built at the same time, as the 1972 excavations seemed to show, makes the variations in size rather odd. What appeared to be a laying-out stone for the north end of the tower was apparent in the excavation, and one would hypothesise a similar stone at the southern end where the wall should continue. So why the difference in shape and size? The towers, each with their internal wall-walk, may well have been designed so that the defenders could enfilade the adjoining sections of wall. Should there be even the slightest of bends in the wall, then the tower would have had to extend further outwards and would thus have had to be of greater internal diameter. Thus the towers to the north of the gatehouse, where the wall curves along its length, are quite large. However, those to the south of the gate house are even larger and they are on relatively straight stretches of wall, whilst the one on School Hill (no. 6), where the wall takes a bend to the east, is the smallest of those surveyed. No detailed survey has been made of the surviving towers to the south and east of the line of Nelson Street. Could the last of the large towers (no. 6) have been placed at the junction of the town and priory grounds, with the priory being responsible for the smaller ones to the south and east? Only a detailed survey, and possibly excavation, can resolve this enigmatic problem.

The wall was built of rubble limestone and has been patched and partially rebuilt in many places. There is a line of square holes in the upper part of the outer face of the wall and towers. These are probably for the provision of bretasches, or projecting wooden galleries, to improve the defences.[53]

There is no documentary evidence to date the construction of the Port Wall, but it has been suggested, by comparison with the castle masonry, that it was probably built in 1272–78 by Roger Bigod, fifth earl of Norfolk.[54]

The next Lord of Chepstow who appears to have taken an interest in the town's defences was Charles Somerset, first Earl of Worcester, to whom the Lordship of Striguil had descended. He granted a Charter of Incorporation to the burgesses on 2 December 1524 'from the love we have and bear to the town which is fallen into great ruin, indigence and decay'.[55] The Charter provided for the appointment of municipal officers, including bailiffs and sergeants at mace.

Somerset also took an interest in the town's defences. The original Town Gate was probably built at the same time as the wall by Roger Bigod, but the design of the present gate indicates a major rebuilding in the 15th or 16th century (Fig. 162). This was probably the work of Charles Somerset, for he allowed the bailiffs 'to have their prison for the punishment of offences within the great gate, which they have builded by our commandment ...'.[56] It would seem likely that the

*Fig. 161 The inside of the Port Wall, looking towards the remains of the rectangular open-backed square tower perched above the Dell. Notice the remains of the wall-walk*

*Fig. 162 Buckler's drawing of the outside of the Town Gate in 1815*

Port Wall, being then some 250 years old, would have had repairs carried out about the same time.

The Town Gate must have been in a similar state for there is no record of repairs after 1310 when 53s. 3¹/₂d. was spent 'on strengthening a new gate of the Borough in boards, ironwork and in other expenses'.[57]

The 16th-century gate stood the test of time—until very recently the only two entrances into the walled town, apart from small postern gates and by boat, were across the bridge over the Wye or through the single Town Gate. There are two coats of arms on the gate, but they are now too weathered to be recognisable. The battlements, archways and windows are all apparently modern replacements installed within the last hundred years or so, whilst the pedestrian passageway on the southern side was constructed in 1928.

There were two small postern gates in the Port Wall. The one on the north-west of the town, giving access to Castle Dell from the present car park, still survives and could be original, but may

*Fig. 163 The exterior of the small postern gate in the Port Wall near the Dell. Notice the square holes in the stonework into which wooden beams were probably inserted to carry additional timber defences projecting over the wall*

well be a 16th-century insertion (Fig. 163). The second, which led from the area of the same car park into the grounds at the rear of the now demolished Congregational Church, was shown to be a 19th-century insertion into an earlier recess and was removed when the wall was breached at this point.[58]

From the square tower opposite Castle Dell the original course of the wall to the west and north is uncertain. At the time of construction of the Port Wall, the castle had already been extended to the west to include the barbican, and the upper gatehouse was probably built about the same time, replacing a simple arched gateway.[59] There are three possible lines which the Port Wall could have taken from the square tower to ensure an adequate defence and, confusingly, all three possibilities are referred to in historical sources.

John Leland wrote of it in 1536–39:

> The towne of Chepstow hath been strongly waulled as yet welle doth appere. The wa(ulles) began at the ende of the great bridge over Wy, and so cam to the castel, the which yet standeth fayr and strong not far from the ruin of the bridge. A [great] part of cumspace withyn the waulles is no[w con]verted to little medows and ga[rdins].[60]

Leland's comment that the wall started at the Wye Bridge and went from there to the castle was accepted by both Wood[61] and Bradney,[62] although the former was quite dogmatic that the wall did not enclose or touch the castle, but followed the south side of Castle Dell towards the bridge. This alignment is not the one shown on the plan by Millerd in 1686 (Fig. 3). This shows the wall joining the castle defences at the south-western corner close to the barbican tower and is taken to be the second possible line. There is some evidence for such a junction in the masonry of the castle (p.115). Otherwise, there is no trace on the ground, but this alignment has generally been accepted until quite recently.[63]

The third line is the one published by Coxe in 1801 (Fig. 164) and accepted by at least one later writer.[64] This takes the line of the postulated earlier defence and leads north-westwards from the square tower. On the ground there is a slight mound with traces of masonry which crosses Castle Dell at right angles to the existing line of the Port Wall, It leads towards the counterscarp of the rock-cut western ditch of the castle. Here, a bridge or drawbridge led into the upper gatehouse of the barbican. This upper gatehouse was built about the same time as the wall and it would seem most likely that this section of the Port Wall was built to enhance this gatehouse, possibly by making use of the postulated earlier defensive work crossing Castle Dell.

A square shape would have been an unusual design for a 13th-century mural tower, particularly on a straight stretch of wall. Such towers do occur in the late 14th and 15th centuries and later,[65] but in an earlier context it would probably only provide a defensive function when built where the wall turns through an acute angle as in the second and third of the possible courses described above.

It is, however, possible that the Port Wall might originally have been built completely separate from the castle following the south side of Castle Dell. At a later date a second wall could then have been built across the Dell with a square tower joining it to the earlier wall. The stone of the redundant section of the wall, between this tower and the bridge, would then have been available for the new work or other building purposes.

Only selective excavation will resolve the problems outlined above and establish the constructional history of the north-western part of the town defences. It is in this area that there is also the best chance of establishing the presence of an earlier defensive line to that of the Port Wall.

The excavation just outside the Port Wall, adjoining the breach made for the car park entry, produced a reasonable quantity of 12th-century pottery, but in the absence of structures this should not be taken as evidence of settled occupation of this part of the town before the wall was built. However, it would not be unusual for a 13th-century defensive wall to exclude some of the inhabitants. Ample evidence has been accrued to demonstrate that a similar policy was followed

in Hereford, where the late 12th-century bank and ditch defence, reinforced with stone in the 13th century, cut across earlier building and property lines.[66] The two main criteria used were apparently the tactical requirements — to ensure that the wall provided a defensive function, and the cost in terms of the length of wall to be built. Such requirements often led to the exclusion of suburbs,[67] and, in the case of Chepstow, the wall would have had to be very much longer had it

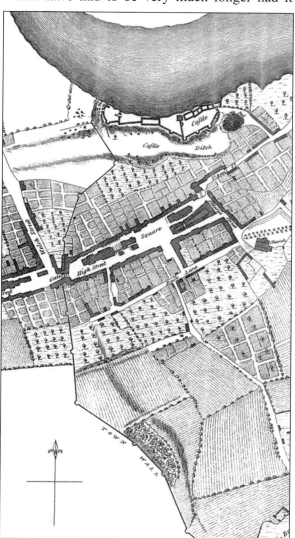

*Fig. 164 An extract from Morrice's plan of Chepstow showing the line of the Port Wall crossing the Dell and running along the north side of the rock cut ditch outside the upper gatehouse (Coxe 1801)*

included even part of Moor Street and Welsh Street, because of the promontory nature of the site. It has been suggested that this latter street could possibly indicate the area occupied by the Welsh after the English borough was founded,[68] extending out towards St. Kynemark's which was possibly a Celtic foundation.[69]

The arrangement of the streets outside the gate suggests that at one time a small extra-mural market occupied the area between St. Thomas Street and Moor Street including Albion Square. The roads leading out of town to the west and south radiated from this market area. A market outside the gate would not be unusual as tolls were collected on merchandise and livestock entering the town. At Chepstow, market tolls continued to be charged until 1874.[70]

Excavations in the Station Road area by the Glamorgan-Gwent Archaeological Trust failed to produce any evidence for occupation in the southern part of the defended area and it would seem that this was always open ground.[71]

**Chepstow Bridge**

The Roman crossing of the Wye has been discussed previously (chapter I). The first direct reference to a bridge at Chepstow is in 1234 when Henry III granted 75 good oaks from the Forest of Dean to repair the bridge, and it would seem likely that there would have been a bridge during the time of William Marshal, if not before. However, repairs were regularly needed and on 22 October 1259 'The constable of the King's castle of St. Briavel's is ordered that in the royal forest of Dean he should let Roger Bigod earl of Norfolk and marshal of England, have 10 good oaks for the bridge of Striguil which is falling down, to be repaired of the King's gift.'[72]

The bridge was associated with a weir which needed repair in 1272.

> For carrying timber from the wood to the weir below the castle 3s. 9d. For the wages of a certain labourer working on the weir for 21 days 5s. 3d at 3d. daily, and for two tides (?) 4d. Also for the wages of another labourer working on the same weir for 17 days 3s. 3d.

> and for two tides 4d. For the wages of a third labourer working on it for three days 9d. and for one tide 2d. Also for two men baulking the weir for four days 2s. Total 16s. 10d.[73]

The bridge is often mentioned in documents such as in Roger Bigod's *Inquisition* of 1306 where there is mention of 'the chantry of the chapel of St. David by the bridge' which was worth nothing beyond the service of the chaplain celebrating there.[74]

In the account of Hugh le Despenser for 29 September 1309 to 7 September 1310, tolls were not collected because 'the bridge ... was damaged by misfortune around Christmas and not rebuilt until 1 August next following'.[74]

By the end of the 14th century, when Richard II passed through Chepstow, the burgesses petitioned that the bridge, on the 'high road passing from England through all South Wales ... is weak and ruinous and on the point of being lost for lack of aid'. They asked the king to allow the collection of tolls for a period of 20 years to pay for the repairs—he granted the request, but only for a period of five years.[75]

The bridge apparently survived into the 16th century, although Leland described it as a ruin, and it seems that a new one was built in 1546. This didn't last long for in an Act of 17 November 1575 'the great bridge of wood called Chepstowe's Bridge ... is of late fallen to great ruin and decay, and is likely daily to fall'. The Act resolved the maintenance problem by stating that 'The County of Gloucester and the County of Monmouth shall stand for ever chargeable for the Maintainance, Repairing and New Making of Chepstow-Bridge'. However, by 1605–6 the bridge 'is of late broken, fallen down and quite carried away ... [and] the said Passage and Highway is utterly taken away'. A new Act provided for a special bridge tax to be charged on the inhabitants of the two adjoining counties. After the Civil War, the bridge continued to be built and maintained in two parts by the respective counties. The present bridge, with stone pillars and cast-iron arches, was opened to traffic in 1816.[76]

# CHAPTER XX

# The Tudor Period

*by* Rick Turner *with contributions by* Dan Miles *and* Stephen Priestley

The lordships of Chepstow and Raglan passed from William Herbert the younger, earl of Huntingdon, to his daughter Elizabeth in 1491. However, the castles of Chepstow and Raglan were held by the earl's younger brother, Sir Walter Herbert (d.1507)[1] and then briefly by his widow Anne, until in 1508 they were acquired through inheritance from Elizabeth (d.1507) by

*Fig. 165  Portarit of Charles Somerset, first earl of Worcester*

her husband, Sir Charles Somerset (*c*.1460–1526) (Fig. 165).[2]

Sir Charles had sailed with Henry Tudor on his return to Britain in 1485 and fought at the Battle of Bosworth Field. As Henry VII, Henry Tudor was to reward Sir Charles in a number of ways. Marriage to the king's ward, Elizabeth in 1492, brought Sir Charles a number of lordships in south Wales to which others were added or given in stewardship. This made him the most powerful man in the region, reflected in his creation as Baron Herbert in 1504. He served the king as an admiral of the fleet and an ambassador to the French court on a number of occasions. He was to remain very influential during the reign of Henry VIII (1509–47), who made him Lord Chamberlain, titular head of the royal household. In 1513, Baron Herbert was one of the commanders of Henry's first military campaign in France for which he was rewarded with the title of earl of Worcester. However, his finest moment came in 1518 when he was put in charge of negotiating the truce between England and France. This culminated in 1520 in the meeting of Henry VIII and François I at the Field of the Cloth of Gold near Guisnes, in the Pas de Calais. This involved the erection of a temporary palace and a host of ancilliary buildings to service the English and French royal courts, who also took part in a great tournament. Worcester had overall responsibility for the construction of what was described as the eighth wonder of the world and stage managing the whole event. When he died in 1526 he was buried in the Beaufort chapel within the royal chapel of St. George at Windsor Castle.[3]

It is almost certain that Sir Charles undertook the remodelling of Chepstow Castle after he acquired the lordship in 1508. In 1524, he had granted a new charter of incorporation to the burgesses of Chepstow 'from the love we have and bear to the town which is fallen into great ruin, indigence and decay'. The earl rebuilt the town gate—which still bears his badly eroded coat of arms—to act as the town's prison and provided for the appointment of a number of municipal officers.[4] His investment in the town perhaps followed his completion of the work to the castle.

### Remodelling the Lower Bailey as a Great Court

There seems to have been no significant new building in the castle since the death of Roger Bigod in 1306 until the time of Sir Charles. Sir Charles remodelled Bigod's buildings in the Lower Bailey to create what in the Tudor period would have been called the Great Court, intended to receive the earl of Worcester, his household and guests in appropriate style and comfort for the period. Superficially, the changes appear to have been limited to the insertion of new windows and some new fireplaces into the main rooms. However on closer examination, there was a fundamental change in plan and circulation, which reflected the changing demands of the age.

The castle remained focussed on Roger Bigod's hall in the Lower Bailey. The changes here were indeed modest with the only visible evidence being the remodelling of the middle window overlooking the courtyard which appears to have been thrust forward to create a bay. The work involved the use of a fine, light-green sandstone which typifies this phase of building. A 16th-century document held by the College of Arms depicts six coats of arms including those of Charles Somerset, earl of Worcester and states that 'from the windows of the castles of Chepstow and Raglan these six have been extracted'.[5] Perhaps at the same time a wooden screen was inserted to hide the three service doorways.

However, the major change which was instituted at this period was that the lord no longer had to leave the hall by walking down its length and climbing the staircase into the Gloriette. Instead he left by walking into the dais chamber and up the spiral staircase. In the late 13th century, this staircase only led to the small room—perhaps an oratory (see pp.138–40 and Fig. 114)—over the dais chamber. However in the Tudor period the staircase was remodelled to emerge in a square, first-floor chamber, contrived in the space between the hall and the Middle Bailey curtain wall, and lit by a large mullioned and transomed window (Figs. 48 and 111). The staircase then continued up to two small chambers over the dais chamber. The main route however for the lord, his family and perhaps his principal guests was to walk across the top of the Middle Bailey gateway—where a passing bay was created (Fig. 166)—into the first floor of the late 12th-century D-shaped tower alongside the Middle Bailey gateway.

This room then became the focus of a new suite of private apartments for Sir Charles Somerset. The arrowloops were blocked or punched out to create new openings, such as the window to the east and doorways to the north and south (Fig. 51). The 12th-century floor levels and the spiral staircase were modified to suit the new arrangements. Most remarkably, two new ranges of buildings were constructed on the two sides of the Middle Bailey curtain wall between the D-shaped and the corner towers. The curtain wall itself was remodelled to insert fireplaces, flues and doorways creating two large rooms on each floor in each range as well as new, heated rooms in the towers. Though the position of the front wall and the pitch of the roof of the range in the Lower Bailey are clear, it is not certain if the new walls were all stone or partly timber-framed. However access to the ground and first floors seems to have been strictly controlled via the D-shaped tower and users will have had to pass from one room into the other.

The ground floor was entered by a new doorway opened up next to the Middle Bailey gateway. The lower room in the D-shaped tower became a small kitchen with a new fireplace and a bread oven. A new two-light window was built into the blocking of the original entrance from the Middle Bailey (Fig. 50) and new passageways partly cut through earlier arrowloops into the ranges built either side of the curtain wall. In the Lower Bailey, there were two large, rectangular rooms each with a large fireplace. One can imagine that these rooms were lit with mullioned and transomed windows overlooking the courtyard. The further room has a doorway and small

cellar within the curtain wall (a fuel store?) and a doorway was punched through into the base of the corner tower. At this date the multi-facetted, rubble-stone vaulting was inserted and the original openings were blocked except for a narrow, round-headed light contained within a former arrowloop. Perhaps this room acted as a wine and beer cellar for this range of buildings. Little of the plan of the ground floor of the Middle Bailey range can be determined, but the ground floor seems to have acted as the service rooms for the earl's main accommodation above, with the two large heated rooms perhaps for the steward of the household.

At first-floor the entrance through the D-shaped tower has already been described. In the Lower Bailey, there were two, large, heated rectangular rooms similar to the ones below (Fig. 48). Access was from the one to the north to that to the south, and then via steps and a doorway through the top of the curtain wall to the first floor of the Middle Bailey range. This seems to have been one long, gallery-like room with a single fireplace with accesses directly from the D-shaped tower and also into an upper room contrived in the corner tower. The receivers for the door latches of the late 12th and early 16th

Fig. 166 The passing bay and entrance into the earl's apartments against the Middle Bailey curtain wall

Fig. 167 The 16th- and 12th-century latch receivers in the Corner Tower of the Middle Bailey. The 16th-century door jamb and carved stone latch receiver is in the centre, and the preceding 12th-century examples are on the extreme right of this photo

215

centuries into this room are neatly juxtaposed (Fig. 167). The room in the tower was provided with a fireplace and a large mullioned and transomed window and a strange void exists between its floor and the top of the newly-vaulted cellar below. The spiral staircases in both towers still gave access to the castellated roof level.

The first floor of this new suite of buildings provided the earl with his private apartments, replacing the Gloriette built by Roger Bigod. The room in the D-shaped tower was an anteroom with the earl's great and privy chambers in the Lower Bailey range. These gave access to a gallery on the other side of the curtain wall, overlooking the Great Tower and the Middle Bailey. The most private room was in the corner tower looking across the Dell into the town and over the quay. There are no latrines in this new range of buildings, which were such a feature of the medieval castle, implying that close stools, containing chamber pots, had come into use in this period.

Elsewhere in the Lower Bailey the changes in the Tudor period were more straightforward. The cellar, buttery, pantry and Gloriette were unchanged except that the 'balcony' below the Gloriette was walled in and roofed, and goods from boats moored within the cave were winched up into this area, rather than directly into the cellar whose doorway seems to have been partly blocked. A massive new fireplace and chimney were built on the outside of the cliff-side wall of the kitchen and the stone base for a boiler was contrived immediately to the west. The upper chambers alongside the kitchen each had new four-light windows inserted looking over the river, the lower with an unusual squint which allowed the first-floor occupants to see who was crossing Chepstow Bridge (Fig. 168). The modifications continued into the upper floors of the Main Gatehouse where Tudor windows were contrived in some of the reveals for the arrowloops.

The New or Marten's Tower underwent similar but more elaborate changes. The first-floor room had a new four-light mullioned and transomed wooden window inserted into the 1280s reveal (Fig. 129). The reveal was remodelled in ashlar oolitic limestone and has finely moulded ribs to a low barrel vault, with a moulded sill beneath the window. A similar but simpler reveal was made for a two-light window looking along the outside of the curtain wall. This room was given a new, smaller fireplace along-

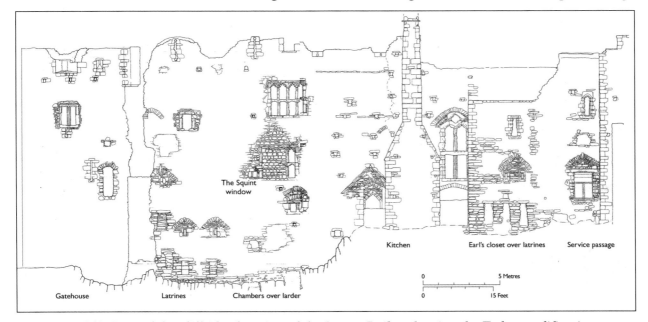

The Squint window

Gatehouse          Latrines          Chambers over larder

Kitchen          Earl's closet over latrines          Service passage

0          5 Metres

0          15 Feet

*Fig. 168 Part of the cliffside elevation of the Lower Bailey showing the Tudor modifications and a detail of the squint window*

side the original (Fig. 132) and it was replastered to hide the late 13th-century decorative scheme. The second-floor room was also provided with a new courtyard window, this time in stone, set in a finely worked reveal. The chapel was made more comfortable with a new fireplace and chimney added to the rear wall. The fireplace is now gone, but was described by Parker in 1853 as 'perfect'.[6] The slots visible in the decorated outer order of the north-east window suggest that it may have been modified in this period. Finally, a room may have been created in the roof space to provide some additional accommodation.

Beyond the Lower Bailey the remainder of the castle rooms were little changed, though there is no evidence to suggest that any of the buildings fell out of use. The present flight of stone steps and the platform were built across the east face of the Great Tower. This structure is earlier than the thickening of the south curtain wall in the second half of the 17th century.

## The Tudor Doors

There are a number of doors which date from this period. The pairs of doors surviving in the Middle and Outer Bailey gateways are identical in construction and are clearly replacements to the originals, although it is thought that at least the iron pintles have been re-used from the original doors. There is, however, a difference in the timber used—those in the Upper Bailey are constructed of oak, whilst those in the Middle Bailey are of elm (Figs. 169 and 170).

The doors consist of two layers of butt-edged 56mm thick planks, the fronts laid vertically and the backs horizontally, and secured with large clenched spikes in a diamond pattern. The gates to the Middle Bailey comprise two-and-a-half boards per leaf, aligned vertically on the outer face, while those to the Upper Bailey have three planks per leaf. These average 450mm wide and are butt-jointed with four sets of 14mm diameter tenons.

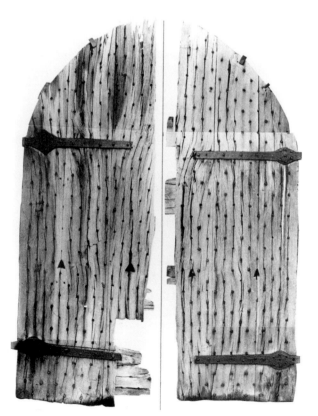

*Fig. 169 The Upper Bailey gateway doors*

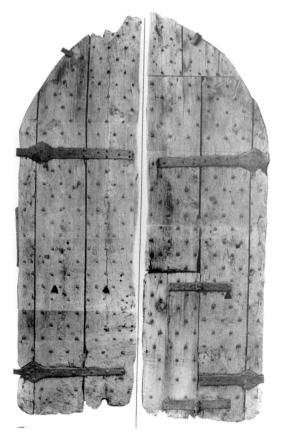

*Fig. 170 The Middle Bailey gateway doors*

An interesting feature of the backing boards is that they have been cut in an alternating, overlapping fashion resulting in every other board protruding 50mm beyond the outer edge of the door centre, with the intervening boards similarly recessed to accommodate those from the opposite door leaf. There do not appear to be any tenons between planks like the vertical boards on the front face.

The timber used for both the vertical and horizontal boards appears to have come from large diameter trees which were sawn into thick (50mm) planks (Figs. 6 and 7). For the Upper Bailey doors, two large oaks 500mm in diameter would have been required to produce the six vertical planks, whilst in theory at least another two trees of 450mm to 600mm diameter would have been needed to produce the backing planks which vary in thickness from 56mm to 75mm. However, dendrochronology has suggested that the rear planks probably came from a least eight or ten different trees. Much of the timber exhibited wide, varied, and in some cases distorted, growth rings, suggesting that the trees came from hedgerows or parkland as opposed to a woodland environment. On the Lower Bailey doors, the elm planks to the front face probably came from one very large tree of at least 625mm to 750mm diameter. The horizontal backing planks probably came from another elm of similar proportions. The elm trees again probably originated from hedgerows or parkland.

The gate to the Upper Bailey has a 150mm x 100mm locking bar which was nailed to the southern leaf and which originally laid in a reciprocal slot in the northern leaf. Here the original nailing pattern continues uninterrupted, the nails being shorter and clenched over the backs of the front layer of planks, illustrating the importance the carpenters placed on symmetry of design over function. When shut, the bar was secured to the northern leaf with a long wrought-iron hasp fastened at the bottom with a padlock and staple.

While the doors to the Upper Bailey remain virtually in their original form, those to the Middle Bailey have been modified, principally through the introduction of a wicket door, prob-ably dating from the late 18th or early 19th centuries and hung on two wrought iron strap hinges. The face of the wicket door has studded nails following the same pattern as the rest of the door, and there is a 75mm iron ring on a staple.

One other modification common to both the Middle and Upper Bailey doors are the provision of 50 to 75mm triangular loop holes cut into the doors, numbering two per leaf. It is clear that these are not primary as the cut sides are perfectly aligned where they cut across different boards. Had they been cut through green or unseasoned timber, then subsequent shrinkage would have been obvious. It is most likely that they were cut during the Civil War as musket or pistol loops.

Whilst it is clear that the iron hinge pintles are the originals set into the stone jambs, the hinges themselves may be replacements. If, as currently thought, the two gateways are from different periods of construction, then it seems surprising that the hinge bands are identical on both doors. However, the position of the fixing holes does not respect the present outer planking, the nails sometimes conflicting with the vertical joints. Also, one or two hinges are not level, suggesting they had worn or distorted to that position from a previous door.

The most notable use of iron in these doors are the spikes or nails used to fix the two layers of boards together. The heads are square with bevelled corners 20 to 25mm across, with 12mm by 8mm shanks drawn out to a point. They are placed in diagonal rows, about 375 being used in the Middle Bailey doors and 480 in the Upper Bailey doors.

Dendrochronological analysis of the doors to the Upper Bailey from the Barbican suggests they were constructed in the first quarter of the 16th century.[7] These gates are virtually identical to those to the Middle Bailey which, being of fast-grown elm, were not suitable for dating, but can now be ascribed to the same construction period.

Two doors survive *in situ* in Marten's Tower, one in the main entrance from the courtyard and one between the spiral staircase and the first-floor room. That to the main entrance measures 1.65m wide by 2.1m high, including 125mm rebates, and was defended by a drawbar internally and a portcullis externally. As with the doors to the Middle and Upper Baileys, the door is comprised of vertical boards to the face, backed by horizontal boards fixed together with 228 nails in 23 staggered rows (Fig. 171). Some of the diagonally-scribed layout lines for the nails are still visible. All of the timber used in the door is of elm, with the exception of the last vertical plank on the locking side of the door face, which is of oak—apparently original as the scribed layout lines run over both this and the adjacent elm planks. There remains within the drawbar socket a length of pine, beyond which is another bulk of more decayed timber, possibly the remains of the original drawbar. Modifications to the door include three musket loops measuring 75mm x 100mm, again probably made during the Civil War.

The upper internal door is of much lighter construction, being formed from four elm boards fixed together with five ledgers of similar thickness. Each of the ledgers is fixed through from the front with three staggered rows of nails, of which the horizontal setting out lines are still visible.

*Fig. 171 The entrance door to Marten's Tower*

Some 156 nails were used in the construction of this door. There remain five keyholes for various replacement stock locks. Like the lower door, the tops of the boards have been cut unevenly rather than at a consistent curve.

Neither door was suitable for dating through dendrochronology, being constructed of fast-grown elm. The one oak timber has wide rings distorted with knots, and was not suitable for analysis. Stylistic dating is difficult, but given the similarity in style and materials to the Middle and Upper Bailey gates, a 16th-century date would not be improbable.

## Conclusions

With the modifications described above Charles Somerset, earl of Worcester, tried to bring his essentially late 13th-century castle up to date (Fig. 172). The conversion of the Lower Bailey into the Great Court hid a radical change in planning and the disposition of the earl's private apartments when compared to Roger Bigod's castle. What was created is reminiscent of the plan of Sir William Herbert's mid-15th-century Raglan Castle.[8] Here too one left the hall to one side of the dais and climbed a staircase to a very fine dining room and parlour looking towards the Great Tower. These rooms led to the state bedrooms and a first-floor gallery across the back of the gatehouse viewing across the courtyard towards the entrance into the hall.

Elsewhere the rooms remained much the same except for new windows and fireplaces. As the detailing is richer in Marten's Tower this may have remained the main guest suite for the castle with senior members of the household and perhaps the more permanent officials of the earl staying in the main gatehouse and chambers alongside the kitchen. The Great Tower remained in use and was apparently unchanged internally from the 1290s. This must have continued to have had ceremonial functions, been the site of the manorial court and perhaps included the main castle chapel.

After Charles' death, later earls of Worcester continued to use the castle periodically. Receiver's accounts for the castle honours and borough of the castle survive for the period 1534–8.[9] These list payments to a number of officials permanently resident in the castle and its appurtenances. They include the seneschel, keeper of the wardrobe, the gatekeeper, the forester, the parker, the clerk, the bailiff of the Barton and beadle of Chepstow. In 1537–8, over £10 was spent preparing the castle for a visit by the earl of Worcester.

From about this date comes the first antiquarian description made by John Leland. He describes the castle 'which yet standeth fayr and strong not far from the ruin of the bridge. In the castel is one tower, as I heard say, by the name of Longine'.[10]

Longinus was the name of the Roman soldier who smote Christ on the Cross with his spear, an incident only attested in the apocryphal *Acts of Pilate*. However, the spear becomes part of Arthurian legend through an association with Joseph of Arimethea who is reputed to have brought the spear and crown of thorns to Glastonbury.[11] The association by antiquarians of the building of the Great Tower with first

Longinus and later Julius Caesar (see pp.35–36, 251) emphasises not only its Roman appearance but also invests the site with mythical qualities.

Perhaps the only illustration of Chepstow Castle from the Tudor period is in the background of what Sir Roy Strong has called the Procession Picture (Plate 13). Painted by Robert Peake (d.1626) about 1600 it shows Edward Somerset, fourth earl of Worcester (d.1628) in the foreground and Queen Elizabeth beneath the canopy. Strong believes the picture alludes to Somerset's role of master of ceremonies at court, though, conventionally, it is thought to represent the wedding procession of his son Henry's marriage to Anne Russell. In the background to the left are two castles—the one to the front is reached by a bridge over a river and is dominated by a large hall with corner turrets. This, Strong takes to be Chepstow whilst in the background the other castle has a tall tower at its centre and is considered to be Raglan.[12] Neither castle is in any way accurately depicted but the whole picture is allegorical. If it is Chepstow, then it helps to show how important this castle was to the Somerset family.

*Fig. 172 A reconstruction of the Tudor castle*

# CHAPTER XXI

# Civil War and Commonwealth

*by* Jeremy Knight

As the country slid towards civil war in the 1630s, the elderly Catholic earl of Worcester in his castle at Raglan was at the centre of puritan propaganda as an alleged harbourer of Jesuits and armed Catholics. Though Monmouthshire had a higher proportion of Catholics than any county in England or Wales, they were concentrated in the north and east of the county. Chepstow had not a single convicted Catholic recusant under Elizabeth or the Stuarts.[1] It was a busy port, with links to puritan Gloucester, Bristol and north Devon. Later in the century, the number of Chepstow tradesmen issuing copper-alloy tokens was matched in Wales only by those from Carmarthen, Haverfordwest and Wrexham.[2]

The Governor of Chepstow Castle and Ranger of Wentwood Forest was a wealthy, middle-aged gentleman, Sir Nicholas Kemeys of Cefn Mably, who had inherited an estate at Llanfair Discoed on the fringes of Wentwood. When war broke out, Kemeys became a Royalist Commissioner of Array for Monmouthshire, concerned with wartime administration, recruitment and tax raising. He was replaced at Chepstow by another Commissioner of Array, Captain Thomas Morgan of Llansôr, outside Caerleon. Morgan had command of part of the county militia. As in all Welsh counties, this was a puny resource, incapable of sustaining prolonged warfare. They comprised 400 'Trained Men', 2,000 reservists, 50 horse and 60 pioneers, with a captain of horse and a professional muster master, and were only liable for service within their own county.[3] Early in 1642, Parliament ordered the removal of the county armoury from Monmouth, a Worcester stronghold, to Newport, where it would be under the control of the parliamentarian earl of Pembroke. A prolonged dispute followed, but when Worcester declared for the King in September, he removed the armoury to Raglan Castle.

Early in 1643, Worcester's eldest son Edward Herbert, earl of Glamorgan set off to besiege Gloucester with two regiments of foot, one of dragoons (mounted infantry) under a professional soldier, Sir Richard Lawdly, and a regiment of cavalry under his brother Sir Charles Herbert, 'a maiden soldier'. This 'Mushroom Army', as Clarendon called it, was encircled and destroyed by Sir William Waller at Highnam outside Gloucester on 25 March.[4] With Herbert's army prisoners, Monmouthshire lay open to attack. Chepstow and Monmouth—the gateways of the county—were garrisoned by the militia. From Gloucester, Waller marched on Monmouth, his approach causing 'the precipitate flight of his Lordship's troops'. Edward Herbert was at Oxford, his army having been left in the hands of supposedly competent professional soldiers. He hurried back to Raglan and by the 28th was sending orders to Thomas Morgan for the disposition of his scanty forces and four cannon. However, he was overtaken by events. With the Wye forced, Morgan fell back on the next river

Fig. 173 Map of Monmouthshire showing the natural features of the county and the houses of the main particpants in the Civil War

**Hundred of Newport**
A  Penllwyn Sarth (Morgan)
B  Machen (Morgan)
C  Gwern Y Cleppa (Pretty)
D  Tredegar (Morgan)
E  Cefn Mably (Kemeys)

**Hundred of Caldicot**
A  Pencoed (Morgan)
B  Pen y Wyrlod (Morgan)
C  Merthyr Geryn (Nicholas)
D  Llanvair Discoed (Kemeys)
E  Dinham (Blethin)
F  Moynes Court (Hughes)
G  St Pierre (Lewis)

**Hundred of Usk**
A  Trostrey (Hughes)
B  Cilfeigan (Morgan)
C  Cefn Ila (Williams)
D  Llangibby (Williams)
E  Llantarnam (Morgan)
F  Penrhos (Morgan)
G  Llansor (Morgan)
H  Pencrug (Morgan)
I  Kemeys Inferior (Kemeys of Kemeys)

**Hundred of Trellech**
A  Llansoy (Jones)
B  Pant Glas (Probert)

**Hundred of Skenfrith**
A  Upper Dyffryn (Gainsford)
B  Treowen (Jones)
C  Wonastow (Milborne)

**Hundred of Abergavenny**
A  Llanfihangel (Arnold)
B  Llantilio Pertholey (Parry)
C  Wernddu (Prodger)
D  Llandewi Rhydderch (Lewis)
E  Coldbrook (Herbert)
F  Hardwick (Jones)

line, at Caerleon. Waller advanced to Usk, but without the numbers or siege train to attempt Raglan, retreated to Chepstow 'very weary of the Welsh ways over the Mountains' (between Usk and Chepstow!). For five days (6–10 April), Waller rested his troops at Chepstow before falling back on Gloucester.[5] At the end of April, he again briefly occupied Monmouth and Hereford and a sea-borne attack was made on Chepstow from Bristol. 'Chepstow taken by Bristow men' noted Walter Powell, the diarist and tax collector, 'and re-taken'.[6]

After the King's unsuccessful siege of Gloucester in the summer of 1643, Chepstow and the Wye Valley became the front line between Royalist Monmouthshire and Parliamentarian Gloucestershire. The following January, Prince Rupert, newly appointed as regional Royalist commander, may have been planning to raise a regiment in Chepstow, for on 20 January, Massey repeated the commando raid of the previous year. This time a Parliamentary warship moored near the Black Rock, troops were transferred to smaller craft and, once landed, killed a Captain Carvine in his chamber at the George Inn in Chepstow and captured twelve other officers and £300 in cash. Edward Herbert of Raglan and his brother William Herbert of the Friars in Cardiff had a narrow escape, for they had only just left the town. Edward Herbert sailed to the Black Rock, unaware of the Parliamentary warship, and almost blundered into it.[7]

Later that summer, the strategic importance of Chepstow and the Severn crossing became even more apparent. Rupert, defeated on Marston Moor outside York on 2 July 1644, retreated via Chester and Monmouth to Bristol. Part of the defeated army, the Northern Horse, marooned in the north, set out to join him. By September they had reached Monmouthshire and Sir John Wintour of Lydney fortified the Beachley peninsula as a crossing point for their evacuation to Bristol. Twice Wintour occupied Beachley and twice Massey, with troops from Gloucester, drove him out. On the second occasion, Prince Rupert himself was nearly captured, for he had planned to join Wintour from Bristol by the next tide.[8] In

the meantime, the last Royalist field army in the west had been destroyed at Montgomery. At Chepstow, Wintour was fearful of direct attack, and in October he wrote to Rupert that he was provisioning and fortifying Chepstow Castle. He had called a meeting of the Commissioners for the county, expecting their help, but it was 'more like a fair than a rendezvous where the enemy is expected'. The following month, with the enemy fortified at Beachley, Wintour prepared two frigates for the defence of the river.[9]

**Chepstow during the war years**
The arrival of the Northern Horse had severe consequences in Monmouthshire, for they were notorious plunderers. One Royalist commander commented '… the ill discipline used by the Northern Horse … hath procured some scandal and much prejudice to his Majesty's affairs here, where neutrality is epidemical'. Another wrote to Rupert that 'since the disaster [at Montgomery] the edge of the gentry is very much blunted … they begin to warp to the enemy's party'.[10] The new burdens imposed by the Northern Horse, on a population already hard pressed by Royalist taxation and billeting at free quarter, led to resistance from the countryfolk, who banded together to resist looting and requisitioning. Royalist commanders, who by this time were not strong enough to overcome such resistance by force, saw these 'Clubmen' simply as a conspiracy against the army and the King.

With the bridge at Chepstow broken down to prevent surprise attack, and trade with Bristol largely stopped, the war was a severe trial for the people of Chepstow. They were crammed within the town walls not only with the castle garrison, but also with large numbers of billeted soldiers. In 1644 exactly half the 44 burials at Chepstow Priory were of soldiers. Some had been killed in action, but many had died of disease: 'John Thomas, a souldier, who died at Widow Rosser's house'; 'Joane, the daughter of a souldier, his name unknowen, but quartered at Edward Phillips's house in Back Lane'; 'A souldier dyinge at the George, his name unknown'; 'Elizabeth, the daughter of a soldier … quartered at the Court House'. A trained band soldier killed by the fall of a wall and two women, Joan Williams, wife of a tiler, and Margaret Winchell, 'killed with the fall of a house' were all buried on 22 January 1645, suggesting a disaster in the overcrowded town. Until his death in September 1646 the registers were kept by the vicar, Abraham Drew, and thereafter by his curate.[11]

## Chepstow Besieged, 1645

The fall of Bristol to Parliament on 10 September 1645 was the signal for many luke-warm Royalists in south Wales to change sides. Within a month, Sir Trevor Williams of Llangibby and the nominally Royalist 'Peaceable Army' in Glamorgan had declared for Parliament. Williams had been commissioned by the King to raise a regiment, which by this stage in the war formed a small private army of both horse and foot. Williams had been secretly nego-tiating with Parliament for some time and now allied himself with the Monmouthshire Clubmen 'those that made rendezvouses in the country'.[12] Anxious to establish his credentials with Parliament, he marched on Chepstow and after a four-day siege forced the town walls and besieged the castle. Williams and Sir Thomas Morgan, the Monmouthshire-born Parliamentarian Governor of Gloucester, both published their own versions of what followed. According to Williams, it was only when he learnt that Royalist forces were mustering to raise the siege, did he seek Morgan's help. Morgan claimed that only on hearing of a rising in Monmouthshire and Glamorgan 'with some shewes of being for the Parliament', did he feel it necessary to intervene. Morgan arrived in Chepstow with 900 horse and foot and summoned the castle governor, Colonel Edmond Fitzmorris, to surrender. Fitzmorris replied that he 'kept it for his master the king'. He had four officers and 106 men within the castle, 18 cannon and two arquebuses. Morgan sent for more men from Bristol and set up two brass culverins and an iron gun in battery. After three days, with the wall breached, Morgan drew up 400 men for an assault. Fitzmorris surrendered.

Colonel Thomas Hughes of Moynes Court, M.P. for the county, replaced him as governor. Morgan's battery, a 'strong wall … on a neigh-bouring hill, the only proper place to annoy the castle' was still there after the Restoration, when nervous royalists in the castle feared that a parliamentary sympathiser, whose house was on the spot, might constitute a security risk.[13]

The stores captured at that time showed Chepstow's importance as a Royalist base and its capacity under siege. There were: 16 barrels of gunpowder, six tons of lead, a 'great store of fire-works', 30 beef in powder, over 400 kilderkins of butter, 4,000 weight each of cheese and biscuit, 30 barrels of salt, three hogsheads of metheglin (mead) and four of beer and ale, 17 bushels of oatmeal, four of peas and beans and 30 of wheat. These were no doubt the stores collected so care-fully by Sir John Wintour.[14]

## The Last Stand: the Siege of 1648

The defeat and capture of the King did not end the political crisis. Divisions within Parliament and the army were exploited by the King and by Royalists hopeful that the Parliamentary cause would dissolve into anarchy. There were army mutinies and in 1647 a Royalist rising in Glamorgan. The following year saw a series of risings, intended to be co-ordinated with a Scots invasion, though on the very day the Scots crossed the border, the rebels in Glamorgan were defeated at St. Fagans.

On 1 May 1648, Oliver Cromwell left London to put down risings by diehard Royalists and disaffected Parliamentarians in Pembrokeshire and Glamorgan. When he arrived at Monmouth on the 10th, he learnt that although the Glamorgan rebels had been defeated two days earlier at St. Fagans, Chepstow Castle had been betrayed by one of its garrison to a party of local Royalists led by Colonel Sir Nicholas Kemeys, with Thomas Lewis of St Pierre as lieutenant-colonel, and his uncle Francis Lewis and Lewis Thomas as majors.[15] Thomas Hughes, the Governor, was apparently absent, perhaps on Parliamentary business. The rising had been care-fully planned. Kemeys's son, Charles Kemeys,

*Fig. 174 A view of the castle from across the Dell where the Parlamentary gun battery was sited*

was one of the insurgents in Pembroke Castle. Sir Nicholas had been replaced as Governor of Cardiff in 1644 under Rupert's policy of replacing local commanders by professional soldiers. Under arrest in London since May 1646, he obtained leave from Parliament to visit Bath for his health and crossed the Bristol Channel to join the rising. Sir Trevor Williams, involved in its planning, was, characteristically, waiting at Llangibby to see how things turned out.[16]

Cromwell's forces marched from Monmouth on 11 May. The town walls of Chepstow were lined with Royalist musketeers, but Colonel Pride's Regiment attacked and after a sharp fire-fight forced the town gate, taking a number of prisoners. Kemeys, with 150 Royalists, retreated to the castle. Cromwell sent in a summons to surrender, but Kemeys' men fired on the drummer who accompanied it and hung out a flag of defiance. That night, Pride's Regiment tried to storm the outer gatehouse of the castle in pouring rain, but were repulsed with four or five men killed, Major Grigson being mortally wounded by a stone dropped from above. Cromwell, anxious to reach Pembroke with the least possible delay, left Colonel Ewer's regiment to complete the taking of Chepstow.[17]

*Fig. 175 'Roaring Meg', a mortar used by Colonel John Birch at the earlier siege of Goodrich Castle towards the end of the First Civil War, now on view at Goodrich Castle*

Ewer had two heavy cannon brought from Gloucester and took two more from a ship. These were set up across the Dell from the south face of the castle, facing it across the steep but narrow valley (Fig. 174). 'We raised [razed] the battlements of the towers with our great guns' he wrote 'and made their guns unuseful to them'. At the same time, mortars bombarded the castle with explosive shells (Fig. 175). One fell in the governor's chamber, forcing him to remove to the upper end of the castle. The 'Governor' was presumably Nicholas Kemeys, reverting to his pre-war role. They then set up the heavy cannons in a siege battery and all morning 'played ... with our great guns very hot '. By midday the cannon had made a breach in the wall 'so low that a man might walk into it'; the south curtain wall opposite the Dell had to be substantially rebuilt after the war. Some Royalists now tried to surrender, but Ewer's men fired on them. Thomas Lewis called to friends of his among the besiegers

offering to surrender at mercy. Ewer replied that he was not interested in individuals, only in the surrender of the garrison, including Nicholas Kemeys and his officers. Lewis was prepared to surrender on terms, for with the wall breached the attackers would be justified under the laws of war in refusing all mercy if they were put to the trouble and bloodshed of a storming. Kemeys rejected Lewis's suggested terms of surrender, but asked to speak with Ewer. Reluctantly, Ewer agreed, 'over-persuaded by some gentlemen of the country who were there'. When they spoke at the drawbridge, through a porthole, the Governor proposed that the garrison surrender, and be allowed to march away. Ewer refused and prepared his men for an assault. The resolve of the defenders was failing, and some tried to run out to surrender. Ewer's men thereupon stormed the breach. After the fall of the castle, Sir Nicholas Kemeys and the man who had betrayed it were shot out of hand (Figs. 176 and 177). The remainder of the prisoners was locked up in Chepstow church pending instructions from Cromwell.[18]

*Fig. 176  Sir Nicholas Kemeys, shot out of hand at the end of the siege of Chepstow Castle in 1648*

*Fig. 177  The memorial plaque to Sir Nicholas Kemeys in the castle*

When the castle fell, papers were found which implicated Sir Trevor Williams and Thomas Morgan of Machen in the plot. On 17 June, Cromwell wrote from 'The Leaguer before Pembroke' to Major Thomas Saunders at Brecon, giving detailed instructions for their arrest. Several people could assist, including Captain John Nicholas, who had replaced Thomas Hughes as Governor of Chepstow.[19]

## Captain John Nicholas and Chepstow under Cromwell

Captain John Nicholas was the third son of Philip Nicholas of Llanpil, Llanfihangel-Tor-Y-Mynydd, and of a family with puritan links. John Nicholas's elder brother, Philip Nicholas of Trellech Grange, and his nephew were married to the widow and daughter of prominent local puritans. At the outbreak of war, many Monmouthshire puritans sought refuge in Bristol or Gloucester. John Nicholas also left the county, and enlisted in Colonel John Okey's Regiment of Dragoons (mounted infantry). Though sometimes dismissed as second-class cavalry, dragoons were valuable specialised troops and Okey's regiment had a distinguished war record, as well as a reputation for radical puritanism. Nicholas fought at St. Fagans in May 1648 in command of Okey's own troop of dragoons, alongside Okey's son. Both were shot through their hats (Civil War muskets were well known for firing high in inexperienced hands), but suffered no other hurt. He was mentioned in despatches and chosen to carry the despatches to Parliament—a traditional honour reserved for an officer who had distinguished himself in battle. This brought him to Cromwell's notice, who appointed him Governor of Chepstow. Nicholas subsequently became Cromwell's trusted lieutenant in Monmouthshire, as Governor of Chepstow Castle, member of various county committees, deputy Major-General (regional governor) for Monmouthshire and M.P. for the county in the Second Protectorate Parliament of 1656–8. Like many of Cromwell's local commanders, his family connections among the minor gentry of the county proved a strong qualification for the job.[20]

Chepstow was still a military arsenal. In 1650 Nicholas was ordered to inspect the mortar piece stored there and if it was defective, put it in condition for service. Five years later, when the royal fort at Bristol was demolished, all provisions of war there were removed to Chepstow. The same year Nicholas was given £300 from the sequestrated estates of Sir Edward Morgan of Llantarnam for repairs to the war damaged curtain walls.[21] This led to complications. The timber on the estate had been sold to a speculator, Samuel Jones, for £600, out of which Nicholas was to receive his £300. He had already spent most of it when Morgan managed to stop the asset stripping. Standing timber on sequestrated estates was often a cause of contention. The lessees wanted the maximum return on their investment, whereas the owners, and even the sequestrators, did not want to diminish the value of the estate permanently. The London-based Sequestration Committee then demanded the £300 from Nicholas, and forced him to give a bond for its payment. He petitioned for the cancelling of the bond, or (he added hopefully) for himself to be admitted as tenant of the estate. In March 1654 he wrote to Cromwell explaining that he had spent the money as ordered, in repairing the fortifications. Cromwell ruled that the accounts should be sent to the committee at Haberdasher's Hall. If they found them satisfactory, they should discharge the payment (which presumably they did, but there is no record).[22]

Chepstow Castle was also a state prison. Bishop Jeremy Taylor, whose sermons made him a focus for London Anglicans, spent two spells there in 1654–5 (Fig. 178). Royalists were held after Penruddock's rising in 1655 and Booth's in 1659. In the spring of 1655, Penruddock's rising in Wiltshire caused a fresh crisis for the Protectorate. Nicholas was ordered to collect 400 horse and foot at Chepstow, reinforce Gloucester, imprison any suspects in Chepstow Castle and seize the horses and arms of local Royalists. He replied that he had heard nothing of any rising, but could collect 500 or 1,000 men at Chepstow if necessary. He reinforced Major Creed at Gloucester with 100 horse and dragoons, kept

*Fig. 178  A portrait of Bishop Jeremy Taylor, who spent two terms of imprisonment in Chepstow Castle*

militia, with a cornet, a quartermaster, three corporals, a trumpeter and 78 troopers—the normal establishment of a New Model Army troop of horse.[24]

Cromwell died in 1658 and Booth's Rising occurred the following year. This was a concerted plan to seize several key English cities whilst Prince Charles and Prince James waited across he Channel with English exiles and French troops. It has come to be known after the only initially successful leader, the Cheshire Royalist Sir George Booth, Chepstow Castle providing accommodation for some of the prisoners taken by Parliament in its suppression. One, John Aylett, was particularly unfortunate. Appointed shadow Governor of Chepstow by the exiled king in 1657, instead of being in command, he spent twenty weeks in prison in the castle. The castle garrison was now strengthened with 40 new recruits, although the pay of the existing troops was over £3,000 in arrears. Royalist prisoners were examined and details (with the value of their estates) sent to London.[25] As late as February 1660, Colonel Okey at Bristol was imprisoning suspected Royalists and threatening to send others to Chepstow Castle, but the Cromwellian regime was unravelling and he was ordered to do nothing without the consent of Parliament.[26] At the Restoration, Okey was executed as a regicide. Nicholas fled abroad, but in 1661, a pass was ordered to be sent to 'Capt. Nicholas, as one of those whom the king wishes to call home'. However, five years later, during the Dutch wars, he was still apparently in Holland, for he was on a list of prominent Cromwellians ordered to return under threat of indictment for treason, the Government fearing that they would aid the Dutch.[27] On his return, he resumed his place among the minor local gentry from among whom he had emerged. When in 1683 his elder brother entered the family pedigree at a Herald's Visitation, he was merely listed in third place among his even more obscure siblings.[28]

others in Monmouth and imprisoned the dissidents whom 'the honest people did judge the most dangerous' in Chepstow Castle.[23] That August, Cromwell reluctantly acknowledged that he could no longer rely on the acquiescence of former Royalists and drew up a scheme of government through regional Major-Generals, with a cavalry militia forming a mounted gendarmerie, funded by a 10% 'decimation' tax on former Royalists. James Berry, Major-General for Wales and the west Midlands, appointed Nicholas, now a Lieutenant Colonel, as deputy Major-General for Monmouthshire, with Colonel Wroth Rogers in a similar post in Herefordshire. Francis Blethin, younger brother of William Blethin of Dinham, was lieutenant of the new

# CHAPTER XXII

# After the Restoration

*by* George Geear, Stephen Priestley *and* Rick Turner

Upon the Restoration of King Charles II to the throne in 1660, the lordship and town of Chepstow were returned to the marquis of Worcester. However, the castle was retained by the king to act as a fort and barracks. In August 1660, Henry, Lord Herbert (1629–1700)—eldest son of the marquis—was appointed Governor of Chepstow Castle and commissioned in the following way:

> And the said garrison with the works and fortifications thereof you are to uphold and maintaine in good repair, which you shall defend for the use of his majestie.[1]

Later he was given power and authority:

> to raise and arme the said company consisting of one hundred men besides officers. And doe hereby constitute and appoint you to be captain thereof and to be imployed in the defence of the place.[2]

A muster roll of this company of men for 1662 survives.[3]

Also in 1662, Henry was granted £500 for the 'repair and mending of the castle of Chepstow', which he described as the key to south Wales and a 'bridle to the ill-affected who abound in these parts'.[4] Following the death of his father in 1667, Henry, now third marquis of Worcester, was released from repaying this grant in 1672.[5]

Earlier his father had submitted a statement of expenses in his service of king and country, which may have been a factor in cancelling the debt.[6] Henry lived in great style, building Castle House and Troy House, Monmouth and a Palladian mansion at Badminton, Gloucestershire. Here he was described as maintaining a 'princely way of living ... above any other, except crowned heads, ... in Europe'.[7]

A number of documents show that, most unusually, the medieval, masonry Chepstow Castle was adapted and maintained in the later 17th century as an artillery fort and barracks. This was not achieved by rebuilding the defences in the manner of Renaissance and later fortifications, which employed low earth-filled bastions arranged in star-shaped batteries.[8] As is described below, it was achieved by extending and developing the repairs initiated by Oliver Cromwell and Parliament, through John Nicholas, in 1650 (see chapter XXI). Chepstow therefore retained its strategic importance at the gateway into south Wales almost to the end of the century.

The inventories of the castle from the 1670s give a very full description of the castle, its contents and how it functioned.[9] Most important are two comprehensive inventories compiled in 1672 and 1679. The latter, dated to 3 May, is given in full, as it not only names different parts of the castle, but it also lists the huge range of munitions and armaments that it contained.

In the drawbridge tower [south-west tower in the Upper Barbican] 2 iron guns the one 6 foote in length to ye base ring, carryes 7 li [libra or pound] bullet ye other 7 foote in length and carryes 9 li bullet both without carriages, the tower wants some repairations.

In ye upper Court lyes 1 iron murthering peece with his Chamber.

In ye litle tower in ye midle court 1 brass field piece 5 foote and a halfe in length carryes halfe a pound bullet mounted upon a decayed carriage and ye platforme much decayed in the said Court. 1 iron gun 7 foot and a halfe in length carryes 9 li bullets lyeing on ye ground.

In Jumper Tower [probably the corner tower of the middle bailey] 2 brass guns each of them 5 foote in length the one carryes a bullet of 4 li and a halfe the other of 3 foote mounted on old carriages, there is an other old carriage and ye plattforme much decayed.

In ye great court 3 iron guns 9 foote and halfe in length of them carrie 18 li bullet 2 of them mounted on old decayed carriages ye other lyes on ye ground. 2 iron guns more there each of them 9 foote and 2 inches and carryes 9 li bullet the one mounted on an old decayed carriage the other lyeing on ye ground. 3 iron guns more there each of them 9 foote long and carryes 5 li bullet the one mounted on a decayed carriage the other lyeing on ye ground 3 iron guns more there each of them 5 foote and halfe in length and carryes 4 li bullet without carriages, 2 brass guns each of them 3 foote in length and carryes 2 bullets both mounted in an old decayed box or carriage in ye said court before the Great Gate. 2 iron morter peeces without carriages each of them 3 foote and 2 inches in length and 12 inches in ye diameter.

In the said Great Court of great shott 1098 of all sorts and sizes from halfe a pound to 20 li fitting ye sizes of all sorts of guns there, there are also 15 great granadoe shells 80 hand granadoes 50 sluggs 30 bullets with iron barrs thorough.

In ye court over ye sellar 1 iron gun 7 foote in length carryes 7 li bullet mounted on an old decayed carriage.

In the plattforme over ye greate gate 2 brass guns of 3 foote in length and carryes 2 li bullet the one mounted on an old decayed carriage,

the other on ye wall. 2 iron guns of 6 foote and a halfe in length and carries 4 li bullet the one is mounted on a carriage, the other lyes on ye platforme.

In ye platforme over ye Greate Tower one brass gun 5 foote in length carryes 3 li bullet mounted on a decayed carriage.

In ye Roome next the Dungeon, 2 brass guns 3 foote in length without any carriages, 13 iron guns of wallpeeces and murtherers out of reparation.

In the binding roome 84 matchlocks fixed, 2 firelocks unfixed one musket without a lock, one firelock gun 9 foote in length for small shot usefull for a wall, another smaller barrill of ye same bore without stock lock or breach.

In ye store roome that is called ye bisket roome. 19 old halberds, 253 pikes, 203 matchlocks indifferently fixed, 323 firelocks, 9 broken musketts, 7 bundles of bandileers, 34 baggs of musket bullets and a barrel and halfe of ye same bullets, 25 peeces of sheetes of lead, 18 sowds of lead, 54 small barrs of lead, 7 bullet moulds, a barrill of brimstone, one fire-lock gun 9 foote in length for small shott usefull for a wall, one broken brass gun in six peeces, 10 quivers of short arrows, 19 single loose arrowes, a heape of match lyeing on a frame in ye said roome, 3 yards in length 2 yardes and halfe in height and 1 yard in breadth most of it all over layne match, with other old decayed necessaryes and 2 old saddles.

In ye Cogloft att ye top of ye Greate Tower 340 sheaves of old over layne match, 15 glaives and 3 broken forest bills, 1 old match lock.

In ye Magazine noe powder but ye Countreys Stock of which there hath bin borrowed for ye use of ye Garryson two barrels, the allowance of powder for the last two yeares are yet undelivered and in arreares.

As to ye walls of ye Castle they are very strong and firme, lined with a wall on ye inner side of 9 or 10 foote in breadth except Longies Tower.

The Company are armed with firelocks besides the aforesaid number of armes.'

For a glossary of the terms used in this inventory see the endnotes for this chapter.[10]

## Artillery of the Period

The artillery listed can be tabulated in the following way:

*Brass ordnance*

| Calibre | Length | Quantity |
|---------|--------|----------|
| ¹/₂pr | 5'6" | 1 |
| 4¹/₂pr | 5' | 1 |
| ? | 3' | 3 |
| 2pr | 3' | 4 |

*Iron ordnance*

| Calibre | Length | Quantity |
|---------|--------|----------|
| 18pr | 9'6" | 3 |
| 9pr | 9'2" | 2 |
| 5pr | 9' | 3 |
| 4pr | 5'6" | 3 |

*Mortars*

| Calibre | Length | Quantity |
|---------|--------|----------|
| 12"diameter | 3'2" | 2 |

Plus '13 iron guns of wall-pieces and murtherers out of reparation'.

From the introduction of the gun in the second quarter of the 14th century until the early 16th century, the majority of guns were either built-up from strips of wrought iron, or cast from bronze. It was only from the early 16th century that iron guns started to be cast. The early guns were predominantly small breech-loaders, but the technology needed to effectively seal the breech against the escape of gas from the exploding gunpowder would not be achieved until the 19th century, and breech-loading was confined to the smaller sizes of gun with reduced powder charges.

Prior to the 16th century there was little attempt at rationalisation and there existed a bewildering variety of cannon which led to complication and confusion in terms of logistics. By the time of the Civil War the variety of pieces in terms of calibre, length and weight had been rationalised, and although not strictly standardised, there were now fewer varieties of cannon that had generally recognised and accepted proportions, but still referred to by name rather than calibre. Designation by calibre would come later in the 17th century.

The thickness of metal from which the gun was formed dictated the powder charge that could safely be used, and hence determined the effective range of the gun. This thickness was normally described as its fortification, and was usually one of three grades—bastard, legitimate or double fortified, in ascending order of fortification.

Brass guns were, in effect, normally cast from a copper/tin alloy—bronze in modern parlance, but the term bronze was only introduced in the 19th century when referring to artillery. Bronze guns were more expensive to cast than iron guns, and became soft when hot and liable to distort when fired rapidly. However, they were safer in use as they normally gave visible warning of impending failure, unlike iron guns, and could be left in the open without suffering corrosion.

Cast-iron guns were cheaper to make, heavier (for a given calibre), rusted when exposed to the weather and could fail explosively with no visible warning in terms of bulging or cracking. Iron guns were, however, capable of firing heavier

| Name | Calibre in inches | Weight in pounds | Length of piece in feet | Weight of shot in pounds |
|------|-------------------|------------------|-------------------------|--------------------------|
| Cannon royal | 8 | 8,000 | 8 | 63 |
| Cannon | 7 | 7,000 | 10 | 47 |
| Demi-cannon | 6 | 6,000 | 12 | 27 |
| Culverin | 5 | 4,000 | 11 | 15 |
| Demi-culverin | 4¹/₂ | 3,600 | 10 | 9 |
| Saker | 3¹/₂ | 2,500 | 9¹/₂ | 5¹/₄ |
| Minion | 3 | 1,500 | 8 | 4 |
| Falcon | 2³/₄ | 700 | 6 | 2¹/₄ |
| Falconet | 2 | 210 | 4 | 1¹/₄ |
| Robinet | 1¹/₄ | 120 | 3 | ³/₄ |

*British Ordnance of the Civil War Period*[11]

shot more rapidly—for this reason they were the cannon of choice for siege operations.

Until the 18th century, wheeled gun carriages were extremely heavy and cumbersome, drawn by teams of horses or oxen. Roads were rutted tracks and mobility was strictly limited. By the time of the English Civil War, cannon used in the field of battle were distributed among infantry regiments where they could be discharged under local command. The lack of light manoeuvrable gun carriages precluded speedy redeployment and prevented local concentration in order to develop a tactical advantage. Some commanders during the Civil War were starting to realise the potential of artillery and Oliver Cromwell's tactical concentration of artillery at Dunbar was an early example of this.[12] Siege artillery relied on heavy and cumbersome carriages fitted with large spoked wheels to cope with the poor roads. By this date guns were fitted with trunnions— pivots close to the centre of gravity to allow the barrel to be elevated or depressed by a quoin or wedge under the breech.

In laying siege to a castle or fortified town, all the necessary troops, guns, ammunition, stores, rations and impedimenta would be formed into a siege train, which could take up several miles of road. Indeed the head of the train could well be arriving at its halt for the night before the last vehicle had left the previous camp.

Siege operations therefore were enormous exercises in terms of planning and logistics, and would only be set up against a fortified position of high tactical and strategic importance.

Mortars were very short-barrelled, large calibre guns—the length of the barrel did not usually exceed three times the calibre (Fig. 175). Usually cast in bronze, they were attached to heavy blocks or beds at a fixed elevation of 45°, the range being altered by varying the powder charge. The mortar bed was wheel-less and laid upon the ground, relying on weight and the high

*Fig. 179 A 17th-century cannon on a double bracket carriage with its trail bogey and wheels in the foreground. The cannon is in the process of being loaded, with ammunition and tools displayed*

angle of elevation to reduce recoil. In the 17th century, mortar calibres ranged from $7\frac{1}{2}$" through 10" and 13" to the huge 18". To give an idea of size, a 13" spherical mortar shell (bomb) weighed some 200lbs.

Mortars were employed where plunging fire was required, for example when there was a need to drop a bomb over a castle wall to attack the garrison, or for a besieged castle to fire over the wall at an attacker without exposing the gun or gun crew to observation or return fire by a cannon. The spherical iron bombs were filled with corned powder and fitted with a fuse. The fuse was cut to a length to explode the bomb at the target, where a combination of blast and fragments would kill or maim the enemy. In extremis, fused mortar bombs (grenadoes in contemporary parlance) could be dropped (or even thrown) onto a besieging force. (At the time of the Civil War the term grenado referred to all types of fused explosive spherical projectiles/missiles, the name deriving from the grenadine or pomegranate owing to the similarity of its seeds to the grains of gunpowder.[13])

It is generally considered that gunpowder was first introduced about the middle of the 13th century. Consisting of a mixture of saltpetre, charcoal and sulphur, its proportions have varied over the years, originally being determined at the whim of the gunners. Those finally settled upon in 1781 were 75% Saltpetre, 15% Charcoal and 10% Sulphur, a mixture ascribed to the Rt. Reverend Richard Watson DD, FRS who was consulted by the government in 1746 for advice on improving the strength of gunpowder.[14] In the preceding 500 years the percentage of saltpetre was generally greater and those of sulphur and charcoal reduced. However, in 1647, Master Gunner Nye[15] records the proportions as:

| Saltpetre | 66.6% |
| Charcoal | 16.6% |
| Sulphur | 16.6% |

The earliest powder had been known as serpentine, so named for its greenish colour. Unfortunately, this mixture would separate into layers of its different components when vibrated or shaken during transportation, and it became the practice for field or siege artillery to be provided with the powder from a pit behind the guns where it was mixed. Early gunpowder was therefore of variable quality and very erratic in its performance.

Great care had to be taken when using serpentine. In particular, care had to be taken when ramming home the powder charge. If the charge was over compressed, then it would burn slowly as the centre of the mass was deprived of the oxygen liberated by the saltpetre. Too loose and similarly, flame propagation was retarded. Serpentine powder also produced inflammable dust and a large quantity of solids as by-products of combustion. These solids would obstruct the bore and require cleaning between shots. The greatest problem, however, was the propensity of gunpowder to absorb moisture from the atmosphere and consequently fail to fire or produce a consistent pressure.

Corned powder, the solution to most of the above problems, was known by the middle of the 15th century in Europe and was introduced into England some time in the early 16th century. Corned powder was made by moistening the mixed ingredients to form a paste, which was compressed between plates or boards and left to dry. When dry, the cakes of gunpowder were broken up and sieved to produce grains or corns of the desired size. The larger the grain size the slower the rate of burning. Large cannon would use the slower burning, large size in order to develop the necessary power in a long barrel, whilst smaller cannon and hand-weapons would use the finer grain, quicker burning powders. There were several advantages of corning: regular grain size promoted more consistent burning rates, whilst the grains themselves resisted over-ramming, which also gave more consistent rates of burning. This consistency in turn led to greater accuracy and consistency in range. Corned powder was also less rapidly affected by water absorption from the air, and so more reliable, whilst more complete combustion was achieved leaving less solid residues/fouling in the barrel.

Such was the increase in the power of corned powder over its predecessors that a reduction in the charge of powder required of about one-third had to be introduced to prevent cannon from bursting. Indeed the introduction into general use of corned powder hastened the demise of the gun built-up of several parts and the breech-loader as they failed to cope with the increases in pressure being generated.

**Analysis of the 1679 Inventory**

A study of the inventories listing the ordnance stored within Chepstow Castle reveals that the castle was used as a repository of obsolescent arms, rather than as an armoury for the issue of serviceable weapons. Indeed many of the weapons would have qualified at the time as having antique status. The inventory of 1672 is also extremely imprecise in terms of both description and quantity. Match for example, being cord treated to burn slowly and used in muskets to fire the charge, is described as being in 'two great heapes' which gives no information as to quantity, condition or length. As match was essential for the firing of muskets this would indicate that the inventory was hardly to be taken as a precise statement of Chepstow's value as a military resource. This is further borne out by the quantity given for pikes as 'about 200 pikes of

ould and new bundles a greate bundle'. This is a most surprising inexactitude, for in the 17th century the pike was still an essential infantry weapon used not only to deter cavalry, but to provide protection in order for the match-lock musketeers to be able to reload their muskets—a time-consuming occupation.

In the 'full and perfect account' of May 1679, we find 'of great shott 1098 of all sorts and sizes' —hardly a full and perfect account! Also 'a heape of match … 3 yards in length 2 yardes and halfe in height and 1 yard in breadth'—this must be one of the earliest examples of a quantity surveyor's nightmare! There are also numerous mentions of things being 'old', 'much decayed' and 'broken'.

Although a large proportion of the weaponry was doubtless capable of use, the inventories suggest that the weaponry in store at Chepstow Castle was to a large extent obsolescent, uncared for, and scarcely to be accepted as a serious tactical reserve in time of war. The statement 'In ye Magazine noe powder but ye Countreys Stock of which there hath bin borrowed for ye use of ye Garrison two barrels, the allowance of powder for the last two yeares are yet undelivered and in arrears', strongly suggests that the military authorities regarded the arming of Chepstow to be extremely low in their list of priorities.

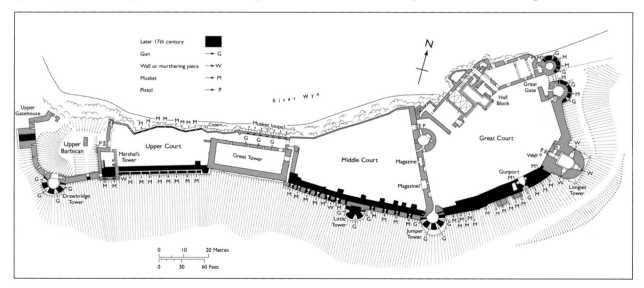

*Fig. 180 Plan of Chepstow Castle showing 17th-century alterations and artillery positions*

234

## From Castle to Artillery Fort

Throughout the castle there were a succession of modifications to the medieval masonry, converting the external defences to mount different types of artillery and to be better prepared to face an artillery attack. Works are documented in 1650 and 1662, but it is impossible to distinguish between the two on site. There may have been works or modifications at other dates. Nevertheless, the 1670s inventories of the castle—particularly that taken in 1679 (see above)—do allow the disposition of the different artillery pieces around the castle to be envisaged.

The 17th-century castle is best described from west to east beginning with the Upper Barbican (Fig. 180). Here the South-West Tower—the Drawbridge Tower of the inventory?—was filled with earth dug from within the Upper Barbican, lowering the original medieval ground levels. Four splayed gunports were constructed within the top of the medieval masonry. They were given oak lintels overbuilt with rubble masonry, to protect the gun crews behind, with the gun or guns standing on the earthen bed. The spiral staircase must have remained open to allow access. To improve the field of fire, the length of town wall running across the Dell to the South-West Tower was probably demolished and the Upper Gatehouse passage was lowered rendering the drawbridge, gates and portcullis useless. Perhaps this end of the castle was blocked restricting access to the Main Gatehouse.

The wall-walk from the South-West Tower towards the Upper Bailey remained largely unchanged, but the front wall of Marshal's Tower was breached. This new opening led onto a radically remodelled south curtain wall. The interior of the tower was dismantled and a platform, reached by stone steps, was built within the south wall (Fig. 58). The two windows overlooking the Dell were partly blocked to create musket loops and a low rectangular opening was punched through the eastern return. This probably contained 'the iron murthering piece in ye Upper Court' described in the inventory, providing covering fire along the face of the south curtain wall. This wall was reduced by about 4m from its original medieval height (Figs. 57 and 181). The stone was used to build an inner skin 1.5m to the rear tapering from 0.75m wide at its base to 0.55m at the top. Connecting the two walls was timber strapping about one third of the way up, whose sockets survive. Six timbers, 0.2m high and 0.15m wide, ran between the two walls. These were halved over a line of semi-circular sectioned timbers—of c.0.3m diameter—built within the rear curtain wall. The void between the two walls was filled with soil and rubble and a

*Fig. 181 A view of the Upper Bailey curtain wall from across the Dell showing the line of musket loops*

single buttress was built to resist the pounding of artillery fire from the opposite side of the Dell, only 65m away. A new 2m high wall was built along the cliff side of the Upper Bailey containing eight musket loops pointing over the river to the opposite bank 160m away (Fig. 181). Four triangular pistol loops were cut through the Tudor doors in the Upper Bailey Gateway.

There are no specific alterations visible on the Great Tower. The inventory refers to 'ye platforme over ye Great Tower' as carrying a brass gun and 'ye Cogloft att ye top of ye Greate Tower' containing sheaves of match and other items. This implies that it was still partly roofed. Also 'ye store roome that is called ye bisket roome' immediately precedes 'ye Cogloft'. Given the vast quantity of stores, this is likely to have been the undercroft of the Great Tower. It is possible that the reason the windows on the north side of the hall in the Great Tower are all missing their lower mullions (Fig. 23) may be that they were converted into gunports. Also the blocking of the arcade on the north side of the Gallery may have created another line of musket loops.

The Middle Bailey is the 'midle court' of the inventory. Its southern curtain wall was treated in a similar way to the Upper Bailey. Using the existing platform and steps in front of the Great Tower for access, the curtain wall was broadened by building an inner, rubble stone skin falling from 6.5m high at its west end to 4.5m high at the east. The rear of this inner wall is supported by buttresses. The two at the west end are narrower and are keyed into the wall. Between these two buttresses are the sockets for timber strapping similar to that in the Upper Bailey. The other six buttresses are more massive and are not keyed into the curtain wall (Fig. 46). They contain large blocks of dressed green sandstone and so may derive from the buildings added to the Middle Bailey curtain wall in the Tudor period (see chapter 18). These buildings would have had to have been demolished to accommodate these later 17th-century alterations.

The new inner curtain wall created a new wall-walk 1.8m wide. This gave access to a line of five musket loops and a small gunport west of the D-shaped tower and four musket loops to the east. These outer curtain walls show some remodelling and patching, which may be repairs following the Civil War sieges. The D-shaped tower is 'ye litle tower'. It was filled with rubble and the top of the tower was remodelled to make three splayed gunports, one of which still contained a brass field piece in 1679. The Jumper Tower of the inventory must be the corner tower of the Middle Bailey. Its walls were breached to create a way from the Middle to the Lower Bailey. It too had some of its openings walled up. The top of the tower was modified to create four gunports with a wooden platform created at wall top level for the guns to stand upon. In 1679, two brass guns and an empty carriage survived in place and the platform was much decayed. The only other visible changes in the Middle Bailey involved the building of a brick-vaulted magazine in the curtain wall and the cutting of four pistol loops into the gates.

The Lower Bailey remained the centre of the 17th-century fort as it had the Tudor castle. It is referred to as the Great Court in the inventory and seems to have had thirteen guns, two mortars and over 1,000 shot and other projectiles lying around. One gun seems to have been mounted on the platform below the Gloriette and four guns on the platform over the Great (or Main) Gate. The south curtain wall between the Middle Bailey and Marten's Tower seems to have been rebuilt. This is the area traditionally believed to have been breached during the second Civil War siege (see pp. 224-26), so the outer curtain wall, which is built on four different alignments, may be of this date. The inner curtain wall is very well built with a moulded plinth, regularly-coursed stone including large and regularly-placed square blocks of limestone. Just east of centre, the stub of an earlier wall is incorporated, but there is no other evidence for earlier buildings in this area.[16]

The inner curtain wall contains an elevated portal with a basket arch to a great gunport (Figs. 182 and 183). This is by far the largest and most sophisticated of the gunports at Chepstow Castle and was built within the void between the inner and outer curtain walls. The outer wall has rotated forward which has split the interior of the gunport in two, and the fill between the two walls has largely been removed. Nevertheless, it has proved possible to reconstruct the form of this remarkable structure (Fig. 182). The rear portal is made of ashlar sandstone, but would have had a massive timber beam across its base to help stop the recoiling gun. The floor of the gunport was also made of massive timbers set on wooden cross beams and low stone walls. The main reveal is built into the outer curtain wall, partly in ashlar and partly in rubble stone. The gun was presented through a rectangular hole, 0.5m wide and 0.6m high. This would have had a massive oak lintel and retains its masonry relieving arch above. The outer splay for the gun was also roofed with wooden beams to absorb the shock of the gun as it leapt on recoil. The gunport ended in an outer portal of a similar shape to that on the inside. This is now blocked by later stonework. The interior of the gunport was roofed with a rubble stone vault, built on massive beams running between the two curtain walls (Fig. 183). To the east is a small chamber 1m wide and 1.3m deep. This may have provided a refuge for the gun crew when the gun was fired. To the west, the arrangements are more complicated. There is an L-shaped space ending in a hatch whose metal hangings suggest they carried a pair of double doors opening out to the gunport. Beyond the L-shaped room, is another room, 1.3m by 2.3m, plastered internally and opening up towards the wall-walk. The setting for some timber strapping in the inner curtain wall suggests that this room may have had a timber ceiling, and may be a small magazine to store charges and shot for the adjacent gun. The charges were protected from the blast of the gun by the L-shaped ante-chamber and the wooden doors on its hatch. There is no special gun identified in the inventories that may have occupied this gunport. However, it is the only large gun position between those mounted on the top of the Jumper Tower and the Main Gatehouse. As such it commanded the lower part of the town and

*Fig. 182 Reconstruction drawing of the rear of the Lower Bailey curtain wall showing the great gunport, with plan opposite*

even the quayside along the river. A line of musket loops was built within the parapet of the new outer curtain wall with two isolated examples visible on the inner curtain wall. These are made of green sandstone and have rectangular surrounds on the outer face. Those over the central section of the curtain wall had to be dismantled in the early 1970s as they were in danger of collapse.

Marten's Tower seems to have remained almost unaltered at this period. It had three pistol

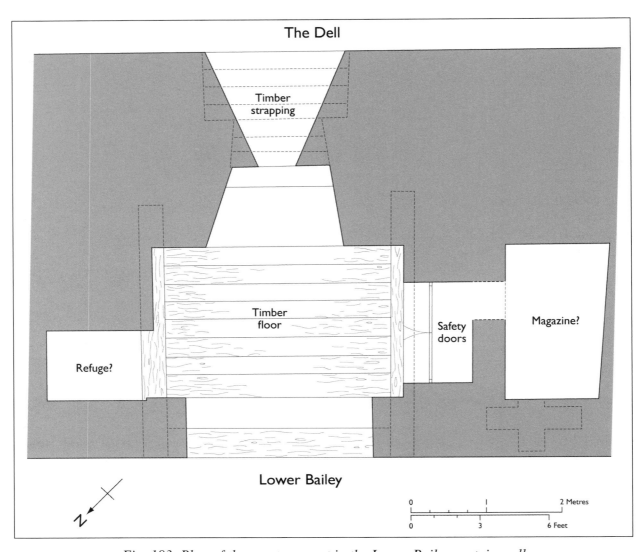

The Dell

Timber
strapping

Timber
floor

Safety
doors

Magazine?

Refuge?

Lower Bailey

| 0 | | 1 | | 2 Metres |

| 0 | | 3 | | 6 Feet |

N

*Fig. 183  Plan of the great gunport in the Lower Bailey curtain wall*

loops cut into the door from the inner courtyard and circular ports were added to the arrowloops at ground floor (Fig. 184), perhaps to house wall or murthering pieces. The top of the towers of the Great Gate were treated in a similar way to the towers along the south curtain wall. A platform was built at wall top level and the existing parapet walls were modified to incorporate alternating musket and gun loops with the four guns apparently being in place in 1679 (Fig. 185).

Whilst the modifications of the castle to take artillery are obvious, less can be said about the accommodation for the soldiers. The inventory of 1672[17] lists a number of rooms and their

contents, almost certainly all lying in the Lower Bailey. In the dining room—the hall—150 new matchlock muskets were stored whilst in the Monmouth-shire magazine there were over 320 muskets and 20 pikes. There was a room for the Governor, Sergeant Miles and Overton (the former prisoner? see p.240), and three other bedchambers. There was also a sparsely furnished barracks. This may have been built against the south curtain wall where floor joist sockets are visible. The wall and a platform in the grass give an outline of this building. The common soldiers would have slept on mattresses made of three 'biskets'. The inventory does not suggest that the accommodation for the garrison was lavish or in good order and there is no evidence of how they were fed and watered.

The structural alterations made to Chepstow Castle to better equip it for defence in an age rapidly becoming dominated by artillery make Chepstow a site of unique interest. At the time of its conversion to both mount and withstand the effects of artillery, it was already appreciated that masonry was greatly inferior to earthworks. Stone could be shattered and walls collapsed by round-shot, whereas earthworks would absorb the impact, and if necessary could be rapidly repaired with the aid of gabions (woven baskets filled with earth) and the use of spades and shovels.

The great gunport in the Lower Bailey curtain wall is a most interesting case in point. The splayed aperture allows movement of the gun in azimuth to give a wide field of fire. The opening is limited in size being only large enough to admit free traverse in elevation, whilst restricting as far as possible the opening available to hostile fire. The provision of storage of 'ready-to-use' ammunition, which is protected from enemy fire, as well as provision for doors to protect it from muzzle-flash or risks from sparks, suggests careful thought in its design.

*Fig. 184 Detail of modified arrowloop in Marten's Tower*

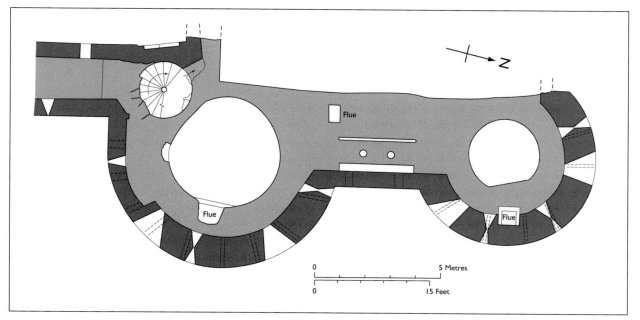

*Fig. 185 Plan of the Main Gatehouse showing the gunports and musket loops*

The service of a muzzle-loading artillery piece in action required a good deal of space around the gun in order to go through the actions of loading, traversing and elevating the gun with the aid of rammers, hand-spikes (levers) etc. (Figs. 179 and 182). At Chepstow the South-West Tower in the Upper Barbican has four gunports on its parapet. This does not necessarily indicate that it provided positions for four guns. On the contrary, it was almost certainly intended for only one gun in time of war, the multiplicity of ports enabling the piece to bring fire over a wider arc than could be covered by only one port. Careful examination of the plans does, however, reveal several areas of 'dead ground' outside the walls, which are not covered by cannon. This provides areas in which an enemy could assemble in safety. Artillery fortifications of the period which were purpose-built, unlike Chepstow, were carefully designed to avoid this weakness.

A besieging battery was always constructed behind earth and gabion works to protect against return fire from the besieged work, and these would in turn provide better protection than the masonry walls which defended Chepstow. The defenders were also at a disadvantage, as mortar bombs landing inside a masonry work would benefit from the stone fragments blasted from the walls. Given also the ability of an attacker to have easy access to reinforcements and resupply, Chepstow could at best only serve to delay an enemy and tie down his troops.

The smaller guns referred to as murthering pieces would have been used to cover approaches to gateways and other vulnerable points. Here their anti-personnel effect when firing sluggs at close range coupled with their higher rate of fire, when compared with heavier artillery, and the facility with which they could be moved would render them invaluable in defence.

## Life in the Castle

The bundle of documents containing the inventory also reveals a little more of the life of the garrison. They include a succession of muster rolls from 1672–8.[18] The marquis was keen to maintain the standard of his company, instructing that those that were useless be discarded. He wanted his soldiers to 'be young lustye fellows and not married'. He also insisted that they were provided with swords, though the money for these was stopped from their pay.[19] The marquis also commissioned an inquiry before the Privy Council to demonstrate that there was no papacy in the garrison.[20] This did not hinder his confirmation as governor of the castle on the accession of the Catholic James II.[21]

As well as acting as a military barracks, Chepstow Castle also acted as a prison for a select group of men who were a potential threat to the crown. The most celebrated of these was Henry Marten (1601/2–1680) — a high-living rake and republican politician in the decades before the Civil War (Fig. 186). He played a prominent role in the establishment of the Commonwealth but turned into an enemy of Cromwell after he dissolved Parliament. Marten was one of fifty-nine people to sign the death warrant of King Charles I, and was one of the few surviving regicides to escape execution following the Restoration, receiving life imprisonment instead. This may have been because he could have become a martyr due to his personal notoriety, or in recognition of his arguing to save the lives of leading Royalists during the Commonwealth. He was first sent to Holy Island, then the Tower of London, was subsequently moved to Windsor Castle and in 1668 finally arrived at Chepstow Castle where he spent twelve years incarcerated in the Tudor apartments in Marten's Tower. He occupied the first floor with his long-time common-law wife, Mary, whilst his servants lived in the room above. This imprisonment was not too harsh as he was allowed to receive visitors and even call upon the neighbouring gentry.[22] Other prisoners included Colonel Robert Overton — an important Parliamentary regimental commander who played a prominent political role during the Commonwealth — who was conveyed from Whitehall to Chepstow in November 1661.[23] However he was either released or escaped, for in

May 1663 he was arrested again and this time imprisoned on Jersey.[24]

The future of Chepstow Castle as a ruin seems to have been sealed by a letter from Mary, duchess of Beaufort, to her husband, Henry, some time after 1682, the year in which he was created duke:

I hope Capt Rider doth not only tell you my house shall be habitable for three yeares, but that it will certainly be safe for you, the truth is if the wind blow anything hard, I cannot sleep for feare of it. I doe most humbly beseech you never to think more of building at Chepstow, now you have told me this, which I never heard one title of before, I believe I should not be my

*Fig. 186 Henry Marten, the regicide imprisoned in Chepstow Castle (where he had been removed from Windsor Castle where he had become 'an eyesore to His Majesty') with his wife and two maidservants until his death in 1680. According to John Aubrey he was 'a great lover of pretty girles ... as far from a Puritaine as light from darkness'. From a painting once in the possession of the Lewis family of St. Pierre*

selfe if I should ever heare of one stone towards building being laid there, therefore lett me beg of you to promise me never to let a thought of it more be, and that you will give me some assurance you are resolved against it, that I may be free from feare. Your son, I dare say for him, was as ignorant as I, for as soone as I had told him what you writ there, he said he had rather pull down this that was there, then add a stone to it, and that he begged of you that you would never think more of it.[25]

The castle is shown at this date in two paintings by Thomas Smith now hanging in Badminton House.[26] They show the castle much as it appears today from the outside, but with roofs on the main gatehouse and Marten's Tower and more chimneys in the Lower Bailey. The Great Tower has been reduced to what survives now. The garrison was disbanded in 1685, and the duke wrote of the 'great rejoicing it will cause among the factions, that have so often bragged they have got me out from my command there'.[27] The buildings were left to fall into further ruin. A letter dated 13 October 1715 written by Mr. Burgh records the seizure of cannon by the government and given by King William III to the duke of Beaufort for the defence of Badminton House: 'the cannon had been in a lumber room since the demolishing of Chepstow Castle, none of the arms were serviceable'.[28]

## Conclusion

The post-Reformation history and development of Chepstow Castle has gone almost unnoted in previous discussions of the site. Very few medieval castles were adapted into 17th-century military forts and barracks. Similar modifications to some of the towers and curtain walls were made at the Tower of London following the Restoration, but grander plans to develop the Tower into a star-shaped fort were never carried out.[29]

Fortifications of this more modern character were built where the strategic need was greater than in south Wales. For example in the Elizabethan period, new defences were created surrounding the town of Berwick on the Scottish border. At Tilbury and other sites at the entrance to the Thames Estuary, new star-shaped artillery forts were built following a raid by the Dutch in 1667.[30]

Nevertheless, the thirty-five years of the occupation of Chepstow Castle as a military fort is an important period in its development. The design of the great gunport with its ancillary chambers presages the design of casemates in the new forts of the 18th century. It also saw the end of the large-scale occupation of the castle given the duchess of Beaufort's insistence that nothing should be done to bring it back into a habitable state. Chepstow's history as a great ruin was about to begin.

# CHAPTER XXIII

# Chepstow Castle as a Picturesque Ruin

*by* Anne Rainsbury

The Dissolution of the Monasteries and the Civil War between them produced a rash of ruins across the face of the country. Abbeys and castles, once the centres of power, wealth and domination that the ideologies of both the Reformation and the Commonwealth had permitted to be plundered and quarried, were mostly abandoned or used for agricultural or even industrial purposes.

The early 18th century was obsessed with ancient Rome and the classical ruins and antiquities encountered by the young nobility on the Grand Tour permeated Georgian taste. Re-creations of temples and pavilions, often built in a ruined state, littered the new landscapes being created around the country house. Alongside the classical, our own native ruins were considered rude. It was the antiquarians who made tours of this country and stimulated the interest in our native antiquities. When the brothers Samuel and Nathaniel Buck began their massive undertaking in the 1720s of illustrating 'the venerable remains of above four hundred Castles, Monasteries, Palaces etc in England and Wales', its appeal was limited to fellow antiquaries.[1] But as the project progressed over the next 20 years, their engravings became more widely popular and it was largely through their work that many people first became acquainted with Britain's rich architectural history. Some knowledge of British antiquities became an essential part of the cultivated person's repertoire.[2] The demand for images and information grew. Gothic architecture was seen to

have a virtue—it was native to Britain, and there were those, like Horace Walpole who sought to promote its revival as the native style.

The classical taste of the early 18th century admired the pastoral idyll, the countryside and landscape which was managed and tamed. On their way to Italy the Grand Tourists rushed through the Alps. Mountains were considered to be the rubbish of creation. They were dangerous and threatening. But there began to be a change too, in the way that Nature was seen, and thought about, and then the reactions that it might stimulate—that there was an emotional response to Nature itself became the subject of philosophical debate and intellectual analysis. A codification of language for the appreciation of Nature was established.[3] Beauty was defined as smooth and gentle—the cultivated valleys, groves, lakes; the Sublime was terrifying—rugged cliffs, mountains, waterfalls. The fashionable interest in painting provided a new medium for expressing what one thought about Nature. A landscape could be compared to the style of a painting, which might in some way go to express what the viewer felt about it. The works of Claude epitomised Beauty, Salvator Rosa the Sublime.[4]

The Picturesque lay somewhere in between. 'Roughness forms the most essential part of the difference between the beautiful and the picturesque' wrote William Gilpin in his *Essay on Picturesque Beauty*.[5] It was roughness and irregularity in every detail, from the trees, to the course of the river (canals of course were anathema) to the buildings. A formal classical building had no place in a picturesque landscape and required beating down with a mallet into a ruin.

> When we introduce a scene on canvas – when the eye is to be confined with the frame of a picture, and can no longer range among the varieties of nature; the aids of art become more necessary; and we want the castle or the abbey, to give consequence to the scene. And indeed the landscape-painter seldom thinks his view perfect without characterising it by some object of this kind.[6]

The Picturesque, as its name implies, was about a way of looking at the landscape as if composing a painting. Nature could, and indeed often did, fail to get the composition right according to the ideals of the Picturesque, in which case reality could be altered by the painter and criticised by the writer.

William Gilpin made his tour down the River Wye in 1770 although his famous book did not appear until 1783. The Wye Tour owes its origins to the Rev. John Egerton, vicar of Ross in the 1740s, who entertained his friends by taking them down the river in a pleasure boat. The commercial version became established as a two-day trip from Ross to Monmouth on the first, Monmouth to Chepstow on the second, at a cost of one and a half guineas for each day. This was not a cheap outing. The boats had a protective awning from sun or rain, and a table, at which the occupants could sketch or write poetry or prose, as the scenery inspired them, and indeed as it became expected for them to do. An itinerary became established to take in the important sites and viewpoints, with stopping places for picnics which were provided as part of the package. This stretch of the Wye had everything to inspire the romantic traveller, the scenery in all its variety, infernal industry, the

*Fig. 187  Chepstow Castle by Paul Sandby. Aquatint in sepia made from his own drawing from his first publication using the aquatint process (Sandby pioneered the use of aquatint in Britain) published by J. Boydell in Cheapside, 1775*

ruins of Tintern Abbey, castles on clifftops, and the wonders of the Piercefield walks. Amidst the ruins their thoughts would be turned to consider the transience of all things, and their own mortality, or to muse on the effects of time and decay, or to imagine what life was once like in the baronial hall. Of course ruins covered with ivy were more picturesque.

The first tourists had no guidebook to tell them where to look. From the 1770s, there were published accounts of some of the high spots. The artist Paul Sandby had been down the Wye, and his aquatints of his Welsh views and the engravings that were published had done much to persuade people to make the tour to see the scenes for themselves (Figs. 187 and 188).[7] Once Gilpin's book was available it became the essential companion for all those who ventured down the Wye, and their numbers increased as the upheavals in Europe and the Napoleonic Wars conspired to make continental travel impossible.

Many of the early tourists to Chepstow thus arrived by boat and the first sight of Chepstow Castle strung out along the cliff top remains to this day a breathtaking one. There was of course always someone who was dissatisfied that nature had again failed to provide the perfect view, Sir Richard Colt Hoare wrote in August 1797:

> ... Chepstow Castle comes in sight. I could wish the bank before it on the left were covered with wood, as it appears in part only over a narrow neck of land not in a very advantageous point of view; whereas it would break on the sight most nobly and surprize every beholder if it could possibly be hidden till the boat turns the angle ...[8]

He conceded that the approach to the town was very picturesque but that the castle was 'not very picturesque within its walls'. A year later, he made the same journey down the river in the company of his son and William Coxe, who seemed more suitably impressed:

*Fig. 188 The Entrance to Chepstow Castle by Paul Sandby. Aquatint made by Sandby after his own watercolour, plate III of his third set of twelve views published in 1777*

In the midst of these grand and picturesque scenes the embattled turrets of Chepstow Castle burst upon our sight; and as we glided under the perpendicular crag, we looked up with astonishment to the massive walls impending over the edge of the precipice, and appearing like a continuation of the rock itself ...[9]

He continued to enthuse; 'I have seldom visited any town whose picturesque situation surpasses that of Chepstow', and went on to quote his friend Mr Wyndham who made his tour in the 1770s:

The beauties indeed are so uncommonly excellent, that the most exact critic in landscape would scarcely wish to alter a single position in the assemblage of woods, cliffs, ruins and water, which form the various prospects around Chepstow.[10]

The second day of the Wye Tour was quite exhausting and most tourists chose to stay the night at one or other of Chepstow's inns and to visit the castle the next day. The approach from Bridge Street would have skirted the Castle Pool, a watering hole for horses that was possibly the remains of the reservoir for the tidal mill. Known more recently as the Dell pond, it was filled in finally in 1964.

Admittance to the castle was obtained by hammering at the oak door with a cannon ball suspended from a chain—'but perhaps it was thought to be more of a battering ram than the superannuated doors could bear, and its place is supplied by a more common-place and quiet performer' noted the sensible Louisa Anne Twamley.[11] If only she could have guessed at the true age of the doors.

The Duke of Beaufort seems to have abandoned interest in Chepstow Castle in the early 18th century when he let it on a lease of three successive lives, the last holder dying at the very end of the century.[12] On John Aram's survey of the Duke of Beaufort's estates at Chepstow, a Mrs Hutton is named as the tenant of the castle and its gardens, which amounted to 2 acres and 26 perches, and also of an 'orchard adjoining the Gate'—a small area in front of the main gate, and another adjoining the river, also just in front of the gate.[13] Stepping through the wicket gate, visitors were met by one the castle's tenants.

It was the last holder of the lease, Mrs Williams, who guided many of the early tourists around the castle. She was remarkable enough to have been written about in her own right. She had been born in the castle and lived to the age of 90, which was in itself unusual, but more so, because her mother, grandmother and great-grandmother had all lived, in good health, to over 100. Her mother, Mrs Hutton, according to Coxe, lived to 101.[14] Her grandmother reached 103 and 'enjoyed such good health and spirits as to be capable of walking, in a morning, from the castle to a farm she rented near the town and returning home again to a very early breakfast within a short period of her death',[15] while the great-grandmother, Mrs Charles, was still acting as midwife to Lady Gage when she was over a hundred and lived until the enormous age of 106!

Mrs Williams had known the women who waited on Henry Marten during his imprisonment in the castle and Charles Heath recorded her recollections on the subject. He also recalled with great enthusiasm his first meeting with Mrs Williams in considerable detail:

The first time I visited Chepstow Castle in the summer of 1790, previous to my becoming a resident at Monmouth, was in the evening of a day after it had been inspected by his Royal Highness the Duke of Gloucester and his son Prince William Henry, accompanied by his Grace the Duke of Norfolk. With a becoming respect to such distinguished characters, Mrs Williams had attired herself in her BEST CLOATHS, – which consisted of a dark-green brocade silk covered with flowers, equal in size to the sunflower, – large worked ruffles, near a quarter of a yard deep, – with other correspondent articles of that age; – and when I walked about the interior, in conversation with her I was more delighted with her appearance added to her attentive manners, than with anything else the building had to offer.[16]

The Hon. John Byng visited in 1787 and, unusually, was shown around by a man (presumably

Mr Williams) who was 'very voluble and ignorant'![17] When Mrs Williams died in 1798, Heath wrote that the castle together with some farmland near Chepstow reverted to the Duke of Beaufort, who 'with his accustomed liberality' allowed Mr Williams to live in the castle for the rest of his life. Coxe states that this was the husband—but the age of the widower of the venerable Mrs Williams surprisingly did not meet with any comment.[18] However it seems that members of the Williams family continued to preside over the castle until the middle of the 19th century.

Visitors after the demise of Mrs Williams seem to have been guided by a 'pretty smiling damsel'. She provided a different kind of distraction for some gentlemen whose 'attention was somewhat divided between the remains of the baronial hall (etc) ... and the well-turned arm that pointed to the several objects'.[19]

By the 1820s, an old Mrs Williams once more held sway, described as a widow, and 'being lame, she employs a young girl to walk round and then at their return she meets them in the first court'.[20] Louisa Anne Twamley in her *Autumn Ramble on the Wye*, published in 1839, was not impressed with the standard of guiding provided by the 'rosy damsel' who then officiated as deputy guide; and 'after listening to some very new and original versions of historic matters from her smiling lips I begged to exchange her company for that of a three-legged stool and enjoyed a long morning of exploring and sketching'. There was also a Miss Williams, 'a daughter not very young & interesting but apparently a genius in drawing & working'.[21]

The tenants lived in Bigod's domestic range in the first court, in a few rooms that were 'less dilapidated than the rest'.[22] The decorated medieval chimney louvre was still being used (see chapter XIV and Fig. 114). Some modern comforts intruded; prints show that sash windows had been installed by the 1770s. Their incongruous appearance was noted by a lady writer, Louisa Anne

*Fig. 189 An inside view of Chepstow Castle drawn by P. Reeves, 1786, showing the First Court in use as a farmyard with the glass factory and malthouse buildings against the Great Hall. The medieval chimney louvre is also visible*

*Fig. 190 'Banquetting Hall' by J. Georges, 1859, showing lean-to buildings which formed part of the custodian's house*

Twamley, who almost fancied that the ancient walls 'looked indignant at a poor little dimity curtain, that was giving itself great airs at an open casement'. These rooms continued to be occupied by the caretakers of the castle well into the 20th century.

To the 18th-century visitor, the appearance of the first court was more that of a working farm-yard, with animals and carts—for the tenants worked what was in effect a smallholding (Plate 11). The second court had been converted into a kitchen garden and, according to Stebbing Shaw who visited in 1788,[23] the last of the lease-holders,[24] made 'a good subsistence by the fruits of the garden, peaches, etc which are plentiful on these warm walls when other places fail'. However the castle towers and apartments around the first court, as well as more recent additional buildings, were being used as industrial units to accommodate a whole range of activities. Heath mentions a stable, dog-kennel, malt-house and a glasshouse. William Beattie, writing later in the 19th century, recorded the areas that had been adapted for commercial and industrial purposes; 'the great kitchen to a sail manufactory; the store-room to a wholesale wine cellar; the grand hall, or banqueting-room was occupied by a glass blower; and the circular tower by the gate leading into the 2nd court, was used as a nail manufactory'.[25] Beattie also remarks that 'one of the principal towers was converted into a glass manufactory, the furnace of which has left its scars deeply indented in the solid masonry'. David Williams writing closer to the time in 1796, stated that the hall was converted into a glasshouse.[26]

A glass factory is known to have been established in Chepstow in 1764, from an advertisement dated 16 October, that appeared in the Bristol papers from 20 October each week until the end of the year. It announced the opening at Chepstow of:

A Flint and Enamel Glass Manufactory where Merchants, Tradesmen, and others may depend on being supplied with all sorts of the best Flint Glass; Also Apothecaries Green Phials and every other article made in the neatest Manner on the lowest terms.[27]

Williams, Dunbar & Co had 'spar'd no pains nor expence to procure the best hands in England' for the enterprise. This notice has acquired considerable significance, as it is the first known advertisement for enamel glass, that opaque white glass for which Bristol became famous in the latter part of the 18th century.[28] This milky-white glass painted with enamels was the glassmakers' attempt to emulate the fine porcelains from the Far East that were so sought after. An additional spur to production was that duty on clear, crystal glass was raised in 1746, but opaque glass, presumably because so little was made, had been left alone. It is thought likely that enamel glass began to be made in Bristol in the 1750s. Whether or not there was a connection between the Chepstow business and any Bristol glassmakers is not known; like-wise it is unclear whether there was any relation-ship with the Williams family who tenanted the castle and the Messrs Williams of the company. It has been suggested that it was the proximity to raw materials, especially coal from the Forest of Dean, which might have made Chepstow a good location for a glasshouse.[29] John Byng also noted in his visit to the ironworks at Tintern in 1781, that the dross was sent to glasshouses at Bristol.

Messrs Williams, Dunbar and Company employed the noted Bristol artist, Michael Edkins, to decorate some of their glass.[30] This he did between 20 February and 23 July 1765, with an additional few items in November of the same year. He painted and gilded mostly blue glass—bottles, basins, pints, salts, beakers, cans, bowls, cream jugs, and decanters. But there were also enamel items—basins, beakers, and jars.[31]

However, in August 1765, another notice appeared in the *Bristol Journal*, dated 5 July, announcing that the partnership of Richard Williams of Tydenham, James Williams and Isaac Hay Dunbar, Glass-Makers of Chepstow, was that day 'dissolved by mutual consent', but that the 'business of glass-making in all its branches is now carried on by the aforesaid Richard Williams'.

Richard Williams was a gentleman farmer of Day House, Tidenham, but he had personal links both with Bristol and several apothecaries, for whom the provision of green glass phials must have been of interest. He had a son, John, who was an apothecary in Bristol and his daughter Sarah was about to marry Thomas Lowder, also an apothecary in Bristol. He did have a son called James, but he also had a brother James who was yet another apothecary, in Chepstow.

This split in the business runs counter to the story told in an article of 1925 by Arthur Powell on Bristol glass-making, from which subsequent articles and accounts seem to derive.[32] He says that in 1765 it was advertised that William Williams had retired and Isaac Hays Dunbar would continue the business, yet no William Williams appears to have been involved. However the only other advertisement it was possible to trace, which appeared in Felix Farley's *Bristol Journal* on 22 November 1766, was yet another notice of the end of a partnership—this time between Messrs Dunbar & Bradley, 'Glass-Makers of Chepstow', announcing that the business was still carried on, but by Dunbar only. Could there have been two glass-making operations in Chepstow, or had Dunbar bought out Richard Williams?[33] Exactly how long the Chepstow glass factory remained in business is unknown, but in the years 1765 and 1766 there are five entries relating to glassmakers in the Chepstow parish records.[34]

No mention is made in any of the advertisements of Chepstow Castle as to the location of the glass factory. The possible site has also become confused by excavations made in 1924 (Fig. 209). Fred Hammond, the engineer who worked with Dr Orville Owen from 1909 to 1911 on his search for the manuscripts that would prove Bacon wrote Shakespeare, became a 'Baconite' and convinced that Bacon's manuscripts were hidden somewhere in Chepstow—and he favoured the castle (see pp. 260-61). The opportunity to excavate the remains of the range of stone buildings that stretched along the south curtain wall was not just an exercise in industrial archaeology but the search for access to a hidden chamber. Fred Hammond wrote on his plans that the building was the Bottle House, but all that he found were fragments of perforated floor tiles which were said to form the floor of the annealing oven (Fig. 191), and the remains of a wooden pipe 8 inches in diameter. These perforated ceramic floor tiles are typical of those used on the floors of malting kilns where the germinated grain was heated to stop it growing. The perforations allowed the combustion gases from the fires in the furnaces below to pass directly through the grain. These kilns usually had a distinctive pyramidal roof—and again there is one shown in the range of buildings against the hall on the other side of the first court (Fig. 189).

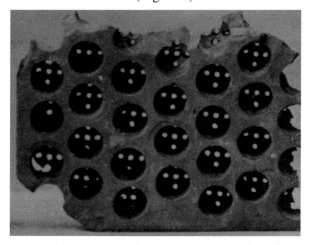

*Fig. 191 Perforated ceramic floor tile found in Fred Hammond's 1924 excavations*

The castle was also providing a base for other industries. Outside, in the ditch, up against the base of the South-West Tower of the Upper Barbican, there were lime kilns in operation. The remains were still visible but overhung with ivy in the late 19th century (Fig. 194).

What role the tenants played in these commercial enterprises is unknown, but they presumably at least profited from sub-letting the various parts of the castle.

Despite these various enterprises and Heath reporting that 'the hand of the spoiler having marked its way through every part of the interior', visitors still seem to have been impressed by the shells of the great hall, kitchens and numerous apartments of considerable size. Vestiges of their baronial splendour 'a few tiles, ornamented with birds and flowers, with which the halls and galleries were paved, have been preserved by affixing them to the walls of the first court' noted Coxe. John Byng had remarked upon them over ten years previously, in 1787, and had been told that a 'pavement was lately knock'd to pieces by some workmen, who threw most of them into the river'. He also noted that coins were often discovered and cannon balls still found in the rubbish.[35]

It was a visit to the 'Dungeon' that was one of the highlights, exciting that frisson of fear and allowing the imagination to run riotously over the plights of prisoners. By the time Louisa Anne Twamley visited in the late 1830s, it was necessary to pay an 'extra douceur' for this privilege! After groping their way in the darkness down a long flight of stairs, they came to:

> a damp and gloomy subterranean vault, with a groined roof, and an aperture for the admission of the few rays of light that struggle through the overhanging and entangled ivy and brushwood of the rock in which this dismal apartment is formed; on peering through the opening, the Wye is seen at a great depth below, rolling heavily along, and the head grows dizzy with gazing from the murky dungeon down the terrific precipice ...[36]

A massive iron ring in the floor was proof indeed that prisoners languished in chains here.

*Fig. 192 'The Dungeon'. Lithograph by John Skinner Prout from* Castles & Abbeys in Monmouthshire, *1838*

However its more prosaic use was as part of the winching system for hauling up provisions directly from boats in the river that could moor safely in the cave immediately below (Figs. 113 and 192). For this was the spacious cellar beneath the great hall, a room for keeping barrels of wine, rather than the 'wretched victims of feudal tyranny'.

Despite the growing number of tourists in the late 18th and early 19th century, still nothing was done to stop the decay of yet more of the castle and the collapse into ruin of the interior of Marten's Tower can be charted through visitors' eyes. When the Hon. John Byng visited in 1781, Marten's Tower was the 'most perfect building ... one floor of which is plank'd and glazed with stairs in good repair ...'. He visited again six years later, and noted that the rooms had become a 'receptacle of sail cloth'. Barber, although greatly distracted by the charms of the pretty young guide, recorded that: '... we entered a Gothic doorway, and, following the taper heels of our gentle conductress up a spiral staircase, visited each apartment in the tower; all of which proved spacious and commodious'. He managed to take a loftier, admonishing tone in a footnote:

> Owing to the neglect of the roof, the upper stories of the building were swimming with water, and perishing very fast. It is hoped, that before this the Duke of Beaufort's agents have looked to their charge, and adopted proper means to prevent the entire loss of a useful habitation, and an interesting remnant of antiquity.[37]

However the warnings went unheeded and Mark Willett, who also remembered seeing the roof and floors of the tower in tolerable repair in about 1797, recorded in 1825 that the floors of the chambers had by then given way, and 'consequently stripped this tower of many traits of its former splendour'.[38]

Most of the 18th-century tourists ventured no further than the Great Tower, which was commonly called the Chapel. It had become associated with the legend of Longinus, father of the soldier who pierced the side of Christ, who was apparently condemned, either for some crime of his own or for having given birth to a criminal, to seek Britain and to erect a religious edifice on the River Wye. The bottom of the tower was overgrown with nettles and brambles—which made inspection 'very inconvenient' if not impossible. Only the intrepid, armed with a machete could have ventured further. When Byng visited in 1781 the two courts beyond the 'Chapel' were sadly overgrown, and impassable, but he could see that if the vegetation were removed, it would be possible to walk around the ramparts, 'and an active man may climb the stone staircases of several towers'. By the 1800s the third court, beyond the 'Chapel', had been converted to a garden which Heath says was filled with fruit and filbert trees. The fourth, however, was shut up by strong doors, and totally overgrown with bushes. Mark Willett noted, in 1810, that it could only be entered by creeping through the sally port in the wall.

In the seventh edition of his book published in 1821, Charles Heath was able to enthuse, with

*Fig. 193 Interior of Chepstow Castle, First Court, lithographed by J. Newman, published by G. Claridge, showing the interior laid out with paths*

almost audible excitement, that 'it gives us pleasure to remark, that the whole of the interior has lately been so effectually cleared of its rubbish, thorns and brambles, (the growth of many years), as to cause them now to be inspected with the greatest ease and convenience ...'. Another exciting addition to the visit was the opening up of the rampart walk along the south wall of the castle: 'cleared of the excrescences of Time we pass along this front of the building on a walk about three feet wide and six above the level of the ground, from one extremity to the other – concluding, by leading to the summit of the Keep' (Marten's Tower). One casualty of this orgy of clearance was the door at the West Gate, which according to Heath was 'a large and curiously constructed wood and iron barred door'. Its replacement was a gate 'more cheerful in its appearance ...'.

Outside the castle, a later guidebook announced: 'the Duke's agents have lately caused a walk to be traced along the ditch to the western tower, and from thence to an eminence on the brink of the river, above the Castle, which presents a pleasing view of several very picturesque objects ...'. The rustic stairway up to the viewpoint is visible in a sketch of 1820 (Fig. 194). The tourist industry had begun to have an effect. At about the same time, the 6th Duke of Beaufort, with the encouragement of his agent, Arthur Wyatt, was tackling clearance work at Raglan Castle, so he most likely instigated all the works at Chepstow.[39] His successors certainly continued them.

Tourists in ever-greater numbers arrived with the steam packets plying between Chepstow and Bristol Hotwells. This led to more changes, so that by the 1840s visitors were greeted by the sight of a bright green lawn interspersed with walnut trees, with all the appearance of a tranquil garden—except on Sundays when the castle was closed.[40] These changes were so marked that an author of another handbook published in 1845 wrote, almost in disbelief of the scene:

The first court is very interesting from the complete metamorphosis it has undergone. The first object that struck me was a gigantic walnut tree, whose nervous branches and eastern foliage spread into the area of the court, dispensing shelter and beauty as if it were the very genius of the place. On a garden seat beneath, a blind harper was carelessly casting his well-tuned fingers over the chords of his instrument to the notes of some ancient ditty and awakening a mournful cadence on the echoing walls. Two or three parties of pleasure-takers were reclining on the sward, surrounded by dishes and flasks, and loudly discoursing with all that joyous hilarity which old English fare never fails to induce.[41]

*Fig. 194  Pencil sketch, dated 9 August 1820, showing the lime kiln under the South-West Tower of the Upper Barbican and the rustic steps up to the viewpoint beyond the west gate*

# CHAPTER XXIV

# The Victorian Period and the 20th Century

*by* Anne Rainsbury *and* Rick Turner

## Festivals, Frolics and Films

The dramatic and romantic setting of the castle ruins have encouraged many local people to stage events within its walls. However, the advantages of the ambience have often been outweighed by the vagaries of the weather—and as the whole area is exposed to the elements, so also have been the scale of the expenses incurred. One of the early events, a public subscription tea to raise money for the widows' and orphans' fund of the Oddfellows on a Monday in late September 1844, tried to take suitable precautions. It advertised that the courtyard was to be boarded to prevent damp and there would also be a covering to prevent inconvenience from rain. The day was lowering and gloomy, but over 700 people came from Coleford, Lydney, Caldicot and Caerwent, and fortunately the tea 'booth' could seat 350, the band played and young people danced.[1]

The newly cleared and more manicured castle became an attractive venue for events, and the Duke of Beaufort seems to have been happy not just to lend the castle, but also his patronage to some of them. The first of the large-scale events were the Chepstow Horticultural Shows. A Chepstow Horticultural Society had held two shows each summer from the late 1830s.[2] In 1845 some local gentlemen decided to re-establish the society and to revive the shows, but on a grander scale. Securing the castle as a venue, and the patronage of the Duke, the Lord Bishop of Llandaff, four MPs and the Lord Lieutenant amongst other members of the local gentry, as well as a large committee composed of most of the local doctors and lawyers, gave a large boost to the enterprise. To attract a good attendance arrangements were made for the Wye steam packet to leave Bristol at 8am and to return at 7pm on the days of the shows.[3]

The second show of 1845 received a lengthy and enthusiastic notice in the *Monmouthshire Beacon*. A large marquee for the fruit and vegetables, and the cottagers' entries, together with a refreshment tent occupied the first court. In the second court, the flowers were shown in the main marquee. Here there were magnificent floral 'devices'—a pelican guarding her young brood, made of dahlias and other flowers; a pillar of red dahlias surmounted by a crown of golden ones; and 'a polite gentleman of the last century, formed of various coloured hollyhocks and seemingly in the act of presenting bouquets to his fair admirers'. The grounds were studded with orange and lemon trees and other portable shrubs, the band of the 37th Regiment of Foot played and more than 2,000 people were believed to have attended during the afternoon, including a fashionable crowd of local gentry.[4] The first show of 1846 received an even more rapturous report, not just in the Monmouthshire newspapers but the pages of the *Illustrated London News*, together with an illustration (Fig. 195).[5] This time far more of the castle had been utilised—there were ornamental flower baskets on the 'greensward exposed for sale' in the first court, but the brilliant

*Fig. 195 Horticultural show in Chepstow Castle, June 1846 (from the* Illustrated London News*)*

spectacle was in the second court, where there was a splendid marquee, and the band of the 37th Foot 'pouring forth the most delicious melodies'. The 'Chapel' (the Great Tower) had been taken over for the refreshments, and there was another large tent in the upper court with specimens for exhibition and a show-table for the cottagers. The whole was deemed to be 'of a character and on an equality with the highest Horticultural Show in the Kingdom'. Expectations were now high, and not disappointed at the September show, where the tentage was again re-arranged, and seems to have settled at fruits in the first court, flowers in the second and vegetables in the 'Chapel'. The stunning floral devices, especially the Chinese pagoda made of 'brilliant china asters, fuchsias, marigolds, dahlias and verbenas', were one of the chief attractions. Another, representing a steamer, had the hull made of moss, the stern ornamented with asters, the body with fuchsias and geraniums, the bow with dahlias and the figurehead representing Flora.[6] With the opening of the railway to Chepstow in 1850 many more visitors came by train, but steamers were still bringing visitors to the shows in the 1860s from Bristol, Cardiff and Portishead.

An event of a very different kind took place in June 1862, when the Duke of Beaufort allowed the castle to be used for the first balloon ascent in the county. This spectacle was provided by Professor Simmons, 'the great American Aeronaut', at a price of 1 shilling a ticket, increasing to 1s 6d three days before the event.[7] It proved a magnificent ascent and the balloon rose almost vertically to a great height, before sailing rapidly east across the river channel. It was a cloudy day and when the balloon emerged from one particularly heavy black cloud, the sun's rays striking the silk caused many of the spectators to think it was on fire. The evening's entertainment was brought to a close by a magnificent display of fireworks produced by the appropriately named Professor Burns.

The coming of age of the Duke of Beaufort's son, Henry, Marquis of Worcester, on Tuesday, 19 May 1868 was marked by a day of celebrations in Chepstow. None of these took place in the castle, but something did happen there to 'mar the day's festivities'. At about 6 o'clock in the evening a local man, Charles Davis, began crawling along the walls on his hands and knees at the top of Marten's Tower, paying no attention to warning calls. Tragically, he fell right down to the basement below, striking the edge of the 'bridge' in his descent. A visitor on the floor below the bridge had a close escape from the falling body. At the inquest it was recommended that the Duke's agent put a railing around the dangerous spot, and a subscription was raised for the widow and an adopted child—to which the jurymen gave their fees, and the doctor 10 shillings.[8]

In his generosity to the town, the Duke of Beaufort responded to a request from the Chepstow Local Board to allow the castle ditch to be used as a public park, leasing it to them for 60 years for the rent of just 1 shilling a year. The opening ceremony in August 1886 began with a huge procession of the tradesmen and shopkeepers, businesses and industries of the town displaying their wares and demonstrating their skills on wagons—all aspects of the working life of the town were exhibited and enacted in this extraordinary cavalcade. Accompanied by three brass bands, the trade unions and friendly societies with their banners and regalia, and followed up at the rear by the inmates from the workhouse and the children from the church Sunday school, the grand parade made its way through the town to the Dell.[9]

In 1887 the Dell was the setting for a programme of sports, promenade concerts and fireworks to mark Queen Victoria's Jubilee. About a month later, Chepstow Castle was the venue for two 'Grand Jubilee Concerts' of National and Patriotic Music, organised by Mr Kingsford (organist and choirmaster at the Parish Church). In the 1880s Wednesday had become the official half-day closing day for shops in the town, but attendance that afternoon was not particularly large, although many of the gentry from the town and neighbourhood were there. In the evening there were around 1,000 to hear the choir of 60 voices and the brass and reed band of the 1st Worcestershire Artillery (Welsh Division). But perhaps the evening spectacle was as much of an attraction. The ivy-clad walls of the castle were illuminated with 'an entirely new and popular means of illumination never before witnessed in Chepstow', Clarke's fairy lamps of 'Queen's Burmese' glassware, which produced an 'exceedingly pretty effect' with the foliage. At the close of the concert, 200 schoolboys walked in procession round the walls carrying 'various kinds of Chinese and other coloured and variegated lamps, producing a fanciful and picturesque effect'. An early version of *son* with *lumière*![10]

Wednesday afternoon and evening musical concerts were obviously considered appropriate entertainments for staging at the castle. In May 1889 the *Chepstow Weekly Advertiser* made the following comment on the activities of Godfrey Seys, warden of the castle for the Duke of Beaufort:

> We are pleased to hear that Mr Godfrey Seys is about to provide a new form of recreation for the inhabitants of Chepstow and visitors for the Wednesday half holiday during the summer months. The noble and interesting ruins have only occasionally been made use of during late years, but now pleasurable opportunity is to be given, to such as choose to avail themselves, of not only promenading the pleasant courts and loitering in the romantic nooks, but listening to strains of music which will be discoursed by the Tidenham Band, and it is to be hoped that the townspeople will appreciate this agreeable mode of spending a Wednesday afternoon.
>
> Arrangements have been made to allow such as desire to partake of tea at the nominal charge of 6d each.

Seys was also giving the castle a thorough clean up and makeover:[11]

> The ruins are literally being swept and garnished, for the grass in the courts is being cut and the place cleaned up generally. Tons of accumulated rubbish have been removed, and the residence has been quite renovated, so as to be quite a comfortable home for the parties who will show over the Castle. Mr Seys has also fitted up a kind of Chapel, with many curiosities dug up in the castle, so that altogether it will take the shine out of Raglan Castle when completed, and from the splendid views will vie with any fortress in the principality.

It was a timely tidying up too for the first major spectacular to be staged by the local community inside the castle—a Grand Historical Fete and Fancy Fair. The Duchess of Beaufort was to open the proceedings, which were to last over three days from 30 July to 1 August. The purpose was to raise money for the restoration of the Parish Church. A huge programme of works was proposed for the church, some of which was to reverse the changes made in the 1840s, and the costs were estimated at some £7,000. Hence this was no ordinary fundraising fair, but a fete on a grand scale, masterminded by Walter Clifford Thomas (Fig. 196), a

*Fig. 196 Walter Clifford Thomas 'pageant master' dressed for his role in the 1890 pageant*

grocer by day, but energetic secretary of sports clubs, the town's volunteer fire brigade, and a member of the local council of the time.

The first fete had a broad historical theme, with a cast of characters from Arthurian legend, through to Tudor and the Civil War, including a number who would have once in reality walked in Chepstow Castle. The stalls in the first court were decorated with heraldic shields and manned by the fashionable ladies of the town. The Duchess of

Fig. 197 *Chepstow Castle Pageant poster, 1893*

Fig. 198 *Chepstow Castle Pageant poster, 1895*

Beaufort arrived in the company of John Loraine Baldwin,[12] with whom she had been staying at Tintern, and took the place of honour on a dais under a canopy beneath the shade of the enormous walnut tree in the first court (Fig. 211). The costumed characters gathered on the rampart walk west of Marten's Tower, and processed along the terrace, through the second court to the first, where they filed into a circle around the Duchess and were joined by the visitors who gathered to hear the opening ceremony speeches. The performance that took place in the second court, consisted of mock tournaments, 'bear baiting', charging at the quintain and maypole dancing. There was a series of five *tableaux vivants* in the banqueting hall, for which the organiser Mrs Maples was much praised, and many sideshows, such as the Prisoner in the Dungeon, to lighten visitors' purses. On the Wednesday, there was also a grand bombardment of the castle by the forces of Oliver Cromwell (mostly made up of the Chepstow Volunteers). There were skyrockets and blank ammunition on both sides, and coloured fires were lit inside the castle.[13]

It was a huge success and raised some £470, which encouraged further and more elaborate events. The vicar, the Rev. E.J. Hensley became actively involved in the pageants, showing a flair for adapting stories into plays. His successor, the Rev. Percy Treasure, was equally enthusiastic and took part in the productions. But the driving force was W.C. Thomas and under his direction the pageants became events attracting large numbers of visitors.

For three days, Chepstow Castle was transformed according to a theme. After the original English medieval pageant in 1884, Norman and Elizabethan themes were gone through in 1889 and

*Fig. 199  Opening of the 1893 pageant under the walnut tree in the castle's Lower Bailey, with the façade of a 'street in Damascus', to house the stalls, created in front of the south curtain wall*

1890, ancient Greece arrived in 1891, eastern tales in 1893 and the legends and histories of Spain in 1895 (Figs. 197–199). The stalls in the first court were imaginatively decorated in keeping with the theme—a street in Damascus, or a Moorish bazaar. The successful formula was repeated: a

*Figs. 200 and 201  Scenes from the 1907 pageant,* The Talisman. *Top: Richard I and his court, lower: the dancing girls performing in the Middle Bailey*

grand procession of all the performers marked the start of the event and allowed the costumes, hired from London, to be properly appreciated. By torchlight at night the effect was dazzling; the opening ceremony each afternoon performed by a lady of the local gentry or nobility under the walnut tree; the main pageant performance, and a series of *tableaux vivants* based on stories of the same period or place. At night the performances were played by limelight, with coloured fires illuminating the castle.[14]

Fund-raising fetes and garden parties for the restoration of the church continued to be held in the castle into the 1900s, many with fancy dress, mounted processions through the town, and performances of plays, as well as more bizarre attractions such as donkey polo! But pageants on the scale of these were not tried again until 1907, when an eastern-themed pageant had a performance of *The Talisman* as its centrepiece (Figs. 200 and 201). It had been done before in 1893, and W.C. Thomas gave freely of his experience to the new organiser Willie Davies, by day a shoe shopkeeper, but also a dance class teacher and organiser of displays and productions. The many splendid photographs from 1907 belie the reality—that the events were cursed by bad weather, with a downpour bringing the first day to an early close, and

torrents of rain and hail turning the ground to a quagmire the next. The last of the great pageants was a revival of *The Siege of Troy* in 1909, when temple-like structures transformed the second court (Fig. 202).

Whether it was the success of the early pageants that emboldened other local groups, or whether it was the burgeoning cultural life of the town in general, that was particularly rich in music and drama, the 1890s saw a much greater use of the castle, and some larger-scale events. There were grand promenade concerts by the Chepstow Orchestral Society on Wednesday afternoons and evenings in June,[15] and then in 1897 band contests and choral competitions—novelties in Chepstow—were staged in the castle as part of a Grand Demonstration of Friendly and Trade Societies on Wednesday, 8 September.[16] The band and choral contests became an annual fixture right up to the First World War, and were resumed for some years after the Armistice. One outcome was the formation of a Chepstow Male Voice Choir in 1899 which went on to give its own promenade concert in the castle in August that year, sadly not well attended.[17]

1899 was a significant year. Following the death of the 8th Duke of Beaufort, a sale of the duke's Chepstow properties brought a huge

*Fig. 202  A scene from the 1909 pageant* The Siege of Troy, *showing the wall-walk used as a viewpoint*

number of commercial and private premises, together with land ripe for development, onto the market. Included in the sale were the Town Gate and the castle. The castle had its own illustrated catalogue and was to be sold with the Castle Ditch (on lease to the council), the Castle Approach and Pond (let to Godfrey Seys) and Guy Meadow (let to W.H. Simkins, the owner of Gwy House), a total of over 10 acres.[18] It was scheduled to be the last lot in the two-day sale on 4-5 October.

In July the Urban District Council had asked Col. Morgan MP to use his influence with the Commissioner of Woods and Forests to try to get Chepstow Castle included with Raglan Castle and Tintern Abbey in the suggested purchase by the Crown. A negative response was received along with the suggestion that a local syndicate should try to buy it privately from the duke before it was put up for auction.[19]

Whilst there was consensus that everyone wanted to secure the castle for the town, there were two camps—one trying to negotiate privately, the other advocating a public meeting. In the end, both attempts were frustrated by each other, and nothing was done towards purchasing the castle for the town, and it remained unsold. The council was, however, determined to acquire the Town Gate, and at the auction, the chairman made an appeal that the representatives of the duke might present it to the town, or allow the council to buy it at a moderate price.[20] The room was filled with cheering and the vendor's solicitor rose to say that he was certain his Grace would agree to grant the Town Gate as a gracious bequest from the late duke, which was met with more cheering. Then came the final lot—Chepstow Castle and surrounding land. No higher offer than £6,000 was made and the castle was 'bought in' at £20,000.

A new player arrived on the scene in 1909, who drew the national press and the nation's attention after him, like a Pied Piper. The charismatic Dr Orville Ward Owen from Detroit came to Chepstow in September to start his search for manuscripts in Francis Bacon's own hand that would prove him to be the real author of Shakespeare's works (Fig. 100). Like other adherents of the theory that Bacon wrote Shakespeare,

he sought the secret in ciphers—of which Bacon himself was a master.[21] He believed he had found their location hidden in cipher in *The Countess of Pembroke's Arcadia* by Sir Philip Sidney. The cipher led him to Chepstow. With the Duke of Beaufort's permission, and with Chepstow engineer, Fred Hammond, employed by the duke to oversee proceedings, make plans of the excavations and ensure that there was no damage to the castle, Dr Owen investigated the cave beneath Chepstow Castle. They found nothing, and Owen spent the winter applying his word cipher to other texts to discover that Bacon had moved the manuscripts to a new place of safekeeping. This was a vault that Bacon had created in a natural rift in the bed of the River Wye in which he had placed 66 lead-lined boxes containing the books and manuscripts. There were clues as to the location of the rift, which led him to a place in the river upstream of the castle. An agreement was made with the Duke of Beaufort, who owned the bed of the river, allowing Owen to dig there and for the duke to have a share in the results. As well as Fred Hammond, the duke's representative, Mr Pirie Gordon was one of the supervisors.

From December 1910 until mid-May 1911 these extraordinary excavations in the bed of the River Wye attracted the attention of the national press with reporters eagerly awaiting the discovery of the documents.[22] In April the focus of attention was moved upstream to the site of

*Fig. 203 Bacon excavations in the River Wye, 1911: pumping out the coffer dam*

the Roman crossing (which featured in the cipher clue). Now interpreting 'below' as 'underneath' rather than 'downstream', excavations uncovered a boat-shaped structure (Figs. 203–205). There was renewed excitement and world-wide press interest. Further evidence finally convinced

*Fig. 204 Bacon excavations in the River Wye, 1911: workmen digging out the pier of the Roman bridge*

*Fig. 205 Bacon excavations in the River Wye, 1911: remains of a pier of the Roman bridge*

Owen's financial backers that this was one of the piers of the bridge and not Bacon's hidden cache and the excavations were abandoned—but not Owen's search. He carried on looking and the cistern at the base of the cliffs below the Great Tower was also subjected to his excavation (chapter XII). Owen and others remained convinced that Chepstow was still the location, and he returned in 1913 focusing on the grounds of Piercefield. Renewed searches resumed after the First World War, and W.R. Lysaght allowed Dr Prescott to dig below the cellar of the castle, until there was concern for its structural safety.

Thanks to Owen, Chepstow and its castle had enjoyed a publicity bonanza, so the choice of it as a film location was not surprising. What seems remarkable now is the incredibly short period of time required to make a great feature film in those early days. The making of *Ivanhoe* in 1913 was not just a memorable event for Chepstow but 'the biggest venture of the kind ever attempted in England'.[23] The first hints of the Imperial Film Company's interest in Chepstow Castle were mentioned in early June, negotiations for its use two weeks later, filming finished on 15 July and the film was released at the beginning of September. The path was more than smoothed by the efforts of Walter Clifford Thomas, who had himself created a version of *Ivanhoe* in the 1890 castle pageant.[24] Because of the pageants, Chepstow people were well used to donning costume and taking part in a big production, so it was not difficult recruiting some 200 local 'supers' or extras, especially as the 5 shillings a day was more than could be earned in Chepstow's Bridge Works. For three or four weeks of the summer of 1913 Chepstow took on 'a state of festival and fancy raiment' as the local extras apparently went about their daily work in costume.[25] The film press gave high praise to the making of the battle scene. The sack of 'Torquilstone' caused two days of excitement involving an army of hundreds of local men, watched and applauded by a crowd of thousands (Fig. 207). Enthusiastic participation resulted in a number of injuries, and the then famous American film star, King Baggot, who played Ivanhoe, fainted from the heat. The whole film, a loose adaptation of Walter Scott's classic, was made under the direction of Herbert Brenon who also played the role of Isaac of York.

When it was released, Chepstow's Electric Picture Hall was packed for four performances each day, and local audiences have had the thrill of re-living their moments of fame for many years since.

Like W.C. Thomas, Willie Davies had also been involved with the film making and had been responsible for the 'effective and tasteful decoration of the stage' in the one of the final big scenes, when Rebecca is to be burnt at the stake. In the spring of 1914 he was presented with gifts and a purse of gold in recognition of his splendid services to the town, before he left for London and a job in films. There he was responsible for the costumes in the film *Jane Shore*, a romanticised story of Edward IV's mistress.[26] In July 1914 the Barker Motion Photography company, through Davies' connections, were busy filming scenes for it at Chepstow Castle and other locations in the district. As no local extras were involved there was a lack of the excitement that *Ivanhoe* had generated.

Nothing like the old historical pageants was seen again until 1937, when as part of Chepstow's celebrations of George VI's coronation, the past master of Chepstow Castle pageants, Walter Clifford Thomas, came out of retirement to mastermind a new event. The theme was Queen Elizabeth I's visit to Kenilworth Castle, where the Earl of Leicester had entertained her in lavish fashion, with masques, balls, pageants and illuminations. However, resources limited the recreation of these events to the day when the queen and her court attended the revels and dances of the country folk. These were reproduced with the help of many

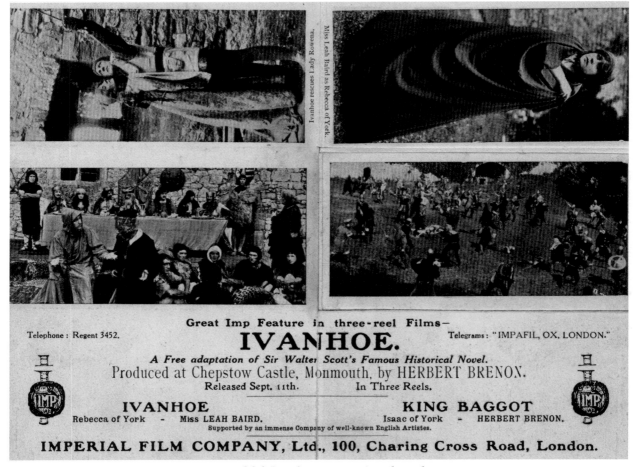

*Fig. 206* Ivanhoe *promotional card*

schoolchildren performing maypole and country dancing. The parts of Queen Elizabeth I and her court were played by members of the Chepstow Operatic & Dramatic Society. Most of the action took place in the Castle Dell close to the west end of the castle.

W.R. Lysaght had the castle floodlit especially for the king's coronation and it was 'the talk of the town. Thousands of people enjoyed the unforgettable thrill' according to the *Weekly Argus*.[27] Desmond Lysaght repeated the idea in 1953 for Queen Elizabeth II's coronation festivities with a scheme that was less elaborate but that he considered equally effective, he told the newspaper. On that occasion most of the activities took place on 2 June either in the Dell or in front of the castle, where a crowd of more than 3,000 lined the slopes beneath the entrance towers to see the crowning of the 'Coronation Queen'. The next day the castle was the scene of a Coronation fair organised by the Urban District Council and local organisations.

Chepstow chose a week in June 1967 to celebrate 900 years of Chepstow Castle. The Chepstow Round Table, formed just five years before, coordinated the programme of events. The official opening ceremony was conducted by the Duke of Beaufort, and for four days, there were afternoon shows of fashion, babies and a carnival and early evening performances of plays, musicals, magic and Adge Cutler and the Wurzels. From 10pm each night there was a *Son et Lumière*, which was written by Howard Moore, the county's drama advisor, based on Arthur Clark's *Chepstow — its Castle and Lordship*.[28]

Chepstow Castle's history has continued to inspire local people, and the ruins of the castle itself to excite the imagination and ambition of generations of enthusiastic organisers to stage events within its walls.

Since the demise of the walnut tree (Fig. 211), which dominated and occupied so much of the Lower Bailey, that too has become a fine arena and stage. The Festival of Castles in Wales in 1983

*Fig. 207 The making of the film* Ivanhoe, *1913: taking a break during the battle scene. The two central Knights Templar on horseback are Chepstow men Robert W. Edgar (left) and Alfred Proctor (right)*

was a spur to persuade people in Chepstow that it was time to revive the great pageants of the past. This time the pageant would celebrate the castle's own history and events that happened in its walls, or by the agency of its great lords. The event was masterminded by Keith Underwood, artist and historian; working with Anna Cassy, Tony Slater and Ann Llewellin, English teacher, musician and writer. Hundreds of people were involved; many working in their own groups, societies, or schools on individual scenes. These were brought together into a massive promenade performance that began in the Middle Bailey and moved into the Lower Bailey, using walls, towers, paths and lawn as acting spaces surrounding the audience, while two narrators maintained the thread of the story.

A few years later, 1986 was the centenary of the grant of the Castle Dell to the town as a public park and the remarkable celebrations that had marked its opening. The curator of Chepstow Museum, Anne Rainsbury, together with Ned Heywood, potter, and many enthusiastic volunteers staged a weekend of events, including a Victorian fair in the Dell, theatre in the castle, and concluding as the original celebrations had done with a grand fireworks display. Such was the enthusiasm created and community spirit engendered, it was suggested that more events over a longer period of time would be an asset to the town, not just for the benefit of the community, but also to attract a wider audience to Chepstow. Thus was born in 1988 the Chepstow Arts and Community Festival, which has become a biennial event over three weeks in July, with the castle the focus of much activity, including plays, music, choral and opera performances. A number of events that began life because of the festival have now become annual fixtures, including a lively programme of theatre. At the heart of the festival is the ethos that many of the events are actually created by members of the community, so that they are active participants in creative endeavour and not just passive audiences.

For the 1990 Festival a *son et lumière*, based on a rich tradition in France, was created for the castle; *Stronghold* told a broad sweep of the castle's story using voices, music, lights and fireworks. Two years later, a small number of costumed performers were added to the production. Emboldened by these successes, 1994 saw the first of the real historical spectaculars: a cast of hundreds of actors performing to a pre-recorded sound track, with a professional script writer, an actor as narrator, specially composed music, a professional director, and as well as lighting effects and fireworks, a few projected images. The result was *Most Loyal Knight*, the story of William Marshal. It was so successful that it was repeated again two years later.

1998 was the 350th anniversary of the siege of Chepstow Castle in the second Civil War, and a new production was created, 1648, *The Tides of War*, with elaborate staging, professional fight direction, pyrotechnics and huge projected images on to the castle walls, with breathtaking effects made possible by the latest technology had to offer![29]

The festivals continue to this day. In 2006, a specially designed, tented canopy will be produced to shelter audiences in the Lower Bailey. It is hoped that this will remove some of the uncertainty and financial risk that have plagued organisers of events in the castle since their beginning in the 1840s.

## Conservation and Custodianship

The failure to sell Chepstow Castle at auction in 1899 saw the Duke of Beaufort remain the owner throughout the Edwardian period. Two of the annual agreements with members of his staff who acted as the castle's custodians survive, and these give an indication of their responsibilities and the restrictions on the use of the castle. In 1902, Godfrey Seys was required to do the following:

> Schedule: notice to be placed at the entrance:
> Visitors to pay doorkeeper 6d, children under twelve 3d, parties of twelve or more 4d each.
> Bazaars and fêtes may be held by arrangement with Custodian.
> Castle open Sundays 2.30 to 5pm.
> No cricket, football, rounders or other games to be played.
> No photographs without permission of Custodian and payment of fee.

No partaking or selling of refreshments, dancing, religious services, speeches, political discussions and singing without consent of Custodian.

No writing on or defacing doors and walls, chipping or removing portions of the fabric, stone or wood, ornamental or otherwise.

Trespassers and others guilty of unseemly conduct or infraction of the above conditions will be expelled and dealt with according to the law.[30]

In 1905, Henry Dyer was also appointed and additional concerns about safety and liability, which are so familiar today, were included in his agreement:

Visitors scaling towers and walls of the ruins do so at their own risk, and neither the Custodian or the owner will be responsible for accident or injury which may occur through faulty masonry, fencing or otherwise.[31]

Both men received an annual salary and pension of £100 and they were supposed to spend any additional visitor income on the repair of the castle. However, in 1914, the castle was bought by William Royse Lysaght, managing director of the Orb Works, Newport. He lived in Castleford in Tutshill and Chepstow Castle was a giant eye-catcher in the view across the River Wye from his house and garden. In 1922–3, Lysaght employed the local architect, Eric Francis, to undertake selective conservation work at the castle.

Francis worked in the Arts and Crafts tradition and was best known for his collaboration with Henry Avray Tipping, the architectural historian and garden designer in building the latter's houses at Mounton and High Glanau.[32] At Chepstow Castle, Francis seems to have overseen the re-facing of the base of the exterior of Marten's Tower in a distinctive red sandstone. He may also have built the two buttresses to stop the Lower Bailey south curtain wall from rotating any further (Fig. 208). Other work, which might be attributed to Francis, was the renewal of the tracery and reveal of the large courtyard window in the kitchen and the insertion of an arch in the opposite wall to support the other window. Works were undertaken to repair the fireplace and oven in the base of the D-shaped tower between the Middle and Lower Baileys. He may have also been responsible for creating the doorway from the Middle Bailey curtain wall into the south-east corner tower.

A good impression of the castle at this date comes from watching the 1913 silent film *Ivanhoe*.[33]

*Fig. 208 Postcard of Chepstow Castle taken soon after Francis' restoration of the base of Marten's Tower and the building of the buttresses against the Lower Bailey curtain wall*

Much of the action takes place in the Middle and Lower Baileys, which remained largely ivy-clad. One area which was much more complete was the Tudor masonry on the natural balcony below the Gloriette in the Lower Bailey. In one scene, Isaac of York[34] was threatened with being thrown through an intact doorway into the river below, of which only the lower half now survives.

The Lysaght family commissioned a new guidebook, the first since Charles Heath's at the beginning of the 19th century. This was written by Noel Somerset and illustrated by a fine series of photographs by Ballard of Chepstow.

The local engineer, Fred Hammond, undertook some excavations inside the Lower Bailey in 1924. Hammond was still searching for the Bacon manuscripts, but these excavations seem to have been linked with the grouting of new foundations below the problematic south curtain wall. A cross-sectional drawing in Chepstow Museum shows six feet of lime concrete underpinning these walls. The photographs of these excavations in the museum show wooden scaffolding on the inner face of Marten's Tower, which may imply that more substantial works were undertaken at this date (Fig. 209). From this period, there are a number of Tudor windows in the Main Gatehouse and Marten's Tower, which had new concrete mullions cast *in situ* to support the surviving tracery. Little more seems to have been done until the Lysaght family put the castle into the guardianship of the Ministry of Works (MOW) in 1953.

*Fig. 209 Hammond's excavations in the Lower Bailey in 1924*

*Fig. 210 A 1956 photograph showing the unpicking of the blocking of the tympanum of the east doorway of the Great Tower*

In the post-war period, the Ministry kept very few records of the work that they undertook to the great monuments in care. This is in contrast to the extensive drawn archives which survive for sites where work was undertaken in the first quarter of the 20th century and in more recent times, where Cadw undertakes comprehensive photogrammetric or hand survey. As well as record drawings, photographs document any conservation work.

The most significant of these alterations were made to the Great Tower. The extent of these alterations has only recently been realised and it does affect our understanding of the two later phases of medieval building. Until the MOW took over, the east end of the Great Tower was partly ivy-covered. An undated photograph, (Fig. 76), shows that the tympanum over the east entrance was blocked with small stones and there are traces of render over this panel extending onto the decorated outer ring and lintel. This much reduces the visual impact of this elevation and explains why earlier authors only give it a summary description.[35] The blocking was carefully unpicked in 1956 (Fig. 210), to reveal the well-preserved carving behind. The joints were re-pointed using an orange-pink mortar made with crushed Roman tile. Also the Ministry unblocked the intact Norman first-floor window in the north wall. Chepstow Castle is not the only site in Britain where the Ministry of Works pealed back layers to reveal what they felt was the more important original fabric.[36] However, this work has compromised the understanding of the appearance of the equally important later phases of the Great Tower and left a construct which would never have existed in the past.

Some idea of progress in other parts of the site can be gained by looking at successive editions of the guidebook. The first edition was printed in 1955.[37] The photographs show areas of the external curtain walls with ivy cladding and wall tops of the taller buildings such as the Great Tower, still with undisturbed vegetation. Soon after the castle was taken into care, the custodian's house was abandoned within the domestic range of the Lower Bailey. Up to that date, visitors used to enter the castle through the open, wicket gate of the original doors, to be greeted by one of the Williams family, long-time custodians for the Lysaght family, sitting below an open canopy, ready to take the entrance fee. The Ministry erected a wooden hut just inside the gatehouse to house its new custodian, Mr Edmunds. In the mid-1950s, the great doors of the Main Gatehouse were taken down and sent up to the joinery shop at Caernarvon Castle for repairs and put into store. On return to Chepstow, they were never re-hung, and in 1964 faithful replicas were made at the Army Apprentices College in Beachley across the river from Chepstow, which remain today. The old doors were kept in the large workmen's shed, which with the public toilet block largely filled Bigod's great hall. The huge walnut tree, whose canopy almost filled the courtyard of the lower

*Fig. 211  The walnut tree in the Lower Bailey supported by a host of wooden props in 1954*

*Fig. 212  View of the Lower Bailey taken in 1966, showing an 18th century doorway into and a bay projecting from the hall (compare with Fig. 189)*

bailey, was reaching the end of its life. It limbs were held up by wooden props and the branches were nearly touching the buildings (Fig. 211). It was felled by Mr Edmunds in 1961.[38]

Another dramatic change followed the collapse of the earth fill from inside the South-West Tower in 1964. All this material was cleared away and the tower consolidated and a walkway created at second floor. The sockets for the large beam, which probably secured the 17th-century timber back to this tower, were filled in by bricks, to distinguish this repair from the original masonry. At the same date, the interior of the south-east corner tower of the Middle Bailey was probably emptied out.

By the time of the publication of the second edition, in 1967,[39] it is evident that the Ministry had worked over much of the interior and some of the exterior of the castle. These areas are free of

vegetation and comprehensively repointed. One feature which survived at that date was the 18th-century doorway in the hall in the Lower Bailey and other masonry which belonged to the glass bottle manufactory (Fig. 212). This included a tall chimney and stepped buttress, which almost obscured the main entrance into the hall porch (Fig. 213). There is no record of their demolition. Also the iron ring in the floor of the cellar (Figs. 113 and 192) was removed as it was considered a trip hazard.

The other major changes following this date concerned the continuing problems with the south curtain wall of the Lower Bailey (Fig. 214).[40] This had rotated to a point where much of the line of musket loops on the wall-walk had to be taken down in 1982. Much of the earth was removed between the two walls and needle piles driven through into the foundations. One of the piles cut through and destroyed a small medieval piscina built into one of the walls. This may be evidence that the castle chapel stood somewhere in this location in the Middle Ages. Finally in 1989, a line of reinforced concrete beams was cast near the wall-top to tie the outer and inner curtain walls together, and partly in hope that a planked wall-walk could be re-opened.

Cadw took over responsibility for Chepstow Castle from its predecessors in 1984, when the castle reflected the Ministry style. A simple wooden shed stood just inside the Main Gatehouse. Here the small entrance fee was taken and the 'blue guide', the only interpretation, apart from cast metal labels on each tower, was sold. In 1985, all the surviving remains of the old custodian's house were stripped out and work began to re-roof the Gloriette and bring the service rooms back into use. Sash windows were replaced by copies of medieval survivors. This allowed a new exhibition to be created undercover. The buttery and

*Fig. 214 A photograph of 1948 showing the walk within the Lower Bailey south curtain wall looking to the doorway into Marten's Tower*

pantry featured the medieval development of the castle, whilst the earl's chamber looked at the Civil War. Crucially the original Main Gatehouse doors were incorporated into this part of the exhibition, when the workmen's shed and toilets were taken out of the hall. There was some danger that the doors would be discarded, but as they were then considered to be 17th century in date, they fitted the theme of the exhibition, only to be revealed as over 400 years older in 1998. In addition to re-roofing and re-flooring the Gloriette, a new visitor centre and shop was created in the larder and custodial facilities in the base of the south tower of the Main Gatehouse. These works were completed in 1989.

By the early 1990s, serious problems had begun to appear with the stability of the cliff face. Successively the visitors had to be kept away from the edge by fencing and gantries, and comprehensive surveys of the cliff face were undertaken by the structural engineers, Ove Arup, sometimes by abseiling from the castle above. This revealed that the limestone cliff face was riddled with cracks and shear planes. Large lumps were in danger of falling away, which would have taken parts of the castle walls with them. Beginning in 1999, a

*Fig. 213 The hall porch obscured by a buttress and chimney before their removal by the Ministry of Works*

series of projects were undertaken by rope-access contractors. They drilled and inserted stainless rock bolts up to 7m long to tie the cliff face back together to a pattern designed by the engineers. To provide additional stability much of the cliff face was held together by a robust galvanised steel mesh. After each phase of cliff stabilisation, a scaffold was cantilevered over or bracketed onto the cliff and the external face of the walls were consolidated and repaired by Cadw's own labour force, Cadwraeth Cymru. In some areas, particularly on the outside of the domestic range in the Lower Bailey, areas were conserved which will not have been repointed or repaired since the Middle Ages, including the vaulting below the cellar (see Fig. 122). When standing out on modern metal scaffolding, securely bolted to the wall face, you could only admire the medieval and Tudor masons who built the original buildings with wooden scaffolding, hemp ropes and simple pulleys to help them manoeuvre the large stones.

In addition to the traditional skills of repointing and stone replacement, the last ten years has also seen the painstaking conservation of the wide range of plaster, painted and carved decoration. Work was undertaken to consolidate the parapet figures on Marten's Tower in 1995.[41] In the Great Tower, the unique plaster decoration in the four niches at the west end had curled off the wall and many fragments had fallen onto the sills (see plate 3). In 1999, what survived was carefully grouted or built up with compatible plasters behind, using crushed Roman tile from Caerwent, to secure this remarkable survival.[42] The conservators also carefully replicated the pattern in Bay 2 in the end niche of the south wall where no plaster survived. The result confirms how relatively clumsy the original must have looked, especially when compared with the chip-carving in the tympanum over the east doorway. At the same time, the painted shields in the hall porch and the associated plaster and carved stonework were consolidated and restored to give the room a more completed feel (see plate 8 for a reconstruction).[43] Similar treatment was under-

taken to the surviving plaster and paintwork in Marshal's Tower. Observation from ground level suggested that the short Purbeck Marble columns in the corbels of the double arch of the Great Tower had thinned to a point where they might collapse. Detailed records were made in 2002 and the extraordinary richness of the carved detail was revealed. Conservation was undertaken in 2003.[44] This involved pinning back the surviving parts of the arches into the body of the wall. The Dundry Limestone was then cleaned of its hard black concretions using ammonium carbonate poultices. The eroded stonework was then carefully built back out using a lime mortar and Bathstone dust mixture and given shelter coats of limewash. The Purbeck marble columns were treated with another mortar using sands to match the colour and texture of the original.

In the summer of 2006, the greatest conservation task will be tackled. This will be to secure the painted and plaster decoration in the first and second floor of Marten's Tower (See plate 9 for its reconstruction). These rooms had only been exposed to the weather in the mid-19th century. However rain and frost has led to the loss of large areas of this unique survival. Fallen plaster can be seen on the corbel tables and within the window reveals. Once the conservation has been completed it is hoped to protect the schemes by erecting a new roof using modern materials to rest on the corbel table at wall-walk level. Combined with a new second floor it will allow visitors to explore this room intended for the visit of King Edward I.

A great ruin like Chepstow Castle will need conservation work for evermore. Decay is inevitable and the original fabric will slowly lose its surface and integrity. Any new work is an intervention that needs to be properly informed and recorded so future generations can assess its success and appropriateness. It is hoped that the research, which makes up this book, will not only be of interest in its own right but also guide the future of this marvellous castle.

# References & Notes

## Abbreviations

| | |
|---|---|
| Acts. Ords. Interr. | C.H. Firth and R.S. Rait (eds.), *Acts and Ordinances of the Interregnum* (1911, 3 vols) |
| Add. Mss. | Additional Manuscripts |
| BL | British Library |
| Bradney | J.A. Bradney, *A History of Monmouthshire* (1904–1933, 12 parts) |
| *CCC* | *Calendar of the Committee for Compounding* |
| *CChR* | *Calendar Charter Rolls* |
| *CCR* | *Calendar of Close Rolls* |
| *CDI* | *Calendar of Documents, Ireland* |
| Clark | G.T. Clark, 'Chepstow Castle', *TBGAS* (1881–2), pp.51-74 |
| *CPR* | *Calendar of Patent Rolls* |
| *CRR* | *Curia Regis Rolls* |
| *CSPD* | *Calendar of State Papers, Domestic* |
| Coxe | William Coxe, *An Historical Tour in Monmouthshire* (London 1801, 2 vols, facsimile reprint 1995) |
| DNB | Dictionary of National Biography |
| GEC | G.E. Cockayne, *The Complete Peerage*, (ed.) V. Gibbs *et al.* (London, 1910–59, 13 vols) |
| Gwent CRO | Gwent County Record Office, Cwmbran |
| HMC | Historical Manuscripts Commission |
| HMSO | Her Majesty's Stationery Office |
| *Ipm* | *Calendar of Inquisitions Post Mortem* |
| *JBAA* | Journal of the British Archaeological Association |
| *JBAS* | Journal of the British Archaeological Society |
| Misc. Mss. | Miscellaneous Manuscripts |
| Morris | M. Morris, *The Bigod Earls of Norfolk in the Thirteenth Century* (Woodbridge, 2005) |
| Newman | P.R. Newman, *Royalist Officers in England and Wales 1642–1660* (1981) |
| NA | National Archives |
| NLW | National Library of Wales |
| Perks | J.C. Perks, 'The Architectural History of Chepstow Castle during the Middle Ages', *TBGAS* (1946–48), pp.307-46 |
| RCAHMW | Royal Commission on the Ancient and Historical Monuments of Wales |
| RCHME | Royal Commission on the Historical Monuments of England |
| Reid | Stuart Reid, *Officers and Regiments of the Royalist Army* (Partizan Press, no date, 5 vols) |
| Siddons | M.P. Siddons, *Visitations by the Heralds in Wales,* Harleian Soc., new series 14 (1996) |
| Strickland | Matthew Strickland (ed), *Armies, Chivalry and Warfare in Medieval Britain and France,* Harlaxton Medieval Studies, vii (Stamford, 1998) |
| *TBGAS* | Transactions of the Bristol and Gloucester Archaeological Society |
| Turner | R.C. Turner, *Chepstow Castle*, Cadw guidebook (Cardiff 2002) |
| Warburton | Eliot Warburton, *Memoirs of Prince Rupert and the Cavaliers* (1849, 3 vols) |
| Webb | J. and T.W. Webb, *Memorials of the Civil War … As it Affected Herefordshire and the Adjacent Counties* (London 1874, 2 vols) |

**Chapter I Introduction**

1. R. Shoesmith, *Excavations at Chepstow 1973-1974*, Cambrian Archaeological Monographs No. 4, (1991), p.3.
2. G. Children. and G. Nash, *A Guide to Prehistoric Sites in Monmouthshire*, Monuments in the Landscape Vol. IV, (Logaston Press 1996), p.3.
3. *Ibid.*, pp.121-4.
4. *Ibid.*, p.40.
5. *Ibid.*, pp.121-4.
6. H.J. Randall, 'Roman Period' *A Hundred Years of Welsh Archaeology*, Centenary Vol, Camb. Arch. Assn., (1946), p.86.
7. L.T. Smith, *The Itinerary in Wales of John Leland in or about the Years 1536–1539*, (London 1906), p.43.
8. Coxe, pp.355-77.
9. Bradney, 4, Pt. 1.
10. Shoesmith (1991), pp.157-8; I. Waters, *The Town of Chepstow* (Chepstow 1975), pp.62-3.
11. G. Ormerod, *Strigulensi: Archaeological Memoirs* (London 1861), p.39.
12. *Ibid.*, p.42.
13. Waters (1975), p.168.
14. Shoesmith (1991), p.159.
15. V.E. Nash-Williams, 'Miscellanea: Harness Trapping from Chepstow, Monmouthshire', *Arch. Camb.*, 82, (1932), pp.393-4; S. Pigggott and G. Daniel, *A Picture Book of British Art* (Cambridge 1951), p.19 and Pl. 43.
16. Shoesmith (1991).
17. *Ibid.*, p.159.
18. J.M.C. Toynbee, *Death and Burial in the Roman World* (London 1971).
19. J.D. Margary, *Roman Roads in Britain* (London 1967), road 60a.
20. I. Waters, 'Shakespear or Bacon?', *Severn and Wye Review,* 1, (1971), pp.85-90; I. Waters, *Chepstow Road Bridges* (Chepstow 1977); Shoesmith (1991).
21. C. Fox, *Offa's Dyke* (London 1955), p.222.
22. Coxe, pp.358-60 and plate opposite.
23. Smith (1906), p.43.
24. Fox (1955), p.222.
25. *Ibid.*, p.196
26. V.E. Nash-Williams, *The Early Christian Monuments of Wales* (Cardiff 1950), p.175.
27. L.A.S. Butler, 'St. Kinemark's Priory Chepstow, An Interim Report on the Excavations from 1962-65', *Monmouthshire Antiq.*, 2, Pt. 1, (1965), pp.33-41.
28. C.J. Delaney and I/N. Soulsby, *The Archaeological Implications of Redevelopment in the Historic Towns of Monmouth District*, Urban Research Unit, University College, Cardiff, (1975).
29. Shoesmith (1991), pp.57-61 and Fig. 30.
30. *Victoria History of Counties of England – Herefordshire*, 1, (London 1908).
31. J. Morris (ed.), *Domesday Book, 15, Gloucestershire* (Chichester 1982).
32. F.B.A. Welch and F.M. Trotter, *Geology of the Country around Monmouth and Chepstow*, Memoirs of the Geological Survey of Great Britain, (London 1961), pp.33-5: Geological Survey Sheets 233, 250.
33. 2.5YR4/3, 5/3.
34. Feldspars are rare (<5%) and the rock fragments (*c*.15-20%) are mostly lavas and tuffs with some schists, phyllites and ferruginous siltstones and silty limestones. Scattered grains of garnet and tourmaline were noted.
35. Welch and Trotter (1961), p.49; J.R.L. Allen, 'Upper Old Red Sandstone (Farlovian) palaeogeography in South Wales and the Welsh Borderland', *J. Sedimentary Petrology*, 35, (1965), pp.167-95.
36. 5YR8/2.
37. 10R3/3.
38. Feldspars, chiefly microcline and orthoclase, and rock fragments, largely siliceous lavas and tuffs with some schists and phyllites, each make up *c*.10% of the rock. There is an incomplete cement of secondary quartz.
39. Welch and Trotter (1961), pp.59-66.
40. 5YR7/1.
41. 5Y8/3.
42. 7.5R5/1.
43. 7.5R5/2, 10R4/2.
44. 10R3/3.
45. 2.5Y7/2.
46. 10YR6/2.
47. 10YR7/3.
48. They are typified by well rounded and sorted, quartz grains, the absence of feldspar, and a low proportion of mainly siliceous rock fragments (*c.* 5%) in a generally incomplete cement of secondary quartz.
49. Welch and Trotter (1961), p.117.

50. J.R.L. Allen, 'Roman and medieval-early modern building stones in southeast Wales: the Sudbrook Sandstone and Dolomitic Conglomerate (Triassic)', *The Monmouthshire Antiquary*, 21, pp.21-44.

51. 10YR7/4-6.

52. Well-sorted and rounded grains of quartz with very little feldspar and rock fragments (<5% together) are set with large subhedral to euhedral dolomite crystals in a variable calcite-dolomite cement.

53. A. Pentecost, 'British travertines: a review', *Proc. Geol. Assoc.*, 104, (1993), pp.23-39; T.D. Ford and H.M. Pedley, 'A review of tufa and travertine deposits of the world', *Earth Science Review*, 41, (1996), pp.117-75.

54. Welsh and Trotter (1961), 135

55. A.N. Coysh, 'A deposit of the shell-bearing tufa near Lydney, Gloucestershire', *Geol. Mag.*, 63, (1926), pp.354-5.

56. 10YR5/3, 4.

57. 7.5YR5/2.

58. 2.5Y7/2.

59. G. Kelling, 'Upper Carboniferous sedimentation in South Wales', in T.R. Owen (ed.), *The Upper Palaeozoic and Post-Palaeozoic Rocks of Wales*, (Cardiff 1974), pp.208, 212-3.

60. F.M. Trotter, *Geology of the Forest of Dean Coal and Iron-Ore Field*, Memoirs of the Geological Survey of Great Britain, (London 1942); Welch and Trotter (1961).

61. F.J. North, 'Building stone', in J.C. Perks, *Chepstow Castle, Gwent*, Ministry of Works guidebook, 2nd ed., (HMSO 1967), pp.34-7.

62. Clark; J.J.K. Knight, *Chepstow Castle*, Cadw guidebook, (Cardiff 1991); Shoesmith (1991); T. Eaton, *Plundering the Past: Roman Stonework in Medieval Britain*, (Stroud 2000); Turner 2002.

63. R.J. Brewer, *Corpus Signorum Imperii Romani, Great Britain, I.5, Wales*, (Oxford 1986); Knight (1991); Eaton (2000), p.38.

64. Allen *et al.* (2003), pp.129-30.

65. Eaton (2000), pp.35-7.

66. This stone is near the base of the west interior elevation.

67. Such decoration is not uncommon in Norman work, for example, the interior of the priory church at Castle Acre, Norfolk, but very rare and a largely northern practice in Roman Britain. T. Blagg, *Roman Architectural Ornament in Britain*, BAR Brit. Ser. 329, (Oxford 2002).

68. The longest (L) and shortest (H) exposed dimension measured on a random sample of 50 blocks gave a mean length of 0.66m (standard deviation 0.17m) and a mean thickness of 0.28m (st. dev. 0.051m). Two derived measures are also of interest. The surface area (i.e. HxL) has a mean of 0.188m$^2$ (st. dev. 0.066m$^2$), while the mean of the form-ratio (L/H), indicative of relative proportions, is 2.42 (st. dev. 0.64).

69. Eaton 2000, p.38.

70. R.J. Brewer, *Caerwent Roman Town*, Cadw guidebook, 2nd ed., (Cardiff 1997).

71. A random sample of up to 50 slabs gave the following mean values: length 0.97m (st. dev. 0.39m), thickness 0.28m (st. dev. 0.053m), area 0.305m$^2$ (st. dev. 0.134m$^2$) and form-ratio 4.04 (st. dev. 1.39).

72. Eaton (2000), p.35.

73. R.E.M. Wheeler and T.V. Wheeler, *Report on the Excavation of the Prehistoric, Roman and Post-Roman Site in Lydney Park, Gloucestershire*, Rep. Res Comm. Soc. Ants. London, 9, (Oxford 1932); P.J. Casey and B. Hoffmann, 'Excavations at the Roman Temple in Lydney Park, Gloucestershire, in 1980 and 1981', *Antiquaries Journal*, 79, (1999), pp.81-143; J.R.L. Allen, 'The building stone at the Roman religious complex, Lydney Park, Gloucestershire: character and fate', *Archaeol. J.ournal*, 160, pp.229-233.

74. Welch and Trotter (1961), p.64.

75. The blocks used at Lydney are of a very fine to medium-grained, dull reddish orange (10R6/4) grading to reddish brown (10R5/4) or dark reddish brown (10R4/3) quartz sandstone. Well-rounded and sorted quartz grain predominate, rock fragments are few (*c.* 5%) and feldspars absent. There is an incomplete quartz cement. The blocks have the following mean properties: length 0.27m (st. dev. 0.071m), thickness 0.12m (st. dev. 0.029m), area 0.033m$^2$ (st. dev. 0.0029m$^2$), and form-ratio 2.26 (st. dev. 0.73).

76. Phase 1 yielded the following mean values: length 0.28m (st. dev. 0.055m), thickness 0.14m (st. dev. 0.022m), area 0.040m$^2$ (st. dev. 0.0095m$^2$) and form-ratio 2.02 (st. dev. 0.62). The corresponding values for the town wall up to eye-height at Caerwent are length 0.34m (st. dev. 0.095m), thickness 0.17m (st. dev. 0.037m), area 0.060m$^2$ (st. dev. 0.0021m$^2$) and form-ratio 2.06 (st. dev. 0.87).

77. F.B.A. Welch and F.M. Trotter, *Geology of the Country around Monmouth and Chepstow*, Memoirs of the Geological Survey of Great Britain, (London 1961), pp.59-66.

78. Welch and Trotter (1961), pp.49, 117.

79. Welch and Trotter (1961), pp. 101-2.

80. A. Heard, 'The petrology of the Pennant Series, east of the River Taf', *Geol. Mag.*, 59, (1922), pp.83-92; G. Kelling, 'Upper Carboniferous sedimentation in South Wales', in T.R. Owen (ed.), *The Upper Palaeozoic and Post-Palaeozoic Rocks of Wales*, (Cardiff 1974), pp.185-224.

81. G.A. Kellaway and F.B.A. Welch, *Geology of the Bristol District*, Memoirs of the Geological Survey of Great Britain, (London 1993).

82. G.W. Green and F.B.A. Welch, *Geology of the Country around Wells and Cheddar*, Memoirs of the Geological Survey of Great Britain, (London 1965).

83. W.J. Arkell, *The Geology of the Country around Weymouth, Swanage, Corfe and Lulworth*, Memoirs of the Geological Survey of Great Britain, 2nd ed., (London 1952).

84. W.F. Whittard, 'Geology of the Aust-Beachley district', *Gloucestershire Geol. Mag.*, 86, (1949), pp.365-76; Welch and Trotter (1961), pp.114, 142.

85. R.A. Waters and D.J.D. Lawrence, *Geology of the South Wales Coalfield. Part III: The Country around Cardiff*, Memoirs of the Geological Survey of Great Britain, 3rd ed., (London 1987).

86. NA SC6/927/24.

87. J.R.L. Allen and M.G. Fulford, 'The distribution of South-east Dorset Black Burnished Category I pottery in south-west Britain', *Britannia*, 27, (1996), pp.223-81.

88. NA SC6/921/24 m.2; SC6/921.26.

89. NA SC6/921/23.

90. NA SC6/921/24 m1.

91. NA SC6/921/26.

92. NA SC6/921/22 f 6; SC6/921/26.

93. NA SC6/921/26.

94. NA SC6/921/22 m6.

95. See Graham Lott's report on Tintern.

96. F.B.A. Welch and F.M. Trotter, *Geology of the Country around Monmouth and Chepstow*, Memoirs of the Geological Survey of Great Britain, (London 1961), pp.59-66.

97. Welch and Trotter (1961).

## Chapter II William the Conqueror, William fitz Osbern and Chepstow Castle

1. *Domesday Book; seu liber censualis Willelmi primi Regis Angliae …*, Abraham Farley (ed.), 2 vols. (London 1783), i, fo. 162r. On what he may have built there, see R.C. Turner *et al*, 'The Great Tower, Chepstow Castle, Wales', *Antiquaries Journal*, lxxxiv, (2004), pp.223-318, and chapter III in this volume.

2. See above all, *The Gesta Guillelmi of William of Poitiers*, (ed and trans) R.H.C. Davis and M. Chibnall (Oxford 1998), p.164 (Hunc prae caeteris familiaribus a pueritia utriusque dilexerat et exaltauerat in Normannia).

3. *William of Malmesbury, Gesta Regum Anglorum*, R.A.B. Mynors, R.M. Thomson and M. Winterbottom (ed.), 2 vols. (Oxford 1998-9), i, p.472; *The Ecclesiastical History of Orderic Vitalis*, M. Chibnall (ed.), 6 vols. (Oxford 1969-81), ii, p.282. On William fitz Osbern, see now, C.P. Lewis, 'William fitz Osbern', in DNB, lix (2004), pp.116-17. Some aspects of his career are treated by Toby Purser, 'William fitz Osbern: Personality and Power on the Welsh Frontier, 1066–1071', in Strickland, pp.133-46.

4. Pierre Bauduin, *La première Normandie (Xe-XIe siècles)* (Caen 2004), p.223, dates the marriage of William's parents to the early 1030s. William the Conqueror's birth is normally dated to 1027 or 1028; for the somewhat inconclusive evidence, see David C. Douglas, *William the Conqueror* (London 1964), p.380.

5. There is an extensive literature on the family, its lands and political importance. See most recently, with references to earlier contributions, Bauduin (2004), pp.219-31. For Osbern's death, *The Gesta Normannorum Ducum of William of Jumièges, Orderic Vitalis and Robert of Torigni*, E.M.C. van Houts (ed.), 2 vols. (Oxford 1992–5), pp.92, 94.

6. *Gesta Guillelmi*, p.164 (see above, note 2).

7. On this period, see now David Bates, 'The Conqueror's Adolescence', *Anglo-Norman Studies*, xxv (2003), pp.1-18.

8. Bauduin (2004), p.225, points out that the marriage is unlikely to pre-date the period between 1040 to 1045.

9. The evidence for the foundation of these two abbeys is surveyed in Véronique Gazeau, *Recherches sur l'histoire de la principauté normande (911–1204). II. Prosopographie des abbes bénédictins (911–1204)*, Dossier présenté devant l'Université de Paris I-Panthéon-Sorbonne en vue d'obtenir l'habilitation à diriger des recherches (2002), pp.64, 149.

10. *Gesta Guillelmi*, p.26. The date of the siege has been much discussed. My own preference remains for 1051-2, see David Bates, *Normandy before 1066* (London and New York 1982), pp.255-6. For 1049, see most recently, G. Louise, *La seigneurie de Bellême Xe-XIIe siècles*, 2 vols. (Flers: Le Pays Bas-Normand 1992–93), i, pp.357-58.

11. Bauduin (2004), pp.223-4, for Breteuil.

12. *Ibid.*, p.224, is the latest supporter of this view.

13. *Gesta Normannorum Ducum*, ii, p.146.

14. For these details, Bauduin (2004), p.229, note 287, citing Louis Régnier, *Notes archéologiques. Excursion à Tillières, Breteuil, Condé et Chambray* (Rouen 1917), p.27.

15. William of Malmesbury, i, p.472; E.M.C. van Houts, 'The Ship List of William the Conqueror', *Anglo-Norman Studies*, x (1988), p.176 (reprinted in E.M.C. van Houts, *History and Family Traditions in England and the Continent, 1000–1200* (Aldershot 1999), chapter VI).

16. *Gesta Guillelmi*, p.164. The evidence for William's role in England is persuasively set out in C.P. Lewis, 'The Early Earls of Norman England', *Anglo-Norman Studies*, xiii (1991), pp.216-17.

17. *The Anglo-Saxon Chronicle*, 'D' s.a. 1066, D. Whitelock, D.C. Douglas and S.I. Tucker (trans.), (London 1961).

18. *Regesta Regum Anglo-Normannorum : The Acta of William I (1066–1087)*, David Bates (ed.), (Oxford 1998), no. 232. For *comes palatii*, see David Bates, 'The Origins of the Justiciarship', *Anglo-Norman Studies*, iv (1982), pp.9-10.

19. 'Qvedam exceptiones de Historia Normannorvm et Anglorvm', in *Gesta Normannorum Ducum*, ii, p.304.

20. *The Chronicle of John of Worcester*, R.R. Darlington and P. McGurk (ed. and trans.), 3 vols. (vol. i not yet published) (Oxford 1998), iii, p.10.

21. For 1068, *Regesta*, nos. 181, 286; for 1069, *ibid*, nos. 138, 232, 254. William also occurs in nos. 216(I) and 345(I), which date from 1067.

22. Orderic, ii, p.222; *Regesta*, Bates (ed.), no. 254.

23. *Ibid*, no. 11; for references to William's activities, Lewis (1991), p.217.

24. See the evidence for William's itinerary during these years, *Regesta*, pp.76, 78-9.

25. For the text of the charter and the arguments for an English location, see Bauduin (2004), pp.382-3.

26. William of Malmesbury, i, pp.472-4; see further, M. Bateson, 'The Laws of Breteuil', *English Historical Review*, xv (1900), pp.73-8, 302-18, 496-523, 745-7; xvi (1901), pp.92-110, 332-45.

27. Domesday Book, i, fos. 162r, 180v, 183r, 183v, 186r; *Liber de Llan Dâv*, J. Gwenogvryn Evans (ed.), (Oxford 1893), p.277.

28. For grants to Walter and Roger de Lacy, Domesday Book, i, fos. 164r, 179v, 181r, 184r, 185r; for Roger des Pîtres, *ibid.*, fos. 164v, 169r; Ralph de Limesy, *ibid.*, i, fos. 162r, 164r; Ansfrid de Cormeilles, *ibid.*, i, fo. 164r; Alvred of Marlborough, *ibid.*, i, fo. 186r; for other grants, *ibid.*, i, fos. 162v, 167r, 179v, 180v, 181r, 183v, 184v, 187r. See in general, C.P. Lewis, 'The Norman Settlement of Herefordshire under William I', *Anglo-Norman Studies*, vii (1985), pp.203-10.

29. Domesday Book, i, fo. 164r.

30. Although it is often unclear which grants should be attributed to William and which to his son, their scale is beyond doubt. For some comment and a gazetteer, S.F. Hockey, 'William fitz Osbern and the endowment of the abbey of Lyre', *Anglo-Norman Studies*, iii (1981), pp.96-8, 104-05.

31. It is overwhelmingly likely that the priory at Chepstow was founded by William fitz Osbern, since after the family's loss of all its English lands in 1075, no one would have granted the priory to Almenèches. This view is taken in Rose Graham, 'Four alien priories in Monmouthshire', JBAS, new series, xxxv (1929), pp.102-03; D.J.A. Matthew, *The Norman Monasteries and their English Possessions* (Oxford 1962), p.56.

32. Orderic, ii, p.260.

33. For modern discussions of William fitz Osbern and Gwent, see Paul Courtney, 'The Norman Invasion of Gwent: a reassessment', *Journal of Medieval History*, xii (1986), pp.297-313; Lewis (1985), pp.201, 213. See also David Crouch's essay in the forthcoming History of Gwent. I am grateful to Professor Crouch for allowing me to see this essay in advance of publication.

34. Domesday Book, i, fos. 187rv.

35. John of Worcester, iii, 4-5; Ann Williams, *The English and the Norman Conquest* (Woodbridge 1995), pp.14-15.

36. Orderic, ii, p.226.

37. *Ibid.*, ii, p.280.

38. *Regesta*, nos. 233, 238. Although it is not certain, there seems to me to be a strong probability that the two charters were confirmed at the same time.

39. The main accounts are Orderic, ii, pp.280-2; William of Malmesbury, i, pp.472-4.

40. The general context is effectively set out in H. Tanner, *Families, Friends and Allies: Boulogne and Politics in Northern France and England, c.879–1160* (Leiden and Boston 2004), pp.102-05.

41. Orderic, ii, p.282; William of Malmesbury, i, pp.472-4.

42. Orderic, ii, pp.282-4. Roger is often called 'Roger de Breteuil' by modern writers. There is in fact no contemporary warrant for the toponymic.

43. Lewis (1985), p.201.

44. For his itinerary, see *Regesta*, pp.75-84.

## Chapter III  The Norman Great Tower

1. Domesday Book, i, f. 162.

2. C.P. Lewis, *The Herefordshire Domesday*, (London 1988), p.16.

3. T. Purser, 'William FitzOsbern, Earl of Hereford: personality and power on the Welsh Frontier, 1066–1071' in Strickland, pp.137-8.

4. *Ibid.*, p.138, though C-L. Salch, *Dictionnaire des Châteaux et des Fortifications du Moyen Age en France*, (Strasbourg 1979), p.198, credits the builder as William the Conqueror after 1054.

5. E. Impey, 'The turris famosa at Ivry-la-Bataille, Normandy', in G. Meirion–Jones, E. Impey and M. Jones (ed.), *The Seigneurial Residence in Western Europe AD c.800–1600*, BAR Int. Ser. 108, (Oxford 2002), pp.197-8.

6. Turner, pp.5-9.

7. H.M. Colvin (ed.), *The History of the King's Works. The Middle Ages*, (HMSO 1963), ii, p.607.

8. The full understanding of the date and function of these circular windows has proved the biggest interpretative problem to the reconstruction of the Norman and Marshal phases of the Great Tower. On the exterior they are contained within rubble walling of soft-edged Carboniferous Limestone. This retains less lichen cover than the rubble limestone walling from the

Marshal phase at a higher level. However, there is no line that represents the gable end of the Norman building and any gable rising from the outer face of the wall below would block any wall-walk. More analysis of this problem is attempted when discussing the interior elevation.

9.  However, there are examples of floors with this structure in 13th-century buildings surviving in the Rows of Chester and elsewhere (A.N. Brown (ed.), *The Rows of Chester: The Chester Rows Research Project*, English Heritage Arch. Res. Rep. 16, (London 1999), p.51). These have heavy wooden ceiling planks resting on the joists, with a layer of bedding sand and thick stone-flagged floors above, providing a fireproof surface.

10. see St. Nicholas's Chapel, Richmond Castle for example (J.A.A. Goodall, *Richmond Castle and St. Agatha's Abbey, Easby*, English Heritage Guidebook, (London 2001), pp.7-8).

11. The sockets have been disrupted by later works at the centre of the elevation.

12. R.J. Brewer, *Corpus Signorum Imperii Romani*, Great Britain, I.5, Wales, (Oxford 1986), pp.35-6, plate 19, cat. no. 51.

13. pers. comm.

14. E. Hirst, *Report on the Conservation Treatment at Chepstow Castle for Cadw: Welsh Historic Monuments*, unpub. Report, Hirst Conservation, (Sleaford 1998).

15. This decoration has been faithfully recreated in a niche where no original plaster had survived in the south wall. This experiment confirms the clumsiness of the original. The decoration in bay 1 repeats the pattern in bay 2, except that the overlying white plaster in the tympanum is too fragmentary to reconstruct the pattern. Bays 3 and 4 have fragments of both plasters only.

16. For Leland see L.T. Smith, *The Itinerary in Wales of John Leland in or about the Years 1536–1539*, (London 1906), p.43 and for Aubrey see R. Legg (ed.), *Monumenta Britannica: a collection of British Antiquities 1665–93*, (London 1980), p.415.

17. W. Camden, *Britain, or a Chorographical Description of the most flourishing kingdoms, England, Scotland and Ireland*, P. Holland (trans.), (London 1610), p.633.

18. H.P. Wyndham, *A Tour through Monmouthshire and Wales*, 2nd ed., (Salisbury 1781), p.2.

19. Coxe, ii, p.365.

20. *Ibid.*, p.368.

21. T. Turner and J. Parker, *Some Account of the Domestic Architecture in England from the Conquest …*, (London 1853), pp.2, 308-10.

22. J. Kenyon, 'Castle Studies and G.T. Clark', in B.Ll. James (ed.), *G.T. Clark, Scholar Ironmaster in the Victorian Age*, (Cardiff 1998), p.100.

23. Clark, *ibid.*

24. *Ibid.*, p.61.

25. *Ibid.*, p.70.

26. Perks.

27. *Ibid.*, p.326.

28. *Ibid.*, p.328.

29. J.C. Perks, *Chepstow Castle*, Ministry of Works guidebook, (London 1955).

30. *Ibid.*, p.5.

31. see C. Platt, *The Architecture of Medieval Britain, a Social History*, (New Haven and London 1990), p.3 for example.

32. E. Fernie, *The Architecture of Norman England*, (Oxford 2000), p.82.

33. J. Goodall, pers. comm.

34. E. Impey and G. Parnell, *The Tower of London, the Official Illustrated Guide*, (London 2000), p.19.

35. G. Coppack, 'The round chapel of St Mary Magdalene', in R. Shoesmith and A. Johnson (eds.), *Ludlow Castle: Its History and Buildings,* (Logaston 2000), pp.147-50.

36. G. Zarnecki, 'The Romanesque sculpture of the Welsh Marches', in G.R. Owen-Crocker and T. Graham (eds), *Medieval Art: Recent Perspectives. A Memorial Tribute to C.R. Dodwell*, (Manchester 1998), p.65.

37. Lewis (1988), p.15.

38. J.K. Knight, *Caerleon Roman Fortress*, Cadw guidebook, (Cardiff 2003), p.3.

39. P.J. Drury, 'Aspects of the origins and development of Colchester castle', *Archaeological Journal*, 139, (1982), pp.302-409.

40. Lectures at the Tower of London conference, Society of Antiquaries, 1999.

41. M.W. Thompson, *The Medieval Hall: the Basis of Secular Domestic Life 600–1600 AD*, (Aldershot 1995), pp.75-7.

42. Impey (2002).

43. D.K. Renn, 'Burgheat and Gonfanon: two sidelights from the Bayeux Tapestry', *Anglo-Norman Studies*, 16, (1994), pp.177-98.

44. *Ibid.*, pp.182-3.

45. P. Dixon and P. Marshall, 'Norwich Castle and its analogues', in G. Meirion-Jones *et al* (eds.), *The Seigneurial Residence in Western Europe AD c.800–1600*, BAR Int. Ser. 108, (Oxford 2002), Figure 4.

46. Colvin (1963), i, pp.19-24.

47. E. Impey, *The White Tower, Tower of London*, (New Haven and London 2006), and P. Marshall, 'The Ceremonial Function of the Donjon in the Twelfth Century', *Château Gaillard*, 20, (2002), pp.141-51.

48. Impey and Parnell (2000), p.18.
49. *Ibid.*, p.17.
50. D. Wilson, *The Bayeux Tapestry: The Complete Tapestry in Colour*, (London 1985).
51. Fernie (2000), p.86.
52. Goodall (2001), pp.9-11.
53. Lewis (1988), p.16.
54. Impey (2002).
55. Colvin (1963), i, p.42.
56. R.R. Davies, *The Age of Conquest: Wales 1063–1415*, (Oxford 1991), pp.33-4.
57. RCAHMW, *Inventory of Glamorgan*, Vol III, Part Ia: The Early Castles, (HMSO 1991), p.164.

**Chapter IV Chepstow under the Marshals**

1. Turner, pp.4-5.
2. A.J. Taylor, 'Usk Castle and the Pipe Roll of 1185', *Archaeologica Cambrensis*, 99, (1948), pp.249-55.
3. D. Crouch, *William Marshal: Knighthood, War and Chivalry 1146–1219* (2nd edn, London 2002).
4. N. Vincent, 'William Marshal, King Henry II and the Honour of Châteauroux', *Archives*, xxv (2000), pp.6-15; Crouch (2002), pp.58-9.
5. A.J. Holden and D. Crouch (eds.), *History of William Marshal*, S. Gregory (trans.), 3 vols, Anglo-Norman Text Society, Occasional Publications Series, 4-6, (2003-5), ii, lines 9294-8.
6. *Brut y Tywysogyon*, s.a. 1175; *Pipe Roll of 21 Henry II*, p.158.
7. For a description of the extent of Edlogan and Lebenydd see Bradney *Vol. 3 The Hundred of Usk*, pp.113-116 and 189-91.
8. A memorandum of 1223 notes that Hywel had died during the late wars and that his lands and revenues were seized by William Marshal, NA E368/5, m. 9d. The most likely date is when William Marshal seized Caerleon in 1217, *Brut y Tywysogyon*, s.a. 1217.
9. Richard of Devizes, *Chronicle of the Time of Richard I*, J.T. Appleby (ed. and trans.), (London 1963), pp.12-13.
10. For William Marshal's career as lord of Striguil, see generally S. Painter, *William Marshal: Knight-Errant, Baron and Regent of England* (Baltimore, 1933), pp.77-169; Crouch (2002), pp.66-119.
11. For Hywel's death 'in guerra', NA E368/5, m. 9d (correcting Crouch 2002, p.137). For the heavy death toll during the hostilities of September 1217 and the siege and fall of Caerleon, *Brut y Tywysogyon*, s.a. 1217; Holden and Crouch (2003-5), ii, lines 17747-84. For Morgan's retreat to Machen and Gwynllwg, into which Marshal pursued him, *Rotuli Litterarum Clausarum*, i, p.330.
12. Holden and Crouch (2003-5), ii, lines 17788-872.
13. For the succession of the Clares to Glamorgan and Newport, *Glamorgan County History*, iii, p.45.
14. For the countess's prompt reclamation of her inheritance in England and Ireland on the elder Marshal's death, see her letter to Hubert de Burgh, NA SC1/1/85. She died on 11 March 1220 and was buried at Tintern Abbey, J. Richardson, 'The Tintern Abbey Chronicles', *The Monmouthshire Antiquary*, xvi (2000), pp.92, 95. A letter to her son was written in haste as he travelled to her sick bed in the last days of February 1220, and it says she was then resident at Chepstow, NA SC1/4/74.
15. *Rotuli Litterarum Clausarum*, i, p.436.
16. For text see NA C53/28, m. 12, inspeximus of 1235.
17. For the course of the war between Richard Marshal and the king, see F.M. Powicke, *The Thirteenth Century, 1216–1307* 2nd edn, (Oxford 1962), pp.53-5; R.F. Walker, 'The Supporters of Richard Marshal, Earl of Pembroke, in the Rebellion of 1233–1234', *Welsh History Review*, xvii (1994), pp.41-65.
18. D. Crouch, 'The Last Adventure of Richard Siward', *Morgannwg*, xxxv (1991), pp.11-15.
19. *CPR*, 1232–47, pp.26, 36; *CRR*, xv, no. 489. Walker (1994), pp.63-4, has a useful analysis of Morgan's behaviour, although the interpretation of the chronology and the position of Caerleon is different from that given here.
20. *CRR*, xv, no. 1154.
21. *CCR*, 1234–37, pp.337, 350, 374; *Brut y Tywysogyon*, s.a. 1236.
22. Text in, Wiltshire Record Office, 1300/159, no. 1 (Seymour deeds), partially printed in Bradney, iv, pt 2, p.191.
23. Matthew Paris, *Chronica Majora*, H.R. Luard (ed.), 7 vols, Rolls Series, (1884-87), iv, pp.135-6.
24. *CPR*, 1232–47, 254, 468; *CCR*, 1242–47, p.447.
25. Richardson, 'The Tintern Abbey Chronicles'. pp.92-5, which gives the places of death and burial; it is not reliable on the dates, however.
26. D. Crouch, *Tournament* (London 2005), p.48.
27. For details of his career, *Llandaff Episcopal Acta, 1140–1287*, D. Crouch (ed.), South Wales Record Society, 5, (1988), pp.xvi-xvii.
28. BL Campbell Charter v 7; BL ms Arundel 19, fo. 26v; NA E368/17, m. 8d.
29. NA C115/K2/6683, fo. 287v.
30. BL ms Arundel 19, fo. 25v.
31. BL ms Arundel 19, fo. 3v.
32. *Ibid.*, fo. 16r.
33. *CRR*, xv, no. 1154.

34. BL Campbell Charter v 7. This compares with a record of a verdict in '*curia comitis apud Strugull*' between Master William of Christchurch and Llanthony Secunda priory, NAC115/K2/6683, fo. 282v, although the land here is not specified.
35. BL ms Arundel 19, fo. 26r.

## Chapter V  The Main Gatehouse
1. For full details of the tree-ring dating of the doors at Chepstow Castle see D.H. Miles and M.J. Worthington, 'List 94: Welsh dendrochronology – phase 2', *Vernacular Architecture* 29, (1998), pp.126-9.
2. A pair of the original pintles is stored loose on site.
3. See J. Geddes, *Medieval decorative ironwork in England*, (London 1999), pp.23-7.
4. For the full discussion of the tree-ring samples and their cross dating see Miles and Worthington (1998).
5. K. Booth, 'Chepstow Castle: excavations in the Great Gatehouse', *Monmouthshire Antiquary* 9, (1993), pp.19-25.
6. A.J. Taylor, 'Usk Castle and the Pipe Roll of 1185, with a note on an expenses account of 1289', *Archaeologia Cambrensis* 99, (1946-7), pp.249-55.
7. D. Crouch, *William Marshal: court, career and chivalry in the Angevin Empire 1147–1219*, rev. ed., (London 2002)
8. See chapter XIV.
9. References to work on the Main Gatehouse in the building accounts of Roger Bigod's lordship are few and none specific. In 1271–2 (NA SC6/921/21), payment was made for repairing and placing joists above the tower beyond the gate. The kitchen and adjacent chambers were being completed in 1283–4 (SC6/921/26). Repairs and propping was necessary to the chamber over the gate at the 'Gloriette' in 1291–2 (SC6/922/3/m.1d), and in 1303–4, the two towers over the gate of the castle were newly joisted (SC6/922/8).
10. For the Tudor period in more general see chapter XX.
11. See chapter XXII.
12. The plain arrowloop with a basal oillet overlooking the cliff on the north side provided light into the prison.
13. The break in the line of beam holes for the roof in the upper part of the east wall may support this argument.
14. A.J. Taylor, *Harlech Castle*, 4th ed., Cadw guidebook, (Cardiff 2002), pp.23-5.
15. G. Parnell, *The Tower of London*, (London 1993), pp.41-2.
16. They are east-facing, so one of them could have served as a private chapel although no evidence of such a function has survived and no concessions appear to have been made in the positioning of the embrasures.

## Chapter VI  The Middle Bailey
1. See discussion by Dan Miles in chapter XX.
2. K. Trott, *Chepstow Castle Middle Bailey excavations, Monmouthshire*, Cambrian Archaeological Projects Report 235, (2003).
3. See chapter XIV.
4. J.K. Knight, 'Usk Castle and its affinities', in M.W. Thompson (ed.), *Ancient Monuments and their interpretation: essays presented to A.J. Taylor*, (Chichester 1977), pp.139-54.
5. J.R. Avent, 'William Marshal's building works at Chepstow Castle, Monmouthshire, 1189-1219', in J.R. Kenyon and K. O'Conor (eds.), *The Medieval Castle in Ireland and Wales*, (Dublin 2003).

## Chapter VII  The Upper Bailey
1. See J.R.L. Allen, *Petrographic Report on Building Stones, Chepstow Castle*, Report to Cadw (2001).
2. NA E372/156 m.49d.
3. Thanks to Peter Brears for making this suggestion.
4. See chapter XIV.
5. W.G. Thomas, 'The Walls of Tenby', *Archaeologia Cambrensis*, cxlii, (1993), p.9 and plate IIIa.
6. N. Ludlow, *Pembroke Castle guidebook* (Pembroke Castle Trust 2001), p.24.
7. *Ibid.*, pp.8-9.
8. D. Thackery, *Corfe Castle*, National Trust Guidebook, (1995), pp.27-34, and J.A. Ashbee, '"The Chamber called Gloriette"; Living at Leisure in Thirteenth- and Fourteenth-Century Castles', JBAA, 157, (2004), pp.17-40.
9. NA SC6/921/21
10. This suggestion comes from Peter Brears' analysis of the inventories of Chepstow Castle from Edward II's reign. See NA E372/156 m.49.

## Chapter VIII  William Marshal's Castle at Chepstow & its place in military architecture
1. M. Prestwich, *Armies and Warfare in the Middle Ages: the English Experience* (London 1996), pp.29-31.
2. N. Jones & D. Renn, 'The military effectiveness of Arrow Loops: Some experiments at White Castle', *Château Gaillard*, 9-10 (1982), pp.445-456.
3. J. Coad, *Dover Castle*, (London 1995), pp.23-37.
4. D. Renn, *Framlingham and Orford Castles* (London 2000), pp.3-13.
5. D. Renn, 'Defending Framlingham Castle', *Proceedings of the Suffolk Institute of Archaeology*, XXXIII, (1973), pp.58-67.

6. The towers at Houdan, Yvelines (1120–37) and Ambleny, Aisne (c.1140) have a rectangular interior plan with chamfered corners and semi-circular turrets clasping the external corners, while at Étampes, Essonne, built around 1150, the keep is constructed of four massive semi-circular towers joined together—see J. Mesqui, *Châteaux et Enceintes de la France Médiévale: de la defense à la résidence* (Paris 1991), pp.113, 133, 135.

7. For comparative plans, see D. Renn, *Norman Castles in Britain* (London 1973), pp.142, 155, 270-71, 322, figs.17, 24, 51, 71.

8. Renn (2000), p.33.

9. S. Johnson, *Conisbrough Castle, South Yorkshire* (London 1997), pp.18-19.

10. Mesqui (1991), pp.261-63.

11. *Ibid.*, pp.167-68, 264.

12. J. Goodall, *Pevensey Castle, East Sussex* (London 1999), pp.12-20.

13. W. Anderson, *Castles of Europe* (London 1980), pp.70-72.

14. Mesqui (1991), pp.38-39, 263.

15. For Marshal's career in France, see D. Crouch, *William Marshal: court, career and chivalry in the Angevine empire 1147–1219* (London 1990), pp.26-88.

16. King and Cheshire in their detailed study of Pembroke Castle (D.J.C. King & M. Cheshire, 'Pembroke Castle', *Archaeologia Cambrensis*, CXXVII (1978), pp.75-121) considered all the defences of both the inner and outer wards to be the work of William Marshal. Subsequently, Ludlow (N. Ludlow, 'Pembroke Castle and Town Walls', *Fortress*, 8 (1991), pp.25-30) has argued for a mid-13th century date for the outer defences and the Dungeon Tower on the inner curtain although, in his more recent guidebook to the castle, the Dungeon Castle is shown as part of Marshal's earlier works on the plan (N. Ludlow, *Pembroke Castle* (Pembroke 2001), opposite p.36).

17. Hodkinson has suggested that attribution of the building of the lower ward defences to Marshal may not be as straightforward as previously thought and the Meyler fitz Henry, who was in possession of the castle from 1200–1208, may be an equally strong contender (B. Hodkinson, 'A summary of recent work at the Rock of Dunamase, Co. Laois', in J.R. Kenyon & K. O'Conor (eds.), *The Medieval Castle in Ireland and Wales: Essays in honour of Jeremy Knight* (Dublin 2003), pp.47-48.

18. C. Colfer, *The Hook Peninsula* (Cork 2004), pp.84-91.

19. For the dating of Usk Castle, see, J.K. Knight, 'Usk Castle and its Affinities', in M.R. Apted, R. Gilyard-Beer & A.D. Saunders, *Ancient Monuments and their Interpretation: Essays presented to A.J. Taylor* (Chichester 1977), p.152.

20. J. Mesqui, *Ile-de-France Gothique 2: Les demeures seigneuriales*, (Paris 1988), pp.262-68; M. Fleury & V. Kruta, *The castle of the Louvre* (Baume-les-Dames 2000).

21. Mesqui (1991), pp.47, 327, fig.407.

22. Clark suggests that Robert de Roos' first work at Helmsley was focused on the southern part of the inner ward and this was then followed by work at the northern end of the inner ward, including the north gate with its D-shaped towers, see J. Clark, *Helmsley Castle, North Yorkshire* (London 2004), pp.20-1, 27.

23. D. Renn, 'An Angevin gatehouse at Skipton Castle', *Château Gaillard*, 7, (1975), pp.173-82.

24. J. Goodall, 'Dover Castle and the Great Siege of 1216', *Château Gaillard*, 19, (2000), pp.91-102.

25. K. Wiggins, *Anatomy of a Siege: King John's Castle, Limerick, 1642*,(Bray 2000), pp.18-21, 38-39, fig.12, plate 5.

26. C. Manning, 'Dublin Castle:The building of a royal castle in Ireland', *Château Gaillard*, 18, (1998), p.121.

27. W. Carrigan, *The history and antiquities of the diocese of Ossory*, (Dublin 1905), 3B; M. Kenealy, 'Plan of Kilkenny Castle 1767', *Old Kilkenny Review*, new ser. 2 (4) (1982), pp.343-46.

28. Kenealy, *ibid.*, p.344.

29. J. Maher, 'Frances Place in Drogheda, Kilkenny and Waterford, etc.', *Journal of the Royal Society of Antiquaries of Ireland*, 64, (1934), pl.12.

30. D. Sweetman, *Medieval Castles of Ireland* (Cork 1999), pp.52-53.

31. C. Manning, 'The Record Tower, Dublin Castle', in J.R. Kenyon & K. O'Conor (eds.) (2003), pp.92-93.

32. Hodkinson (2003), pp.39-40.

33. H. Summerson, *Warkworth Castle, Northumberland*, (London 1995), pp.12-13.

34. Goodall (1999), pp.6-7.

35. Thackray (1995), p.20.

36. J. Goodall, *Scarborough Castle, North Yorkshire* (London 2000), pp.8-9, 12-13, 24.

37. See footnote 16, above.

38. Mesqui (1991), p.137, fig.152.

39. For a full discussion of these towers, see, Mesqui (1991), pp.162-66.

40. See footnote 18, above.

41. For a discussion of this form of gate with particular reference to Pembroke Castle but without reference to Saranda Kolones, see, D.J.C. King, 'Pembroke Castle', *Château Gaillard*, 8, (1977), pp.164-65, figs 10, 11.

42. A.H.S. Megaw, 'Excavations at "Saranda Kolones", Paphos, Preliminary report on the 1966-67 and 1970-71 seasons', *Report of the Department of Antiquities Cyprus, 1971* (Nicosia 1971), p.120; F.G. Mair & V. Karageorghis, *Paphos: History and Archaeology* (Nicosia 1984), pp.308-10; A.J. Boas, *Crusader Archaeology: The Material Culture of the Latin East* (London 1999), pp.108-09.

## Chapter IX  The Marshals' use of the Great Tower

1.  A.J. Taylor, 'Usk Castle and the Pipe Roll of 1185', *Archaeologia Cambrensis*, 99, (1948), pp.249-55.
2.  J.R. Avent, 'The late twelfth-century gatehouse at Chepstow Castle, Monmouthshire, Wales', *Château Gaillard*, 20, pp.27-40; Turner.
3.  This has been described in detail in chapter VII.
4.  Documents concerning this succession can be found in the *CCR*, 1247–55, p.110, and in J. Goronwy Edwards, *Calendar of Ancient Correspondence concerning Wales*, Board of Celtic Studies, University of Wales History and Law Series II (Cardiff 1935), p.29.
5.  *CCR*, 1227–31, p.31..
6.  *CCR*, 1231–34, p.343.
7.  *CCR*, 1231–34, p.504.
8.  *CCR*, 1234–37, p.28.
9.  Perks, p.316.
10.  See chapter XI.
11.  An analysis undertaken by Peter Brears in a report to Cadw.
12.  See for example Winchester Castle hall, the Bigod Hall in the lower bailey, Chepstow Castle and the Great Hall, St. Davids Bishops Palace.
13.  C. Platt, *The Architecture of Medieval Britain, a Social History*, (New Haven and London 1990), p.39, and P. Marshall, 'The Ceremonial Function of the Donjon in the Twelfth Century', *Château Gaillard*, 20, (2002), pp.141-51.

## Chapter X  The Architecture and Decoration of the Marshals' Great Tower

1.  The following text is an edited and revised version of the authors' contribution to Turner *et al*, 'The Great Tower, Chepstow Castle, Wales', *Antiquaries Journal*, 84, (2004), pp.270-97, to which reference should be made for additional information and illustrations of details. Their acknowledgements are also recorded there.
2.  R.R. Davies, *The Age of Conquest: Wales 1063–1415* (Oxford 1991), p.279.
3.  DNB, 36, pp.819-24.
4.  J. Rady, T. Tatton-Brown and J.A. Bowen, 'The Archbishop's Place, Canterbury', *JBAA*, 114, (1991), pp.43-54.
5.  See further T.B. James and A.M. Robinson, *Clarendon Palace: the History of a Medieval Palace and Hunting Lodge near Salisbury, Wiltshire* (London 1988).
6.  The term coined by H. Brakspear, 'A West Country School of Masons', *Archaeologia*, 81, (1931), pp.1-18.
7.  A term used by V. Jansen, 'Lambeth Palace Chapel, the Temple choir and the southern English Gothic architecture of *c*.1215-1240', in W.M. Ormrod (ed.), *England in the Thirteenth Century* (Woodbridge 1985), pp.95-9.
8.  For mouldings terminology, see R.K. Morris, 'An English glossary of medieval mouldings, with an introduction to mouldings c.1040-1240', *Architectural History,* 35, (1992), pp.1-17.
9.  R. Stalley, 'The Construction of the Medieval Cathedral', in K. Milne (ed.), *Christ Church Cathedral Dublin: a History* (Dublin 2000) pp.53-74. Richard Morris is most grateful to Roger Stalley for discussion of the dating evidence.
10.  R Stalley, 'The medieval sculpture of Christ Church, Dublin', *Archaeologia,* 106, (1979), pp.117-18.
11.  For Lichfield, see M. Thurlby, 'The early Gothic transepts of Lichfield Cathedral', in J. Maddison (ed.), *Medieval Architecture an Archaeology at Lichfield*, British Archaeol. Assn. Conference Trans. XIII, (Leeds 1993), p.50. The transepts are problematic owing to the extensive restoration, but 19th-century depictions indicate that G.G. Scott reconstructed the original design.
12.  For a discussion of the dating, see W. Rodwell, *Wells Cathedral: Excavations and Structural Studies 1978–93*, 2 vols, English Heritage Arch. Rep. 21, (London 2001), ch.8.
13.  D. Robinson, *Tintern Abbey*, Cadw guidebook, 4th edn (Cardiff 2002), p.12.
14.  *Ibid.*, pp.12, 30.
15.  D. Welander, *The History, Art and Architecture of Gloucester Cathedral* (Stroud 1991), pp.110-111.
16.  A. Brodie, 'The sculpture of Burmington Manor, Warwickshire', in E. Fernie and P. Crossley (eds), *Medieval Architecture and its Intellectual Context. Studies in Honour of Peter Kidson* (London 1990), pp.91-110.
17.  For dating see most recently J. Newman, *Glamorgan*, The Buildings of Wales (London 1995), pp.245-6. The Llandaff stiff-leaf is not in the Chepstow style.
18.  V. Jansen, 'Henry III's Windsor: castle-building and residences', in L. Keen and E. Scarfe (eds), *Windsor: Medieval Archaeology, Art and Architecture of the Thames Valley*, British Archaeol. Assn Conference Trans, XXV, (Leeds 2002), pp.102-104.
19.  H.M. Colvin, *The History of the King's Works: the Middle Ages*, 2 vols (London 1963), I, pp.137-41.
20.  A. Hastings, Elias of Dereham, *Architect of Salisbury Cathedral* (Salisbury 1997), p.17. For a more restricted view of Elias' involvement in architectural practice, see Peter Kidson in T. Cocke and P. Kidson, *Salisbury Cathedral: Perspectives on the Architectural History* (London 1993), pp.50-2; and N. Coldstream, 'Architectural designers in the thirteenth century', in M. Prestwich *et al* (eds), *Thirteenth-Century England IX*, Proceedings of the Durham Conference, (Woodbridge 2003), pp.201-207.
21.  D. Crouch, *William Marshal: Knighthood, War and Chivalry 1147–1219* 2nd edn., (London 2002), p.140.

22. J. Ashbee, *Goodrich Castle*, English Heritage Guidebook (London 2005), pp.32-33; C.M. Woolgar, *The Great Household in Late Medieval England* (New Haven and London 1999), pp.50-4.

## Chapter XI  The Upper Barbican

1. *CCR*, 1234–7, p.28.
2. NA SC6/922/6 and 7. Fuller discussion of these accounts is undertaken in chapters XIII, XIV and XV.
3. Badminton Muniments (Duke of Beaufort) FmE 2/5/12.
4. Some modern brickwork fills beam holes on the rear of the tower at second floor. However these probably relate to a timber back, added in the 17th century to retain the earth fill on which a gun platform was created at wall-walk level (see chapter XXII).
5. See Ellis and Frame's plan in Clark.
6. See the discussion in chapter XXII.
7. RCAHMW, *An Inventory of Ancient Monuments in Glamorgan, Volume III — the Later Castles* (Llandudno 2000), part Ib, p.97.
8. J. Coad, *Dover Castle*, (English Heritage 1995), pp.34-5.
9. D. Renn, *Framlingham Castle*, English Heritage guidebook, (London 2000), pp.3-7.
10. See chapter XIX.

## Chapter XII  The Sub-tidal Cistern

1. See for example O.W. Owen, *Sir Francis Bacon's Cipher Story*, 1, and *Sir Francis Bacon's Cipher Story*, 2, (Howard Publishing Company 1893 and 1894).
2. Chepstow Museum acc. nos CH/1968-40 (39-40).
3. Hammond's notebooks are reported to be in Newport Museum or Library but they could not be traced. These may contain a description of what was found during the emptying out of the cistern.
4. The team consisted of John Godbert, Nigel Nayling, Bevis Sale and the author, who were dropped and collected by the kindness of the Severn Area Rescue Association.
5. R.C. Turner, 'A sub-tidal cistern at Chepstow Castle', *Archaeology in the Severn Estuary 2002*, 13, (2003), pp.123-31.
6. This was acquired by the National Museum and Gallery of Wales in 2004, through their librarian, John Kenyon, acc. no. NMGW 18800.
7. Pers. comm.
8. J.R. Avent, 'The Late Twelfth Century Gatehouse at Chepstow Castle, Monmouthshire, Wales', *Château Gaillard*, 20, p.32.

## Chapter XIII  The Life of Roger Bigod, Fifth Earl of Norfolk

1. In general, see Morris; for the surrender of 1302, see idem, 'The "Murder" of an English Earldom: Roger IV Bigod and Edward I', *Thirteenth-Century England*, ix, (Woodbridge 2003), pp.89-99.
2. *Ipm*, i, p.239. For a fuller proof of his date of birth, see Morris p.102.
3. Matthaei Parisiensis, *Monachi Sancti Albani, Chronica Majora*, H.R. Luard (ed.), 7 vols., Rolls Series, (1872–83), iv, p.491; I.J. Sanders, *English Baronies* (Oxford 1960), pp.63-4.
4. The relationship of the two families is discussed in Morris, pp.2-3, 8-14, 18-20, 25.
5. *Calendar of Papal Registers*: Papal Letters, 1198–1342, W.H. Bliss (ed.), 2 vols., (HMSO 1893–5), p.253; *Chronica Majora*, v, pp.382-3.
6. *CCR*, 1264–8, p.500; Morris, p.198; *Chartularies of St Mary's Abbey, Dublin with the register of its house at Dunbrody and Annals of Ireland* , J.T. Gilbert (ed.), 2 vols., (Rolls Series 1884), ii, pp.143-4.
7. *CPR*, 1266–72, p.460.
8. A detailed account of the build-up of the estate is given in Morris, pp.31-42, 102-6; for the Marshal inheritance, see *CPR*, 1364–7, pp.263-75.
9. For the castles, see F.J. Raby and P.K.B. Reynolds, *Framlingham Castle* (London 1959) and H. Braun, *Bungay Castle: Historical Notes and an Account of the Excavations* (new edn, Bungay 1991). For the under-tenants, see *Ipm*, iv, pp.297-303.
10. W.F. Nugent., 'Carlow in the Middle Ages', *Journal of the Royal Society of Antiquaries of Ireland*, 4th series, lxxxv, pp.62-76; E. St John Brooks, *Knights' Fees in Counties Wexford, Carlow and Kilkenny* (Dublin 1950), pp.1-91; B. Colfer, 'Anglo-Norman Settlement in County Wexford', *Wexford: History and Society* (Dublin 1987), pp.65-101.
11. Morris, pp.205-6.
12. NA SC12/22/13; *CPR*, 1364–7, pp.266, 269, 271, 274; Morris, pp.33-40.
13. *CPR*, 1301–7, p.460.
14. J.L. Bolton, *The Medieval English Economy, 1150–1500* (London 1980), p.95.
15. *CPR*, 1364–7, pp.263-75; Cf. N. Denholm-Young, *Richard of Cornwall* (Oxford 1947), p.163; J.R. Maddicott, *Thomas of Lancaster* (Oxford 1970), p.23.
16. M. Altschul, *A Baronial Family in England: The Clares, 1217–1314* (Baltimore 1965), p.205.
17. *CPR*, 1258-66, pp.459-60; *Ipm*, ii, p.228; Morris, pp.104-5.

18. *Calendar of Fine Rolls*, 1272–1307 (HMSO 1911), p.146; *Ipm*, ii, pp.227-9; *Select Cases in the Court of King's Bench*, G.O. Sayles (ed.), 7 vols., (Selden Soc., lv, lvii, lviii, lxxiv, lxxvi, lxxxii, lxxxviii, 1936-71), i, p.81; *Placitorum in Domo Capitulari Westmonasteriensi Asservatorum Abbreviatio* (Record Commission 1811), p.272.

19. *CCR*, 1242–7, pp.443, 454-5; *Chronica Majora*, iv, p.548.

20. For a full discussion of the Marshal's rights and responsibilities, see Morris, pp.26-31.

21. e.g. M. Prestwich, *Edward I* (London 1988), pp.413-4.

22. *Letters of Medieval Women*, A. Crawford (ed.), (Stroud 2002), pp.191-2; F.M. Powicke, *King Henry III and the Lord Edward* (Oxford 1947), pp.615-6; GEC, ix, p.593.

23. E368/44, mm.4d-6d; *Calendar of Fine Rolls*, 1272-1307, p.50. For full details of the saga of the Bigod debts to the Crown, see Morris, *passim*.

24. *CPR*, 1272–81, pp.166, 170; *CCR*, 1272–9, pp.360, 371; *Calendar of Fine Rolls*, 1272–1307, pp.75, 217; *CPR*, 1281–92, p.183.

25. *CDI*, 1252–84, pp. 459-61.

26. *Itinerary of Edward I*, E.W. Safford (ed.), 3 vols., (List and Index Society, 103, 132, 135, 1974–77), i, p.200. *CPR*, 1281–92, p.149. See also *CDI*, 1252–84, p.435, where Edward describes Roger as 'bearing himself well and laudably on the king's service in Wales'.

27. *CPR*, 1281–92, p.277; *CPR*, 1292–1301, p.126; M.C. Prestwich, *War, Politics and Finance under Edward I* (London 1972), p.249; Morris, pp.153-61.

28. *Edward I and the Throne of Scotland, 1290–1296. An Edition of the Record Sources for the Great Cause* , E.L.G. Stones and G.G. Simpson (eds.), 2 vols., (Oxford 1978), ii, p.81; for the 1296 Scottish campaign, see in particular 'A Plea Roll of Edward I's Army in Scotland, 1296', C.J. Neville (ed.), *Miscellany of the Scottish Historical Society*, XI, (Scottish Historical Society, 5th series, iii, 1990), pp.7-133.

29. *CDI*, 1293–1301, p.73; J.E. Morris, *The Welsh Wars of Edward I* (Oxford 1901), pp.244, 248. Stephen Priestley has discovered more information about the earl's movements during this campaign in NA SC6/859/24, SC6/920/7 and E101/531/12.

30. W.M. Ormrod, 'Love and War in 1294', *Thirteenth-Century England*, viii, (Woodbridge 2001), pp.143-52.

31. *The Chronicle of Walter of Guisborough*, H. Rothwell (ed.) (Camden Society, lxxxix, 1957), pp.289-90.

32. E. Miller, 'War, Taxation and the English Economy in the Late-Thirteenth and Early-Fourteenth Centuries', *War and Economic Development: Essays in Memory of David Joslin* , J.M. Winter (ed.), (Cambridge 1975), pp.20, 27; *The Chronicle of Bury St. Edmunds, 1212–1301* (ed) A. Gransden (London 1964), pp.138-9; *Documents Illustrating the Crisis of 1297–98 in England* (ed) M. Prestwich (Camden Society, 4th series, xxiv, 1980), pp.105-6.

33. Prestwich (1988), pp.419-20; NA SC6/1020/23.

34. Prestwich (1988), pp.525-7; J.R. Maddicott, "1258' and '1297': Some Comparisons and Contrasts', *Thirteenth-Century England*, ix, (Woodbridge 2003), p.13.

35. For a full analysis see Morris (2003), pp.89-99.

36. *Flores Historiarum* , H.R. Luard (ed.), 3 vols. (Rolls Series 1890), iii, p.125 (for 'earl of Warwick' read 'earl of Norfolk'). This story is repeated in the later *Willelmi Rishanger, Chronica et Annales*, H.T. Riley (ed.), (Rolls Series 1865), p.227.

37. *Chronicle of Walter of Guisborough*, pp.352.

38. *CPR*, 1301–7, pp.29-31; *CChR*, 1300–1326, pp.25-6.

39. *Flores Historiarum*, iii, pp.328-9 (for *Julii* read *Junii*); Prestwich (1988), p.556.

40. Morris (1901), p.304; W. Stubbs, *The Constitutional History of England*, 3 vols., (Oxford 1880), ii, p.158.

41. F.M. Powicke, *The Thirteenth Century, 1216–1307*, 2nd edn, (Oxford 1962), p.227. Cf. Prestwich (1988), p.108; M.T. Clanchy, *England and Its Rulers, 1066–1272*, 2nd edn, (Oxford 1998), pp.208-12; T.F. Tout, 'The Earldoms under Edward I', *Transactions of the Royal Historical Society*, 2nd series, 8 (1894), pp.129-55, notes the 'healthy monotony' of Edward's earls.

42. *The Chronicle of William de Rishanger of the Barons' Wars*, J.O. Halliwel (ed.), (Camden Soc. 1840), pp.19, 49-50; *Chronica Majora*, iv, pp.182-4.

43. e.g. *Chronica Majora*, iii, p.404; iv, pp.478-9; v, pp.85-6, 530.

44. A. Gransden, *Historical Writing in England, c.550 to c.1307* (London 1974), pp.470-76; *Chronicle of Walter of Guisborough*, pp.xxvii-xxxi.

45. *Flores Historiarum*, ii, p.426; above, n.28; *Rishanger*, p.404; BL Royal 20 D ix.

46. *Chronica Majora*, iv, pp.182-4, 478-9; *CPR*, 1247–58, pp.561, 594. Cf. the earls of Lincoln or Lancaster: Prestwich (1988), pp.130, 153, 378.

47. R. Frame, 'The Justiciar and the Murder of the MacMurroughs in 1282', *Irish Historical Studies*, xviii (1972), pp.223-30.

48. Morris, pp.188-9.

49. B.M.S. Campbell, *English Seigniorial Agriculture, 1250–1450* (Cambridge 2000), p.172.

50. J.H. Denton, 'The Crisis of 1297 from the Evesham Chronicle', *English Historical Review*, xciii (1978), p.577; *Documents Illustrating the Crisis of 1297–98* , pp.137-9.

51. They are kept in the class SC6 (Special Collections: Ministers' Accounts). For printed examples, see F.G. Davenport, *The Economic Development of a Norfolk Manor, 1086–1565* (London 1906) and *Medieval Framlingham,* J. Ridgard (ed.), (Suffolk Records Society 1985).

52. e.g. J.E.T. Rogers, *History of Agriculture and Prices in England from 1259 to 1793*, 7 vols., (London 1866–90), ii, passim; E.A. Kosminsky, *Studies in the Agrarian History of England in the Thirteenth Century* (Oxford 1956), pp.58-67, 164-7; Campbell, *English Seigniorial Agriculture*, pp.172, 232-3.

53. NA SC6/873/7; SC6/837/13. SC6/932/12 records the following expenses consecutively: 'Sir Reginald de Grey and Sir Amaury de St Amand, staying for the tournament, £12 17s'. 'Sir A. de St Amand, from Thursday after St Bartholomew the Apostle [27 August 1271] until the Nativity of the Blessed Virgin Mary [8 September 1271], when his leg was broken, 64s 6$^{1/2}$d'.

54. NA SC6/1020/22; SC6/922/3.

55. *CPR*, 1292–1301, p.68; Braun (1991), p.20.

56. NA SC6/1007/13-19; J. Fairclough and S.J. Plunkett, 'Drawings of Walton Castle and other Monuments in Walton and Felixstowe', *Proceedings of the Suffolk Institute of Archaeology and History*, 39, (2000), pp.419-59.

57. NA SC6/1237/42; SC6/1239/1. Cf. T. O'Keeffe, 'Ballyloughan, Ballymoon and Clonmore: Three Castles of *c*.1300 in County Carlow', *Anglo-Norman Studies*, xxiii (Woodbridge 2001), p.185.

58. NA SC6/748/21; SC6/1020/17; SC6/936/16; SC6/937/2; SC6/997/5; SC6/1020/20; SC6/1006/6.

59. Building at Tintern was said to have begun in 1269, the same year Roger was said to have taken over the running of his uncle's estate (*Chartularies of St Mary's Abbey* m Gilbert (ed.), ii, pp.143-4). Before 1276 he had granted the monks his church of Halvergate in Norfolk, as well as half an acre of marshland in the same vill (Morris, p.220; RBIV 4; see also RBIV 1 and RBIV 13); William Worcestre, *Itineraries,* J.H. Harvey (ed.), (Oxford 1969), pp.60-61; Cf. D.M. Robinson, *Tintern Abbey,* 4th edn., (Cardiff 2002), pp.14, 32.

60. Similarly, see his gifts to the friars: NA SC6/837/12; SC6/873/18; SC6/921/26-7; SC6/922/22; SC6/1239/3; SC6/1239/9. Note also his foundation of a chantry and construction of a shrine in Tidenham Park. *Calendar of Chancery Warrants*, 1244–1326 (HMSO 1927), pp.346-7. See also chapter XV p.160.

61. Turner, p.44.

62. Ridgard, *Medieval Framlingham,* pp. 48-50; for Seagrave's expectations, see N. Denholm-Young, *Seignorial Administration in England* (Oxford 1937), pp.167-8. Morris, pp.138-53 has a full analysis of the earl's household.

63. R.R. Davies, *Conquest, Coexistence and Change: Wales, 1063–1415* (Oxford 1987), pp.380-81.

64. NA SC6/922/6; Turner, p.17.

65. A total itinerary for the earl, of the kind obtainable for the king, is impossible to reconstruct (*pace* Denholm-Young, *Seignorial Administration*, p.19n). An itinerary based on the earl's datable appearances appears in Morris, pp.198-204.

66. E32/30, m. 10; R.R. Davies, *Lordship and Society in the March of Wales, 1282–1400* (Oxford 1978), pp.3-4, 120, 149-75, 217-21.

67. On one occasion we find Roger feasting on porpoise: NA SC6/922/7. Cf. W. Rees, *South Wales and the March, 1284–1415* (Oxford 1924), pp.43-4.

68. For a full description of Cas Troggy see chapter XVIII.

69. Morris (2003), p.89. He did not, however, entirely forsake East Anglia: Morris, p.204.

**Chapter XIV  The 'Gloriette' in the Lower Bailey**

1. NA SC6/921/21.

2 NA SC6/859/19 m.6.

3. NA SC6/921/23.

4. Morris, p.122.

5. NA LR 12/43/1938.

6. NA SC6/1020/15 and SC6/1020/20.

7. D.M. Robinson, *Tintern Abbey*, Cadw guidebook, 4th edn., (Cardiff 2002) pp.14-15, 32 and Morris, p.134.

8. NA SC6/921/24 m. 1 and 2.

9. NA SC6/921/26.

10. NA SC6/921/28.

11. Morris, pp.130-1.

12. NA SC6/921/28.

13. NA SC6/922/3 m.1d.

14. NA SC6/922/5 m. 1d.

15. J. Alexander and P. Binski (eds.), *Age of Chivalry, Art in Platagenet England 1200–1400* (London 1981), Royal Academy exhib. cat. nos.56-57.

16. NA E372/156 M.49 and M.49d.

17. Clark, p.69

18. J. Givens, *Observation and Image-Making in Gothic Art* (Cambridge 2005), p.5.

19. R. Cassanelli (ed.), *La Méditerranée des Croisades* (Paris 2000), pp.217 and 223.

20. Coxe, p.367 footnotes.

21. L.F. Salzman, *Bulding in England down to 1540*, (Oxford 1967), rev. edn., pp.94-5; and M. Wood, *The Englsh Medieval House* (Oxford 1965), p.99.

22. There was no wooden screen in this hall. These features did not commonly appear before the end of the 14th century.

23. C.M. Woolgar, *The Great Household in late Medieval England*, (London and New Haven 1999), pp.136-165.
24. A. Emery, *Greater Medieval Houses of England and Wales 1300–1500: volume II East Anglia, Central England and Wales*, (Cambridge 2000); M.W. Thompson, *The Medieval Hall: the Basis of Secular Domestic Life 600–1600 AD* (Aldershot 1995).
25. Wood (1965), pp.261-5.
26. It still does today and this may reflect poor design originally.
27. J.A. Ashbee, '"The chamber called *Gloriette*": Living at Lesiure in Thirteenth- and Fourteenth-century castles', JBAA, 157, (2004), pp.17-40.
28. *Ibid.*, pp.31-33.
29. The authors would like to thank Peter Brears for allowing them to quote from his report on the kitchen at Chepstow Castle and other Cadw sites. His work is unravelling the complexity of household management in the great castles of Britain.
30. The manorial account for the Barton—the castle's home farm—shows that part of the labour dues of the tenants for the year 1286/7 was to transport the earl's wardrobe and kitchen from Chepstow to his manor house at Hamstead Marshall., NA SC6/922/22.
31. Ullage is the filling-up of a barrel of the wine lost to evaporation or leakage in transit.
32. NA SC6/920/2.
33. NA E 372/156 M.49.
34. See the *Ipm* of Roger Bigod NA C133/127.
35. BL Add. Ms. 36371, f.478 and 50, and J.H. Parker, *A Concise Glossary of Architecture*, (Oxford 1869), pl.228.
36. Coxe, p.367 footnote.
37. NA E/101/531/12.
38. Morris, pp.138-9.
39. *Calendar Memoranda Rolls*, 1326-7, p.359.
40. Thanks to Ed Peach and Bevis Sale for their persistence.
41. For a discussion of pentices and the source of this quotation see Wood (1965), p.336.
42. A.N. Brown (ed.), *The Rows of Chester: The Chester Rows Research Project*, English Heritage Report 16, (London 1999).
43. Morris, pp.27-31.
44. RCAHMW, *The Inventory of Glamorgan — the Later Clares* (Llandudno 2000), pp.51-104.
45. M. Altschul, *A Baronial Family in England: The Clares, 1217–1314*, (Blatimore 1965).
46. KJ.R. Kenyon, *Kidwelly Castle*, Cadw guidebook, (Cardiff 2002), rev. edn.
47. See chapters XVI and XVII in R. Shoesmith and A. Johnson (eds.), *Ludlow Castle: its History and Buildings*, (Logaston 2000).
48. Emery (2000), pp.537-40.
49. Morris, p.156.
50. M. Prestwich, *Edward I* (London 1988).

**Chapter XV  The New or Marten's Tower**
1. R.A. Brown, *English Castles*, (London 1976), p.54.
2. See chapter XXII pp.240 and 241.
3. NA SC6/921/24 m.2.
4. NA SC6/922/1.
5. NA SC6/922/3 m.1d.
6. NA SC6/922/5.
7. NA SC6/922/7.
8. NA LR 12/43/1938.
9. Perks, p.321; J.K. Knight, *Chepstow Castle*, Cadw guidebook, (Cardiff 1986), p.29.
10. Clark, p.66.
11. British Library Add. Ms. 36371, f.38
12. J.H. Parker, *Some Account of Domestic Architecture in England*, (Oxford 1853), II, pp.308-10.
13. Galeries Nationales du Grand Palais, L'Art du Temps des Rois Maudits, Philippe le Bel et ses fils, 1285–1328, (Paris 1998, exhib. cat. nos.85, 92, 93 and 100. For slightly later English examples see John de Grandisson Ivories in J. Alexander and P. Binksi (eds), *Age of Chivalry, Art in Plantagenet England 1200–1400*, (London 1987), Royal Academy exhib. cat. nos.593-6.
14. N. Coldsteram, *The Decorated Style, Architecture and Ornament 1240–1360*, (British Museum 1994), pp.24-28 and fig.12.
15. D.M. Robinson, *Tintern Abbey*, Cadw guidebook, (Cardiff 2002), 4th edn., pp.40-41.
16. The crown of his head was repaired with cement at some time. See A. Teagle, *Conservation Work to the carved Human Figures at the Marten's Tower, Chepstow Castle*, (report to Cadw, undated).
17. Parapet figures were placed outside the nave of York Minster from c 1310, with standing figures in the triforium; at Beverley Minster and Selby Abbey, both probably 1330s (N. Coldstream, 'York Minster and the Decorated Style in Yorkshire', *Yorkshire Archaeological Journal*, 52, 1980, p.110). Small soldiers holding small stone missiles; and later figures famously survive on the Bars of York and at Alnwick Castle.

18. NA E372/121, rot comp 22; E101 468/20 f3r. We are very grateful to Jeremy Ashbee for this information in advance of the publication of his Ph D thesis.

19. A.J. Taylor, *Caernarfon Castle*, Cadw guidebook, (Cardiff 2002), 6th edn., pp.27-9.

20. N. Orme, *From Childhood to Chivalry. The education of the English Kings and aristocracy 1066–1530*, (London and New York 1984), pp.166-7, 170-205.

21. St. Johns College, Cambridge MS K.26, f.10v. Illustrated in N.J. Morgan, *Early Gothic manuscripts (II) 1250–1285*, (London 1988), fig.383.

22. NA SC6/922/5.

23. This hall was built for Bishop Carew (1256-80), R.C. Turner, *The Bishop's Palace, Lamphey and Llawhaden Castle*, Cadw guidebook, (Cardiff 2000), p.17.

24. See E.W. Tristram, *English Wall Painting of the Fourteenth Century*, (London 1955) for a range of examples.

25. RCHME, *Salisbury: The Houses in the Close*, (London 1993), pp.234-9.

26. A.J. Taylor, *Caernarfon Castle*, Cadw guidebook, (Cardiff 2004).

27. J.R. Mathieu, 'New Methods on Old Castles: Generating New Ways of Seeing', *Medieval Archaeology*, (1999), XLIII, pp.115-142.

28. J. Munby and H. Summerson, *Stokesay Castle*, English Heritage guidebook, (London 2002), pp.35-6. Edward I spent the night at Clun Castle.

29. *Ibid.*, pp.19, 29.

30. For the significance of licences to crenellate see C. Coulson, 'Structural Symbolism in Medieval Castle Architecture', *JBAA* (1979), 132, pp.73-86.

31. D.K. Renn, *Caerphilly Castle*, Cadw guidebook, (Cardiff 1997) rev. edn. pp.36-9 and RCAHMW, *The Inventory for Glamorgan – the Later Castles*, (Llandudno 2000), pp.78-83.

32. S. Thurley, 'Royal Lodgings at the Tower of London 1216–1327', *Architectural History*, 38, (1995), pp.47-52.

33. J. West, 'Acton Burnell Castle, Shropshire', in A. Detsicas (ed), *Collectanea Historica, Essays in Memory of Stuart Rigold*, (London 1981), pp.85-92.

34. Despite spending over £21,000 on works at the Tower of London, including St Thomas' Tower, he was only a rare visitor between 1275-99. See Thurley (1995), p.46.

35. R.R. Davies, *The Age of Conquest, Wales 1063–1475*, (Oxford 1991), pp.354-7.

**Chapter XVI  Roger Bigod's Great Tower**

1. NA SC6/922/5.

2. NA LR 12/43/1938.

3. R.R. Davies 1991, *The Age of Conquest 1063–1415*, (Oxford 1991), pp.382-5.

4. Morris, pp.151-3 and 156.

5. NA SC6/859/24.

6. NA E101/531/12.

7. NA SC 6/922/6 Expense of the engine. 'For the wages of master Reginald the Engineer making four engines called Springalds in the Castle from Michelmas to Sunday on the feast of St Peter in Cathedra for 21 weeks 55s 1$^{1}$/2d. who took for himself and his boy weekly 2s 7$^{1}$/2d. For six quarters and one bushel of oats bought for feeding the horse of the said Master Reginald 11s 2$^{3}$/4d at 22d the price of a quarter, which received one bushel nightly. For shoeing of the said horse 10d. For the wages of carpenters felling and cutting timber for the said engines and for joists and planks for raising, setting up and covering the said engines on the towers 55s 9$^{1}$/4d. For the wages of two sawyers sawing timber for the same 5s 6d. For 500 nails bought for the same 12$^{1}$/2d. For the wages of smiths for forging and making the ironwork of the engines from the said feast of michelmas to Christmas for 12$^{1}$/2 weeks 34s 6d. For iron bought for the same 23s 5$^{1}$/2d. For steel bought for the same 6d. For three horse-loads (seams) of coal bought for the same 9d. For 350 lbs of rope 'de pilo' (literally 'of hair' ie. horse-hair) bought at Bristol for the said engines 35s at a price of 1d a pound. For canvas string bought in the same place for the same 2s. For carriage and porterage of the said cord and string 10d on two occasions. For wax and 'coda' bought for the rope 4$^{1}$/4d. For an assistant to string the cords 6d. For withies bound together to make hurdles and for making hurdles and for dragging timber to the castle and hauling it up onto the towers by the labourers of Tudenham 7s 8d. For 200 large quarrels bought at London for the engine £4 3s 4d at 5d the price of a quarrel. For 150 smaller quarrels bought in the same place £3 7s 6d. For obtaining the said quarrels in London on two occasions 12s. For tallow bought for the engines 2d. For an assistant for lifting up the engines 18d (by one indenture). For the wages of Philip Danyel carpenter completing and putting right the timber of the great engine upon the Great Tower for one week 21d after the departure of master Reginald. For binding withies and carrying them to the said engine to make hurdles 12$^{1}$/2d (as appears by the particulars). Total £18 11s 6$^{1}$/4d.

8. Late May to late July.

9. NA SC6/922/7.

10. Clark, plate 1.

11. For the context see R.K. Morris, 'The development of later Gothic mouldings in England *c*.1250–1400, Part I', *Architectural History*, 21, (1978), pp.35-7.

12. M. Wood, *The English Medieval House*, (London 1965), p.157 and fig.8.

13. Turner, p.43.
14. For example in 1309, the chapel is recorded as containing: 'one pair of decrepit vestments, three towels, one altar frontal, one super altar, one corporal cloth, one silver chalice, one missal, one antiphonary, one breviary, one psalter except the first return, one statue of the Virgin Mary, two crosses, one leaden vessel for holy water'. NA E372/156 m.49.
15. G. Coppack, *Helmsley Castle*, English Heritage guidebook, (London 1997).
16. J. Munby and H. Summerson, *Stokesay Castle*, English Heritage guidebook, (London 2002), pp.35-6.
17. Morris, pp.118-19.
18. *Ibid*, pp.161-71.
19. C. Platt, *The Architecture of Medieval Britain, a Social History*, (New Haven and London 1990), p.103 and fig.117.
20. NA E372/156 m.49 covering the years 1308–10.
21. R.K. Morris, 'The architecture of Arthurian Enthusiasm: castle symbolism in the reigns of Edward I and his successors', in Strickland.
22. D.D.R. Owen (ed.), *Chrétien de Troyes: Arthurian Romances*, rev. ed., (London 1995), pp.374-495.
23. *Ibid*, p.469.

## Chapter XVII  From Edward II to the Later Middle Ages

1. Perks, pp.34-42.
2. NA C133/127.
3. NA E371/68, E372/153, 156 m.34d and m.46.
4. NA SC 1/48 no.14; NA SC/8/327, C47/10/43 no.20, C145/71/14, SC 1/16 no.25, E101/14/20; NA SC6/922/10; *Calendar of Fine Rolls*, 1307–19, p.3, 17, 24, 67; *CCR*, 1307–13, pp.7, 29, 34, 279, 288, 378, 429; *CPR*, 1307–13, pp.68, 278, 312, 313, 331, 333, 353, 366, 599; *Cal. Chancery Warrants I*, pp.322, 347, 359.
5. Abstract in *CPR*, 1301–7, p.460.
6. *Cal. Fine Rolls* 1307–19, p.18, *Cal. Fine Rolls* 1319–27, p.63. T.F. Tout, *The Place of Edward II in English History*, (Manchester 1936), pp.315n, 323n. J.R. Medlicott, *Thomas of Lancaster*, (Oxford 1970), pp.78n, 118.
7. NA E372/156 m.49.
8. NA C145/71/14. The inquisition is summarised in *Calendar of Inquisitions Miscellaneous*, Vol. II, no.112.
9. Perks, p.342.
10. Cardiff Public Library Philipps ms 30341 rot 3 m.2d. Printed in T. Pugh (ed), *The Marcher Lordships of South Wales 1415–1536*, (Cardiff 1963), p.75.
11. NA E 372.156 m.49d.
12. NA E372/156 m.49d.
13. NA C145/71/14.
14. M. Vale, *The Princely Court*, (Oxford 2004), p.245 citing NA E101/374/19, f.3r.
15. NA E101/14/20; BL Additional Charters 26052; NA SC6/922/10.
16. *CPR*, 1307–13, p.547.
17. *CPR*, 1307–13, p.599.
18. The original deed of Thomas de Brotherton granting Chepstow to Despenser is in NA E 40/4880.
19. For a recent account of the younger Despenser's territorial acquisitions in Wales and the Marches, see R.R. Davies, *Lordship and Society in the March of Wales* (Oxford 1978), pp.279-81.
20. *CPR*, 1324–7, p.359.
21. NA E101/17/20; Society of Antiquaries MS.122 (Household Account Book of Edward II 1325–26).
22. E.M. Thompson (ed), *Chronicon Galfridi le baker de Swynbroke*, (Oxford 1889), p.23.
23. A surviving account book of the household of Margaret Countess of Norfolk for 1394–95 (College of Arms, Arundel ms 49).
24. NA SC6 922/10-12.
25. *CPR*, 1340–43, p.93.
26. See ref. 10.
27. Arundel Castle Muniments W.61 m.5.
28. J. Waurin, *Recueil des Croniques et archivinnes istoires de la Grant Bretaigne*, (ed) W. Hardy, 5 vols., (Rolls Series 1864–91), Vol. 5, p.580.

## Chapter XVIII  The Hunting Preserves

1. See for example M. Vale, *The Princely Court*, (Oxford University Press 2004), pp.179-84.
2. References to hunting are made in the laws of Hywel Dda and hunting scenes are depicted on some Early Christian Monuments such as V.E. Nash-Williams, *The Early Christian Monuments of Wales*, (Cardiff 1950), no.234, fig.165 and pl.XXXVIII now at Margam Stones Museum.
3. See O. Rackham, *Trees and Woodland in the British Landscape*, (London 1976), pp.152-65 for a discussion of Royal Forests and their origins.
4. W.A. and F. Baillie-Grohman (eds.), *The Master of Game*, by Edward, 2nd Duke of York, (London 1909).
5. R. Hands (ed.), *English Hawking and Hunting in 'The Boke of St Albans'*, (Oxford 1975).

6. See R.K. Morris, 'The Architecture of Arthurian Enthusiasm: Castle Symbolism in the Reigns of Edward I and his Successors', in Strickland, pp.63-81.
7. D.D.R. Evans (ed.), *Chrétian de Troyes: Arthurian Romances*, rev. ed., (London 1993).
8. *Ibid.*
9. W.R.J. Barron (ed.), *Sir Gawain and the Green Knight* (Manchester 1974).
10. *Ibid.*, p.81.
11. *Ibid.*, p.89.
12. *Ibid.*, p.117.
13. J.M. Gilbert, *Hunting and Hunting Reserves in Scotland* (Edinburgh 1979).
14. C.M. Woolgar, *The Great Household in Late Medieval England* (London and New Haven 1999).
15. Bradney, 4, part 1, pp.146-7.
16. NA SC6/921/24 m.2.
17. See for example NA SC6/859/19 m.6, NA SC6/921/26 and NA SC6/922/24 m.1.
18. NA SC6/921/28.
19. NA SC6/922/3 m.1d.
20. NA SC6/920/5.
21. NA SC6/859/23 and NA SC6/922/3 m.1 respectively.
22. NA SC6/921/24 m.1 and NA SC6/922/1.
23. *CCR*, 1300–1326, p.31.
24. NA SC6/922/8.
25. NA SC6/858/22.
26. NA C/133/127.
27. NA E372/156 m.49.
28. L. Toulmin Smith (ed.), *Itinerary of John Leland in England and Wales*, ii, (London 1906), p.42.
29. T. Churchyard, *The Worthiness of Wales, a poem* (London 1587, reprinted 1776), p.20.
30. W. Camden, *Britain, or a Chorographical Description of the most flourishing kingdoms, England, Scotland and Ireland*, P. Holland (trans.), (London 1610), p.633.
31. J. Ogilvy, *Britannia, volume the first* (London 1676), plate 16, discussed in D.P.M. Michael, *The Mapping of Monmouthshire* (Bristol 1985), p.38.
32. NLW, Badminton Estate Maps, album 1.
33. Coxe, i, pp.32 and 36-8.
34. O. Morgan and T. Wakeman, *Notes on Wentwood, Castle Troggy and Llanvair Castle*, Monmouthshire and Caerleon Antiquarian Association, (Newport 1863).
35. See S.G. Priestley and R.C. Turner, 'Three Castles of the Clare family in Monmouthshire during the thirteenth and fourteenth centuries', *Archaeologia Cambrensis*, 152, (2005), pp.9-51.
36. See NA E 372/156 m.49 for example.
37. T.B. Pugh (ed.), *The Marcher Lordships in South Wales 1415–1536*, selected documents, University of Wales Press, (Cardiff 1963), pp.15-6.
38. Bradney, pp.147-8.
39. See Bradney, p.148; Morgan and Wakeman, pp.20-3: N. Rogers, *Memoirs of Monmouthshire*, reprinted 1978 by Moss Rose Press, (Chepstow 1708).
40. The Forestry Commission undertook consultation on its new Forest Design Plan for the Wentwood in 2005.
41. NA SC6/921/24 m.1.
42. NA SC6/859/80 and NA SC6/859/27.
43. NA SC6/859/27.
44. NA SC6/921/24 m.1-2.
45. NA E 372/156 m.34d and m.46 and 49.
46. NA C/133/127.
47. R.C. Turner, *Lamphey Bishop's Palace and Llawhaden Castle*, rev. ed., Cadw guidebook, (Cardiff 2000), p.8.
48. NA SC6/921/28.
49. *CPR*, 1340–3, p.93. A William of Dernford had been a high-ranking member of Roger Bigod's household and this outlaw may have been a direct descendant with a grudge.
50. NLW Badminton Ms 8924/5.
51. HMC, *The Manuscripts of the Duke of Beaufort etc*, twelfth report, appendix, part IX, (HMSO London 1891), p.4.
52. Quoted in N. Cooper, *Houses of the Gentry 1480–1680*, (New Haven & London 1999), p.110. The chapter on lodges in this book, pp.109-122, shows how widespread lodges were on the estates of the nobility and gentry in the 16th and 17th centuries and illustrates how experimental they were in their plans, elevations and external decoration when compared to their parent great houses.
53. M. Girouard, *Life in the English Country House*, Penguin edn., (London 1980), p.108.
54. J.R. Kenyon, *Raglan Castle*, rev edn, Cadw guidebook, (Cardiff 2003), and E. Whittle 1989, 'The Renaissance Gardens of Raglan Castle', *Garden History*, 17, (1989), pp.83-94.

55. See J. Harris 1985, *The Artist and the Country House*, rev. edn., Sothebys, (London 1985). Troy is shown on plate 122, p.123, and Badminton on plate 125, p.125.
56. NA SC6/859/20.
57. NA SC6/859/24.
58. NA SC6/859/23.
59. NA SC6/859/19 m.6.
60. NA SC6/921/27.
61. NA LR/12/43/938.
62. NA SC6/859/24.
63. NA SC6/921/26.
64. NA SC6/922/3 m.1d.
65. NA SC6/922/3 m.1.
66. NA E/101/91/14.

## Chapter XIX Chepstow Town, Priory and Port Wall

1. *Giraldus Cambrensis, Itinerarium Cambrae*, J.F. Dimock (ed.), Rolls Series, Vol. VI, (1868). Dated to *c*.1188-91.
2. R. Shoesmith, *Excavations at Chepstow 1973-1974*, Cambrian Archaeological Monographs No. 4, (1991).
3. J.C. Perks, *Chepstow Castle* Ministry of Works guide (London 1967), p.5.
4. R. Shoesmith, *Hereford City Excavations Vol. 2 – Excavations on and close to the defences*, CBA Res. Rep. 46, (1982), p.82.
5. P.E. Curnow and M.W. Thompson, 'Excavations at Richard's Castle, Herefordshire, 1962-64', *JBAA*, 32, (1969), pp.105-27.
6. I. Soulsby, *The Towns of Medieval Wales* (Chichester 1983), pp.36-9.
7. T.J. Miles, 'Chepstow – The Port Wall, Interim note, *Archaeology in Wales: CBA Group 2 Newsletter,* 11, (1971), p.33.
8. C.J. Delaney and I.N. Soulsby, *The archaeological implications of redevelopment in the historic towns of the Monmouth district*, Urban Research Unit, University College, Cardiff, (1975), 4.4.3.
9. W.H. St. John Hope, 'The Ancient Topography of the Town of Ludlow, in the County of Salop', *Archaeologia*, 11, (second series) (1909) pp.383-88.
10. Shoesmith (1982), p.93
11. I. Waters, *The Town of Chepstow* (Chepstow 1972), p.50.
12. *IPM* of Roger Bigot, earl of Norfolk (NA C133/127).
13. Letter from the bailiffs, Good Men, and all the Community of the Town of Chepstow to King Edward II (NA SC 1/16 no. 25).
14. R. Graham, 'Four Alien Priories in Monmouthshire', *J.BAA*, 35, (1929-30), p.102.
15. F.G. Cowley, *The Monastic Order in South Wales 1066-1349* (Cardiff 1977), p.10.
16. *Ibid,*, p.13.
17. Graham (1929-30), p.105.
18. *Cal. Let. Pat.*, v, p.258.
19. Cowley (1977), p.40.
20. *Ibid.*, Apps. II and III.
21. G.F. Duckett, (ed.), *Charters and Records of Cluny* (Lewes 1888), p.136.
22. Clerical Subsidy, NA Bundle 33/1.
23. *Cal. Let. Pat. 1385-88*, pp.252, 511.
24. *Calendar of Papal Letters*, v, p.258.
25. *Calendar Rotuli Clausarum 1399-1401*, NA C54, p.72
26. L.T. Smith, *The Itinerary in Wales of John Leland in or about the Years 1536–1539*, 2, (London 1906), p.43.
27. W. Dugdale, *Monasticum Anglicanum*, Vol. 4, (1846), p.652.
28. *Ibid.*, pp.653-4.
29. W. Camden, *Brittannia* (London 1607), p.9.
30. E.A. Freeman, 'Chepstow Parish Church', *Archaeologia Cambrensis,* 2, (second series), (1851), pp.1-8.
31. Shoesmith (1991).
32. Cowley (1977), p.270.
33. Waters (1972), pp.128-33.
34. Account of Elias Pouger from 2 June – 29 September 1307. NA E372/156 m.46.
35. S. Clarke, 'The Beaufort Hotel, Archaeological Evaluation' internal report by Monmouth Archaeology (1999).
36. Coxe.
37. Waters (1972), pp.119-20.
38. Information kindly supplied by Rick Turner.
39. Account of Henry le Fox reap-reeve (messor) of Tidenham of works from Michaelmas, 7 Edward I (29 Sep 1279) to Michaelmas, 8 Edw I (29 Sep 1280). NA SC6/859/19 m.6.
40. Account of John Ailward receiver ... 1279-80. NA SC6/921/26.
41. Account of the Beadles of the Town of Chepstow, 15-16 Edward I (1287-88), NA SC6/921/29.

42. Account of Walter de Gloucester escheator ... 6 December 1306-2 June 1307. NA E372/156; Account of Elias Pouger from 2 June – 29 September 1307. NA E372/156 m.46; Indenture between John Prior of Striguil ... to repairs carried out by John de Patishull. n.d., but shortly after 23 August 1311. NA E101/14/20.

43. Waters (1972), p.120.

44. Accounts of the Beadles 1285-90. NA SC6/921/29.

45. A.N. Brown (ed.) *The Rows of Chester: the Chester Rows Research Project*, English Heritage Archaeological Report 16, (1999), pp.15-18.

46. J. Schofield, *The Building of London from the Conquest to the Great Fire* (London 1984), 77-8

47. E.J. Bettington, 'Old Cellars in Widemarsh Street [Hereford]' *Trans Woolhope Natur. Fld. Club,* v–x, (1939); R. Shoesmith, *The Pubs of Hereford City*, 3rd edn., (Logaston 2004), pp.172-3.

48. J. Morris (ed.), *Domesday Book 15, Gloucestershire*, (Chichester 1982).

49. I. Waters, *Chepstow Road Bridges*, (Moss Rose Press 1977); I. Waters, *The Wine Trade of the Port of Chepstow*, n.d. wine and port.

50. Smith (1906), p.43.

51. Waters (1977) & n.d.

52. Waters (1972), pp.48 and 218.

53. Shoesmith (1991), pp.21-6; H.L. Turner, *Town Defences in England and Wales* (London 1970), 64

54. J.C. Perks (1967), p.33.

55. NLW Badminton MS 1790 ff.70-75.

56. *Ibid.*; Perks (1967), p.33; Waters (1972), p.138.

57. Indenture between John Prior of Striguil ... to repairs carried out by John de Patishull. n.d., but shortly after 23 August 1311. NA E101/14/20.

58. Shoesmith (1991), p.19.

59. Perks (1967), p.32.

60. Smith (1906), p.43.

61. J.G. Wood, *The Lordship, Castle and Town of Chepstow, otherwise Striguil* (Newport 1910), p.35.

62. Bradney, 1, p.14.

63. R.E. Wilson, *Archaeological Implications of Development in Chepstow,* MS, (1974); Delaney and Soulsby (1975).

64. Perks (1967), p.33.

65. Turner (1970), p.60.

66. Shoesmith (1982); R. Shoesmith and R. Morriss 'The later medieval defences' in A. Thomas and A. Boucher, *Hereford City Excavations, Vol. 4, 1976-90,* (Logaston Press 2002), pp.169-82.

67. Turner (1970), pp.55-6.

68. Soulsby (1983), p.108.

69. L.A.S. Butler, 'St. Kinemark's Priory Chepstow, An Interim Report on the Excavations from 1962-65', *Monmouthshire Antiq.*, 2, Pt. 1, (1965), pp.33-41.

70. Waters (1972), p.140.

71. Clarke (1999).

72. *CCR* 1256-59, p.454.

73. Account of Henry le Fox and Robert Suel reap-reeves (messor) of Tidenham Michaelmas 56 Henry III (29 Sep. 1272) – Mich 1 Edw I (29 Sep 1273). NA SC6/879/17.

74. *Ipm* of Roger Bigod; Account of Hugh le Despenser from 24 April 1308 to 7 September 1310. NA E372/156 m.49.

75. NA SC/8/221 (AP 11002); W. Rees (ed.), *Calendar of Ancient Petitions relating to Wales* (1975), p.371.

76. Waters (1977).

**Chapter XX  The Tudor Period**

1. In 1502 Queen Elizabeth of York was sailed across the Severn to Chepstow where one of Sir Walter Herbert's servants brought her a goshawk before she moved onto Raglan. N. Harris Nicholas, *Privy Purse Expenses of Elizabeth of York,* (London 1830), p.43.

2. J.R. Kenyon, *Raglan Castle*, rev. edn., Cadw guidebook, (Cardiff 2003), pp.12-13.

3. J. Hughes, 'Charles Somerset, first earl of Worcester (*c.*1460–1526)', *DNB online*, (Oxford 2004).

4. NLW Badminton Ms 1790, ff 70-5.

5. College of Arms Ms R.22, f 79.

6. T. Turner and J.H. Parker, *Some Account of Domestic Architecture in England …*, (London 1853), ii, p.309.

7. For full details of the tree-ring dating of the doors at Chepstow Castle see D.H. Miles and M.J. Worthington, 'List 94: Welsh dendrochronology – phase 2', *Vernacular Architecture* 29, (1998), pp.126-9.

8. Kenyon (2003).

9. NA E 315/448, ff 17-20.

10. L. Toulmin Smith, *Itinerary of John Leland in England and Wales*, 2, (London 1906), p.43.

11. B. Kirkpatrick (ed.), *Brewer's Concise Dictionary of Phrase and Fable*, Cassell, (London 1992), pp.562 and 624.

12. R. Strong, 'Eliza Triumphans', *The Cult of Elizabeth*, Thames and Hudson, (London 1977), pp.17-55.

## Chapter XXI  Civil War and Commonwealth

1. F.H. Pugh 'Monmouthshire Recusants in the reigns of Elizabeth 1 and James I, from the returns in the Public Record Office', *South Wales and Monmouthshire Record Society*, 4, (1957), pp.59-110.
2. G.C. Boon, *Welsh Tokens of the Seventeenth Century* (Cardiff 1973), pp.99-101.
3. There are two muster rolls of the Monmouthshire militia, of 1634 (Gwent CRO Misc. Mss 648 Letterbook of Richard Herbert, 10) and 1638 (NA State Papers 16 381/66, Joyce Malcolm, *Caesar's Due* (1983), pp.234-5). Militia strengths in Welsh and English counties, Malcolm (1983), pp.234-5.
4. William Waller. *The Victorious and Fortunate Proceedings of Sir William Waller and his Forces in Wales*, John Wright, 17 April 1643.
5. *Ibid*. The Caerleon letter, now Gwent CRO Misc. Mss 1357, was found at the Priory, Caerleon, concealed in the slates of the roof, with other papers which were not preserved. J.E. Lee, *Isca Silurum* (London 1862), p.121 and pl. 50, 1.
6. *The Diary of Walter Powell of Llantilio Crossenny in the County of Monmouth, Gentleman, 1603–1654* (ed.) J.A. Bradney (Bristol 1907). 23-28 April 1643.
7. *CSPD* 1644, p.8. Chepstow Parish Register (Gwent CRO D/ Pa. 86.1) 20 January 1644 (burial of Captain Carvine).
8. J. Corbett, *Diary of the Campaigns of Massey West of Severn* (ed.) J. Washborne, (1825), pp.117, 356-7. *CSPD* 1644–5, p.42. HMC 14th Report (Portland Mss 3), p.127. *Moderate Intelligencer*, 19 October 1644.
9. Wintour to Prince Rupert, 26 October, 20 November 1644. Warburton, ii, p.525.
10. T. Carte, *A Collection of Original Letters and Papers* (1739), pp.61-2. BL Add. Mss. 18981, f. 259, Warburton, i, p.519.
11. Gwent CRO D/Pa.86.1. W.H. James, *The Registers of Chepstow Parish Church* (Chepstow 1913). Ivor Waters, *Chepstow Parish Records* (Chepstow 1955).
12. Bodleian Library, Tanner Ms 60 ff. 440-441.
13. HMC 13th Report (Portland Mss part 1) pp.286-7 (10 October 1645). *CSPD* 1661–2, p.184.
14. *The True Informer*, Wednesday, 22 October 1645.
15. *A Full Relation* (n. 18 below). Bradney, 4.1 Hundred of Caldicot, pp.76-7. Reid, iii, p.105. Lewis Thomas (? of Peterston Wentloog), a Captain at Highnam and a Major at Raglan during the siege, compounded April 1649 in respect of both wars. Newman no.1413, p.369, *CCC* 1980
16. For the background see R. Ashton, *Counter Revolution : The Second Civil War and its Origins* (1994); G.E. Aylmer (ed), *The Interregnum : The Quest for A Settlement 1645–1660* (1972) and Austin Woolrych, *Britain in Revolution 1625–1660* (Oxford 2002), pp.402-33.
17. *Moderate Intelligencer*, 18 May 1648.
18. R.W. *A Great Fight at Chepstow Castle betwixt the forces under Lt. General Cromwell and the Cavaliers commanded by Sir William Kelmish, Governor of the said Castle* (R. Williamson, 13 May 1648). BL Thomason Tracts E. 443 (14). *A Full and Particular Relation of the Manner of the late besieging and taking of Chepstow Castle in Wales … expressed in a letter from Col. Ewer to the … Speaker of the House of Commons* (Matthew Simmons, 25 May 1648). BL Thomason Tracts E 445 (6). J.R. Phillips, *Memoirs of the Civil War in Wales and the Marches*, Vol 2 (1874), pp.375-6. Few junior officers can be identified, but Captains John and Christopher Harris were possibly neighbours of Nicholas Kemeys in Wentwood. The former had been a Captain in the Marquis of Worcester's Foot at Raglan. Reid,iv, p.193.
19. W.C. Abbott (ed.), *Letters and Speeches of Oliver Cromwell* (4 vols, Harvard 1937–47), Vol 1, pp.615-16.
20. Letter from Colonel Okey, printed W.N. Johns, *Historical Traditions and Facts Relating to Newport and Caerleon* (Newport 1885), pp.147-8. Bradney, ii, part 2, Hundred of Trellech, pp.230-5. Siddons, pp.198-9. Bradney's version of the pedigree (pp.225-6) differs and omits John Nicholas. Acts. Ord. Interr ii, p.973.
21. *CSPD* 1650, p.381; 1655, p.256. Further repairs costing £500 were made in 1661–2 by Lord Herbert of Raglan. *CSPD* 1661–2, p.490; Addenda 1660–1670, pp.353-4.
22. *CCC* Vol 43, 2311. *CSPD* 1649–50, pp.176, 504 do 1654, p.52. Webb, ii, pp.322-3.
23. *CSPD* 1655–6, pp.644, 651. C. Durston, *Cromwell's Major Generals: Godly Government during the English Revolution* (Manchester 2001), pp.140-47.
24. J. Berry and S.G. Lee, *A Cromwellian Major General: The Career of Colonel James Berry* (Oxford 1938), Appendix E, from NA State Papers, Interregnum 25/77.
25. *CSPD* 1659–60, pp.114, 205, 578.
26. *CSPD* 1659–60, p.374.
27. W.R. Williams, *The Parliamentary History of the Principality of Wales 1541–1855* (Brecon 1895), p.125. CSPD Addenda 1660–70, pp.342, 358 (printed proclamation).
28. Siddons, pp.198-9.

## Chapter XXII  After the Restoration

1. Badminton Muniments, FME 2/5/1.
2. Badminton Muniments, FME 2/5/2.
3. Society of Antiquaries, London, Wakeman Ms. 790/1.
4. M. McClain, 'Henry Somerset, first duke of Beaufort (1629–1700)', *DNB online*. (Oxford 2004).
5. Badminton Muniments, FME 2/5/5.
6. NLW Badminton Ms. 11718-9.

7. Lord Keeper Guilford quoted in McClain (2004)

8. A. Saunders, *Fortress Britain: Artillery Fortification in the British Isles and Ireland* (Liphook 1989), pp.53-69.

9. Badminton Muniments, FME 2/5/12.

10. *Bandileares/Bandoliers*: a leather belt worn across the chest, from which were suspended, on cord, small wooden cylinders each one holding a single powder charge.

    *Bill*: a pole-arm originally favoured by the Anglo-Saxons, developed from an agricultural implement. It is characterised by the broad blade with a cutting edge and a variety of hooks and spikes projecting from the back end of the blade.

    *Brimstone*: sulphur.

    *Bullets*: in early times this was often used to refer to artillery balls as well as the balls for small arms. Artillery would have fired balls of stone or in smaller calibres of lead before cast iron projectiles became a practical proposition.

    *Bullets with iron bars thorough* (*sic*): bar-shot—a ball pierced by a length of bar, which on exiting the barrel would become unstable and cause terrible wounds. Alternatively an incendiary projectile, around which flammable material was wrapped.

    *Chamber*: in this context, a removable chamber shaped like a pewter tankard which was loaded with powder and projectile(s) and locked into place with a wedge. The oldest form of breechloader. This system was obsolete by 1660, breechloading not reappearing in British Service until the mid-19th century.

    *Fire locke*: flintlock.

    *Glaive*: a broad bladed pole-arm in which the edge curves backwards near the point (usually 12th-13th century).

    *Great granadoe shells*: mortar projectiles.

    *Harkibus/Harquebus*: archaic—a generic term for all forms of portable firearms. In 1630 official English measurements classified an harquebus as being a shoulder arm of 3' overall with a 2' 6" barrel of 17 bore (approx .65").

    *Ladle/Ladel*: a long wooden stave with a metal scoop at one end. This was filled with loose gunpowder, passed down the bore to the breech end, then turned so the gunpowder was deposited under the vent (touch-hole).

    *Li*: probably 'pound' from *livre*.

    *Match locks*: muskets fired by a mechanism which held a piece of match (q.v.) which, when the trigger was pressed was brought down into the priming powder in the pan.

    *Match*: cotton cord boiled or soaked in potassium nitrate (saltpetre) which burns slowly and reliably, and is used to set off the priming powder in the cent. The match (later called slow-match) was held in a metal fitting on the end of a pole, the whole being referred to as a linstock.

    *Morterpeeces*: mortars—short barrelled, large calibre artillery pieces for firing bombs at high angles of elevation so as to fall inside fortifications or behind hills.

    *Murderes/Murderers*: a short, light gun for firing shot to clear attacking troops from an approach.

    *Murthering pieces*: see murderers above.

    *Sluggs*: small projectiles as fired from murthering pieces etc, usually roughly formed from lead and up to approximately $^3/_4$" diameter.

    *Tamprings*: probably tampeons—muzzle-stoppers to prevent the ingress of rain etc when not in use.

    *Wallpeeces/Wallpieces*: a long-arm in the form of an enlarged musket (or harquebus) fitted with a yoke, which in turn fitted into a prepared hole on the ramparts of a fortification. Wallpieces were used for 'picking off' individual soldiers of an enemy who were beyond the range of ordinary long-arms. They usually fired a heavier ball, which for a given velocity would carry further.

11. William Eldred, William, *The Gunner's Glasse* (1646).

12. Brig. O.F.G. Hogg, *English Artillery 1362–1716*, Royal Artillery Institute, (London 1963).

13. Master Gunner Nye, *Art of Gunnery*, (London 1647).

14. Brig. O.F.G. Hogg, *Artillery: its Origin, Heyday and Decline* (London 1970).

15. *Ibid.*

16. Peter Humphries of Cadw photographed a small medieval piscina found *in situ* between the two curtain walls when the fill was removed in the 1970s. The item is now lost.

17. Badminton Muniments, FME 2/5/6.

18. Badminton Muniments, FME 2/5/6 and 2/5/14.

19. Badminton Muniments, FME 2/5/6.

20. Badminton Muniments, FME 2/5/1.

21. Badminton Muniments, FME 2/5/13.

22. S. Barber, 'Henry Marten', *DNB online*, (Oxford 2004), and C. Heath, *Accounts of the Ancient and Present State of Chepstow Castle etc.* (Monmouth 1801).

23. BL Egerton Ms. 2618.

24. B. Taft, 'Robert Overton (1608/9–1678/9)', *DNB online*, (Oxford 2004).

25. Badminton Muniments, FME 4/1/13.

26. J. Harris, *The Artist and the Country House*, rev. edn., (London 1981), fig.123.

27. BL Add. Ms. 15892, f. 241.

28. Badminton Muniments, PA 1/3 1714/15-1718/19. Book of Mr. Burgh's letters pp.79, 83-5.

29. E. Impey and G. Parnell, *The Tower of London: the official illustrated history* (London 2000), pp.74-8.

30. See A.D. Saunders, *Fortress Britain*, (Liphook 1989) and G. Williams, *Stronghold Britain*, *four thousand years of British fortifications* (Stroud 1999), pp.178-90.

**Chapter XXIII Chepstow Castle as a Picturesque Ruin**

1. Published as two volumes. S. and N. Buck, *Perspective Views of the Ruins of the Most Noted Abbies and Castles of England*, (1726–42).
2. R. Sweet, *Antiquaries: The discovery of the past in eighteenth-century Britain* (London and New York 2004).
3. E. Burke, *A Philosophical Enquiry into the Origins of our Ideas of the Sublime and the Beautiful* (London 1756).
4. D. Jacques, *Georgian Gardens: the Reign of Nature*, (London 1983).
5. W. Gilpin, *Essay on Picturesque Beauty - Three Essays: on Picturesque Beauty; on Picturesque Travel; and on Sketching Landscape*, (London 1792). For a discussion of Gilpin's impact see D. Jacques, *Georgian Gardens: the Reign of Nature*, (London 1983), pp.95-101.
6. W. Gilpin, *Observations on the River Wye, and Several Parts of South Wales etc. Relative Chiefly to Picturesque Beauty: Made in the Summer of the Year 1770* (London 1782).
7. R. Russell, *A Guide to British Topographical Prints* (1979).
8. M.W. Thompson, *The journeys of Sir Richard Colt Hoare through Wales and England 1793–1810* (Stroud 1983).
9. Coxe.
10. H.P. Wyndham, *A Gentleman's Tour through Monmouthshire and Wales, in the Months of June and July 1774* (London 1775).
11. L.A. Twamley, *An Autumn Ramble on the Wye* (1839).
12. Ivor Waters states that the castle was originally let to a Mr Hutton whose granddaughter married a merchant named Williams, I. Waters 'Chepstow Castle from Cromwell to Picturesque Ruin', *Chepstow Packets* (Chepstow 1983).
13. The plan is undated, but there is a clue in an advertisement in Felix Farley's *Bristol Journal* of 4 July 1767, where John Aram announced that he had opened the half-way house from Chepstow to Newport, the Rock and Fountain, and in addition to the best sorts of wines and spirits on offer to gentlemen and travellers he sought custom for his professional skills being 'obliged to any Nobleman, Gentleman etc, who would employ him in Land-Measuring, as he has now nearly completed that of his Grace the Duke of Beaufort'. Felix Farley's *Bristol Journal* and the *Bristol Journal* printed by S. Farley, Bristol Reference Library.
14. Heath says just 100.
15. C. Heath, *Historical & Descriptive Accounts of the Ancient & Present State of the Town & Castle of Chepstow etc*, various editions, (Monmouth 1793–1828).
16. *Ibid.*
17. Hon. J. Byng, *'The Torrington Diaries"* containing the tours through England & Wales 1781–94, C.B. Andrews (ed.), (London 1934).
18. Ivor Waters suggests it was the son.
19. J.T. Barber, *A Tour throughout South Wales & Monmouthshire etc* (1803).
20. From the diary of Judith Beecroft, 1827, by kind permission of of Cardiff Libraries & Information Service, MS2.325.
21. Quotation from the diary of Anne Porter 1824 (by kind permission of Major H.R.M. Porter and Liz Pitman). The 1841 census lists both an Elizabeth Williams, aged 50, and a Mary Williams, 40, together with their 15-year-old servant Mary Dodd in the castle. Miss Mary Williams died in 1852, aged 62, her death announced in the *Monmouthshire Beacon* noted that formerly for many years she had resided in Chepstow Castle. (By that time according to Lascelles Directory the family of Mr Vincent Corbett were the tenants.)
22. Coxe, II, pp.365-77.
23. Rev. S. Shaw, *A Tour to the West of England in 1788* (London 1789).
24. The elderly Mrs Williams.
25. W. Beattie, *The Castles & Abbeys of England* (1844).
26. D. Williams, *History of Monmouthshire* (1796).
27. Felix Farley's *Bristol Journal* and the *Bristol Journal* printed by S. Farley, Bristol Reference Library.
28. J. Bedford, *Bristol and Other Coloured Glass* (London 1964).
29. K.M. Evans, 'Glassmaking in Chepstow', *Severn & Wye Review* (Autumn 1971).
30. Edkins was a painter of delftware, porcelain and glass but as his business ledger testifies he was a craftsman painter, and shop fronts, inn signs, lettering, coach painting as well as the interior decorations at the Theatre Royal in Bristol, were all part of his varied business. He painted glass for several other Bristol firms over a 20 year period from the 1760s–80s. *Michael Edkins Ledger Book* (1761–86), Bristol Reference Library : acc. no.20196.
31. The prices he charged range from 2d for a beaker to 9d for a quart decanter of blue glass, and enamel ware at 4s for 2 long dozen (ie 13) basins and beakers could not represent the elaborate painting in colours that appears on some of the work attributed to him and must surely be more simple gilding and lettering—by comparison, he charged 1d for 2 inch high capital letters in his signwriting. His total earnings from Williams & Dunbar amounted to £4 18s 8d.
32. A.C. Powell, 'Glass-Making in Bristol', *TBGAS*, XLVII, (1925).
33. Williams makes no mention of it in his will made in 1774. What of Bradley? A Robert Bradley & Co had been in possession of a glasshouse on Temple Backs in Bristol but that was back in 1750. Dunbar apparently ended up in Dublin as a

glassmaker and appeared in a list of insolvent debtors there in 1778, see Westropp's Irish Glass, 1913 quoted in Powell (1925).

34. Thomas Wells buried his wife, and William Gordon was buried during 1765, and three glass makers, John Barnet, John Dunkisson and Richard Sanders all had daughters who were baptised in 1766. K.M.Evans, 'Glassmaking in Chepstow', *Severn & Wye Review* (Autumn 1971).
35. Byng (1934).
36. T. Roscoe, *Wanderings and Excursions in South Wales, including the Scenery of the River Wye,* (1837).
37. Barber (1803).
38. M. Willett, *An Excursion from the source of the Wye* (1810), *The Stranger in Monmouthshire & South Wales* (1825), and *The Strangers Guide to the Banks of the Wye* (1845 edition).
39. J.R. Kenyon, *Raglan Castle*, Cadw guidebook, (Cardiff 2003), p.23.
40. Although William Makepeace Thackeray managed to gain entry, using a few persuasive tactics.
41. T.P. Farrar, *The Stranger's Hand-Book to the Chepstow and the Wye* (1845).

## Chapter XXIV The Victorian Period and the 20th Century

1. *Monmouthshire Beacon* 14 & 21 September 1844.
2. The venue for these exhibitions was the nurseryman James Morgan's gardens in Mead's Lane (a nursery which became better known under its subsequent proprietor, Pillinger, and the road as Station Road). They soon seem to have attracted interest from beyond the neighbourhood, but for some reason they foundered in the early 1840s.
3. Two shows were planned, for weekday afternoons, one in June the other in September, the latter to be followed by a dinner of the new 'Chepstow United Horticultural Society at the Beaufort Hotel' . *Monmouthshire Beacon* 19 April, 10 & 17 May 1845.
4. *Monmouthshire Beacon* 6 & 13 September 1845.
5. *Illustrated London News* 20 June 1846, *Monmouthshire Beacon* 13 June 1846 'Chepstow ... was the scene of one of the most magnificent spectacles it has ever been our lot to witness in a provincial town'. The whole town had a 'gay appearance', the castle towers were decorated with flags, as also was the shipping in the river. The visitors who arrived on the steam packet wiled away the time before the castle gates opened at one o'clock, with trips to Tintem and the Wyndcliff.'
6. *Monmouthshire Beacon* 12 September 1846.
7. The inflation of the balloon began at noon but it was not until 7 o'clock that the balloon assumed a beautifully symmetrical form' (fortunately there was a band to entertain and some people danced the polka) and a little before 8pm when 'the Aeronaut took his seat in the car and amid the cheering of thousands of spectators, who had crowded every available eminence, the Professor gave the word to let go.' *Chepstow Weekly Advertiser* 14 Jun & 5 July 1862.
8. *Chepstow Weekly Advertiser* 23 May 1868. The Duke of Beaufort 'with his usual desire to meet the wishes of the public and his promptness in taking action, immediately sent instructions to his agents, the Messrs J & T Evans. Chepstow, to inspect the spot where the accident happened and to have a barrier fixed there, and also to have protecting rails placed underneath the Bridge in the Tower, at the same time, with a Beaufort's noble liberality, not forgetting the widow and orphan' — to whom he gave two guineas, and for which she gave grateful thanks — *Chepstow Weekly Advertiser* 6 June 1868.
9. Programme, 'Public Opening of the Chepstow Castle Dell', 11 August 1886, Chepstow Museum; *Chepstow Weekly Advertiser* 14 August 1886.
10. *Chepstow Weekly Advertiser* 16 & 23 July 1887.
11. *Chepstow Weekly Advertiser* 11 & 18 May 1889. Ivor Waters speculated that Seys knew of an impending visit by the ex-Empress Eugénie on 11 May 1889. I. Waters 'Chepstow Castle from Cromwell to Picturesque Ruin', *Chepstow Packets* (1983). She was travelling incognito, and took a boat down the Wye from Monmouth to Chepstow.
12. John Loraine Baldwin, warden of Tintern Abbey from 1873 until his death in 1896, lived at St Ann's, Tintern, one of the founders of the I Zingari Cricket Club in 1845, authority on whist and other card games, a Society figure.
13. *Chepstow Weekly Advertiser* 3 August 1889.
14. Pageant posters, programmes, Parish Magzines, reports in *Chepstow Weekly Advertiser*, in Chepstow Museum; A. Rainsbury, *Chepstow and the River Wye in Old Photographs* from the collections of Chepstow Museum (1989).
15. Programmes 1891, 1892 Chepstow Museum.
16. An address on 'Friendly Societies and State Aided Pensions' was part of the days programme, which was curtailed due to torrential rain. But despite that, and the abandonment of the village-choir contest as the only entrants failed to turn up, the day was considered a great success and moved to Whit Tuesday. *Chepstow Weekly Advertiser* 4 & 11 September 1897.
17. *Chepstow Weekly Advertiser* 27 May, 1 July & 16 August 1899; programmes 1899 & 1901 in Chepstow Museum.
18. Copies of the sale catalogue are in the collections of the Chepstow Museum and Newport Reference Library.
19. *Chepstow Weekly Advertiser* 22 July 1899.
20. This was to be by way of a 'parting gift' with the town, as it had according to tradition at one time belonged to the town. From report of auction, *Chepstow Weekly Advertiser* 7 October 1899.
21. Owen had already spent eight years developing his Word Cipher with some 'spiritual guidance' from Bacon himself. He had made a 'Wheel which he said was Bacon's design - two large spools around and between which rolled a thousand feet of canvas two feet wide. On this he stuck individual pages of the complete works of Bacon, as well as Shakespeare,

Marlowe, Greene, Peele and Spenser and Burton's *Anatomy of Melancholy*, all of which he attributed to Bacon. At the turn of the wheel the works rolled out beneath his eyes. He could pick out 'Guide Words' he had been 'given': Fortune, Honour, Nature, Reputation and Pan. These led to 'key' words and they in turn to significant phrases. These extracts were colour coded to classify them. When arranged in the 'correct order', according to Dr Owen, they made a story, the story of Bacon's life; that he was the secret child of Queen Elizabeth I and Robert Dudley and therefore an heir to the throne. Owen published Bacon's story in six volumes. But he needed the proof to convince people of his theory, and that could only be Bacon's account of his life in his own hand and all the manuscripts of Shakespeare's plays. J. Michell, *Eccentric Lives and Peculiar Notions* (1984); I.Waters, 'Shakespeare or Bacon?' *A Chepstow Notebook* (Chepstow 1980).

22. Newspaper cuttings archive, Chepstow Museum. Because of the extremely high tides of the river, work was restricted to a short interval when the tide went out—day or night—and water had to be pumped out before work could begin. A number of holes were dug, excavations and workforce enlarged, coffer dam built, steam-driven pump installed.

23. *South Wales Weekly Argus* June 28 1913.

24. His input was acknowledged by the producer/director and actor, Herbert Brenon, 'never in the history of any film has a gentleman taken so much interest and devoted so much of his time to it as has Mr Thomas.' Apart from his personal passions, W.C. Thomas had the vision to see how much publicity it could bring to the town, and how it could attract more film makers to the area. *Cinematograph Exhibitors Mail* 9 July 1913; *South Wales Weekly Argus* 7 & 21 June 1913.

25. *The Bioscope* 3 July 1913.

26. National Film Archive catalogue. Over half a century later Chepstow people had the chance to rub shoulders with stars again when scenes for *Jabberwocky* were filmed on location at Chepstow Castle over a week in September 1976. Some 276 local people auditioned for about 60 parts as 'extras' in Terry Gilliam's, (of Monty Python fame), zany film of medieval life and myth.

27. Chepstow's Coronation Celebrations May 1937 programme, Chepstow Museum; *Weekly Argus* 15 May 1937; *South Wales Argus* 2 June 1953, *Western Mail* 3 & 4 June 1953.

28. Ian Wilcox worked with Moore on the artistic and technical direction, Alan Matthews was the producer, Weekly Argus 8 June 1967, Castle Week 1967 programme, Chepstow Museum;.

29. A small team of four have been responsible for devising and planning the productions, working with script writers and visualising and plotting the shows—Ned Heywood and Anne Rainsbury together with Keith Underwood and Ann Llewellin—but it would not be possible without the many stalwart volunteers who have been involved over the years making costumes, props, images, and performing before audiences now numbering tens of thousands.

30. Badminton Ms 10,776, National Library of Wales.

31. Badminton Ms 10,777.

32. J. Newman, *The Buildings of Wales, Gwent/Monmouthshire*, (Penguin 2000), pp.67-8. Francis was a pupil of Guy Dawber and listed his restoration of Chepstow Castle on his RIBA application in 1923. He also did conservation work at Pencoed Castle and St Pierre House.

33. D. Berry, *Wales and Cinema: the first hundred years* (Cardiff 1996).

34. Played by Herbert Brenon, the producer and director.

35. See Clark, pp.55-7 and Coxe, II, p.369, fig. 1, which shows the chip-carving on the rear doorcase only.

36. A. Keay, 'The presentation of guardianship sites', *Transactions of the Ancient Monuments Society*, (2004), 48, pp 7-20.

37. J.C. Perks, *Chepstow Castle*, Ministry of Works Official Guide-book, (HMSO 1955).

38. Ivor Waters recorded that four workmen with an 8-ton pulley uprooted the tree on 9 December 1961. (*South Wales Argus* 9/12/1961) He went on to say that the Forestry Commission district officer Mr S.J.C. West said the tree was 80 feet high, 11 feet 3 inches around the trunk and 600 years old. The tree had been attacked by honey fungus and pronounced dead.

39. Perks (1955).

40. Part of the outer curtain wall against Marten's Tower had collapsed in 1872, and stone and the earth fill had fallen into the Dell. It was soon rebuilt and is easy to distinguish from the 17th-century masonry.

41. A. Teagle, *The Conservation of the Parapet Figures on Marten's Tower, Chepstow Castle*, Report to Cadw, 1995, held in Cadw's archive.

42. Hirst Conservation, *Report on the Conservation Treatment at Chepstow Castle*, (1999), Report to Cadw, held in Cadw's archives.

43. Nimbus Conservation, *Chepstow Castle, Report on the Conservation of Wallpainting*, (1998), Report to Cadw, held in Cadw's archive.

44. Nimbus Conservation, *Report on the Conservation of Decorative Corbels and Arches within the Great Hall*, (2003), Report to Cadw, held in Cadw's archive.

# Index